# The
# Great American
# Cookbook

# *The*
# Great American Cookbook

INTERNATIONAL
CULINARY
SOCIETY

First impression 1990

Text copyright © 1990 The National Magazine Company Ltd
Illustrations © 1990 Gill Tomblin and Susan Robertson
Photographs © 1990 The National Magazine Company Ltd

This 1990 edition published by International Culinary Society
a division of dilithium Press, Ltd
distributed by Crown Publishers, Inc.,
225 Park Avenue South
New York, New York 10003

Published by arrangement with Ebury Press
an imprint of The Random Century Group Ltd
20 Vauxhall Bridge Road
London SW1V 2SA

ISBN 0 517 68831 X
hgfedcba
Library of Congress Cataloging-in-Publication Data
Great American cookbook: traditional recipes for everyday cooking,
holidays, and celebrations.
p.    cm.
Reprinted from the Ebury Press ed.
Includes index.
ISBN 0-517-68831-X
1. Cookery, American.   2. Holiday cookery.   I. International
Culinary Society.
TX715.G81126   1989
641.5973 — dc20                                        89-32300
                                                            CIP

Edited by Carol Hupping Fisher
Illustrated by Gill Tomblin, Susan Robertson and Kate Simunek
Photographed by Jan Baldwin, Martin Brigdale, Laurie Evans,
Melvin Grey, John Heseltine, James Jackson, David Johnson,
Paul Kemp

Filmset in Monophoto Ehrhardt by Advanced Filmsetters (Glasgow) Ltd
Printed and bound in Yugoslavia

# CONTENTS

# COOKERY NOTES

All spoon measures are level unless otherwise stated. All fruits and vegetables are medium size, unless indicated.

- Large eggs should be used, except when otherwise stated.
- Granulated sugar is used, unless otherwise indicated.
- Flour is all-purpose, pre-sifted, unless otherwise mentioned.

Some recipes call for self-rising flour. This flour is available in all supermarkets, but, if desired, for each cup of self-rising flour you can substitute 1 cup of all-purpose flour and 1 teaspoon baking soda.

> All recipes in this book serve SIX PEOPLE unless otherwise indicated.

## KEY TO SYMBOLS

$\boxed{1.00*}$ Indicates minimum preparation and cooking times in hours and minutes. They do not include prepared items in the list of ingredients, calculated times apply only to the method. An asterisk * indicates extra time should be allowed, so check the note below symbols.

$ Indicates a recipe which is good value for money. $ $ indicates an expensive recipe. No $ sign indicates an inexpensive recipe.

$\boxed{309 \text{ cals}}$ Indicates calories per serving, including any serving suggestions (for example, cream, to serve) given in the list of ingredients.

# S·P·R·I·N·G

*S*pring is in the air, at last! The days are really getting longer now, and you can feel the warm weather starting to settle in. What a fine time to make plans for getting together with those you enjoy being with, for marking special dates and celebrations of all kinds on your calendar.

Here, and in the other three front sections of this book, you will find menus and recipes to match the season, to give you suggestions for entertaining in style.

We start spring with an Easter Brunch, a fancy breakfast affair, dressed up in flowers and other spring finery.

A Family Picnic follows, with lots of ideas for preparing and packing good take-along foods that everybody will like.

Spring gardens bring lots of salad foods, and our Spring Salad Sampler gives you a great reason for trying them all, with a little help from your friends. There are some tips, too, for making and serving salads of all sorts.

What's spring without a wedding, and our spring concludes with a self-catered, garden wedding celebration, complete with delectable foods and lots of champagne.

# BORSCH

2.00 | $ | 137 cals

*Serves 6*

8 oz chuck steak

1 carrot, peeled and sliced

1 onion, skinned and stuck with a
   few cloves

2 celery sticks, chopped

1 bouquet garni

salt and freshly ground pepper

12 oz raw beets

8 oz ripe tomatoes

2 Tbsp tomato paste

1 Tbsp red wine vinegar

1 bay leaf

1 tsp sugar, to taste

$\frac{2}{3}$ cup sour cream and *pirozhki*
   (see box), to serve

*1* Put the beef in a large saucepan with the carrot, onion and
celery. Pour in 5 cups water and
bring to a boil. Skim off any scum,
add the bouquet garni and salt and
pepper to taste. Lower the heat,
cover the pan and simmer for
1 hour until the meat is just
becoming tender.

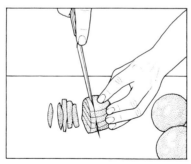

*2* Meanwhile, peel the beets and
cut into thin, matchstick strips
with a very sharp knife.

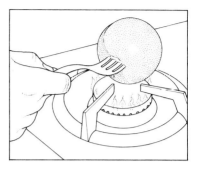

*3* Skin the tomatoes. Do this by
holding them, one at a time,
over a gas flame until the skin
blisters. Cool and peel.
Alternatively, plunge into boiling
water for 1 minute, then into cold
water. The skin will crack and peel
easily. Chop the tomato flesh
roughly.

*4* Remove the beef from the pan
and slice into thin matchstick
strips, as with the beets. Remove
the vegetables and bouquet garni
with a slotted spoon and discard.

*5* Return the beef to the pan and
add the beets, tomatoes,
tomato paste, wine vinegar and
bay leaf. Simmer for another
50 minutes to 1 hour, until the
beef and beets are really tender.
Discard the bay leaf, then adjust
seasoning, adding sugar to taste.
Serve the borsch hot, with the
sour cream and *pirozhki* handed
separately.

**Menu Suggestion**
When served with sour cream and
*pirozhki*, this soup is substantial
enough to be served on its own as
a lunch or supper dish.

---

**BORSCH**

*Pirozhki*, little crescent-shaped
pastries, are the traditional
accompaniments to borsch.
Authentic recipes for *pirozhki*
involve making a yeast pastry
and a filling of either meat,
cabbage and onion or
mushrooms, eggs and onions. A
quick alternative is to use bought
puff pastry and a filling of
packet stuffing mix enriched with
vegetables.

# STUFFED MUSHROOMS

| 1.05* | 642 cals |
| --- | --- |

* plus 1 hour or overnight chilling;
freeze mushrooms and the dip
separately in step 6

*Serves 4*

| 2 Tbsp olive oil |
| --- |
| 1 small onion, chopped |
| 2 garlic cloves, crushed |
| 14-oz can tomatoes |
| 1 tsp dried oregano |
| 1 tsp dried basil |
| 2 Tbsp chopped fresh parsley |
| $\frac{1}{4}$ tsp sugar |
| salt and freshly ground pepper |
| 32 even-sized button mushrooms, wiped |
| $\frac{3}{4}$ cup unsalted butter, softened |
| 2-oz can anchovies in olive oil, drained and chopped |
| finely grated rind of 1 lemon |
| 2 eggs, beaten |
| 1 cup dried breadcrumbs |
| vegetable oil for deep frying |

*1* *To prepare* (40 minutes): Make the tomato dip. Heat the oil in a saucepan, add the onion and half the garlic and fry gently for 5 minutes until soft but not colored.

*2* Add the tomatoes, dried herbs, half the parsley, the sugar and seasoning to taste. Bring to the boil, stirring constantly with a wooden spoon to break up the tomatoes. Lower the heat and simmer, covered, for 30 minutes, stirring occasionally.

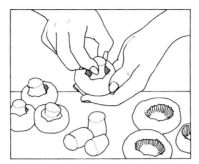

*3* Meanwhile pull the stems carefully from the mushrooms with your fingers. Chop the stems finely, then place in a bowl with the butter, anchovies, lemon rind, remaining garlic and parsley. Beat the ingredients together until well combined, then add pepper to taste (do not add salt because of the saltiness of the anchovies).

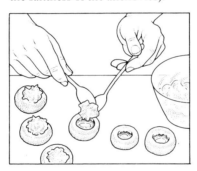

*4* Spoon the butter mixture into the cavity of each of the mushrooms.

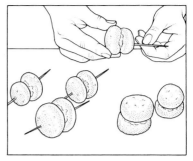

*5* Sandwich the mushrooms together in pairs and pierce through the center of each pair with a wooden toothpick. Dip the mushrooms in the beaten eggs, then in the breadcrumbs until evenly coated.

*6* Chill in the refrigerator for 1 hour, or overnight if more convenient. Remove the tomato dip from the heat, leave to cool, then chill in the refrigerator at the same time as the mushrooms.

*7* *To serve* (25 minutes): Work the tomato dip in a blender or food processor, then sieve to remove the tomato seeds. Taste and adjust seasoning, then pour into a serving bowl. Return to the refrigerator while frying the mushrooms.

*8* Heat the oil in a deep frier to 375°F and deep fry the mushrooms in batches for about 5 minutes until golden brown and crisp on all sides. Drain quickly on absorbent paper, then remove the toothpicks. Serve immediately, with the chilled tomato dip handed separately.

**Menu Suggestion**
This dinner party appetizer is so substantial that it needs no accompaniment other than chilled dry white wine.

# CURRIED POTATO AND APPLE SOUP

| 0.50 | $ | 267 cals |

*\* freeze at step 3, after puréeing*

*Serves 4*

$\frac{1}{4}$ cup butter or margarine

4 medium potatoes, peeled and diced

2 eating apples, peeled, cored and diced

2 tsp curry powder

5 cups vegetable stock or water

salt and freshly ground pepper

$\frac{2}{3}$ cup yogurt, at room temperature

*1* Melt the butter or margarine in a large saucepan. Add the potatoes and apples and fry gently for about 10 minutes until lightly colored, shaking the pan and stirring frequently.

*2* Add the curry powder and fry gently for 1–2 minutes, stirring. Pour in the stock or water and bring to a boil. Add salt and pepper to taste. Lower the heat, cover the pan and simmer for 20–25 minutes or until the potatoes and apples are really soft.

*3* Sieve or purée the soup in a blender or food processor, then return to the rinsed-out pan.

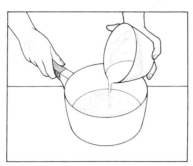

*4* Stir the yogurt until smooth, then pour half into the soup. Heat through, stirring constantly, then taste and adjust seasoning.

*5* Pour the hot soup into warmed individual bowls and swirl in the remaining yogurt. Serve immediately.

**Menu Suggestion**

This soup is delicately spiced, with a sweet flavor of apples.
Serve with French bread and chilled beer for an informal supper or lunch.

---

**CURRIED POTATO AND APPLE SOUP**

It is important to fry the curry powder in step 2 of the recipe, or the spices will taste raw in the finished soup. Yogurt has a tendency to curdle when stirred into very hot liquids. This problem can be overcome if the yogurt is brought to room temperature and stirred well before use.

# FRESH FISH MOUSSE

| 0.40* | $ $ | 359 cals |

* plus 30 minutes cooling, 2 hours chilling and 30 minutes to come to room temperature

*Serves 6*

12 oz fresh haddock fillet
1 cup milk
1 bay leaf
6 peppercorns
salt and freshly ground pepper
2 Tbsp butter or margarine
2 Tbsp flour
1½ tsp gelatine
1 Tbsp Dijon mustard
1 tsp tomato paste
1 tsp Worcestershire sauce
6 Tbsp heavy cream
⅔ cup mayonnaise
1 Tbsp lemon juice
cucumber, to garnish

*1* Place the haddock in a sauté or frying pan. Pour in the milk and add the bay leaf, peppercorns and a good pinch of salt. Bring slowly to a boil, cover and simmer for 5–10 minutes, or until the fish flakes easily when tested with a fork.

*2* Strain the cooking liquid from the fish and reserve. Skin and flake the flesh, discarding any bones.

*3* Melt the butter in a saucepan, add the flour and cook gently, stirring for 1–2 minutes. Remove from the heat and gradually blend in the strained cooked liquid. Bring to a boil, stirring constantly, then simmer for 3 minutes until thick and smooth. Remove the pan from the heat and sprinkle in the gelatine. Stir briskly until dissolved.

*4* Work the sauce in a blender or food processor with the fish, mustard, tomato paste, Worcestershire sauce and salt and pepper to taste. Transfer to a bowl and leave to cool for 30 minutes.

*5* Lightly whip the cream and stir it into the fish mixture with the mayonnaise and lemon juice. Check the seasoning.

*6* Spoon the mousse into 6 individual ramekins or soufflé dishes and chill in the refrigerator for at least 2 hours until set. Leave at cool room temperature for 30 minutes before serving, garnished with cucumber.

**Menu Suggestion**
This mousse is light and delicate in flavor. Serve for a dinner party appetizer with Melba toast; followed by a main course of chicken or veal, then a fresh, fruity dessert.

13

# EASTER BRUNCH

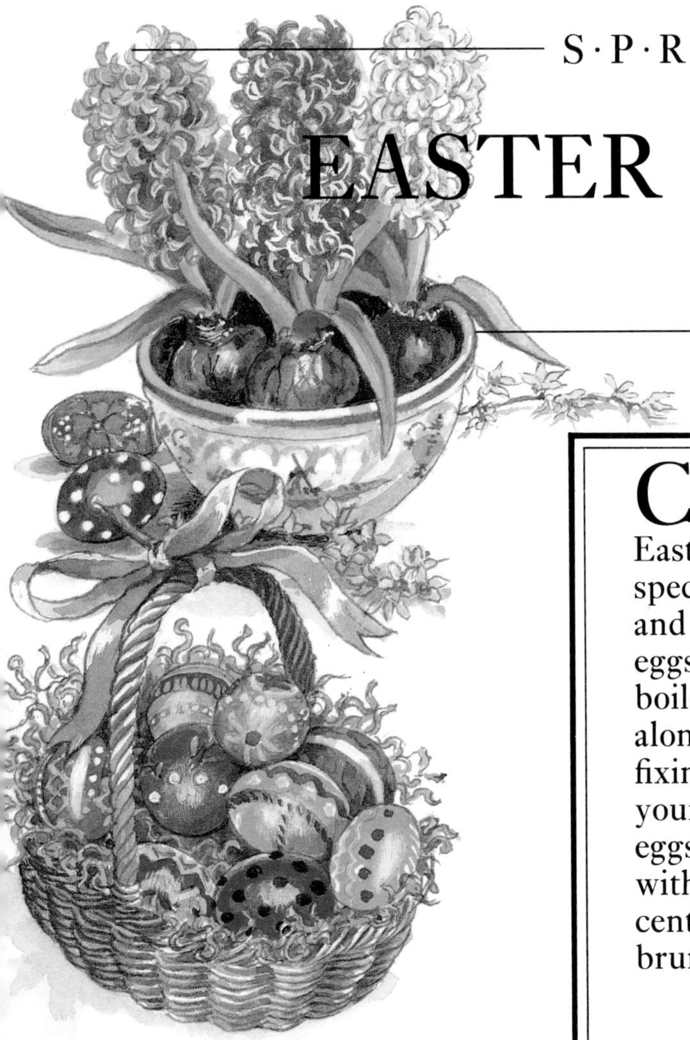

Celebrate the egg in its many forms this Easter Sunday with a special brunch for family and friends. Serve the eggs scrambled, hard-boiled and in quiche, along with all the fixings. Save some of your gaily colored Easter eggs and arrange them with fruit in an edible centerpiece for your brunch table.

Easter, whether it comes in early March or late April, marks for many the real beginning of springtime. It's the holiday of rebirth—the beginning of a new season, the start of new growth.

So it is no coincidence that the egg, which symbolizes a new life, is so closely connected with Easter. We hard-boil them and paint the rainbows of color. Then we nest them in ribboned baskets stuffed with cellophane grass, to sit cozily next to chocolate rabbits and pink marshmallow chicks. And we save some to hide outdoors for family Easter egg hunts.

Easter Sunday is traditionally a big family day and one to show off the new spring finery. For many, the day begins with Easter service at church and continues with a day of visiting grandma and grandpa. If the weather is obliging, perhaps there's the "Easter parade" down Main Street or a stroll in the park.

How nice it is to invite some close friends and a few relatives over in mid-morning for a big Easter brunch. An invitation to arrive at 11 or 12 gives everyone time to have their early morning themselves, to attend church and/or open the Easter baskets (but not to have the egg hunt, which will be in your yard as the grand finale). But it's not so late in the day that it interferes with afternoon outings.

## MENU

◆

*Kir (see featured recipe here)*
*orange juice*
*scrambled eggs with bowls of chopped*
*smoked salmon, cream cheese and chives,*
*for garnishes*
*Herbed Brie Quiche*
*(see featured recipe here)*
*broiled breakfast sausages and bacon*
*assorted muffins and croissants*
*mixed fruit salad*
*Banana Cheesecake (see page 54)*
*coffee with cinnamon sticks, tea*

◆

## Welcome In Spring

To put yourself and your guests in the proper mood, cast off winter by filling the house with baskets and bowls of the flowers we all associate with early spring: golden daffodils, sweet-smelling hyacinths, delicate narcissi, forsythia and pussy willows.

## The Meal That Celebrates the Egg

As for the meal itself, of course you'll serve eggs. There may be simple, scrambled eggs that can be adorned with garnishes of smoked salmon, and cream cheese and chives (include some of the chive flowers if they're blooming already). Scramble the eggs by themselves and have the chopped salmon, cream cheese and chives on the side in bowls so that guests can garnish the eggs as they wish. Also serve a fancy quiche or two, like the Herbed Brie Quiche featured here. They can be made ahead of time, freeing you up for other last-minute tasks. And whatever you have left over can be refrigerated now and brought back to room temperature later, to be finished then. Accompany the egg dishes with juicy breakfast sausages and broiled bacon, a big fruit salad, and muffins and croissants piled high in an Easter basket.

Have glasses of Kir and orange juice on a tray near the door so that guests can help themselves as they enter. Luscious Banana Cheesecake is just right for the finish—and to fortify all for the egg hunt.

## KIR

*Makes 1 serving*

| |
|---|
| 4 parts dry white wine |
| 1 part blackcurrant-flavored liqueur |

1 Thoroughly chill the wine before combining it with the liqueur; serve in a wine glass.

## HERBED BRIE QUICHE

*Serves 4–6*

| |
|---|
| 1 cup flour |
| 1 tsp dried mixed herbs |
| salt |
| 4 Tbsp butter |
| 2 Tbsp lard |
| 1 egg yolk |
| a little beaten egg white |
| 8 oz ripe Brie |
| $\frac{2}{3}$ cup heavy cream |
| 3 eggs, lightly beaten |
| 2 Tbsp chopped fresh mixed herbs (e.g., thyme, marjoram, parsley, chives) |
| freshly ground pepper |

1 Make the pastry. Sift the flour into a bowl with the herbs and a pinch of salt. Add the butter and lard in small pieces and cut into the flour with a knife. Rub the fat into the flour until the mixture resembles fine breadcrumbs, then stir in the egg yolk. Knead lightly until smooth.

2 Roll out on a floured surface. Use to line an 8-inch tart ring set on a baking sheet. Refrigerate for 20 minutes.

3 Prick the base of the dough lightly with a fork, then line with foil and weight down with baking beans. Bake blind in the oven at 400°F for 10 minutes.

4 Remove the foil and the beans, brush the inside of the pastry shell with the beaten egg white, then return to the oven and bake for a further 5 minutes.

5 Remove the rind from the cheese, cut into squares and place in the base of the pastry case. Soften the cheese with a fork and gradually work in the cream to make a smooth mixture. Whisk in the beaten eggs, and seasonings.

6 Pour the filling into the pastry case. Bake in the oven at 350°F for 30 minutes until the filling is just set and the rind from the cheese has formed a golden crust.

# TURKEY ROQUEFORT SALAD

| 0.15* | 375 cals |

* plus 30 minutes chilling

*Serves 4*

$\frac{2}{3}$ cup sour cream

4 oz Roquefort or any other blue cheese, crumbled

salt and freshly ground pepper

1 lb cold cooked turkey, skinned and cut into pieces

lettuce or chicory leaves, washed and trimmed

snipped chives, to garnish

*1* Mix the sour cream and Roquefort together to make a dressing. Season to taste. Add the turkey and coat well in it. Cover and chill in the refrigerator for 30 minutes.

*2* To serve, arrange the lettuce or chicory leaves in a serving bowl. Spoon the turkey mixture in the center and sprinkle with chives. Serve chilled.

**Menu Suggestion**
Serve for a summer luncheon with fresh French bread or rolls and a bottle of dry sparkling white wine.

# HAM AND CHEESE SALAD WITH AVOCADO

| 0.15 | $ $ | 502 cals |

*Serves 4*

2 ripe avocados

4 Tbsp yogurt

1 garlic clove, skinned and crushed

a few drops of Tabasco sauce

salt and freshly ground pepper

8 oz lean cooked ham, cubed

8 oz Emmenthal or Gruyère cheese, cubed

1 red pepper, cored, seeded and diced

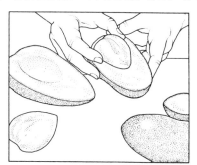

*1* Halve the avocados and remove the pits, then peel and mash the flesh. Mix quickly with the yogurt, garlic and Tabasco, seasoning to taste.

*2* Fold the ham, cheese and red pepper (reserving some pepper to garnish) into this dressing and pile into a salad bowl. Serve immediately, or the avocado flesh may discolor the dressing. Sprinkle with the reserved red pepper.

**Menu Suggestion**
This salad is incredibly quick to prepare. Serve it for a healthy lunch, with wholewheat rolls.

# Pan Bagna with Avocado

| 0.30 | $ | 316–421 cals |

*Serves 6–8*

| 2 ripe avocados |
| 1 Tbsp lemon juice |
| 1 Tbsp vegetable oil |
| garlic salt and black pepper |
| two 14-inch French loaves |
| 8 oz tomatoes, sliced |
| 1 small green pepper, cored, seeded and sliced into thin rings |
| 2½-oz can anchovies, drained |
| few capers and black olives, pitted |

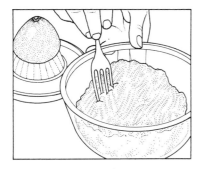

*1* Halve avocados and remove pits. Mash flesh with lemon juice, oil and seasoning. Cut anchovies in thin strips.

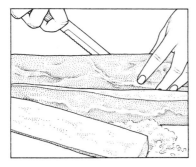

*2* Halve loaves lengthwise; discard some of crumbs. Spread bases with avocado. Top with tomatoes and pepper. Lattice with anchovies, capers and olives. Close up and serve, in chunks.

# PAN BAGNA WITH MUSHROOMS

| 0.30 | $ | 317–422 cals |

*Serves 6–8*

8 oz button mushrooms

4 Tbsp olive oil

2 Tbsp butter

1 garlic clove, crushed

salt and freshly ground pepper

two 14-inch French loaves

8 oz tomatoes, sliced

4 stalks celery, washed and sliced

2½-oz can anchovies, drained and cut into thin strips

few capers

black olives, pitted or green stuffed olives

*1* Wipe and slice the mushrooms. Heat 2 Tbsp oil and butter in a pan, add the mushrooms and garlic and cook gently for 5 minutes until soft. Season with salt and pepper.

*2* Halve loaves lengthwise, discarding some of the crumbs. Sprinkle the halves with the remaining oil.

*3* Spoon the mushrooms on the bases. Top with the tomatoes, celery, anchovies, capers and olives. Close up and serve, in hunks.

## PAN BAGNA

Provençal *Pan Bagna* is the ideal picnic food with which you can ring many changes. French bread or a small, round country bread should traditionally be used (in the Nice area a loaf is specially baked for this purpose) and the filling very moist. Translated, *Pan Bagna* means "wet bread." Often the bread is sprinkled with olive oil. Other filling ingredients could include hard-boiled eggs, tuna fish, French beans, broad beans or globe artichokes.

## PREPARING AVOCADOS

To prepare avocados, use a stainless steel knife, cut the avocados in half lengthwise, through to the pit. Hold the pear in both hands and gently twist. Open the halves and remove the pit. If necessary, the peel can either be removed with a potato peeler or lightly score the skin once or twice and peel back the skin. Always brush the exposed flesh immediately with lemon juice to prevent discoloration.

# SHEPHERD'S PIE

| 1.00 | $ | ✳ | 524 cals |

*Serves 4*

1½ lb potatoes, peeled

salt and freshly ground pepper

1 lb cooked lamb

2 Tbsp vegetable oil

1 medium onion, skinned and chopped

2 Tbsp all-purpose flour

1¼ cups lamb or beef stock

1 Tbsp Worcestershire sauce

6 Tbsp chopped fresh parsley

1 tsp dried marjoram

2 oz Cheddar cheese, grated

chopped fresh parsley, to garnish

*1* Cook the potatoes in a saucepan of boiling salted water for about 20 minutes until tender.

*2* Meanwhile, trim the excess fat from the lamb and discard. Chop finely.

*3* Heat the oil in a frying pan, add the onion and fry for about 5 minutes until lightly browned. Stir in the flour and fry for 2–3 minutes. Add the stock and simmer, stirring until thickened.

*4* Stir in the lamb, Worcestershire sauce, parsley, marjoram and salt and pepper. Spoon into a 5-cup shallow pie pan.

*5* Drain the potatoes. Mash well, then gradually beat in the cheese and salt and pepper. Spoon or pipe over the lamb.

*6* Bake in the oven at 400°F for 30 minutes until well browned. Serve hot, sprinkled with chopped parsley.

**Menu Suggestion**

Traditional vegetables to serve with Shepherd's Pie are cabbage or spring greens. To ensure that the nutrients are retained, shred the leaves, blanch and stir-fry rather than boiling.

### SHEPHERD'S PIE

Although not traditional, Shepherd's Pie tastes extra good if you add mashed carrots or turnips to the potato topping. You can add as many or as few as you like, but a good proportion is half the weight of root vegetable to potato. Carrots and turnips not only add flavor, they also give the topping a warming golden-yellow color.

# PAPRIKA BEEF

| 2.15 | $ | 213 cals |

*Serves 4*

1 lb lean shin of beef
1 Tbsp wholewheat flour
1½ tsp mild paprika
¼ tsp caraway seeds
¼ tsp dried marjoram
salt and freshly ground pepper
1 large onion, sliced
2 medium carrots, peeled and
  sliced
1 cup beef stock
1 Tbsp tomato paste
1 garlic clove, crushed
1 whole clove
4 oz button mushrooms, wiped
  and sliced
chopped fresh parsley, to garnish

*1* Trim the fat from the beef. Cut the meat into large cubes. Mix together the flour, paprika, caraway seeds, marjoram and seasoning to taste. Toss the beef in the seasoned flour.

*2* Layer the meat, onion and carrots in a 2-quart flameproof casserole.

*3* Whisk together the stock, tomato paste, crushed garlic and clove. Pour into the casserole. Bring to the boil and simmer, uncovered, for 3–4 minutes.

*4* Cover the casserole tightly and cook in the oven at 350°F for about 1½ hours, stirring occasionally.

*5* Remove the casserole from the oven and stir in the mushrooms. Cover again and return to the oven for a further 15 minutes or until the meat is tender. Taste and adjust seasoning. Garnish.

**Menu Suggestion**
Serve with layered sliced potatoes and onions, moistened with stock and baked in the oven.

# COCOTTE EGGS

| 0.35 | 310 cals |

*Serves 4*

2 Tbsp butter

1 small onion, skinned and finely chopped

4 slices of lean bacon, finely chopped

$\frac{1}{4}$ lb button mushrooms, finely chopped

2 tsp tomato paste

2 tsp chopped fresh tarragon or 1 tsp dried tarragon

salt and freshly ground pepper

4 eggs

$\frac{1}{2}$ cup heavy cream

chopped fresh tarragon, to garnish

*1* Melt the butter in a small saucepan, add the onion and fry gently until soft. Add the bacon and fry until beginning to change color, then add the mushrooms and tomato paste. Continue frying for 2–3 minutes until the juices run, stirring constantly.

*2* Remove from the heat and stir in the tarragon and seasoning to taste. Divide the mixture equally between 4 cocottes, ramekins or individual soufflé dishes. Make a slight indentation in the center of each one.

*3* Break an egg into each dish, on top of the mushroom and bacon mixture, then slowly pour 2 Tbsp cream over each one. Sprinkle with salt and freshly ground pepper to taste.

*4* Place the cocottes on a baking tray and bake in the oven at 350°F for 10–12 minutes until the eggs are set. Serve immediately.

**Menu Suggestion**
Serve for breakfast, brunch, lunch or supper, with triangles of whole-wheat toast and butter.

---

**COCOTTE EGGS**

As an alternative to the mushrooms in this recipe, you can use fresh tomatoes. At the end of the summer when they are often overripe, they are best used for cooking rather than in salads, and this baked egg dish is a good way to use them up. Skin them first if you have time as this will make the finished dish more palatable. A quick way to skin a few tomatoes is to pierce one at a time with a fork in the stalk end and then hold in the flame of a gas stove. Turn the tomato until the skin blisters and bursts, leave until cool enough to handle, then peel off the skin with your fingers. To replace the mushrooms, use 4 medium tomatoes, chopped, and substitute basil for the tarragon, if available.

# NOODLES IN WALNUT SAUCE

| 0.20 | 730 cals |

*Serves 4*

1 cup walnut pieces
¼ cup plus 2 Tbsp butter, softened
1 small garlic clove, skinned and
  roughly chopped
2 Tbsp flour
1¼ cups milk
10 oz green tagliatelle
1 tsp vegetable oil
salt and freshly ground pepper
4 oz Cheddar cheese, grated
freshly grated nutmeg

*1* In a blender or food processor, mix together the walnuts, ¼ cup of the butter and the garlic. Turn into a bowl.

*2* Put the remaining 2 Tbsp of butter in the blender or food processor. Add the flour and milk and work until evenly mixed.

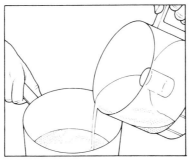

*3* Turn the mixture into a saucepan and bring slowly to a boil, stirring. Simmer for 6 minutes.

*4* Meanwhile, cook the tagliatelle in plenty of boiling salted water, adding the oil to the water (this prevents the pasta from sticking together).

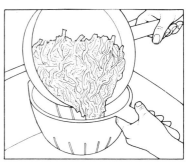

*5* For the timing, follow the pack instructions and cook until *al dente* (tender, but firm to the bite). Drain the pasta thoroughly, then return to the pan. Add the nut butter and heat through gently, stirring all the time.

*6* Divide the pasta mixture equally between 4 large, individual gratin-type dishes. Add seasoning to the white sauce, then use to coat the pasta.

*7* Scatter the grated cheese on top, sprinkle with the nutmeg, then broil for 5–10 minutes until brown and bubbling. Serve immediately.

**Menu Suggestion**
Serve for a supper dish followed by a tomato and fennel salad dressed with olive oil, lemon juice and chopped fresh basil.

---

**NOODLES IN WALNUT SAUCE**

Making velvety smooth sauces is not the easiest of culinary tasks, and most cooks seem to have problems with them at some time or another. Even French chefs have been known to sieve their sauces before serving to remove lumps! The French method of cooking a roux of butter and flour, then gradually adding milk, requires a certain amount of skill and judgement, whereas the all-in-one method in this recipe is quick and easy to do if you have a blender or food processor—and just about foolproof!

# MEAT LOAF

| 1.35* | 494–659 cals |
|-------|--------------|

* plus cooling and overnight chilling
*Serves 6–8*

2 lb boneless leg or shoulder of pork, ground

8 oz mushrooms, finely chopped

8 oz bacon, finely chopped

2 medium onions, skinned and finely chopped

1 large garlic clove, skinned and crushed

2 cups fresh breadcrumbs

$\frac{2}{3}$ cup sour cream

3 Tbsp dry white wine

1 tsp dried mixed herbs

$\frac{1}{2}$ tsp ground allspice

$\frac{1}{4}$ tsp grated nutmeg

salt and freshly ground pepper

*1* In a large bowl, mix all the ingredients together until evenly combined.

*2* Pack the mixture into a 6-cup loaf pan and cover with foil.

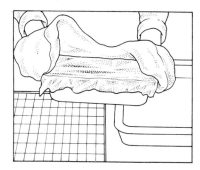

*3* Half fill a roasting pan with water and place the loaf pan in the water bath. Cook in the oven at 375°F for 1 hour.

*4* Uncover the pan, increase the oven temperature to 400°F and cook the meat loaf for a further 30 minutes.

*5* Remove the pan from the water bath and leave to cool for 30 minutes. Cover with foil and place heavy weights on top. Chill in the refrigerator overnight.

*6* To serve, turn the meat loaf out of the pan and cut into slices for serving.

**Menu Suggestion**
Thickly sliced Meat Loaf is similar to a pâté or terrine. Serve as a lunch dish with a potato or rice salad and sprigs of watercress.

# SPICY SCOTCH EGGS

| 0.40* | $ | 927 cals |

\* plus 30 minutes chilling

*Makes 4*

2 Tbsp vegetable oil

1 onion, skinned and very finely chopped

2 tsp medium-hot curry powder

1 lb pork sausagemeat

4 oz mature Cheddar cheese, finely grated

salt and freshly ground pepper

4 eggs, hard-boiled

flour, for coating

1 egg, beaten

1–1½ cups dried breadcrumbs

vegetable oil, for deep-frying

*1* Heat the 2 Tbsp oil in a small pan, add the onion and curry powder and fry gently for 5 minutes until soft.

*2* Put the sausagemeat and cheese in a bowl, add the onion and salt and pepper to taste. Mix with your hands to combine the ingredients well together.

*3* Divide the mixture into 4 equal portions and flatten out on a floured board or work surface.

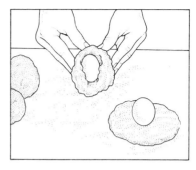

*4* Place an egg in the center of each piece. With floured hands, shape and mold the sausagemeat around the eggs. Coat lightly with more flour.

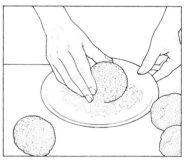

*5* Brush each Scotch egg with beaten egg, then roll in the breadcrumbs until evenly coated. Chill for 30 minutes.

*6* Heat the oil in a deep-fat fryer to 325°F. Carefully lower the Scotch eggs into the oil with a slotted spoon and deep-fry for 10 minutes, turning them occasionally until golden brown on all sides. Drain and cool on paper towels.

**Menu Suggestion**

Home-made Scotch eggs are quite delicious, with far more flavor than the commercial varieties. Serve them cut in halves or quarters with a mixed salad for lunch, or wrap them individually in plastic wrap or foil and pack them for a picnic or packed lunch—they are easy to eat with the fingers. Scotch eggs can also be served hot for a family meal.

## MEAT LOAF

The method of cooking meat loaves, pâtés and terrines in a roasting pan half filled with water is called *au bain marie* in French. It is a very simple method, but an essential one if the finished meat mixture is to be moist in texture. If the loaf pan is placed directly on the oven shelf, the mixture will dry out and the top will form a hard, unpleasant crust. A *bain marie* creates steam in the oven, which gives a moist heat. Special pans called water baths can be bought at kitchen shops for cooking *au bain marie*, but an ordinary roasting pan does the job just as well.

# FIRST-OF-THE-SEASON FAMILY PICNIC

A picnic is a wonderful way to welcome in spring. A leisurely walk in the park that's paced for the little ones as well as the adults lets everyone dust off the cobwebs of winter and search for the first signs of greenery. Plan a Saturday that promises sunshine (but choose a raindate just in case!) and set out with just the children—or a bunch of fit friends. Take a filled picnic basket with you and make a day of it.

Spring weather has finally arrived and everybody is itching to get outdoors to see the new arrivals: fiddlehead ferns beginning to unfurl, wild narcissi dotting the greenery, the pungent shoots of wild spring onions and garlic grass poking up through the leftover autumn leaves. Don't wait any longer.

A country park or rural woodland is the best. If you start off early in the morning you can enjoy the serene beauty that only the very beginning of a new day can offer. A picnic basket filled with goodies is the reward for all that exercise.

### Light Foods That Travel Well

At lunchtime (which will probably come early; fresh air and long walks make for hearty appetites) choose a spot that the sun's shining on, roll out the blanket and open up your basket. What have we here?

Delicious foods that travel well like bite-sized pieces of raw vegetables, crusty French bread and ripe cheeses, grapes and apples (prewashed, of course), and something more substantial, like Devilled Chicken Drumsticks and Spicy Scotch Eggs. Maybe there's a simple marinated vegetable salad made earlier and packed in plastic containers like Tomato Salad. A

## — MENU —

◆

*carrot, celery and cucumber sticks*

*a selection of cheeses, perhaps Camembert, Saga Blue, Cheddar and Gouda*

*loaves of French bread*

*apples and grapes*

*Devilled Chicken Drumsticks (see featured recipe here)*

*Spicy Scotch Eggs (see page 27)*

*Tomato Salad (see page 382)*

*Peanut Crunchies and Honey Jumbles (see pages 228 and 229)*

*cranberry juice cocktail*

— ◆ —

arinated salad like this is a good aveler because there's nothing to o limp, and it gets better the nore it marinates.

Then cookies for dessert. ranberry juice cocktail is very efreshing because it's not articularly sweet, and it holds up ery well when mixed with parkling water.

Don't choose a menu that's too eavy, unless you've got an after-unch nap on the grass scheduled which is not such a bad idea, if ou can get the children to go off y themselves and play Frisbee or game of catch).

Picnic meals should be easily ansportable, which means that hey keep their shape well even if hey do get jostled and squashed a it on the way. Sandwiches, of ourse, are regular picnic fare, and an be easy to make and bring ong, and quite good to eat, so ng as they don't contain fillings at get the bread soggy quickly, ke tuna and chicken salad. But, as he menu here shows, picnics can way beyond sandwiches.

**Packing For a Picnic**
When packing food for a picnic, se small plastic bags for items ich as cheese, cooked meats and lid salad ingredients. For more elicate foods like quiches, pizzas, rd-boiled eggs and open tarts, se cake tins or rigid plastic boxes.

To keep these bags and boxes cool, pack pre-frozen ice packets or ice blocks in with the food.

For taking liquids on picnics, the thermos or insulated jug is great. (Wine, soda and mineral water should be carried in their bottles; this may be the one time you want to look for them in plastic rather than glass bottles— they're lighter and they don't break.) When using a thermos or insulated jug, fill it as much as possible; any air trapped at the top will reduce the container's insulating qualities. Don't plan to keep food or drink in either one for more than 8 hours.

## DEVILED CHICKEN DRUMSTICKS

* plus at least 4 hours marinating; freeze in marinade, before cooking
*Makes 6*

| |
|---|
| $\frac{2}{3}$ cup vegetable oil |
| 1 tsp mild curry powder |
| 1 tsp paprika |
| $\frac{1}{2}$ tsp ground allspice |
| $\frac{1}{2}$ tsp ground ginger |
| 6 chicken drumsticks |

1  Make the marinade. Whisk together the oil and spices.

2  Skin the chicken drumsticks. Using a sharp knife, make 3 shallow slashes in the flesh of each one.

3  Spoon the marinade over the chicken, cover and chill in the refrigerator for 4–5 hours, turning occasionally.

4  Place the chicken drumsticks in a roasting tin just large enough to hold them in a single layer. Pour over the marinade.

5  Bake in the oven at 400°F for 40–45 minutes, basting frequently and turning once. Cool on a wire rack.

6  When completely cool, wrap a little foil over the end of each drumstick, or top with a cutlet frill. Pack together in a rigid container for transporting.

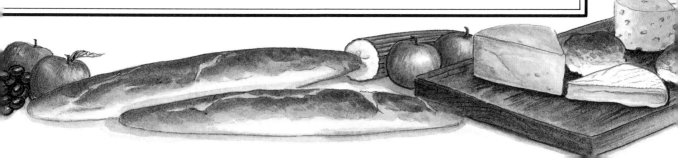

# SPICY LAMB CASSEROLE

| 2.00 | $ | 710 cals |

**MILD**

*Serves 6*

1 lb basmati rice

1 medium onion, skinned and roughly chopped

2 garlic cloves, skinned

1 inch piece of fresh ginger root, peeled and roughly chopped

$\frac{2}{3}$ cup ghee or vegetable oil

1 lb boned shoulder of lamb, trimmed of excess fat and cut into 1-inch cubes

$\frac{2}{3}$ cup yogurt

$\frac{1}{2}$ cup ground almonds

4 whole cloves

2 black cardamoms

4 green cardamoms

1 tsp cumin seeds

1 inch stick cinnamon or 4 pieces of cassia bark

$\frac{1}{3}$ cup light raisins

1–2 tsp salt

large pinch of saffron threads, or 1 tsp each yellow and orange food colorings

1 tsp rose water

can French fried onions, to garnish

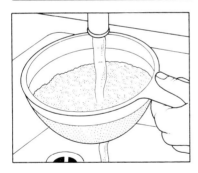

*1* Put the rice in a sieve and wash well under cold running water until the water runs clear. Transfer the rice to a bowl, cover with cold water and leave to soak.

*2* Meanwhile, put the onion, garlic and ginger in a blender or food processor and work until smooth. Set aside.

*3* Heat 4 Tbsp of the ghee in a large flameproof casserole. Add the cubes of lamb and fry over high heat until well browned on all sides. Transfer to a plate with a slotted spoon.

*4* Add the onion purée to the residual ghee in the pan and fry over high heat for 2 minutes, stirring constantly. Return the meat to the pan, then stir in the yogurt one spoonful at a time. Cook each addition over high heat, stirring constantly, until the yogurt is absorbed.

*5* Add the ground almonds and $\frac{2}{3}$ cup water. Bring to a boil, cover and simmer gently for 30 minutes, stirring occasionally to prevent sticking.

*6* Heat another 4 Tbsp ghee in a large heavy-based frying pan, add the cloves, cardamom pods, cumin seeds and cinnamon and fry gently for 1 minute.

*7* Drain the rice well and add to the spices, stirring until the rice absorbs all the fat. Stir in the raisins and salt to taste.

*8* Sprinkle the spiced rice evenly over the meat in the casserole. Carefully pour in enough water to just cover the rice. DO NOT STIR. Bring to a boil, cover and bake in the oven at 300°F for 30 minutes.

*9* Meanwhile, if using saffron threads, soak them in 4 Tbsp boiling water.

*10* Remove the casserole from the oven, uncover and drizzle over the saffron water or food colorings. Recover tightly and bake for 15 minutes.

*11* To serve, uncover the casserole and carefully fork up the meat and rice. Sprinkle with the rose water and, finally, the onion garnish.

# ROLLED STUFFED BREASTS OF LAMB

| 1.55 | $ | 925 cals |

\* freeze at end of step 4

*Serves 4*

2 Tbsp butter or margarine

1 medium onion, skinned and chopped

1 oz bacon slices, chopped

$\frac{1}{2}$ lb frozen spinach, thawed

$1\frac{1}{2}$ cups fresh breadcrumbs

3 Tbsp chopped fresh parsley

finely grated rind of $\frac{1}{2}$ lemon

1 Tbsp lemon juice

pinch of grated nutmeg

1 egg, beaten

salt and freshly ground pepper

2 large breasts of lamb, boned and trimmed, total weight about $2\frac{1}{2}$ lb

3 Tbsp vegetable oil

watercress, to garnish

*1* Melt the butter in a saucepan, add the onion and bacon and fry for about 5 minutes until lightly browned.

*2* Drain the spinach and chop roughly. Place in a bowl with the onion and bacon, breadcrumbs, parsley, lemon rind and juice, nutmeg and egg. Mix together well, adding salt and pepper to taste.

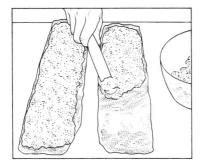

*3* Lay the breasts of lamb fat side down on a work surface and spread the stuffing evenly over them with a frosting knife.

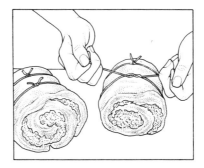

*4* Roll up the lamb breasts loosely and tie in several places with string to hold their shape.

*5* Weigh each roast and calculate the cooking time, allowing 25 minutes per 1 lb plus 25 minutes for each roast. Heat the oil in a roasting pan and place the roasts in the pan. Roast in the oven at 350°F for the calculated cooking time, basting occasionally. Serve hot, garnished with watercress.

## Menu Suggestion

Breast of lamb makes an economical midweek roast. This recipe has a spinach stuffing, therefore only one or two additional vegetables are necessary. New potatoes tossed in mint butter would go well, with glazed carrots.

### ROLLED STUFFED BREASTS OF LAMB

Breast of lamb is one of the fattier cuts, but it is excellent cooked in this way with a tasty and substantial stuffing. When buying breasts of lamb, look for the leanest ones possible—not all lamb breasts are very fatty. Any visible fat should be white and dry, whereas the meat should be pink and moist. Most lambs are aged between 3 and 6 months at the time of slaughtering; after this time the meat darkens in color and becomes more coarsely grained.

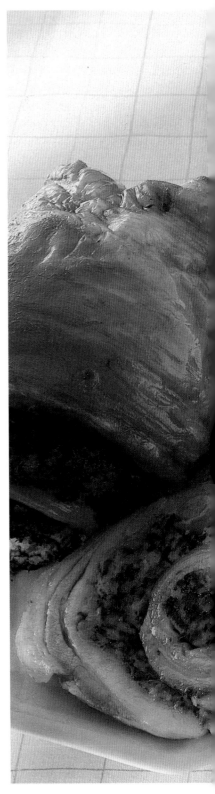

# GOLDEN BAKED CHICKEN

| 1.15 | $ | 324 cals |

*Serves 4*

4 chicken portions

1 small onion, skinned and finely chopped

salt and freshly ground pepper

1 cup fresh white breadcrumbs

1 Tbsp chopped fresh parsley and thyme or 1 tsp dried mixed herbs

$\frac{1}{4}$ cup butter or margarine, melted

*1* Wipe the chicken portions and season well with salt and freshly ground pepper.

*2* Mix the breadcrumbs with the onion and herbs.

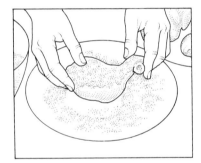

*3* Brush the chicken all over with the butter or margarine; toss them in the herbed breadcrumbs and place in a buttered ovenproof dish.

*4* Bake in the oven at 375°F for about 1 hour or until golden. Baste occasionally during cooking. Serve hot, straight from the dish.

**Menu Suggestion**
Serve with baked potatoes cooked in the oven at the same time, and a salad of tomato and raw onion with a lemony vinaigrette dressing.

# GINGERED CHICKEN

| 1.00 | $ | 361 cals |

*Serves 4*

3 lb oven-ready chicken
1 Tbsp flour
1 Tbsp ground ginger
4 Tbsp vegetable oil
1 onion, peeled and sliced
10-oz can bamboo shoots
1 red pepper, halved, seeded and sliced
$\frac{2}{3}$ cup chicken stock
3 Tbsp soy sauce
3 Tbsp medium dry sherry
salt and freshly ground pepper
4 oz mushrooms, sliced

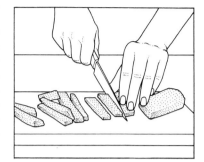

*4* Cut up the canned bamboo shoots into $\frac{1}{2}$-inch strips; add to the pan, together with the sliced pepper. Then stir in stock, soy sauce, sherry and seasoning. Bring to boil, cover, simmer 15 minutes.

*5* Add the sliced mushrooms, cover again with lid and cook for a further 5–10 minutes, or until the chicken is tender.

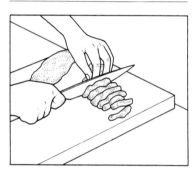

*1* Cut all the flesh off the chicken and slice into chunky "fingers," discarding the skin.

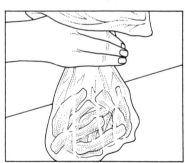

*2* Mix the flour and ginger together in a plastic bag and toss the chicken in it to coat.

*3* Heat the oil in a very large sauté or deep frying pan and fry the chicken and sliced onion together for 10–15 minutes until they are both golden.

## BAMBOO SHOOTS

These are used extensively in oriental cooking, although the Chinese and Japanese use fresh shoots rather than the canned ones specified in this recipe. If fresh bamboo shoots are not obtainable, buy canned ones which are available at oriental specialist stores, large super-markets and delicatessens. These make a very convenient substi-tute—they are pre-cooked, so all they need is draining and heating through.

The flavor of bamboo shoots is very difficult to describe. Some say they taste like mild asparagus, although asparagus aficionadoes would probably disagree! Look for those canned in water rather than those canned in vinegar — they will have a milder flavor.

# MACARONI BAKE

| 1.10 | $ | 587 cals |

*Serves 6*

$\frac{1}{2}$ cup plus 1 Tbsp butter

2 Tbsp olive oil

1 small onion, skinned and finely
  chopped

2 garlic cloves, skinned and
  crushed

14-oz can tomatoes

1 tsp chopped fresh basil or $\frac{1}{2}$ tsp
  dried, or mixed herbs

salt and freshly ground pepper

$\frac{1}{2}$ lb large macaroni

$\frac{2}{3}$ cup all-purpose flour

$2\frac{1}{2}$ cups milk

3 oz Gruyère cheese, grated

$\frac{1}{4}$ tsp freshly grated nutmeg

4 Tbsp freshly grated Parmesan
  cheese

3 Tbsp dried breadcrumbs

*1* Make the tomato sauce. Melt
  $\frac{1}{4}$ cup of the butter in a heavy-
based saucepan with the olive oil.
Add the onion and garlic and fry
gently for 5 minutes until soft but
not colored.

*2* Add the tomatoes and their
  juices with the basil and
seasoning to taste, then stir with a
wooden spoon to break up the
tomatoes. Bring to a boil, then
lower the heat and simmer for 10
minutes, stirring occasionally.

*3* Meanwhile, plunge the
  macaroni into a large pan of
boiling salted water, bring back to
a boil and cook for 10 minutes
until just tender.

*4* Make the cheese sauce. Melt
  the remaining butter in a
separate saucepan, add the flour
and cook over low heat, stirring
with a wooden spoon, for about
2 minutes. Remove the pan from
the heat and gradually blend in the
milk, stirring after each addition to
prevent lumps forming. Bring to a
boil slowly, stirring all the time
until the sauce thickens. Add the
Gruyère cheese and seasoning to
taste and stir until melted.

*5* Drain the macaroni and mix
  with the tomato sauce.
Arrange half of this mixture in a
large buttered ovenproof dish.

*6* Pour over half of the cheese
  sauce. Repeat the layers, then
sprinkle evenly with the Parmesan
and breadcrumbs.

*7* Bake the pie in the oven at
  375°F for 15 minutes, then
brown under a preheated broiler
for 5 minutes. Serve hot.

# STUFFED TURKEY LEGS

| 2.00 | 459 cals |

*Serves 6*

2 turkey legs (drumsticks), at least 2 lb total weight

8 oz pork sausagemeat

1 Tbsp chopped fresh tarragon or ½ tsp dried tarragon

2 tsp chopped fresh parsley

salt and freshly ground pepper

1 cup button mushrooms, sliced

3 Tbsp flour

1 egg white, beaten

⅔ cup fresh white breadcrumbs

½ cup butter or margarine, softened

1 Tbsp French mustard

watercress, to garnish

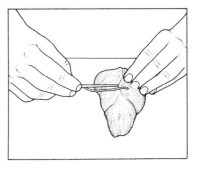

*3* Reshape the stuffed turkey legs, then sew them up neatly, using fine string.

*4* Dip the legs in flour, brush with beaten egg white and place seam side down in a greased roasting pan.

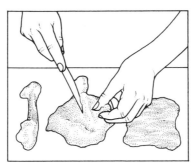

*1* Skin the turkey legs, slit the flesh and carefully ease out the bone and large sinews.

*2* Mix the sausagemeat, herbs and seasoning, and spread one quarter of the mixture over each boned leg. Cover with a layer of sliced mushrooms, then top with more sausagemeat stuffing.

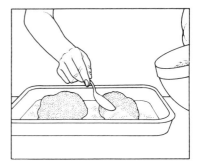

*5* Beat together the breadcrumbs, butter and mustard. Spread over the tops and sides only of the legs.

*6* Bake in the oven at 375°F for about 1 hour 40 minutes, until tender with a crisp, golden crust. Remove the string, slice, and serve with gravy made from the pan juices. Garnish with a sprig of watercress.

**Menu Suggestion**
Serve these roasted turkey legs sliced, as an unusual alternative to the traditional Sunday roast, with vegetables, roast potatoes and gravy made from the turkey's cooking juices.

# A WEDDING GARDEN PARTY

**A** fancy garden party is romantic, especially when the guests of honor are the new bride and groom. The champagne flows, there's music in the air, and of course, an abundance of scrumptious foods. Gardens are at their best this time of year. There's every shade of spring green, light and new and fresh. Spring flowers are the most fragile and often the loveliest flowers of the year.

A wedding celebration is special enough in itself, but there is something extra festive about a wedding party in a garden on a bright late spring or early summer day. People seem more relaxed and more alert outside in the fresh air. There's more room to move and mingle, more things about— trees, flowers, puffs of clouds against a (hopefully) blue sky—to catch the eye and give one reason to be happy.

If you have a big enough backyard and are willing to take your chances with the weather, having it outdoors can mean less wear and tear on the house and give you room for more people.

**Fancy Finger Foods, and More**
Finger foods, like little tea sandwiches, are perfect. Don't make them up too far ahead of time; they'll get soggy. Use one slice of wholewheat or rye bread and one slice of white in each sandwich for an interesting effect, or make small double or triple deckers with 3 or 4 slices of bread and 2 or 3 different fillings.

There are many elegant fillings you can concoct for something as special as a wedding spread: chopped roasted lamb with sour cream and chopped mint leaves, smoked salmon with thin slices of cucumber and lemon juice, egg salad with avocado or capers,

---

### MENU

◆

*Champagne Cocktail*
*(see featured recipe here)*

*fancy tea sandwiches*

*cold boiled and peeled shrimp with*
*cocktail sauce*

*cold lightly steamed asparagus with*
*Hollandaise Sauce (see page 375)*

*Ramekins of Baked Crab*
*(see featured recipe here)*

*fresh whole strawberries*

*Yogurt and Orange Whip (see page 52)*

*Black Forest Trifles (see page 52)*

*champagne*

*chilled dry white wine*

— ◆ —

cottage cheese and watercress or bean sprouts, Brie and tomatoes.

If sandwiches are not food enough, bring out cold boiled shrimp heaped on silver platters accompanied by cocktail sauce, and fresh asparagus (that have been quickly steamed so they still have some crunch left in them) with Hollandaise Sauce. Individual Baked Crab Ramekins will further delight your guests. Big, ripe strawberries, all by themselves in a crystal bowl, individual Yogurt and Orange Cream Whip cups and Black Forest Trifles make for a memorable ending.

Champagne is indisputably the best thing with which to toast the newlyweds, and champagne cocktails are the best of the best. Follow them with more champagne, chilled dry white wine, and sparkling water.

## CHAMPAGNE COCKTAIL

*Serves 6–8*

| |
| --- |
| 6–8 small sugar lumps |
| Angostura bitters |
| juice of 1½–2 lemons, strained |
| 6–8 Tbsp brandy |
| 1 bottle of champagne, chilled |
| wafer-thin lemon slices, to decorate (optional) |

**1** Put 1 sugar lump in the bottom of 6–8 tall champagne flutes and pour 4 dashes of Angostura bitters over each.

**2** Add the strained lemon juice and brandy to each and top up with champagne. Float a thin slice of lemon on top of each glass, if desired. Serve immediately.

## RAMEKINS OF BAKED CRAB

*Serves 6*

| |
| --- |
| 2 Tbsp butter or margarine |
| ⅓ cup onion |
| 8 oz crab meat |
| 1 cup fresh wholewheat breadcrumbs |
| 2 tsp French mustard |
| ⅔ cup yogurt |
| 3 Tbsp light cream or milk |
| cayenne |
| salt |
| about 1½ oz Cheddar |
| lime slices and parsley sprigs, to garnish (optional) |

**1** Melt the butter in a saucepan. Skin and finely chop the onion and fry it gently in the butter until golden brown.

**2** Flake the crab meat, taking care to remove any membranes or shell particles. Mix it into the cooked onions and add the breadcrumbs. Mix well together. Stir in the mustard, yogurt and cream. Sprinkle generously with cayenne, then add salt to taste.

**3** Spoon the mixture into 6 individual ramekins or individual soufflé dishes. Grate the cheese thinly over the surface of each dish. Stand the dishes on a baking sheet. Place on the top shelf in the oven and cook at 325°F for 25–30 minutes, or until really hot. Garnish with lime slices and parsley, if desired.

**Menu Suggestion**
Serve with triangles of crisp hot wholewheat toast for an informal dinner party appetizer, or for a tasty lunch or supper snack.

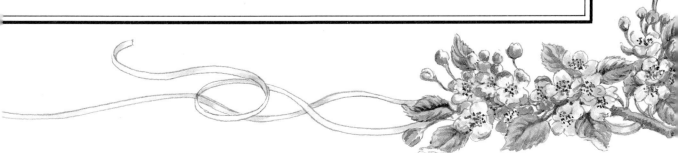

# PETITS POIS WITH PROSCIUTTO

| 0.25 | $ $ | 206 cals |

*Serves 4*

2 oz Prosciutto

4 Tbsp butter or margarine

2 lb fresh young peas, shelled

12 scallions, washed, trimmed and sliced

1 firm lettuce, washed and shredded

1 tsp sugar

salt and freshly ground pepper

$\frac{3}{4}$ cup chicken stock

sprig of mint, to garnish

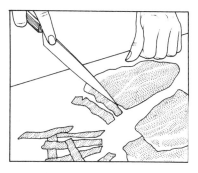

*1* Using a sharp knife, cut the prosciutto into small strips. Then melt the butter in a large pan, add the peas, ham and the next 6 ingredients.

*2* Bring to the boil, cover and simmer gently for 15–20 minutes. Serve in a warm serving dish with the cooking liquid. Garnish with a sprig of mint.

## PETITS POIS

These are small, sweet, tender young peas, much used in Europe. The term literally means "little peas" in French. This recipe, with Prosciutto, is claimed by the Italians. The ham can be omitted if desired, or other varieties of ham used. Without the addition of ham it is known as *petits pois à la française*, a traditional, well-known French dish.

This recipe can only be made in spring and summer, when all the vegetables are fresh and young. Fresh young peas should be eaten with their cooking liquid so that their full flavor is appreciated.

It is essential to cook peas as soon as possible after they are picked, as the sugar in them begins to "die" and turn to starch the moment they leave the parent plant. When you are picking or buying fresh peas, the pods should be crisp, young and well-filled.

If fresh peas are unavailable, good-quality frozen varieties are available, and make a good substitute. Ordinary frozen peas, however, cannot be substituted for *petits pois*.

# FRENCH BEANS IN SOUR CREAM WITH PAPRIKA

| 0.25 | $ | 141 cals |

*Serves 4*

| 1½ lb French green beans |
| 2 Tbsp butter or margarine |
| 1 small onion, chopped |
| 1 tsp paprika |
| salt and freshly ground pepper |
| ¾ cup chicken stock |
| ¾ cup sour cream |

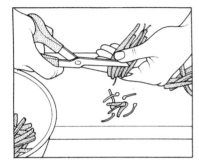

*1* Using kitchen scissors, top and tail the French beans and cut them into 1-inch lengths. Melt the butter in a pan, add the onion and cook gently for 5 minutes until soft and golden, but do not brown.

*2* Stir in ½ tsp paprika, beans, seasoning and stock. Bring to the boil, cover and simmer for 5–10 minutes until the French beans are tender.

*3* Stir the cream into the pan and reheat without boiling. Turn into a heated serving dish and dust the top with the remaining paprika.

# NEW POTATOES WITH TARRAGON CREAM

| 0.15 | $ | 204 cals |

*Serves 4*

**1 Tbsp butter or margarine**

**4 scallions, washed, trimmed and chopped**

**$\frac{3}{4}$ cup sour cream**

**salt and freshly ground pepper**

**3 sprigs of fresh tarragon**

**$1\frac{1}{2}$ lb cooked new potatoes, drained and kept hot**

*1* Melt the butter in a pan, add the scallions and cook for 5 minutes until soft. Stir in the cream, seasoning, and two tarragon sprigs and heat without boiling.

*2* Add the cooked potatoes to the creamy onion and tarragon mixture in the pan. Reheat gently, do not boil.

*3* Turn the potatoes and the sauce into a warm serving dish and serve garnished with a sprig of fresh tarragon.

# CABBAGE WITH CARAWAY

**0.15** | **110 cals**

*Serves 6*

3 lb green cabbage

salt

4 Tbsp butter or margarine

1 tsp caraway seeds

freshly ground pepper

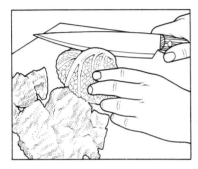

*1* Shred the cabbage finely, discarding any core or tough outer leaves. Wash well under cold running water.

*2* Cook in a large pan of boiling salted water for 2 minutes only—the cabbage should retain its crispness and texture. Drain well.

*3* Melt the butter in the saucepan; add the drained cabbage with the caraway seeds and seasoning. Stir over a moderate heat for 2–3 minutes until the cabbage is really hot. Adjust seasoning and serve immediately.

# PEPPERED CARROTS

| *0.20* | 157 cals |

*Serves 4*

**4 Tbsp butter or margarine**

**1 tsp sugar**

**1 lb carrots, peeled or scrubbed and thinly sliced**

**3 spring onions, washed and trimmed**

**$\frac{1}{4}$ tsp cayenne pepper or to taste**

**3 Tbsp sour cream**

**salt and freshly ground pepper**

*1* Melt the butter with the sugar in a deep sauté pan which has a tightly fitting lid. Put the carrots into the pan, cover tightly and cook gently for 10–15 minutes until tender.

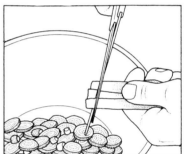

*2* Remove the lid from the pan and snip in the spring onions with a pair of sharp kitchen scissors. Transfer carrots and onions with a slotted spoon to a serving dish and keep warm.

*3* Stir the cayenne pepper and sour cream into the pan. Taste and adjust seasoning, and warm through for 1–2 minutes. Pour over the carrots and serve.

# SPRING SALAD SAMPLER

Many people still tend to think of salads as boring mixtures of raw green "rabbit food." If you know people who think this way, invite them to a salad sampler party and expand their horizons. The choice of foods that can be used to make super salads is endless, with ingredients ranging from the usual lettuce, cucumber and tomato, to exotic fruits and vegetables such as avocados, artichokes and mangos; and cold cooked foods like rice, pasta, fish and spicy cooked meats.

Make your party interesting and have each guest bring a salad. Suggest to them the main ingredient in their salad, and ask them to create the dish around that. That way, there's little chance of duplication and lots of opportunity for variety. This is one time when it helps to know t culinary skills and creativity of your guests. It allows you to suggest a more exotic main ingredient to those you know are comfortable trying new things ar save the more familiar foods for those who like to stick with the tried and true. You may want to have a few good salad recipes on hand, to give out to anyone who seems at a loss for what to bring.

### Your Contributions

As host or hostess you might war to make up a many-layered salad because it looks so pretty and is a bit difficult for someone to transport to your party. Choose a high-sided glass bowl (a trifle bo is perfect) so that you can see the layers. Build up the salad by starting with a layer of shredded green or red lettuce and top it wi layers of any number of things th are so plentiful in springtime: fresh asparagus chunks, snow peas, sweet peas, scallions, radishes, baby carrots, watercres and spinach. Finish off with a layer of diced cooked meat and

nother of shredded cheese. Have
small pitcher of Sour Cream and
Watercress Dressing on the side.

Have a few kinds of bread on
and to serve along with the salads
and to scoop up particularly good
alad dressings). This is one time
when you can serve a rich dessert,
ike Marbled Chocolate Ring,
without feeling like you're
verloading your guests.

### Salad Making Tips

resh green salads should be crisp
nd cool. Wait until close to
erving time to trim and wash the
reens because breaking the tender
eaf tissues exposes more surface
rea to the air, causing them to go
imp and turn brown faster. And
vater, after a while, will make
hem soggy. If you do need to
repare lettuce and other greens
head of time, wrap them gently in
clean dish towel after washing
hem and keep them wrapped up
n the refrigerator. When you take
hem out to serve, wipe off each
eaf gently to remove any water;
alad dressing will not stick to
eaves coated with water. Then
reak them into smaller pieces, if
eed be, as you place them in the
alad bowl for tossing and serving.
low really cool and delightful
our green salad will be if you can
nanage to chill the salad bowl—
nd even the individual salad
lates—beforehand.

## FRENCH SPINACH SALAD WITH HOT BACON DRESSING

### Serves 4

| |
|---|
| 8 oz fresh young spinach, washed and trimmed |
| 2 large slices of white bread |
| 3 Tbsp vegetable oil |
| 1 garlic clove, crushed |
| 8 strips bacon, chopped |
| 1 Tbsp white wine vinegar |
| salt and freshly ground pepper |

**1** Shred any large spinach leaves
into small strips and place in a
salad bowl. Set aside until
required.

**2** Make the croûtons. Remove the
crusts from the bread and cut the
bread into $\frac{1}{2}$-inch cubes. Put the
oil in a frying pan and fry the
bread cubes until golden brown.

**3** Stir the crushed garlic into the
bread croûtons, then drain them
on paper towels.

**4** Add the bacon to the pan and
fry for about 5 minutes until crisp
and golden brown. Pour the fried
bacon and any fat over the spinach
leaves.

**5** Add the vinegar to the pan, stir
well to deglaze, then pour over the
salad. Add seasoning, toss quickly,
scatter the croûtons on top and
serve at once.

### ——— RAW SPINACH ———

Raw spinach makes a perfect
summer salad ingredient—it
requires very little preparation and
no cooking, therefore very little
time needs to be spent in the
kitchen. Raw spinach is also
excellent from a nutritional point
of view: rich in calcium and iron
and a good source of vitamins A
and C as well as dietary fiber.

# BLACK FOREST TRIFLES

| 0.20 | 266 cals |
|------|----------|

*Serves 4*

¾ lb fresh cherries or 15-oz can cherries

3 oz sponge cake

⅔ cup sour cream

1 Tbsp kirsch or orange-flavored liqueur (optional)

1 egg white

1 Tbsp sugar

chocolate curls, to decorate

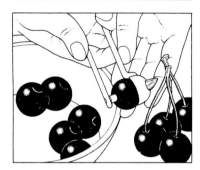

*1* If using fresh cherries, pit them, then simmer them gently in a little water for 2–3 minutes. Leave to cool. If using canned cherries, drain and pit them, reserving the juice.

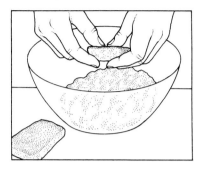

*2* With your fingers, break the sponge cake roughly into a bowl. Stir in 2 Tbsp of the sour cream and the liqueur, if using.

*3* Divide the sponge mixture between 4 stemmed glasses. Spoon the cherries on top, with 8 Tbsp of the cooking liquid or reserved juices from the canned cherries.

*4* Whisk the egg white until stiff, add the sugar and continue whisking until very stiff. Fold into the remaining sour cream.

*5* Top each glass with the sour cream mixture and chill in the refrigerator until ready to serve. Decorate with chocolate curls just before serving.

**Menu Suggestion**
Exceptionally quick to prepare, these trifles make a delicious dessert for Sunday lunch, when there's no time to bake something special.

---

**BLACK FOREST TRIFLES**
Kirsch is a cherry brandy that comes from the border area of France, Germany and Switzerland. The Germans call their version *kirschwasser*, and it is traditional to use it in the famous Black Forest chocolate and cherry gâteau, Schwarzwalder Kirschtorte. These Black Forest Trifles are a variation on the theme, so the addition of kirsch gives them authenticity.

---

# YOGURT AND ORANGE WHIP

| 0.15 | $ | 225 cals |
|------|---|----------|

*Serves 4*

2 eggs, separated

2 oz sugar

finely grated rind of 1 orange

1 Tbsp orange-flavored liqueur

¼ pint natural yogurt

orange shreds, to decorate

*1* In a deep bowl, whisk the egg yolks with half of the sugar until pale and creamy. Whisk in the orange rind and liqueur.

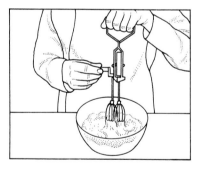

*2* In a separate bowl, whisk the egg whites until stiff but not dry, add the rest of the sugar and whisk again until stiff.

*3* Fold the yogurt into the egg yolk mixture, then fold in the whisked egg whites until evenly incorporated.

*4* Spoon the mixture into 4 individual glasses and decorate with orange shreds. Serve immediately, or the mixture will begin to separate.

**Menu Suggestion**
Yogurt and Orange Whip makes the perfect last-minute cold dessert. Serve with sponge fingers.

# BANANA CHEESECAKE

$\boxed{0.40^*}$ $ $ $\boxed{428\text{--}570 \text{ cals}}$

\* plus 3–4 hours chilling; freeze after step 5. Defrost in refrigerator overnight, then continue with step 6.

*Serves 6–8*

18 gingersnaps

½ cup unsalted butter, melted and cooled

8 oz cream cheese

⅔ cup sour cream

3 bananas

2 Tbsp honey

1 Tbsp chopped preserved ginger (with syrup)

3 tsp gelatine

4 Tbsp lemon juice

banana slices and preserved ginger slices, to decorate

*1* Make the crust. Crush the gingersnaps finely using a food processor or blender. Stir in the melted butter.

*2* Press the mixture over the base of an 8-inch springform pan. Chill in the refrigerator for about 30 minutes.

*3* Meanwhile, make the filling. Beat the cheese and cream together until well mixed. Peel and mash the bananas, then beat into the cheese mixture with the honey and ginger.

*4* Sprinkle the gelatine over the lemon juice in a small heat-proof bowl. Stand the bowl over a saucepan of hot water and heat gently until dissolved.

*5* Stir the dissolved gelatine slowly into the cheesecake mixture, then spoon into the crumb-lined pan. Chill in the refrigerator for about 3–4 hours until the mixture is set.

*6* To serve, remove the cheesecake carefully from the pan and place on a serving plate. Decorate around the edge with banana and ginger slices. Serve as soon as possible or the banana will discolor.

# CHOCOLATE MOUSSE CAKE

1.30* $ $ 586 cals

* plus 1 hour cooling and overnight
chilling; freeze after stage 6

*Serves 8*

1 lb semisweet chocolate

3 Tbsp orange-flavored liqueur

9 eggs, 5 of them separated

¾ cup sugar

½ cup unsalted butter, softened

blanched julienne strips of orange
    rind and grated chocolate, to
    decorate

*1* Grease an 8-inch spring-form
pan, line with waxed paper and
grease the paper.

*2* Break half the chocolate into a
heatproof bowl and place over
a pan of simmering water and stir
gently until the chocolate has
melted. Stir in 1 Tbsp liqueur,
then remove from the heat.

*3* Using an electric whisk, whisk
five egg yolks and the sugar
together until thick and creamy,
then beat in the butter a little at a
time until smooth. Beat in the
melted chocolate until smooth.

*4* Whisk the five egg whites until
stiff, then fold into the chocolate mixture. Turn into the prepared pan and bake in the oven at
350°F for 50 minutes until risen
and firm. Leave the cake to cool in
the pan for 1 hour.

*5* Make the top layer: melt the
remaining chocolate as before,
then stir in the remaining liqueur.
Remove from the heat, cool for
1–2 minutes. Separate the remaining eggs and beat the egg yolks
into the chocolate mixture. Whisk
the egg whites until stiff, then fold
into the chocolate mixture.

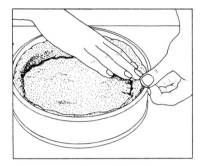

*6* Press the crust down on the
baked cake with your fingers
and pour the top layer over it.
Refrigerate overnight.

*7* The next day, remove the cake
carefully from the pan and put
onto a serving plate.

*8* Arrange blanched strips of
orange rind around the outside
edge and decorate with grated
chocolate.

# CHOCOLATE VIENNESE FINGERS

| 1.00* | $ | 89 cals |

\* plus 1 hour cooling and setting; freeze after stage 5

*Makes about 18*

½ cup butter or margarine

½ cup confectioners sugar

3 oz semisweet chocolate

¾ cup all-purpose flour

¼ tsp baking powder

1 Tbsp sweetened milk chocolate powder

few drops of vanilla extract

*1* Grease two baking sheets. Put the butter into a bowl and beat until pale and soft, then beat in the confectioners sugar.

*2* Break 1 oz chocolate into a heatproof bowl and place over simmering water. Stir until the chocolate is melted, then remove from heat and leave to cool for 10 minutes.

*3* When the chocolate is cool, but not thick, beat it into the creamed mixture.

*4* Sift in the flour, baking powder and milk chocolate. Beat well, adding a few drops of vanilla extract.

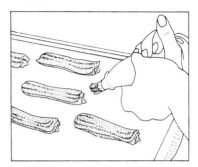

*5* Spoon into a piping bag fitted with a medium star vegetable nozzle and pipe finger shapes about 3 inches long onto the pre-pared baking sheets, allowing room between each for the mixture to spread. Bake at 375°F for 15–20 minutes until crisp and pale golden. Cool on a wire rack for 30 minutes.

*6* When the fingers are cold, break the remaining 2 oz chocolate into a heatproof bowl. Stand the bowl over a pan of simmering water and stir until the chocolate has melted. Remove from the heat and dip both ends of the fingers into the melted chocolate. Leave on a wire rack for 30 minutes to set.

# MARBLED CHOCOLATE RING CAKE

| 2.00* | $ $ | 775 cals |

\* plus 1¼ hours cooling and 1 hour
setting; freeze after stage 6

*Serves 8*

| 8 oz semisweet chocolate |
| 1 tsp vanilla extract |
| 3 Tbsp water |
| 1½ cups butter |
| 1¼ cups sugar |
| 4 eggs, beaten |
| 1½ cups all-purpose flour |
| 2 tsp baking powder |
| ½ tsp salt |
| ½ cup ground almonds |
| 2 Tbsp milk |

*1* Grease a 2-quart ring mold.
Break 2 oz chocolate into a
heatproof bowl. Add the vanilla
extract and 1 Tbsp water and
place over simmering water. Stir
until the chocolate is melted, then
remove from heat and leave to cool
for 10 minutes.

*2* Put 1 cup butter and the sugar
into a bowl and beat together
until pale and fluffy. Beat in the
eggs one at a time.

*3* Fold the flour, baking powder,
and salt into the creamed mixture with the ground almonds.
Stir in the milk. Spoon half the
mixture into base of ring mold.

*4* Stir the cooled but still soft
chocolate into the remaining
mixture. Spoon into the mold.

*5* Draw a knife through the cake
mixture in a spiral. Level the
surface of the mixture again.

*6* Bake in the oven at 350°F for
about 55 minutes or until a
fine warmed skewer inserted in
the center comes out clean. Turn
out onto a wire rack to cool for
1 hour.

*7* Make the chocolate frosting.
Break 5 oz chocolate into a
heatproof bowl with 2 Tbsp water
and the remaining butter. Place
over simmering water and stir
until the chocolate is melted, then
pour over the cooled cake, working quickly to coat top and sides.
Leave to set for 1 hour.

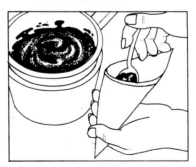

*8* Melt the remaining chocolate
over simmering water as before. Spoon into a waxed paper
piping bag, snip off the tip and
drizzle chocolate over the cake.

# S·U·M·M·E·R

*T*he lazy days of summer have arrived. School's out, vacations are in. Here come the clambakes, barbecues and backyard parties.

Our summer menus are filled with summer salads, foods for the broiler, and refreshing, fruity desserts that cool off the hottest of days.

We begin with a backyard barbecue that lets each person there custom-make their own main course from the bowls of marinated meats, fish and vegetables ready to be skewered for kabobs.

Fourth of July is celebrated with a clambake, complete with corn on the cob and cole slaw. It's sure to be a great success, even if there is no beach in sight.

After all the excitement of barbecues and clambakes we settle into a quiet Patio Supper. This is a barbecue of sorts, but one that's ideal for a lazy summer night. The fish practically broils itself while you and your guests relax with some wine and a cool cucumber soup.

Summer has almost come to a close as we end with a Late Summer Potluck. It's the ideal meal for bringing together the neighbors for one last summer fling.

# ICED TOMATO AND HERB SOUP

| 0.20* | $ | 133 cals |

* plus 2 hours chilling

*Serves 4*

1 lb ripe tomatoes

1 small onion, skinned and sliced

4 tsp tomato paste

14$\frac{1}{2}$-oz can chicken consommé

2 Tbsp chopped fresh herbs, e.g.
  basil, coriander, parsley

salt and freshly ground pepper

$\frac{1}{2}$ cup fresh white breadcrumbs

$\frac{2}{3}$ cup sour cream

fresh basil leaves, to garnish

*1* Roughly chop the tomatoes and process them with the onion, tomato paste, consommé and herbs until smooth.

*2* Rub the tomato mixture through a nylon sieve into a saucepan. Heat gently to remove the frothy texture, then add plenty of salt and pepper.

*3* Pour the soup into a large serving bowl and stir in the breadcrumbs. Chill in the refrigerator for at least 2 hours.

*4* Stir the sour cream until smooth, then swirl in. Float the fresh basil leaves on top.

**Menu Suggestion**
Serve this elegant soup for a summer dinner party appetizer.

# COLD CUCUMBER SOUP

| 0.20* | $ | 267 cals |
|---|---|---|

\* plus 8 hours chilling

*Serves 4*

2 medium cucumbers, peeled

1 cup walnuts, chopped

2 Tbsp olive oil or a mixture of walnut and olive oil

$1\frac{1}{4}$ cups chicken stock, skimmed

1 garlic clove, skinned and crushed

2 Tbsp chopped fresh dill or 2 tsp dried dill

salt and freshly ground pepper

$1\frac{1}{4}$ cups yogurt or sour cream

sprigs of fresh dill, to garnish

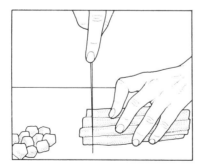

*1* Dice the cucumbers and place in a bowl. Add the walnuts, oil, stock, garlic and chopped dill and season to taste with salt and pepper.

*2* Stir the soup well, cover the bowl with plastic wrap and chill in the refrigerator for at least 8 hours, or overnight.

*3* To serve, uncover and whisk in the yogurt or sour cream. Ladle into individual soup bowls surrounded by crushed ice and garnish with the sprigs of dill.

**Menu Suggestion**
Cool, creamy and refreshing, this cucumber soup is best served with crisp Melba toast and chilled dry white wine.

# HUMMUS
## (MIDDLE EASTERN CHICK PEA AND TAHINI DIP)

| 1.20* | $ | 277–416 cals |

* plus overnight soaking and a few hours chilling; freeze without the garnish

*Serves 4–6*

1 cup chick peas, soaked in cold water overnight

about ⅔ cup lemon juice

⅔ cup tahini paste

3 garlic cloves, skinned and crushed

salt

2 Tbsp olive oil

1 tsp paprika

crudités, to serve (see box)

*1* Drain the soaked chick peas and rinse well under cold running water. Put the chick peas in a large saucepan and cover with plenty of cold water.

*2* Bring slowly to a boil, then skim off any scum with a slotted spoon. Half cover the pan with a lid and simmer gently for about 1 hour, until the chick peas are very tender.

*3* Drain the chick peas, reserving 4 Tbsp of the cooking liquid. Set a few whole chick peas aside for the garnish, then put the remainder in a blender or food processor. Add the reserved cooking liquid and half of the lemon juice and work to a smooth paste.

*4* Add the tahini paste, garlic and 1 tsp salt and work again. Taste and add more lemon juice until the dip is to your liking, then blend in 2 Tbsp hot water.

*5* Turn into a serving bowl and cover with plastic wrap. Chill in the refrigerator until serving time. Before serving, mix the oil with the paprika and drizzle over the Hummus. Arrange the reserved whole chick peas on top.

# PAPA GHANOOYE
## (ARABIC EGGPLANT DIP)

| 0.50* | $ | 322–483 cals |

* plus a few hours chilling; freeze without the garnish

*Serves 4–6*

2 large eggplants

salt

2–3 garlic cloves, skinned and roughly chopped

2 tsp cumin seeds

½ cup olive oil

⅔ cup tahini paste

about ½ cup lemon juice

thin tomato slices, to garnish

crudités, to serve (see box)

*1* Slice the eggplant, then place in a colander, sprinkling each layer with salt. Cover with a plate, put heavy weights on top and leave to drain for 30 minutes.

*2* Meanwhile, crush the garlic and cumin seeds with a pestle and mortar. Add 1 tsp salt and mix well.

*3* Rinse the eggplant under cold running water, then pat dry with paper towels. Heat the oil in a large, heavy-based frying pan until very hot. Add the eggplant slices in batches and fry until golden on both sides, turning once. Remove from the pan with a slotted spoon and drain again on paper towels.

*4* Put the eggplant slices in a blender or food processor with the garlic mixture, the tahini paste and about two-thirds of the lemon juice. Work to a smooth paste, then taste and add more lemon juice and salt if desired.

*5* Turn into a serving bowl, cover with plastic wrap and chill in the refrigerator until serving time. Serve chilled, garnished with tomato slices.

# SKORDALIA
## (GREEK GARLIC DIP)

| 0.30* | $ | 381–572 cals |

* plus a few hours chilling

*Serves 4–6*

1½ cups crustless white bread

4 Tbsp milk

6 garlic cloves

1 cup olive oil

¼ cup lemon juice

salt and freshly ground pepper

black olives and finely chopped parsley, to garnish

crudités, to serve (see box)

*1* Tear the bread into small pieces into a bowl. Add the milk, mix and soak for 5 minutes.

*2* Skin the cloves of garlic, chop roughly, then crush with a pestle and mortar.

*3* Squeeze the bread with your fingers, then mix with the crushed garlic. Add the olive oil a drop at a time to form a paste.

*4* When the mixture thickens, add a few drops of lemon juice, then continue with the olive oil. Add more lemon juice and salt and pepper. Turn into a bowl and cover with plastic wrap. Chill in the refrigerator and garnish with olives and parsley before serving.

---

**VEGETABLE DIPS**

Dips make good appetizers for informal supper parties, or to serve at a cocktail party. Crudités (raw vegetables) are ideal for dipping and dunking. To serve 4–6 people: 4 carrots, peeled and cut into thin sticks, 1 small cauliflower, divided into florets, 4–6 celery sticks, halved, ½ cucumber, seeds removed and cut into sticks, 1 red and 1 green pepper, cored, seeded and sliced, 1 bunch of radishes, trimmed. Fingers of hot pita bread can also be served.

---

# INDONESIAN PORK SATÉ

0.40* $ $ 468 cals

* plus 30 minutes marinating

*Serves 4*

1 lb pork tenderloin

2 Tbsp dark soy sauce

3 Tbsp lemon juice

1½ tsp ground ginger

¾ cup unsalted peanuts

2 Tbsp oil

1 garlic clove, skinned and crushed

½ tsp ground coriander

¼ tsp chili powder

¼ tsp salt

2 cups coconut milk

1 tsp brown sugar

freshly ground pepper

½ cucumber

*1* Cut the pork tenderloin into small cubes. Thread onto 8 long saté sticks, or metal skewers.

*2* Mix together the soy sauce, lemon juice and 1 tsp of the ginger. Pour over the pork skewers and leave to marinate for at least 30 minutes, turning occasionally.

*3* Meanwhile, finely chop the peanuts or grind them in a nut mill. Heat the oil in a saucepan. Add the peanuts, garlic, coriander, chili powder, remaining ginger and salt and fry for about 4–5 minutes until browned, stirring.

*4* Stir in the milk and sugar. Bring to a boil and simmer for about 15 minutes or until the sauce thickens. Check the seasoning, adding pepper to taste.

*5* Broil the pork skewers for about 6 minutes, or until the meat is tender, turning occasionally.

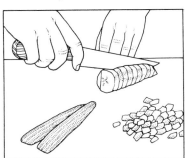

*6* Meanwhile, chop the cucumber finely. Serve the saté hot, with the chopped cucumber, and the peanut sauce for dipping.

**Menu Suggestion**
These kabobs come with their own sauce for dipping and so need no accompaniment. Follow with an Indonesian-style main course of whole steamed or baked fish, or a fish curry.

# SPICY SPARERIBS

$0.20*$ $ 274 cals

* plus 2 hours marinating
*Serves 4*

4 lb pork spareribs
1 onion, skinned and sliced
1½ cups tomato juice
3 Tbsp cider vinegar
2 Tbsp clear honey
2 tsp salt
1 tsp paprika
¾ tsp chili powder

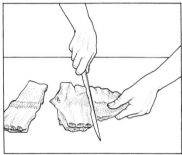

*1* Separate the spareribs into sections of 2–3 ribs. Place in a shallow dish. Mix all the remaining ingredients together and pour over the ribs. Cover and marinate in the refrigerator for 2 hours.

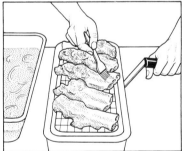

*2* Place the spareribs under a preheated broiler. Brush with the marinade. Broil for 20 minutes, brushing occasionally with the marinade and turning. Heat the marinade and serve as a sauce.

**Menu Suggestion**
Serve as a first course for a Chinese-style supper party.

# BACKYARD BARBECUE

**S**ummer means barbecues, barbecues and more barbecues. But they don't all have to be hamburgers and hot dogs or even steaks. Today's barbecues might be anything from marinated meats, to grilled fish steaks, to chunks of firm vegetables—or all three mixed on skewers.

The backyard barbecue is the on sure time that cooking is pleasur Rather than standing solitary ove a hot stove, the cook is out in the fresh air, right in the center of activity. It hardly seems like wor at all.

**Make-Your-Own Kabobs**
It can be even less work for the cook if family and friends are invited to do their own cooking over the coals. Set out plates heaped with meats, fish and vegetables, give each a skewer or two and have them make their ow kabob creations, with chunks of foods that hold their shape as the grill: beef, lamb, chicken, meaty fish like tuna, swordfish or salmo zucchini, eggplant, semi-cooked potatoes, peppers, small onions, even tofu.

It's best to have marinated all the meat and fish for a few hours and preferably overnight (always in the refrigerator); they'll be mo tender and less apt to dry out as they grill. Even the vegetables wi improve if they are placed in a marinade for an hour or two. You can make a simple marinade that' good with meat, fish and vegetables by mixing 2 Tbsp lemon juice, $\frac{1}{2}$ cup olive oil, $\frac{1}{2}$ tsp salt, $\frac{1}{8}$ tsp pepper, 1 minced garlic clove and $\frac{1}{4}$ tsp dried rosemary. This makes enough marinade for each pound of food. For 8 people

---

## MENU

◆

*Spicy Spareribs (broiled or barbecued)*
*(see page 67)*

*chunks of meat, fish and vegetables for kabobs*

*Rice Salad Ring (featured recipe here)*

*Barbecued Beans (see page 101)*

*Poppy Seed Rolls (see page 385)*

*Green Salad (see page 382)*

*Orange Sherbet (see page 113)*

*a light red wine*

*beer*

◆

ou will need about 2½ lb of meat, hicken or fish, and about 4 lb of egetables.

Grill the the kabobs about inches from the heat source and rush now and then with leftover narinade or olive oil or vegetable il.

**The Rest of the Meal**

To stave off hunger pains as the abobs cook, serve an appetizer, ke Spicy Spareribs, that has lready been cooked, either on the arbecue or under the broiler. When the kabobs are just about eady, set out the accompaniments: dinner rolls, tossed salad, Rice Salad Ring and Barbecued Beans. Orange Sherbet is a nice ght dessert to an otherwise filling neal.

**Grilling Tips**

Get ready well ahead of time by hecking your barbecue quipment. Roughly figure that ou'll need a barbecue grill with a iameter of at least 18 inches to ook enough food for 8 people. or this make-your-own kabob arbecue you'd be wise to have nore than one grill going at the ame time. This will prevent bottlenecks" at the grill.

Have plenty of metal skewers on and, too. Assume that each erson will want to make up 2 kewers each. They should be at least 12 inches long; this will enable everyone to put on several chunks of food and still leave room at the end so that food will not slide off as it's being handled.

## *RICE SALAD RING*

*Serves 8*

| |
|---|
| 8 oz long-grain rice |
| salt and freshly ground pepper |
| 1 green pepper, seeded and diced |
| 3 caps canned pimento, diced |
| 7 oz canned corn, drained |
| 5 Tbsp chopped fresh parsley |
| 2 oz salted peanuts |
| 3 Tbsp lemon juice |
| celery salt |
| watercress, to garnish |

**1** Cook the rice in plenty of boiling salted water for 10–15 minutes until tender, then tip into a sieve and drain.

**2** Rinse the rice through with hot water from the kettle, then rinse under cold running water and drain thoroughly. Leave to cool completely.

**3** Blanch the green pepper in boiling water for 1 minute, drain, rinse under cold running water and drain again.

**4** In a large bowl, mix the cold rice, pepper and pimento, corn, parsley, peanuts and lemon juice, and season well with celery salt and pepper.

**5** Press the salad into a lightly oiled 6-cup ring mold and refrigerate for 1 hour.

**6** Turn the rice salad ring out onto a flat serving plate and fill with watercress. Serve chilled.

# KABOBS WITH CUMIN

| 0.30* | $ | 280 cals |
|---|---|---|

\* plus overnight chilling; freeze after shaping in step 3

*Serves 4*

12 oz finely ground veal or beef

finely grated rind of 1 small lemon

1 Tbsp lemon juice

1 garlic clove, skinned and crushed

1 tsp ground cumin

$\frac{1}{2}$ tsp salt

$\frac{1}{2}$ tsp freshly ground pepper

1 small onion, skinned

vegetable oil, for broiling

lemon wedges, to serve

*1* Put the ground meat in a bowl with the lemon rind and juice, the garlic, cumin and salt and pepper. Mix well together, preferably by hand.

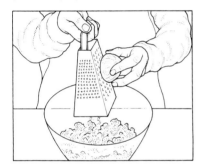

*2* Grate in the onion and mix again. (The longer the mixture is stirred, the drier it becomes and the easier it is to handle.) Cover the bowl and chill in the refrigerator, preferably overnight.

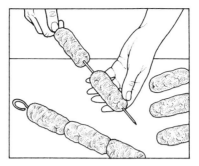

*3* Divide the mixture into 12 pieces and form into small sausage shapes. Chill again if possible, then thread onto 4 oiled kabob skewers.

*4* Place on a baking sheet. Brush with oil and broil evenly for 10–12 minutes, turning frequently until browned. Serve hot, with lemon wedges.

**Menu Suggestion**

Serve on a bed of rice or pilaf, or serve in pockets of warm pita bread with salad.

# FRIKADELLER
## (DANISH MEAT PATTIES)

| 0.30 | $ | 243 cals |
|---|---|---|

*Serves 6*

1 egg

$1\frac{1}{4}$ cups milk

12 oz ground veal

4 oz ground pork

1 small onion, skinned and finely chopped

$\frac{3}{4}$ cup flour

1 Tbsp chopped fresh thyme or $\frac{1}{2}$ tsp dried

$\frac{1}{2}$ tsp grated nutmeg

salt and freshly ground pepper

3 Tbsp vegetable oil

*1* Break the egg into a small bowl, add the milk and beat lightly with a fork.

*2* Put the ground veal and pork in a separate bowl. Add the onion, flour, thyme, nutmeg and salt and pepper to taste. Mix well together with a wooden spoon.

*3* Gradually stir the egg and milk into the meat mixture, then beat well until smooth.

*4* Heat the oil in a heavy-based frying pan. Fry heaped tablespoonfuls of the mixture for 5 minutes on each side, or until brown.

*5* Remove with a slotted spoon and drain on paper towels. Keep hot while cooking the remainder.

71

# QUICK CHICKEN AND MUSSEL PAELLA

| 0.50 | $ | 520–780 cals |

*Serves 4–6*

4 Tbsp olive oil

about 1 lb boneless chicken meat, skinned and cut into bite-sized cubes

1 onion, skinned and chopped

2 garlic cloves, skinned and crushed

1 large red pepper, cored, seeded and sliced into thin strips

3 tomatoes, skinned and chopped

2 cups white rice, preferably Valencia or risotto

5⅔ cups boiling chicken stock

1 tsp paprika

½ tsp saffron powder

salt and freshly ground pepper

two 5-oz jars mussels, drained

lemon wedges, peeled shrimp and fresh mussels (optional), to serve

*1* Heat the oil in a large, deep frying pan, add the cubes of chicken and fry over moderate heat until golden brown on all sides. Remove from the pan with a slotted spoon and set aside.

*2* Add the onion, garlic and red pepper to the pan and fry gently for 5 minutes until softened. Add the tomatoes and fry for a few more minutes until the juices run, then add the rice and stir to combine with the oil and vegetables.

*3* Pour in 4½ cups of the boiling stock (it will bubble furiously), then add half the paprika, the saffron powder and seasoning to taste. Stir well, lower the heat and add the chicken.

*4* Simmer, uncovered, for 30 minutes until the chicken is cooked through, stirring frequently during this time to prevent the rice from sticking. When the mixture becomes dry, stir in a few tablespoons of boiling stock. Repeat as often as necessary to keep the paella moist until the end of the cooking time.

*5* To serve, fold in the mussels and heat through. Taste and adjust seasoning, then garnish with lemon wedges, mussels in their shells and a sprinkling of the remaining paprika.

**Menu Suggestion**
Serve for a substantial supper dish with fresh crusty bread and a mixed green salad.

---

### QUICK CHICKEN AND MUSSEL PAELLA

Spain's most famous dish, paella, gets its name from the pan in which it is traditionally cooked—*paellera*. The pan is usually made of a heavy metal such as cast iron, with sloping sides and one flat handle on either side. The *paellera* is not only the best utensil for cooking paella, it is also the most attractive way to serve it, so if you like to make paella fairly frequently it is well worth investing in one—they are obtainable from specialist kitchen shops and some large hardware stores.

# STUFFED POTATOES

| 1.30 | $ | 346 cals |

*Serves 4*

4 medium baking potatoes

¼ cup butter or margarine

1 small onion, skinned and finely chopped

1 lb fresh spinach, cooked, drained and chopped, or 8 oz frozen chopped spinach

4 oz cream cheese

¼ tsp freshly grated nutmeg

salt and freshly ground pepper

2 oz Gruyère or Emmental cheese, grated

pinch of paprika or cayenne

*1* Scrub the potatoes under cold running water, then pat dry with paper towels.

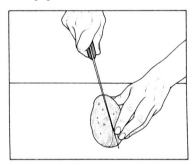

*2* With a sharp, pointed knife, score a line in the skin around the middle of each potato.

*3* Place the potatoes directly on the oven shelf and bake at 400°F for 1¼ hours or until tender.

*4* About 15 minutes before the end of the cooking time, melt the butter in a heavy-based saucepan, add the onion and fry gently for about 5 minutes until soft and lightly colored. Add the fresh spinach and cook gently for 2–3 minutes, stirring frequently. (If using frozen spinach, cook for 7–10 minutes until thawed.) Remove from the heat.

*5* When the potatoes are cooked, slice in half lengthwise. Scoop out the flesh into a bowl and add the spinach mixture, the cream cheese, nutmeg and salt and pepper to taste. Mix well.

*6* Spoon the mixture into the potato shells, mounding it up in the center. Stand the stuffed potatoes on a baking sheet. Sprinkle over the cheese and finally the paprika or cayenne. Return to the oven for 10–15 minutes, until the cheese topping is bubbling and golden. Serve hot.

## Menu Suggestion

These stuffed baked potatoes are very filling. Serve them on their own for a hearty lunch or supper, followed by a crisp salad.

# MEXICAN BAKED POTATOES

| 1.25 | $ | 367 cals |

*Serves 4*

4 medium baking potatoes

2 Tbsp vegetable oil

1 medium onion, skinned and finely chopped

1 garlic clove, skinned and crushed

14-oz can tomatoes

2 tsp tomato paste

$\frac{1}{2}$ tsp chili powder

pinch of sugar

salt and freshly ground pepper

15-oz can red kidney beans, drained

2 Tbsp chopped fresh parsley

2 oz Monterey Jack or Cheddar cheese, coarsely grated

*1* Scrub the potatoes under cold running water, then pat dry. Brush with a little vegetable oil, prick all over with a skewer or fork. Bake at 400°F for $1\frac{1}{4}$ hours or until tender.

*2* Meanwhile, make the stuffing. Heat the remaining oil in a saucepan, add the onion and garlic and fry gently until soft.

*3* Add the tomatoes with their juice and stir to break up with a wooden spoon. Add the tomato paste, chili powder, sugar and salt and pepper to taste and bring to a boil, stirring. Simmer, uncovered, for about 20 minutes, stirring occasionally. Add beans and parsley and heat through.

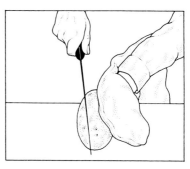

*4* When the potatoes are cooked, slice off the top third of each one and reserve for lids. Scoop out some of the potato from the bottom third of each one and add to the tomato sauce.

*5* Place 1 potato on each serving plate and spoon the chili bean mixture into each one, letting it spill out onto the plate. Sprinkle grated cheese on top, then replace the lids at an angle. Serve immediately.

**Menu Suggestion**

This vegetarian dish is hot, spicy and substantial. Serve for a hearty supper, accompanied by a crisp green salad and glasses of chilled beer.

# SPANISH OMELETTE

| 1.00 | $ | 376 cals |

*Serves 4*

1 pint (16 oz) vegetable or olive oil, for frying

1 medium Spanish onion, skinned and thinly sliced

salt and freshly ground pepper

4 medium potatoes, about 1 lb total weight, peeled

4 eggs

*1* Heat 4 Tbsp of the oil in a large, heavy-based frying pan or omelette pan. Add the sliced onion and a pinch of salt and fry gently, stirring frequently for 10–15 minutes until soft and a light golden brown. Remove with a slotted spoon and drain on paper towels.

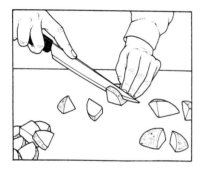

*2* Cut the potatoes into small wedges. Dry well with a clean dish towel. Pour the remaining oil into a deep-fat fryer and heat to 375°F. Fry the potatoes in batches for 5 minutes in the hot oil, covering the pan so that they become soft. Remove with a slotted spoon, place on paper towels, sprinkle with salt and leave to drain.

*3* Beat the eggs lightly in a large bowl with salt and pepper to taste. Stir in the onion and potatoes.

*4* Reheat the oil remaining in the frying pan until smoking. Pour all but 2 Tbsp of the egg and potato mixture into the frying pan. Turn the heat down to low and let the mixture run to the sides. Cook for 3–5 minutes until the underneath is just set.

*5* Turn the omelette out upside down onto a plate. Heat 1 Tbsp of the deep-frying oil in the frying pan.

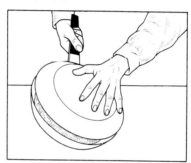

*6* Pour the reserved egg mixture into the pan and tip and tilt the pan so that the egg covers the base and forms a protective layer on which to finish cooking the omelette.

*7* Immediately slide in the omelette, set side up. Make the edges neat with a spatula and fry for 3–5 minutes until set underneath. Slide onto a serving plate and cut into wedges to serve.

## Menu Suggestion

Spanish Omelette can be served hot or cold as a main course with a tomato or green salad. It is also delicious cold as an appetizer with drinks before a meal, in which case it should be sliced into thin wedges.

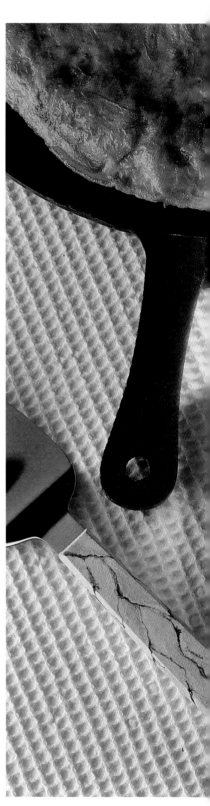

# FOURTH OF JULY CLAMBAKE

Clambakes are best at the beach, of course. All the accessories can be found there: the sweet salt air, sun, surf and sand. You also usually have two traditional clambake cooking aids at hand—seaweed and saltwater—and maybe even the clams. But alas, beach access, even on July 4th, is at a premium for most of us. Our clambake, complete with corn on the cob and "baked" potatoes, can be set up anywhere.

Be creative and use your backyard instead of the sandpit. Our clambake will feature an old-fashioned water boiler, the kind earlier Americans used to use to heat up their wash water. Alternatively you can use an old water trough or a large metal canning kettle, depending upon the size of your party. Any cooking container you choose should be big enough to hold all the food (you might want to make a dry run to be sure it will all fit, with at least 6 inches of boiling room to spare at the top), made of metal, and clean and free from holes. You should have a lid of some sort, even if it's just a piece of clean sheet metal cut to size. (Don't use anything that isn't fire-resistant.) Instead of the seaweed, we'll have lots of clean corn husks. (You might still be able to have seaweed; check with the people that sell you the clams because they might just have some on hand for the purpose.)

If you're using seaweed, rinse it well several times. Soak the corn husks or seaweed in clean water for at least an hour, then put down about a 6-inch layer of either in the bottom of the water boiler or trough. Pour in about an inch of water. Then put the whole thing over an open wood or coal fire or even a large charcoal grill and bring the water to a boil. For 10 people, put in 10 scrubbed

## MENU

◆

*whole potatoes*

*corn on the cob*

*clams*

*chicken*

*coleslaw*

*Tomato, Basil and Onion Salad
(featured recipe here)*

*Refrigerator Cookies (see page 117)*

*watermelon*

*beer*

*lemonade*

*iced tea*

— ◆ —

potatoes that have been wrapped in foil and 3 frying or broiling chickens, cut up and wrapped in cheesecloth. Cover and simmer for 5 minutes.

If yours is a fancy clambake, now is the time to add the lobsters, one per person. Cover again and cook for another 10 minutes. Then add another layer, this time of cleaned ears of corn that have been wrapped in foil. Cook for 10 minutes and, finally, add the clams: maybe half a dozen for each person. Cover and cook again, peeking in at them every few minutes after the first 5 minutes have gone by. When the shells have opened (this shouldn't take more than 10 minutes total) the clams—and the clambake—are ready.

#### And the Extras

Get out the melted butter, plenty of napkins, rolls, coleslaw and perhaps a lighter salad not so weighted down with mayonnaise, like Tomato, Basil and Onion Salad. Beer is a must. Iced tea for adults and lemonade for the kids are good nonalcoholic beverages that will quench thirsts throughout the big meal.

If anyone has room left, you could pass around something simple like Refrigerator Cookies and watermelon for dessert.

## TOMATO, BASIL AND ONION SALAD

*Serves 8*

| 8 large tomatoes |
| 1 large purple onion |
| 4 large handfuls fresh basil leaves |
| $\frac{1}{3}$ cup virgin olive oil |
| 2 tsp freshly squeezed lemon juice |
| salt and freshly ground pepper |
| Parmesan cheese for garnish, if desired |

1 Wash and thickly slice the tomatoes. Peel the onion and thinly slice it. Place tomatoes and onions in a serving bowl.

2 Wash and pat dry the basil. Tear it by hand into small pieces or mince with a knife. Then toss it with the tomatoes and onions.

3 Add the oil and lemon juice to the serving bowl and toss until the tomatoes and onions are evenly covered.

4 Cover and let sit in the refrigerator for at least one hour to marinate. Serve as is or with a sprinkling of Parmesan cheese.

### BASIL

Basil is the one herb that tomatoes can't do without. If you like tomatoes, then grow some basil to go with them so that you'll have it fresh all summer long. Basil grows very easily from seed in any sunny spot. Since it takes up little room, you can grow it anywhere you have a little space, even in a large flower pot. Plant it as soon as the soil has warmed up, which is late May in most parts of the country, and you'll have basil plants big enough to pick leaves from by the time tomatoes are in full season. Keep pinching off the top of the plants so they don't go to seed and you'll have basil from them until frost.

#### Frozen Basil Leaves

Dried basil will do in a pinch, but it is no real substitute for fresh basil in salads. Anticipating the long, cold winter ahead, you can freeze your fresh basil. Chop up cleaned and trimmed leaves with a knife or grind them in a food processor. Then place them in the squares of an ice cube tray and cover them with water or olive oil. When frozen pop the basil cubes out of the tray into a plastic bag. Defrost a cube at a time as needed.

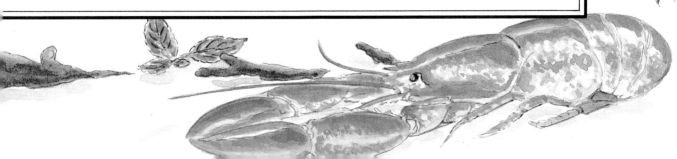

# *Spicy Lamb Kabobs*

| 0.45* | 516 cals |
|---|---|

\* plus 2–3 hours marinating

*Makes 8*

1½ lb boneless leg of lamb

1 lb small zucchini

8 tomatoes, halved

1 large corn on the cob

8 shallots

salt

⅔ cup plain yogurt

1 garlic clove, crushed

2 bay leaves, crumbled

1 Tbsp lemon juice

1 Tbsp vegetable oil

1 tsp ground allspice

1 Tbsp coriander seeds

freshly ground pepper

lemon wedges, to garnish

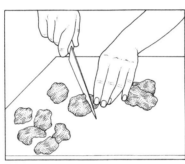

*1* Using a sharp knife, cut the lamb into 1-inch cubes, making sure to trim off any excess fat from the meat.

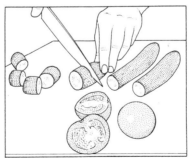

*2* Cut the zucchini into ¼-inch slices, discarding the tops and tails. Halve the tomatoes.

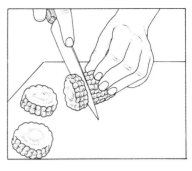

*3* Cut the corn into eight slices. Blanch in boiling salted water, drain well and set aside.

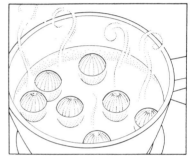

*4* Blanch the shallots in boiling, salted water, skin and set aside. Make the marinade. Pour the yogurt into a shallow dish and stir in garlic, bay leaves, lemon juice, oil, allspice, coriander seeds and seasoning.

*5* Thread the lamb cubes on to eight skewers with zucchini, tomatoes, corn and shallots. Place in dish, spoon over marinade, cover and leave for 2–3 hours, turning once to ensure even coating.

*6* Cook the kabobs for about 15–20 minutes, turning and brushing with the marinade occasionally. To serve, spoon remaining marinade over the kabobs and garnish.

# LAMB AND SPINACH LASAGNE

| 1.45 | $ | 799 cals |

\* freeze at the end of step 6

*Serves 6*

1 lb fresh spinach, washed
2 Tbsp vegetable oil
1 medium onion, skinned and
   chopped
1 lb ground lamb
8-oz can tomatoes
1 garlic clove, skinned and crushed
2 Tbsp chopped fresh mint
1 tsp ground cinnamon
freshly grated nutmeg
salt and freshly ground pepper
$\frac{1}{4}$ cup butter or margarine
6 Tbsp flour
$3\frac{3}{4}$ cups milk
$\frac{2}{3}$ cup yogurt
12–15 sheets cooked lasagne
   noodles
6 oz Feta or Cheddar cheese,
   grated

*1* Put the spinach in a saucepan with only the water that clings to the leaves and cook gently for about 4 minutes. Drain well and chop finely.

*2* Heat the oil in a large saucepan, add the onion and fry gently for 5 minutes until softened. Add the lamb and brown well, then drain off all the fat.

*3* Stir in the spinach with the tomatoes and their juice, the garlic, mint and cinnamon. Season with nutmeg, salt and pepper to taste. Bring to a boil and simmer, uncovered, for about 30 minutes. Leave to cool while making the white sauce.

*4* Melt the butter in a saucepan, add the flour and cook gently, stirring, for 1–2 minutes. Remove from the heat and gradually blend in the milk. Bring to a boil, stirring constantly, then simmer for 3 minutes until thick and smooth. Add the yogurt and salt and pepper to taste.

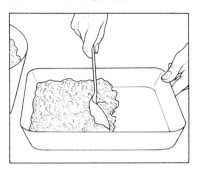

*5* Spoon one-third of the meat mixture over the base of a rectangular baking dish.

*6* Cover with 4–5 sheets of lasagne and spread over one-third of the white sauce. Repeat these layers twice more, finishing with the sauce, which should completely cover the lasagne noodles. Sprinkle the cheese on top.

*7* Stand the dish on a baking sheet. Bake in the oven at 350°F for 45–50 minutes, or until the top is well browned and bubbling. Serve hot.

**Menu Suggestion**
Lamb and Spinach Lasagne is rich and filling. Serve with a tomato salad dressed with oil, lemon juice and raw onion rings, chopped spring onion or snipped fresh chives.

# BEEF PATTIES

2.00* $ 637 cals

* plus overnight soaking and 2–3 hours cooling

*Serves 6*

2 cups rolled oats

1¼ cups milk

2 medium onions, roughly chopped

2 lb lean ground beef

salt and freshly ground pepper

3 tsp caraway seeds (optional)

5 Tbsp seasoned flour*

4 Tbsp vegetable oil

2 Tbsp butter

3 Tbsp flour

2 cups beef or chicken stock

2 Tbsp tomato paste

1¼ cups sour cream

parsley sprigs, to garnish

* Flour seasoned with salt, pepper and paprika

*1 To prepare* (40 minutes): Soak the oats in the milk overnight. Squeeze out excess milk and mix the oats with the onions, ground beef and seasoning to taste.

*2* Put this mixture twice through a grinder or mix in a food processor until smooth. Beat in 2 tsp of the caraway seeds, if using.

*3* Shape into 18 round flat cakes, or bitkis. Coat with seasoned flour.

*4* Heat the oil in a large frying pan and brown the bitkis well. Place in a single layer in a large shallow ovenproof dish.

*5* Melt the butter in a saucepan, add the flour and cook over low heat, stirring with a wooden spoon, for 2 minutes. Gradually blend in the stock, stirring after each addition to prevent lumps forming. Bring to the boil slowly, then simmer for 2–3 minutes, stirring. Stir in the tomato paste, sour cream and remaining caraway seeds, if using.

*6* Pour the sauce over the bitkis and cool for 2–3 hours. Cover with foil and chill in the refrigerator until required.

*7 To serve* (1 hour 20 minutes): Bake in the oven at 350°F for about 1¼ hours or until the juices run clear when the bitkis are pierced. Garnish with parsley just before serving.

**Menu Suggestion**
Serve these Russian beef patties for a family meal with noodles and a mixed salad which includes grated or chopped beets.

# BEEF KABOBS WITH HORSERADISH RELISH

| 0.45 | $ | 399 cals |

*Serves 6*

1½ lb lean ground beef
2 cups grated onion
9 Tbsp prepared horseradish
3 Tbsp chopped fresh thyme
3 cups fresh white breadcrumbs
salt and freshly ground pepper
1 egg, beaten
flour, for coating
⅔ cup plain yogurt
8 Tbsp finely chopped fresh parsley

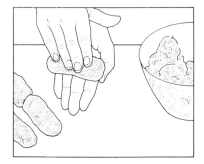

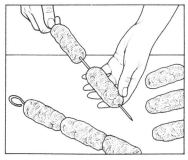

*1 To prepare* (20 minutes): Place the ground beef in a large bowl and mix in the onion, 6 Tbsp of the horseradish, thyme, bread-crumbs and seasoning to taste.

*2* Add enough egg to bind the mixture together and, with well-floured hands, shape into 18 even-sized sausages. Cover and chill in the refrigerator until required.

*3 To serve* (25 minutes): Thread the kabobs lengthwise onto 6 oiled skewers. Place under a pre-heated broiler and broil for about 20 minutes, turning frequently.

*4* Meanwhile, mix the yogurt with the remaining horse-radish and parsley. Serve the kabobs hot, with the sauce handed separately.

**BEEF KABOBS WITH HORSERADISH**

Kabobs are very popular in Indian and Middle Eastern cooking, and this method of threading ground meat on skewers is a very common one. In India, such kabobs are cooked on the street, and passers-by stop to buy them and eat them as they are going along. A charcoal grill is used for cooking, which gives them such a wonderful aroma that they are hard to resist if you are hungry when walking by a kabob stall. If you have a barbecue, then cook the kabobs on it, and you will understand why!

# MUSHROOM QUICHE

| 0.45 | $ | 303 cals |

*Serves 4*

**1 cup wholewheat breadcrumbs**

**1¼ cups plain yogurt**

**salt and freshly ground pepper**

**4 eggs**

**⅔ cup milk**

**6 oz mushrooms, wiped and sliced**

**4 spring onions, trimmed and chopped**

**¾ cup grated Cheddar cheese**

*1* Mix the breadcrumbs and half the yogurt to a paste. Add seasoning to taste.

*2* Use the mixture to line a 9-inch quiche dish or tin, pressing the paste into shape with the fingers. Set aside.

*3* Whisk the eggs and milk together with the remaining yogurt and seasoning to taste.

*4* Arrange the mushrooms, spring onions and half the cheese on the base of the quiche. Pour the egg mixture over the top and then sprinkle with the remaining cheese.

*5* Bake the quiche in the oven at 350°F for about 30 minutes or until brown and set. Serve warm.

## MUSHROOM QUICHE

The unusual base for this quiche is made simply from wholewheat breadcrumbs and yogurt—less fattening than a conventional pie pastry base—and with healthier ingredients. If you prefer to use a pastry base, however, then use your own favorite recipe, or try the following recipe for wholewheat pastry, which is sufficient to line a 9 inch dish. Mix 1¼ cups wholewheat flour and a pinch of salt in a bowl, add 3 Tbsp each butter or margarine and lard in small pieces and rub in with the fingertips until the mixture resembles fine crumbs. Sprinkle about 8 tsp ice-cold water into the bowl and mix it in with a knife. Draw the mixture together with the fingers of one hand, then chill or leave to rest for 30 minutes.

# SWEDISH MEATBALLS

| 0.15* | $ $ | 492 cals |
|---|---|---|

\* plus 1 hour chilling; freeze after
step 5

*Serves 4*

**1 lb lean veal, pork or beef (or a
 mixture of these)**

**4 oz bacon**

**$\frac{1}{2}$ small onion, skinned**

**1 large slice of stale wholewheat
 bread**

**$\frac{1}{2}$ tsp ground allspice**

**salt and freshly ground pepper**

**$\frac{1}{4}$ cup plus 2 Tbsp unsalted butter**

**2 cups chicken stock**

**juice of $\frac{1}{2}$ lemon**

**2 tsp chopped fresh dill or 1 tsp
 dried**

**$\frac{3}{4}$ cup sour cream**

**dill sprigs, to garnish (optional)**

*1* Put the meat, bacon, onion and
 bread through the blades of a
grinder twice so that they are
ground very fine. (Or work them
in a food processor.)

*2* Add the allspice to the mixture
 with seasoning to taste, then
mix in with the fingertips to bind
the mixture. (Pick up a handful
and press firmly in the hand—it
should cling together, but not be
too wet.) Chill in the refrigerator
for 1 hour.

*3* Melt the butter gently in a
 large flameproof casserole. Dip
a tablespoon in the butter, then
use to shape a spoonful of the
ground mixture.

*4* Add the meatball to the
 casserole and then continue
dipping the spoon in the butter
and shaping meatballs until there
are 12–14 altogether.

*5* Fry the meatballs half at a
 time, if necessary, over moderate heat until they are browned on
all sides. Return all the meatballs
to the casserole, pour in the stock
and lemon juice and bring slowly
to boiling point. Lower the heat,
add the dill and seasoning to taste,
then cover the casserole and
simmer gently for 30 minutes.

*6* Stir the sour cream into the
 casserole and mix gently to
combine evenly with the meatballs
and cooking liquid. Taste and
adjust the seasoning of the sauce
and then garnish with dill sprigs, if
desired. Serve hot.

**Menu Suggestion**
In Sweden and other parts of
Scandinavia, these meatballs are
traditionally served with boiled
potatoes and creamed spinach.

---

**SWEDISH MEATBALLS**

Egg-shaped meatballs like these
are popular all over Scandinavia,
where they are served for the
evening meal with hot vegetables. Our version is casseroled, but they are often served
simply fried in butter, with a
gravy made from the pan juices.
In Denmark, these are known as
frikadeller, and are immensely
popular. The Danes use ground
pork to make them, and sometimes they add a little smoked
bacon to the mixture, for extra
flavor. Some Scandinavian cooks
stir a little soda water into the
meat mixture before it is shaped.
If you have soda water at hand,
you can add up to 3 Tbsp for a
lighter result.

# *ROAST CHICKEN*

2.00  351–526 cals

*Serves 4–6*

4–5 lb chicken

sage and onion stuffing

1 medium onion, skinned

$\frac{1}{2}$ lemon

$\frac{1}{4}$ cup butter

salt and freshly ground pepper

4 bacon slices

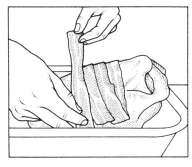

*1* If the chicken is frozen, allow it to thaw out completely. A 4-lb bird will take 8–10 hours at room temperature.

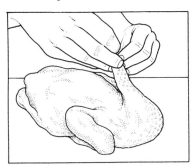

*2* Wash the bird and dry thoroughly. Spoon the stuffing into the neck end, then fold over the neck skin. To add flavor, put the onion and lemon in the body of the bird.

*3* Weigh the chicken and place it in a deep roasting pan. Spread with the butter and sprinkle with salt and pepper.

*4* Place the bacon slices over the breast of the bird, to prevent it from becoming dry.

*5* Roast in the oven at 400°F, basting from time to time, and allowing 20 minutes per 1 lb plus 20 minutes extra.

*6* Put a piece of foil over the breast if it shows signs of becoming too brown. The chicken is cooked if the juices run clear when the thickest part of the leg is pierced with a knife or skewer.

**Menu Suggestion**
The traditional British accompaniments to sage-and-onion-stuffed roast chicken are roast and creamed potatoes and fresh vegetables such as Brussels sprouts and carrots. Bread sauce and giblet gravy are also traditional, as are chipolata sausages and bacon rolls which have been cooked around the chicken.

---

**ROAST CHICKEN**

No roast is complete without a well-flavored gravy to accompany it. You can either make a giblet gravy as suggested above, or for a change make a gravy or "jus" in the French style, adding a little wine to enhance the flavor of the chicken.

To make this gravy pour off as much fat from the roasting pan as possible. Place the pan over

the heat on top of the stove and let the sediment bubble up for a few minutes, stirring until nicely colored. Add about $1\frac{1}{4}$ **cups home-made chicken stock** or vegetable cooking water and a dash of **red or white wine**. Boil rapidly, stirring occasionally to mix well, until reduced by almost half. Season and strain.

# MARINATED CHICKEN WITH PEANUT SAUCE

| 1.15* | 685 cals |
|---|---|

* plus 24 hours marinating; freeze in the marinade

*Serves 4*

**4 large chicken pieces**
**5 Tbsp soy sauce**
**2 Tbsp sesame or vegetable oil**
**2 Tbsp clear honey**
**juice of 1 lemon**
**½ tsp chili powder**
**1 red pepper**
**1 green pepper**
**3 oz cream of coconut**
**5 Tbsp crunchy peanut butter**
**2 tsp dark brown sugar**

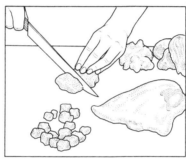

*1* Skin the chicken pieces. Cut away the flesh from the bones with a sharp, pointed knife and slice the flesh into small cubes.

*2* Put 3 Tbsp of the soy sauce in a bowl with the oil, honey, lemon juice and chili powder. Whisk with a fork until well combined.

*3* Add the cubes of chicken to the marinade, stir well to coat, then cover and leave to marinate for 24 hours. Turn the chicken occasionally during this time.

*4* When ready to cook, cut the red and green peppers in half, remove the cores and seeds and cut the flesh into neat squares.

*5* Thread the chicken cubes and pepper squares on 4 oiled kabob skewers, place on a rack in the broil pan and brush liberally with the marinade.

*6* To make the peanut sauce. Grate the cream of coconut into a heavy-based saucepan. Add ⅔ cup boiling water and bring slowly back to the boil, stirring constantly. Simmer, stirring, until the coconut has dissolved.

*7* Add the peanut butter, remaining soy sauce and the sugar to the pan and whisk to combine. Simmer very gently over the lowest possible heat, stirring occasionally until smooth.

*8* Meanwhile, broil the chicken under moderate heat for 15 minutes, turning the skewers frequently and brushing with the remaining marinade. Serve hot.

**Menu Suggestion**
Serve the kabobs on a bed of brown rice or noodles, with a little of the sauce poured over. Hand the remaining sauce separately in a bowl. A cool, crisp salad of cucumber strips, spring onions and beansprouts tossed in oil, lemon juice and seasoning would make a refreshing follow-up to this dish.

# BAKED TURKEY ESCALOPES WITH CRANBERRY AND COCONUT

| 0.50 | 391 cals |

*\* freeze after step 2*

*Serves 4*

1 lb boneless turkey breast

salt and freshly ground pepper

4 tsp Dijon mustard

4 Tbsp cranberry sauce

$1\frac{1}{2}$ Tbsp flour

1 egg, beaten

2 Tbsp shredded coconut

$\frac{3}{4}$ cup fresh breadcrumbs

$\frac{1}{4}$ cup butter or margarine

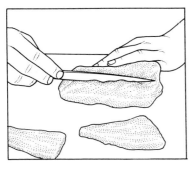

*1* Thinly slice the turkey breast to give four portions.

*2* Pound the escalopes between two sheets of waxed paper or plastic wrap. Season, then spread each portion with mustard and cranberry sauce.

*3* Roll up, starting from the thin end, and secure with a cocktail stick or toothpick. Dust each portion with flour, then brush with egg. Combine the coconut and breadcrumbs then coat the turkey with the mixture.

*4* Melt the fat in a frying pan, add the turkey portions, and fry until brown on both sides. Transfer to a baking tin just large enough to take the turkey in a single layer and baste with more fat. Bake in the oven at 350°F for about 40 minutes until tender.

**Menu Suggestion**
Serve these scrumptiously crisp escalopes with a salad of chopped and grated raw vegetables (e.g., celery, peppers, white cabbage, carrot and onion) tossed in a mayonnaise, sour cream or yogurt dressing. Alternatively, serve with a simple green salad.

**BAKED TURKEY ESCALOPES WITH CRANBERRY AND COCONUT**

Cranberries are a distinctively sharp-tasting fruit which make a delicious sauce, used here to add zest to turkey meat. The fresh fruit have a limited season, but they can also be bought frozen or canned throughout the year. Cultivated mainly in America, the ruby red berries grow on vines in flooded marshy soil. To harvest them, the water is whipped up by machine. This dislodges the fruit which floats to the surface and is separated off from the leaves and other debris. The sorting process includes a special machine which bounces the berries over a barrier seven times—if the berries don't bounce they are rejected as unsound!

Cranberry sauce is good mixed with fresh orange juice and poured over vanilla ice-cream, sweet pancakes or waffles, and whole berries are good in beef and pork casseroles.

# STIR-FRIED CHICKEN WITH WALNUTS

0.20* | 358 cals

* plus at least 1 hour marinating

*Serves 4*

4 boneless chicken breasts,
    skinned and cut into thin strips

2-inch piece of fresh ginger, peeled
    and thinly sliced

4 Tbsp soy sauce

4 Tbsp dry sherry

1 tsp five-spice powder

3 Tbsp sesame or vegetable oil

2 Tbsp cornstarch

$\frac{2}{3}$ cup chicken stock

salt and freshly ground pepper

$\frac{1}{3}$ cup walnut pieces

$\frac{1}{4}$ cucumber, cut into chunks

scallion tassels, to garnish

*1* Put the chicken in a bowl with the ginger, soy sauce, sherry and five-spice powder. Stir well to mix, then cover and marinate for at least 1 hour.

*2* Remove the chicken and ginger from the marinade with a slotted spoon. Reserve marinade.

*3* Heat 2 Tbsp of the oil in a wok or large heavy-based frying pan. Add the chicken and stir-fry over brisk heat for 5 minutes until well browned.

*4* Mix the marinade with the cornstarch, then stir in the stock. Pour into the pan and bring to the boil, then add salt and pepper to taste and stir-fry for a further 5 minutes or until the chicken strips are tender.

*5* Heat the remaining oil in a separate small pan, add the walnuts and cucumber and stir-fry briefly to heat through.

*6* Transfer the chicken mixture to a warmed serving dish and top with the walnuts and cucumber. Garnish with scallion tassels and serve.

**Menu Suggestion**
Serve with Chinese egg noodles, followed by a mixed salad of beansprouts, grated carrot, chopped celery and onion tossed in a dressing of oil, lemon juice and soy sauce.

# CHICKEN FLORENTINE

| 1.00 | $ | 527 cals |

*Serves 4*

1 lb fresh spinach

salt and freshly ground pepper

4 boneless chicken breasts, skinned

6 Tbsp butter or margarine

1 Tbsp vegetable oil

$\frac{1}{4}$ tsp freshly grated nutmeg

2 Tbsp flour

2 cups milk

$\frac{1}{4}$ lb Cheddar cheese, grated

pinch of ground mace

a little paprika

*1* Wash the spinach, put into a pan with a pinch of salt. Cook over low heat for 7 minutes until just tender. Drain well.

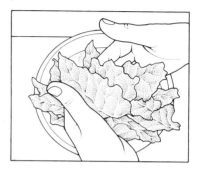

*2* Meanwhile, cut each chicken breast in two horizontally. Melt 2 Tbsp of the fat in a frying pan with the oil. Fry the chicken for 3 minutes on each side.

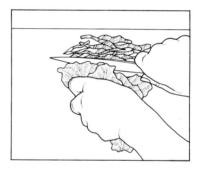

*3* Chop the drained spinach. Mix with half of the remaining fat, the nutmeg and salt and pepper to taste. Put the spinach in the base of an ovenproof dish, then arrange the chicken on top.

*4* Melt the remaining fat in a pan. Add the flour and stir for 2 minutes. Gradually add the milk, then the cheese, mace and seasoning. Simmer until thick.

*5* Pour over the chicken, then sprinkle with the remaining cheese and a little paprika. Bake at 375°F for 30 minutes.

**Menu Suggestion**
Serve with mashed potatoes.

# PATIO SUPPER

This late supper on the patio or deck is a treat for adults only. The children are in bed and all is peaceful in the night—the perfect setting for a leisurely meal under the summer stars.

As the midsummer sun gets lowe in the sky and dusk approaches, you can feel yourself beginning to unwind. The busy activities that so quickly fill up a summer day at over; the evening is ahead, ready to relax and refresh you. Summer nights are heavenly—cool, fresh and peaceful—the perfect time to linger over a meal with friends.

**Creating the Atmosphere**
If you've got the picture-perfect backyard setting for your supper, great. If not, you can help it along a bit with some "special effects."

**Homemade Candle Protector**
Use candles to light up the assets of your supper setting and create party mood. If there's a breeze, you might want to protect the candle flames with simple homemade candle protectors. Gather together some plain glass jars, like mayonnaise jars. Pour a few inches of moist sand in each and insert a candle firmly in the sand. Be sure that the candle is n touching the sides of the jar; otherwise the heat of the flame could crack the glass.

In daylight your homemade candle stand might look pretty crude, but at night about all you' see is the flickering candle flame, which is now protected from the wind and from accidentally being knocked over. Because they cost

## MENU

◆

Cold Cucumber Soup *(see page 63)*

Bass on the Barbecue
*(featured recipe here)*

tossed salad with Blender Tomato
Dressing *(see page 288)*

mixed wild and white rice

Strawberries with Raspberry Sauce
*(see page 112)*

a medium white wine

——— ◆ ———

nothing to make, you can afford to have lots of them around, to light up a patio path, illuminate some particularly lovely potted flowers in the corner, or to place around a fountain or pool.

For the table itself, you might want to be a bit more fussy about your candle protectors and buy glass globes or hurricane lamps.

### A Dish That Cooks Itself

Once you've taken care of creating the mood, concentrate on the meal—a lazy, leisurely supper. Barbecuing is a natural, but choose a dish that doesn't need a lot of attention. Remember, this is supposed to be a relaxing occasion. Bass on the Barbecue is just right, because the fish, which is seasoned with flavorful butter, is grilled in foil. It doesn't need to be watched carefully as it cooks. That gives you time to enjoy your guests, and time to serve a summery first course like Cold Cucumber Soup.

When the fish is ready, bring out a tossed salad with Blender Tomato Dressing. Serve mixed wild and white rice with the fish. Don't butter or season the rice; there will be plenty of buttery sauce from the fish to do that. End with some summer fruit, like Strawberries with Raspberry Sauce.

## BASS ON THE BARBECUE

*plus 2–3 hours chilling time; freeze before cooking*
*Serves 4*

| |
|---|
| ½ cup unsalted butter |
| 4 tsp dillweed |
| finely grated rind and juice of 1 lemon |
| salt and freshly ground pepper |
| 3-lb sea bass, cleaned |
| ⅓ cup dry white wine |
| lemon slices and dill sprigs, to garnish |

1 Work the butter with the dillweed, lemon rind and salt and pepper to taste. Form into a roll, wrap in foil and chill in the refrigerator for 2–3 hours until firm.

2 Cut a sheet of foil large enough to enclose the fish. Place the fish in the center of the foil.

3 Using a sharp knife, cut the flavored butter into slices. Peel off and discard foil after cutting.

4 Place the butter slices inside the belly of the fish. Sprinkle the outside of the fish with salt and pepper, then slowly pour over the wine and lemon juice.

5 Fold the foil over the fish to form a loose package so that the wine and juices do not leak out. Place the foil package on the barbecue and grill for 45 minutes. Serve hot, straight from the foil, garnished with a few lemon slices and fresh dill sprigs.

# BARBECUED BEANS

**4.20\*** $ 213 cals

\* plus overnight soaking

*Serves 6*

| |
|---|
| **12 oz red kidney beans, soaked overnight** |
| **5 cups tomato juice** |
| **1 large onion, skinned and sliced** |
| **2 Tbsp soy sauce** |
| **4 Tbsp cider vinegar** |
| **1 Tbsp Worcestershire sauce** |
| **1 Tbsp mustard powder** |
| **1 Tbsp honey** |
| **$\frac{1}{2}$ tsp chili powder** |
| **salt and freshly ground pepper** |

*1* Drain the beans and place in a saucepan. Cover with cold water, bring to a boil and boil rapidly for 10 minutes then drain.

*2* Put the tomato juice, onion, soy sauce, vinegar, Worcestershire sauce, mustard, honey and chili powder in a flameproof casserole. Bring to a boil then add the beans.

*3* Cover and cook in the oven at 275°F for about 4 hours until the beans are tender. Season well with salt and freshly ground pepper.

**Menu Suggestion**
Serve as a vegetable accompaniment to any roast or broiled meat or poultry.

# SAUTÉED CUCUMBER WITH HERBS

| 0.45 | $ | 101–151 cals |

*Serves 4–6*

1 cucumber

salt

4 Tbsp butter or margarine

2 shallots or 1 small onion, finely
chopped

1 Tbsp fresh chopped
rosemary or 2 tsp dried

$\frac{1}{2}$ tsp sugar

freshly ground pepper

4 Tbsp sour cream

fresh rosemary sprigs, to garnish

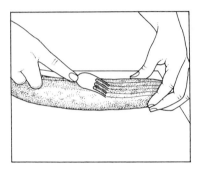

*1* Using a sharp fork, run the
prongs down the length of the
cucumber to score. (This will give
an attractive effect.)

*2* Using a sharp knife, cut the
cucumber into 2-inch lengths,
then cut each piece lengthwise
into quarters.

*3* Remove the seeds from the
cucumber, then put the cucumber in a colander and sprinkle
with the salt. Cover with a plate
and leave to drain for 30 minutes,
pressing the plate down occasionally to press out the liquid from
the cucumber. Rinse and pat dry
with absorbent paper.

*4* Melt the butter in a large,
heavy-based frying pan. Add
the shallots and fry gently for
5 minutes until they are soft and
lightly colored.

*5* Add the cucumber pieces to
the pan, together with the
rosemary, sugar and pepper to
taste. Cook for 5 minutes only,
stirring frequently to ensure even
cooking.

*6* Remove the pan from the heat
and stir in the sour cream.
Taste and adjust seasoning.
Garnish with rosemary sprigs and
serve immediately.

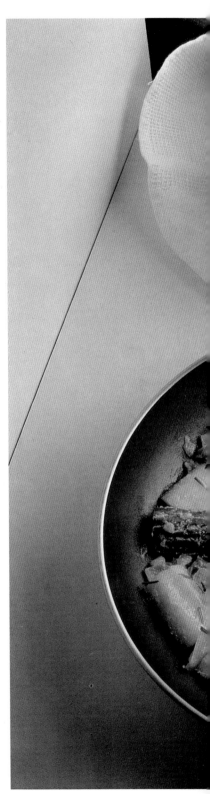

# SAUTÉED ZUCCHINI WITH CHIVES

| 0.15 | $ | 105 cals |

*Serves 4*

1 lb small zucchini
2 Tbsp butter
1 Tbsp vegetable oil
grated rind and juice of $\frac{1}{2}$ lemon
salt and freshly ground pepper
1 Tbsp fresh chives

*1* Wash the zucchini and pat dry with absorbent paper. Top and tail them and thinly slice.

*2* Heat the butter and oil in a pan, add the zucchini and cook over medium heat, uncovered, for 5–8 minutes. When tender but still slightly crisp, add the lemon rind and juice and seasoning to taste.

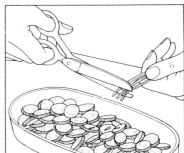

*3* Turn into a heated serving dish. Snip fresh chives over the zucchini and serve immediately, while still hot.

# CHICORY, ORANGE AND WALNUT SALAD

| 0.30 | $ | 160 cals |

*Serves 8*

2 heads chicory

6 oranges

$\frac{1}{4}$ cup walnut pieces

1 Tbsp sugar

$\frac{2}{3}$ cup sour cream

4 Tbsp vegetable oil

2 Tbsp lemon juice

salt and freshly ground pepper

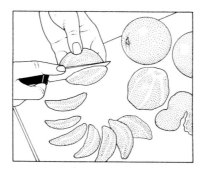

*2* Remove peel and white pith from remaining oranges. Segment oranges and add segments to chicory. Add the walnuts.

*3* Just before serving, combine the sugar, sour cream, reserved orange juice and rind. Beat in the oil gradually and stir in the lemon juice. Season well. Spoon dressing over chicory, oranges and walnuts and toss together lightly.

*1* Pull the chicory apart, wash and dry thoroughly. Tear into pieces and place in a salad bowl. Grate the rind of one orange into a bowl and squeeze in the juice.

## ENDIVE AND CHICORY

There is always confusion over chicory — because in England it is called endive, yet in France and the US it is called chicory!

The chicory used in this recipe is the large, rather wild-looking salad vegetable; it has crinkly or frondy leaves, which vary in color from dark green on the outside to pale green, almost yellow, in the very center.

The flavor of chicory is rather bitter — like endive. For this reason it is most successfully used with other ingredients in a mixed salad, and its unusual looks also add interest. The combination of bitter chicory with a sweet-tasting fruit such as orange is a good one, as this helps to take the edge off the chicory. Adding a little sugar to the dressing ingredients — as in this recipe — also helps.

Like lettuce and most leafy salad vegetables, chicory does not keep well — its curly fronds quickly go limp and sad-looking. Some greengrocers sell a half head, or even a quarter, so check before buying because whole heads can be expensive. Store, loosely wrapped in a plastic bag or in a rigid container, in the salad drawer of the refrigerator. Chicory has too high a water content to freeze successfully.

# TOMATO, AVOCADO AND PASTA SALAD

0.20 | $ | 626 cals

*Serves 4*

6 oz small wholewheat pasta shells
salt and freshly ground pepper
7 Tbsp olive oil
3 Tbsp lemon juice
1 tsp wholegrain mustard
2 Tbsp chopped fresh basil
2 ripe avocados
2 red onions
16 black olives
8 oz ripe cherry tomatoes, if available, or small salad tomatoes
fresh basil leaves, to garnish

*1* Cook the pasta in plenty of boiling salted water for about 5 minutes until just tender. Drain in a colander and rinse under cold running water to stop the pasta cooking further. Cool for 20 minutes.

*2* Meanwhile, whisk the oil in a bowl with the lemon juice, mustard, chopped basil and salt and pepper to taste.

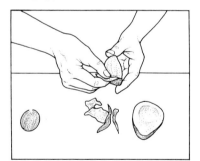

*3* Halve and pit the avocados then peel off the skins. Chop the avocado flesh into large pieces and fold gently into the dressing.

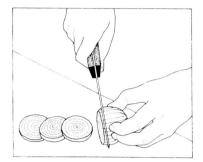

*4* Slice the onions thinly into rings. Pit the olives. Halve the tomatoes and mix them with the onion rings, the olives and the cold pasta shells.

*5* Spoon the pasta and tomato onto 4 individual serving plates. Spoon over the avocado and dressing and garnish with fresh basil leaves. Serve immediately.

**Menu Suggestion**
This pretty salad makes a delicious summer appetizer. Serve with chunky slices of fresh wholegrain bread and butter, with a chilled dry white wine to drink. Alternatively, serve the salad as an accompaniment to barbecued or broiled meat.

# RAW SPINACH AND MUSHROOM SALAD

| 0.50 | \$ | 402–604 cals |

*Serves 2–3*

8 oz young spinach leaves
8 oz button mushrooms
2 thick slices of white bread
6 Tbsp olive oil
2 Tbsp butter or margarine
1 garlic clove, skinned and crushed
2 Tbsp tarragon vinegar
1 tsp tarragon mustard
salt and freshly ground pepper

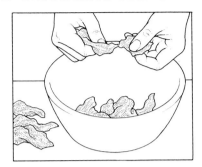

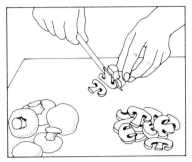

*1* Wash the spinach well, discarding any damaged or yellowing leaves. Cut out and discard any thick ribs.

*2* Tear the spinach leaves into a large salad bowl, discarding any thick stalks.

*3* Wipe the mushrooms but do not peel them. Slice them thinly into neat "T" shapes.

*4* Add the mushrooms to the spinach. Using your hands, toss the 2 ingredients together. Set aside while making the croûtons and dressing.

*5* Cut the crusts off the bread and cut the bread into $\frac{1}{2}$-inch cubes. Heat the oil and butter in a frying pan, add the garlic and the cubes of bread and fry until crisp and golden. Remove the croûtons with a slotted spoon and drain well on paper towels.

*6* Add the vinegar to the oil in the pan, with the mustard and salt and pepper to taste. Stir well to combine, then remove the pan from the heat and leave to cool for 5 minutes.

*7* Add the croûtons to the salad, then the dressing. Toss well to combine and serve immediately.

**Menu Suggestion**
This nutritious salad of raw ingredients tossed in a warm oil and vinegar dressing makes an unusual light lunch or supper. Serve with hot crusty rolls.

# LATE SUMMER POTLUCK GET-TOGETHER

A potluck party is a delightful meal of surprises for all involved, including the host or hostess. The menu here is simply a suggestion, because there's no way to know just what will wind up on the table.

Late summer days are not for cooking. There are too many mor important things to do than be in the kitchen, like floating in the pool, taking a few swipes at the birdie with the old badminton racket or catching up on neighborhood gossip over glasses of iced tea.

But that doesn't mean you don get to eat. Give yourself a little vacation from the kitchen and socialize over a meal at the same time—throw a potluck get-together.

**Planning the Potluck**

It's potluck because no one know what the others are bringing; you take your chances and hope five potato salads won't show up. If they should, you could always have an impromptu potato salad-tasting. Or you could take some precautions to avoid such a misha by dividing the meal into main course, side dish and dessert and ask each guest to bring a specific course.

**Save a Special Dish to Prepare Yourself**

Since you don't have to go anywhere you might want to choose a dish to make that no one else could easily bring. Perhaps it something that could serve as a main course or dessert centerpiec

If you're planning a main

## MENU

◆

Quick Chicken and Mussel Paella
*(see page 73)*

Tomato, Avocado and Pasta Salad
*(see page 106)*

Raw Spinach and Mushroom Salad
*(see page 107)*

Chicory, Orange and Walnut Salad
*(see page 104)*

Salad Niçoise *(see page 382)*

Caesar Salad *(see page 382)*

Potato Salad *(see page 381)*

Fruit Salad *(featured recipe here)*

Grandma's Cookies *(see page 114)*

beer

◆

course, consider a warm dish; it will probably be the only one served since people don't generally bother to bring something that needs to be heated up, especially in summertime. Choose something, too, that's more substantial than most salads and double or triple the recipe so that you're sure there will be plenty of it to go around. Quick Chicken and Mussel Paella is a good choice.

A fruit salad, served in a carved-out melon shell, looks beautiful on the table during the meal and is a delicious dessert afterwards. Usually fruit salads like this are served in large watermelon shells, but if you want something extra special, have small, individual shells filled with fruit salad for each guest. Buy small cantaloupes, cut them in half and scoop out the flesh with a melon baller so you're left with little melon baskets. Serve cookies along with the fruit salad.

## SUMMER FRUIT SALAD

*plus 30 minutes cooling
*Serves 4–6*

| |
|---|
| $\frac{2}{3}$ cup sugar |
| 1 cup water |
| few fresh mint sprigs |
| 1 strip of orange peel |
| 8 oz fresh strawberries |
| 8 oz fresh raspberries |
| 1 small cantaloupe |
| 2 Tbsp orange-flavored liqueur |
| 2 Tbsp finely chopped fresh mint |
| few whole fresh mint leaves, to decorate |

**1** Put the sugar in a heavy-based pan, add the water and heat gently for 5–10 minutes until the sugar has dissolved, stirring occasionally.

**2** Add the mint sprigs and orange peel, then boil the syrup rapidly for 5 minutes, without stirring. Remove from the heat and leave for about 1 hour until completely cold.

**3** Meanwhile, prepare the fruit. Hull the strawberries, then slice them lengthwise.

**4** Leave the raspberries whole. Cut the melon in half, scoop out and discard the seeds.

**5** Cut the flesh into balls using a melon baller. Remove the mint sprigs and orange peel from the cold syrup, then stir in the liqueur and chopped mint.

**6** Put the fruit in a serving bowl, pour over the syrup, then carefully fold together. Chill in the refrigerator for at least 30 minutes. Serve chilled, decorate with whole fresh mint leaves.

# ICED TUTTI FRUTTI PUDDING

0.30* $ $ 624 cals

* plus 2–3 hours soaking fruit, 6–7 hours freezing and 20 minutes standing before serving

*Serves 8*

½ cup glacé cherries

1½ oz angelica

½ cup blanched almonds

4 canned pineapple rings, drained

½ cup orange-flavored liqueur

3¾ cups heavy cream

⅔ cup sugar

6 eggs, beaten

*1* Cut the cherries in half, finely chop the angelica, almonds and roughly chop the pineapple.

*2* Pour over the liqueur, cover and leave to steep for 2–3 hours, stirring occasionally.

*3* Meanwhile, put the cream, sugar and eggs in a heatproof bowl standing over a saucepan of gently simmering water (or in the top of a double boiler). Place over gentle heat and cook until the custard is thick enough to coat the back of a wooden spoon, stirring all the time. Do not boil.

*4* Pour the custard into a large bowl, cover and leave to cool for about 1 hour. When cold, freeze the custard for about 2 hours until mushy in texture.

*5* Mash the frozen mixture with a fork, then freeze again for about 2 hours until slushy.

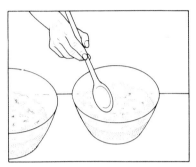

*6* Mash the frozen mixture again and stir in the fruit mixture. Mix well and pack into a 6- or 7-cup pudding mold, lined with aluminum foil. Return to freezer for 2–3 hours until firm.

*7* About 1 hour before serving, remove from the freezer and leave to soften slightly at room temperature. Turn out and serve immediately.

**ICED TUTTI FRUTTI PUDDING**

*Tutti frutti*, which literally translated means "all fruit" in Italian, was originally an American invention. Assorted fruits such as cherries, currants, raspberries, strawberries, apricots, peaches and pineapple were steeped in brandy in a stone crock for at least 3 months.

# RASPBERRY REDCURRANT FREEZE

| 0.30* | 284–392 cals |

* plus 1 hour chilling, 4 hours freezing
and 1 hour standing before serving

*Serves 4–6*

**12 oz fresh or frozen raspberries**

**8-oz jar redcurrant jelly**

**1¼ cups sour cream**

**small crisp cookies, to serve**

*1* Put the raspberries and jelly in a saucepan and heat gently, stirring frequently, until the fruit is soft. Transfer to a blender or food processor and work to a purée. Sieve to remove the seeds. Chill in the refrigerator for about 1 hour until cold.

*2* Whisk in the sour cream, then pour into a freezer container (not metal) at least 2 inches deep. Freeze for about 2 hours until firm but not hard.

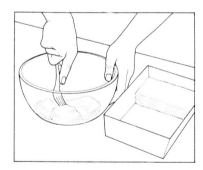

*3* Turn the frozen mixture into a bowl and break into pieces. Beat until smooth, creamy and lighter in color. Return to the freezer container and freeze for a further 2 hours until firm.

*4* Allow to soften slightly in the refrigerator for about 1 hour before serving with cookies.

**Menu Suggestion**
Serve for a cool and refreshing dessert after a rich main course.

# STRAWBERRIES WITH RASPBERRY SAUCE

**0.20\*** | 91 cals

\* plus at least 30 minutes chilling

*Serves 6*

2 lb small strawberries

1 lb raspberries

½ cup confectioner's sugar

*1* Hull the strawberries and place them in individual serving dishes.

*2* Purée the raspberries in a blender or food processor until just smooth, then work through a nylon sieve into a bowl to remove the seeds.

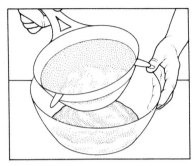

*3* Sift the confectioner's sugar over the bowl of raspberry purée, then whisk in until evenly incorporated. Pour over the strawberries. Chill in the refrigerator for at least 30 minutes before serving.

**Menu Suggestion**
This dessert is so simple to make, yet it's absolutely delicious. Serve it at a summer dinner party after a simple main course.

## STRAWBERRIES WITH RASPBERRY SAUCE

Freshly picked raspberries freeze successfully (unlike strawberries which tend to lose texture and shape due to their high water content). If you have raspberries which are slightly overripe or misshapen, the best way to freeze them is as a purée; this takes up less space in the freezer and is immensely useful for making quick desserts and sauces at the last minute. For this recipe, for example, you can freeze the purée up to 12 months in advance, then it will only take a few minutes to put the dessert together after the purée has thawed. The purée can be frozen with or without the sugar.

# ORANGE SHERBET

| 0.10* | $ | 268 cals |
|---|---|---|

* plus 4–5 hours freezing

*Serves 8*

6¼-oz carton frozen orange juice

⅞ cup sugar

3 Tbsp corn syrup

3 Tbsp lemon juice

2½ cups milk

1¼ cups light cream

shreds of orange rind and sprigs of
   mint, to decorate

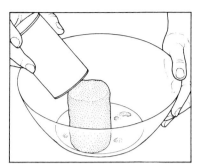

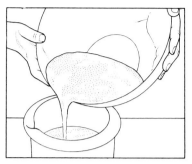

*1* Tip the frozen, undiluted orange juice into a deep bowl. Leave until beginning to soften, then add the sugar, corn syrup and lemon juice. Whisk until smooth.

*2* Combine the orange mixture with the milk and cream and pour into a deep, rigid container. Cover and freeze for 4–5 hours. There is no need to whisk the mixture during freezing.

*3* Transfer to the refrigerator to soften 45 minutes–1 hour before serving. Serve scooped into individual glasses or orange shells, decorate with orange shreds and sprigs of mint.

**Menu Suggestion**

Make up a batch or two and keep in the freezer for dinner parties. It makes a tangy and refreshing end to a rich meal.

**ORANGE SHERBET**

There is always some confusion over the terms "sherbet" and "sorbet" when used to describe a dessert. The word "sherbet" is in fact the American term for the European word "sorbet", although it is often mistakenly used to describe a water ice. Water ices are simple concoctions of sugar syrup and fruit purée or fruit juice, sometimes with liqueur or other alcohol added. Sorbets or sherbets are a smoother version of water ices. They are made in the same way, with sugar syrup and fruit, but at the half-frozen stage they have whisked egg whites or other ingredients folded into them.

# GRANDMA'S COOKIES

| 0.35* | $ | 101 cals |
|---|---|---|

* plus cooling time

*Makes 35*

| $\frac{1}{4}$ cup butter or margarine |
| $\frac{7}{8}$ cup dark brown sugar |
| 2 Tbsp corn syrup |
| 1 cup self-rising flour |
| $\frac{1}{2}$ tsp baking soda |
| $\frac{1}{2}$ cup rolled oats |
| 1 cup shredded coconut |
| 1 egg, beaten |

*1* Put the fat, sugar and corn syrup in a heavy-based pan and heat gently until melted, stirring occasionally.

*2* Meanwhile, put the flour, baking soda, oats and coconut in a large mixing bowl and stir well to mix.

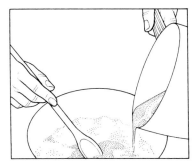

*3* Pour the melted mixture onto the dry ingredients and stir well to mix. Add the beaten egg and stir again until all of the ingredients are evenly combined.

*4* With the palm of your hands, shape and roll the mixture into about 35 small, walnut-sized balls.

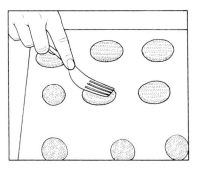

*5* Place the balls slightly apart on greased baking sheets to allow for spreading during baking, then flatten with the back of a fork to make an attractive pattern.

*6* Bake in the oven at 350°F for 12–15 minutes until browned. Leave to settle on the baking sheets for a few minutes, then transfer to a wire rack and leave to cool completely before serving. To keep crisp, store in an airtight container.

**Menu Suggestion**
Crisp, crunchy and wholesome, these old-fashioned cookies are a great hit with children—ideal for packed lunches.

# REFRIGERATOR COOKIES

| 0.35* | 37–49 cals |

* plus overnight chilling and about 30 minutes cooling; freeze dough at the end of step 3

*Makes 50–60*

$1\frac{1}{2}$ **cups all-purpose flour**

**2 tsp baking powder**

$\frac{1}{2}$ **cup butter or margarine**

$\frac{7}{8}$ **cup sugar**

**1 tsp vanilla extract**

**1 egg, beaten**

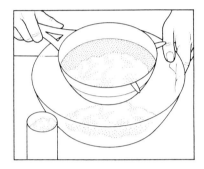

*1* Sift the flour and baking powder into a bowl. Rub in the fat until the mixture resembles breadcrumbs, then add the sugar and stir until evenly combined.

*2* Add the vanilla extract and egg and mix to a smooth dough with a wooden spoon.

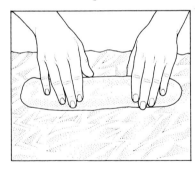

*3* Turn the dough onto a large sheet of foil and shape into a long roll about 2 inches in diameter. Wrap in the foil and chill in the refrigerator overnight.

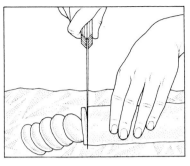

*4* To shape and bake: slice the roll very thinly into as many cookies as required. (The remainder of the roll can be wrapped again in the foil and returned to the refrigerator for up to 1 week.)

*5* Place the cookies well apart on a buttered baking sheet. Bake in the oven at 375°F for 10–12 minutes until golden.

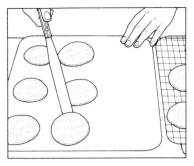

*6* Leave the cookies to settle on the baking sheet for a few minutes, then transfer to a wire rack and leave to cool completely. Store in an airtight container if not eating immediately.

**Menu Suggestion**
Serve for children's snacks or when unexpected visitors call. Keep a roll of dough in the refrigerator ready to make a batch of cookies at a moment's notice.

--- VARIATIONS ---

Walnut: add $\frac{1}{2}$ **cup very finely chopped walnuts** with the sugar in step 1.
Coconut: add $1\frac{1}{2}$ **cups shredded coconut** with the sugar in step 1.
Raisins: add $\frac{1}{3}$ **cup very finely chopped light raisins** with the sugar in step 1.
Chocolate: add **2 oz very finely grated semisweet chocolate** with the sugar in step 1.
Spicy: omit the vanilla and sift in **2 tsp ground mixed spice** with the flour in step 1.
Lemon: omit the vanilla and add the **finely grated rind of 1 lemon** with the sugar in step 1.
Ginger: omit the vanilla and sift in $1\frac{1}{2}$ **tsp ground ginger** with the flour in step 1.
Cherry: add $\frac{1}{4}$ **cup very finely chopped glacé cherries** with the sugar in step 1.
Orange: omit the vanilla and add the **finely grated rind of 1 orange** with the sugar in step 1.

# F·A·L·L

*T*he arrival of cool weather again means back to work and school and the more serious stuff of everyday. But every season of the year, even the quietest one, contains good reasons for getting—and eating—together. There are school receptions and church suppers and Indian summer outings. Halloween, football games, even Election Day and Columbus Day, are good excuses for parties. And, of course, fall ends with a bang—the biggest American feast day of all, Thanksgiving.

This season we have four more menus for you. The Sunday Night Fireside Supper is meant to be a quiet, comforting meal for the family and maybe a few friends.

Our Tailgate Party is not nearly so quiet, and it's got the hearty food and drink to match the hearty appetites and thirsts that come so predictably with the big Saturday afternoon game.

Halloween is mostly for kids (and the kids in us all), and so is our Halloween Treats Party, complete with treats and sweets for all ages. It will give you ideas for children's party foods that can be put to good use any time of the year.

And then comes Thanksgiving, with a meal that you won't forget, featuring the traditional bird, cranberry relish, sweet potatoes, pumpkin pie, and some new dishes that might very well find a permanent place on your annual turkey day menu.

# CHICKEN AND CORN SOUP

| 1.45 | 331 cals |

\* freeze after step 4

$3\frac{1}{2}$ lb chicken

$4\frac{1}{2}$ cups water

salt and freshly ground pepper

1 stalk celery, roughly chopped

1 sprig parsley

1 medium onion, roughly chopped

1 bay leaf

10 peppercorns

two 8-oz cans corn, drained

6 hard-boiled eggs

3 Tbsp chopped fresh parsley

$\frac{2}{3}$ cup light cream, to serve

*1* Place the chicken in a large saucepan with the water, salt, celery, parsley sprig, onion, bay leaf and peppercorns.

*2* Bring to the boil and simmer gently for $1–1\frac{1}{2}$ hours until the chicken is completely tender.

*3* When cooked, remove the chicken from the pan and cut the meat into large bite-size pieces. Discard skin and bones.

*4* Strain the chicken stock, return it to the saucepan and add the chicken meat and corn. Simmer for about 5 minutes.

*5* Chop the hard-boiled eggs. Add to the soup with the chopped parsley and salt and pepper to taste. Heat through gently, then pour into warmed individual bowls.

*6* Swirl cream into each portion and serve the chicken and corn soup immediately.

**Menu Suggestion**

This is a substantial meal-in-itself soup. Serve for a warming supper with garlic bread or French bread and butter, and a sharp, hard cheese such as Vermont Cheddar.

---

**QUICK CHICKEN AND CORN SOUP**

If time is short, you can make a quick chicken soup by using cooked chicken, skinned, boned, and cut into pieces. Simmer in 4 cups stock (made from cubes if necessary), with the vegetables and seasonings in the recipe above for 20 minutes. Drain, discarding the vegetables and seasonings and simmer the chicken pieces and stock with the corn for 5 minutes, then follow the recipe exactly as from step 5.

# WATERCRESS SOUP

| 0.25 | $ | 325 cals |

*Serves 4*

$\frac{1}{2}$ cup butter or margarine

1 medium onion, skinned and
    chopped

2 bunches watercress

$\frac{1}{2}$ cup flour

3 cups chicken or veal stock

$1\frac{1}{4}$ cups milk

salt and freshly ground pepper

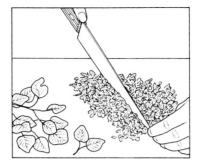

*1* Melt the butter in a saucepan,
add the onion and cook gently
for 10 minutes until soft but not
colored.

*2* Meanwhile, wash and trim the
watercress, leaving some of the
stem, then chop roughly.

*3* Add the chopped watercress to
the onion, cover the pan with a
lid and cook gently for another
4 minutes.

*4* Add the flour and cook gently,
stirring, for 1–2 minutes.
Remove from the heat and gradually blend in the stock and milk.
Bring to a boil, stirring constantly,
then simmer for 3 minutes. Season
to taste.

*5* Sieve or purée the soup in a
blender or food processor.
Return to the rinsed-out pan and
reheat gently, without boiling.
Taste and adjust seasoning, if
necessary. Serve hot.

**Menu Suggestion**
Watercress soup makes a delicious
appetizer for a winter dinner
party. Follow it with roast game
and end with fruity dessert.

# CREAM OF CARROT WITH ORANGE SOUP

| 0.55 | $ | 73–110 cals |

*Serves 4–6*

2 Tbsp butter or margarine

$1\frac{1}{2}$ lb carrots, peeled and sliced

8 oz onion, skinned and sliced (2
    medium onions)

$4\frac{1}{2}$ cups chicken or ham stock

salt and freshly ground pepper

1 orange

*1* Melt the butter in a saucepan,
add the vegetables and cook
gently for 10 minutes until
softened slightly.

*2* Add the stock and bring to a
boil. Lower the heat, cover and
simmer for about 40 minutes, or
until the vegetables are tender.

*3* Sieve or purée the vegetables
with half of the stock in a
blender or food processor. Add
this mixture to the stock remaining
in the pan.

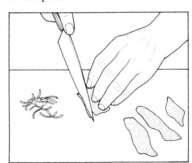

*4* Meanwhile, pare half of the
orange rind thinly, using a
potato peeler, then cut it into
shreds. Cook the shreds in gently
boiling water until tender.

*5* Finely grate the remaining
orange rind into the soup. Stir
well to combine with the ingredients in the pan

*6* Squeeze the juice of the orange
into the pan. Reheat the soup
gently, then taste and adjust
seasoning. Drain the shreds of
orange rind and use to garnish the
soup just before serving.
Serve hot.

**Menu Suggestion**
This is an everyday soup made
from basic ingredients, but the
orange rind and juice give a
delicious "kick" to the flavor.

# Coarse Liver Pâté

| 3.20* | 454 cals |

*plus cooling and overnight chilling
*Serves 8*

½ lb sliced bacon

1¼ cups milk

slices of onion, bay leaf, peppercorns and 1 or 2 cloves, for flavoring

2 Tbsp butter or margarine

1½ Tbsp flour

1 lb slab uncured bacon

1 lb pig's liver

1 small onion, skinned and quartered

2 garlic cloves, skinned and crushed

2 Tbsp medium dry sherry

salt and freshly ground pepper

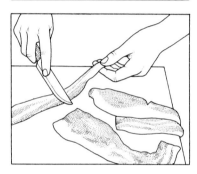

*1* Put the bacon slices on a board and stretch, using the back of a knife. Use to line the base and sides of a 6-cup dish or terrine.

*2* Pour the milk into a saucepan, add the flavoring ingredients and bring slowly to a boil. Remove from the heat, cover and leave to infuse for 15 minutes.

*3* Strain the milk and reserve. Melt the butter in the rinsed-out pan, add the flour and cook gently, stirring, for 1–2 minutes. Remove from the heat and gradually blend in the milk. Bring to a boil, stirring constantly, then simmer for 3 minutes until thick and smooth. Cover and leave to cool slightly.

*4* Cut the pork and liver into small pieces. Pass the meats and onion through a grinder, fitted with the coarsest blade. Alternatively, chop in a food processor.

*5* Put the ground mixture into a bowl, add the garlic, then stir in the sherry and plenty of salt and pepper. Gradually beat in the cooled sauce and continue beating until well mixed. The mixture may seem a little sloppy, but it will firm up on cooking.

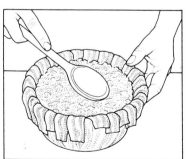

*6* Spoon the mixture into the prepared dish and press down with the back of the spoon. Fold over any overlapping bacon. Cover the dish tightly with foil.

*7* Place the dish in a roasting pan and half fill with boiling water. Bake in the oven at 350°F for about 2¼ hours until firm to the touch and the juices run clear when the center of the pâté is pierced with a fine skewer.

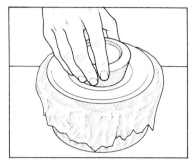

*8* Remove the dish from the roasting pan and replace the foil with a fresh piece. Place a plate or dish, small enough just to fit inside the dish, on top of the pâté. Cover with heavy weights.

*9* Leave the pâté to cool for 1 hour, then chill overnight. To serve, dip the dish into hot water for about 30 seconds then invert the pâté onto a plate.

**Menu Suggestion**
Coarse Liver Pâté makes a substantial appetizer for an informal supper party, served with salad, French bread and a full-bodied red wine. Alternatively, cut the pâté into thick slices and use for packed lunches and picnics, with a selection of salads.

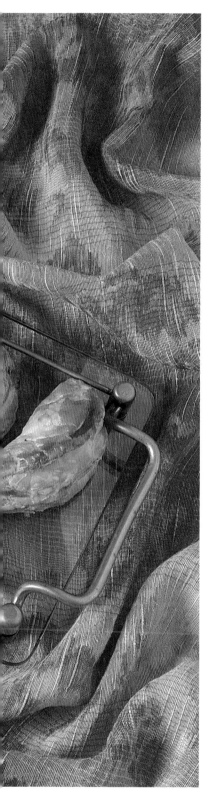

# CREAMY HAM AND MUSHROOM PUFFS

| 1.00* | 430–645 cals |

* plus cooling; freeze at the end of step 5

*Serves 4–6*

3 oz button mushrooms

1 small onion, skinned

3 Tbsp butter or margarine

2 Tbsp flour

$\frac{1}{3}$ cup milk

$\frac{1}{2}$ cup heavy cream

3 oz boiled ham, finely diced

2 tsp chopped fresh tarragon or 1 tsp dried

salt and freshly ground pepper

12 oz packet frozen puff pastry, thawed

1 egg, beaten, to glaze

*1* Chop the mushrooms and onion very finely. Melt half of the butter in a pan, add them to it and fry over moderate heat for 2–3 minutes. Remove and drain.

*2* Melt the remaining butter in the pan, add the flour and cook gently, stirring, for 1–2 minutes. Remove from the heat and gradually blend in the milk. Bring to a boil, stirring constantly. Add the cream and simmer for 3 minutes until thick. Off the heat, fold in the mushroom mixture, ham and seasonings.

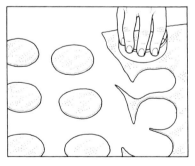

*3* Roll out the pastry on a lightly floured surface and cut out 12 rounds using a 4-inch plain round cutter.

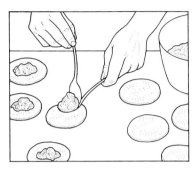

*4* Put spoonfuls of the ham and mushroom filling on one half of each pastry round.

*5* Brush the edges of the pastry rounds with beaten egg, then fold the plain half of the pastry over the filling. Seal the edges and crimp with the prongs of a fork.

*6* Place the turnovers on a dampened baking sheet. Brush with beaten egg to glaze, then bake in the oven at 425°F for 15–20 minutes until puffed up and golden. Serve hot.

**Menu Suggestion**

These puff pastry turnovers are rich and filling. Follow with a light main course such as broiled or barbecued fish kabobs. A tangy lemon or orange soufflé or mousse would make the ideal dessert.

127

# SUNDAY FIRESIDE SUPPER

Ah, Sunday night. The last of the weekend. A time for an easy meal with family and maybe a few friends. Nobody feels like cooking much on Sunday night. You'd much rather have time to finish (or start) reading the Sunday paper, catch the last of the football game on TV, or linger at the kids' Sunday afternoon soccer match. This meal fits the mood.

Casseroles, stews and soups are the ideal make-ahead foods. They actually taste better if they're left in the refrigerator for a day before serving. It gives the spices time to mellow and blend together and the other ingredients time to marinate in the stock or sauce.

Our fireside supper features one of these make-ahead dishes, a hot and flavorful casserole called Three-Cheese Lasagne. It's the perfect dish for taking the chill of the cool fall evening and a comforting conclusion to a busy week.

### The Antipasto

While the lasagne is baking, you can bring out a serving platter of antipasto to nibble on. Antipasto means "before the meal" in Italian, and it can be anything from one or two slices of salami to a huge selection of cold meats, fish, eggs, vegetables and fresh or marinated salads.

Knowing this, your antipasto can include any of the above, as little or as much as you wish. Preparing an antipasto is a good excuse for exploring the interior of your refrigerator in search of some little leftovers that would fit in very nicely.

If you're planning to buy the ingredients expressly for making up an antipasto and want to have nice substantial platter to bring

---

## MENU

◆

*antipasto*
*Breadsticks (see page 385)*
*Three-Cheese Lasagne*
*(featured recipe here)*
*tossed salad with Yogurt Dressing*
*(see page 288)*
*Garlic Bread (see page 384)*
*Apple Sauce Cake (see page 353)*
*a full-bodied red wine*

◆

ut, then you should figure that
or 10 servings you will roughly
eed the following, or similar
ubstitutes: 1 small head of
ettuce, 20 slices of Italian salami,
0 slices of cooked Italian sausage,
0 slices of prosciutto, 12 oz
Mozzarella cheese, 5 quartered
ard-boiled eggs, 5 sliced
omatoes, 1 jar of marinated
rtichoke hearts, 1 jar of roasted
eppers, olives and anchovies for
arnish. Line the platter with
ettuce leaves and group the other
oods on top.

You won't need a vinaigrette if
here are a few marinated foods,
ke the ones suggested above, on
our platter; otherwise serve some
n the side, along with breadsticks.

### Accompaniments

The lasagne is complete with
ossed salad and maybe some
arlic bread warmed by the fire.
Keep glasses filled with a hearty
ed Italian wine.

People will probably say they
ave no room left for dessert —
ntil you tell them that you've got
warm Apple Sauce Cake, topped
ith heavy cream. (You can make
his, too, ahead of time. Bake it
nd then freeze it; take it out to
haw in the morning and heat it up
hile dinner is being eaten.)

## THREE-CHEESE LASAGNE

*Serves 10*

| |
|---|
| one 16-oz can tomatoes |
| small onion, chopped |
| 1 celery stalk, trimmed and chopped |
| garlic clove, crushed |
| bay leaf |
| salt and freshly ground pepper |
| 1 lb ground beef |
| 1 egg |
| $\frac{1}{2}$ cup grated Parmesan cheese |
| $\frac{3}{4}$ cup all-purpose flour |
| 4 Tbsp olive or vegetable oil |
| $\frac{1}{3}$ cup butter or margarine |
| $2\frac{1}{2}$ cups milk |
| 4 oz mild cured ham, chopped |
| 4 oz Mozzarella cheese, thinly sliced |
| 4 oz Bel Paese cheese, cut into strips |
| $\frac{2}{3}$ cup light cream |
| 1 lb lasagne noodles |

**1** Prepare the tomato sauce by
placing the tomatoes, onion,
celery, garlic and bay leaf in a
small pan, bring to a boil and
simmer, uncovered, for 30
minutes. Stir occasionally to
prevent sticking.

**2** Discard the bay leaf and rub
mixture through a sieve or purée
in a blender. Season. Combine
beef, egg, half the Parmesan and
seasoning. Shape the mixture into

twenty-four meatballs. Roll lightly
in a little seasoned flour.

**3** Heat the oil in a pan and cook
the meatballs for about 5 minutes
until brown. Remove with slotted
spoon and drain.

**4** Melt the butter in a pan, add
$\frac{1}{2}$ cup flour and stirring, cook
gently for 1 minute. Remove from
the heat and gradually stir in the
milk.

**5** Bring to a boil and cook, stirring
all the time, until the sauce
thickens. Stir in the ham,
Mozzarella, Bel Paese, cream and
seasoning.

**6** Prepare the lasagne as directed
on the packet. In a large, greased,
oval or rectangular ovenproof dish,
layer up the lasagne, meatballs,
tomato and white sauces, finishing
with a layer of lasagne topped with
white sauce.

**7** Sprinkle over the remaining
Parmesan cheese, then bake in the
oven at 400°F for 20–25 minutes
until golden brown.

# RED FLANNEL HASH

| 0.45 | $ | 380 cals |

*Serves 4*

1 lb potatoes, scrubbed

salt and freshly ground pepper

8 oz corned beef, chopped

1 medium onion, skinned and
finely chopped

1 tsp garlic salt

8 oz cooked beets, diced

2 Tbsp chopped fresh parsley

$\frac{1}{4}$ cup beef drippings or lard

*1* Cook the potatoes in their skins in lightly salted boiling water for about 20 minutes or until tender when pierced with a fork.

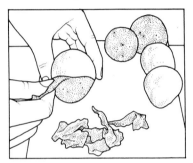

*2* Drain the potatoes, leave until cool enough to handle, then peel off the skins with your fingers. Dice the flesh.

*3* Put the diced potatoes into a large bowl, add the beef, onion, garlic salt, beets and parsley and toss to combine. Add pepper to taste.

*4* Heat the drippings or lard in a heavy-based skillet or frying pan until smoking hot. Add the hash mixture and spread evenly with a spatula.

*5* Lower the heat to moderate and cook the hash, uncovered, for 10–15 minutes. Break up and turn frequently with the spatula, so that the hash becomes evenly browned. Serve hot.

**Menu Suggestion**
Red Flannel Hash is a traditional dish from New England. Serve it topped with fried or poached eggs, for a quick evening meal or snack.

# SIZZLING STEAK SANDWICHES

**0.15** $ 605 cals

*Serves 2*

2 "flash-fry" steaks, about 3 oz each

1 Tbsp vegetable oil

salt and freshly ground pepper

4 slices of wholemeal bread, from a large loaf

butter or margarine, for spreading

2 Tbsp mayonnaise

about 4 small lettuce leaves, shredded

1 tomato, skinned and sliced

2 tsp Dijon-style mustard

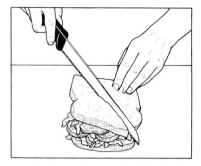

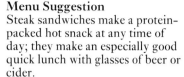

**Menu Suggestion**
Steak sandwiches make a protein-packed hot snack at any time of day; they make an especially good quick lunch with glasses of beer or cider.

*4* Cut each sandwich in half with a serrated knife to make 2 triangles and place on individual plates. Serve immediately.

*1* Brush the steaks on one side with half of the oil and sprinkle with pepper to taste. Broil under a preheated hot broiler for 3 minutes, then turn them over, brush with the remaining oil, sprinkle with more pepper and broil for another 3 minutes, or until done to your liking.

*2* Meanwhile, toast the bread on both sides, removing the crusts if desired. Spread one side of each slice with butter, then with the mayonnaise. Top 2 slices of toast with the shredded lettuce and sliced tomato and sprinkle with salt and pepper to taste.

*3* Place the steaks on top of the salad and spread evenly with the mustard. Cover with the remaining 2 slices of toast.

# STUFFED EGGPLANT

| 1.30 | $ | 524 cals |

*Serves 4*

2 medium eggplants

salt and freshly ground pepper

5 Tbsp olive oil

1 medium onion, skinned and
  finely chopped

1–2 garlic cloves, skinned and
  crushed

1 red or green pepper, cored,
  seeded and finely diced

6 oz button mushrooms, wiped
  and finely chopped

4 ripe tomatoes, skinned and finely
  chopped

1 Tbsp tomato paste

$\frac{1}{2}$ cup long-grain rice

$\frac{1}{3}$ cup chopped mixed nuts

2 Tbsp chopped fresh parsley

4 oz Cheddar cheese, grated

$1\frac{1}{2}$ cups fresh wholewheat
  breadcrumbs

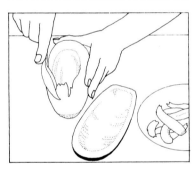

*1* Slice the eggplants in half
lengthwise. Scoop out and
reserve the flesh, leaving a narrow
margin inside the skin so that the
eggplants will hold their shape.

*2* Sprinkle the insides of the
eggplant shells with salt and
stand upside down to drain for 30
minutes.

*3* Dice the scooped-out eggplant
flesh, then place in a colander,
sprinkling each layer with salt.
Cover with a plate, place heavy
weights on top and leave to drain
for 30 minutes.

*4* Meanwhile, heat 4 Tbsp of the
oil in a heavy-based saucepan.
Add the onion and garlic; fry
gently for 5 minutes until soft.
Add the diced pepper to the pan
and fry gently for 5 minutes.

*5* Rinse the diced eggplant under
cold running water then pat
dry with paper towels. Add to the
pan with the mushrooms,
tomatoes and tomato paste.
Simmer for about 5 minutes, then
add the rice, nuts, parsley and salt
and pepper.

*6* Rinse the eggplant cases and
pat dry with paper towels.
Brush a baking dish with the
remaining oil, then stand the
eggplant cases in the dish. Fill
with the stuffing mixture.

*7* Mix the grated cheese and
breadcrumbs together, then
sprinkle evenly over the top of the
eggplants. Bake uncovered in the
oven at 350°F for 45 minutes.
Serve hot.

**Menu Suggestion**

Eggplants stuffed with rice and
vegetables make a most nutritious
main course dish for a family
supper or an informal party.

# MEAT LOAF WITH ONION SAUCE

| 2.00 | $ | 511 cals |

*Serves 4*

¼ cup butter or margarine

2 medium onions, skinned and
    finely chopped

1 tsp paprika

1 lb ground beef

1¼ cups fresh breadcrumbs

1 garlic clove, skinned and crushed

4 Tbsp tomato paste

1 Tbsp chopped fresh mixed herbs
    or 1 tsp dried

salt and freshly ground pepper

1 egg, beaten

1½ Tbsp flour

1¼ cups milk

*1* Grease a 1 lb loaf pan, then line the base with greased waxed paper. Set aside.

*2* Melt 2 Tbsp of the butter in a frying pan, add half of the onions and cook until softened. Add the paprika and cook for 1 minute, stirring, then turn the mixture into a large bowl.

*3* Add the beef, breadcrumbs, garlic, tomato paste, herbs and salt and pepper to taste. Stir thoroughly until evenly mixed, then bind with the beaten egg.

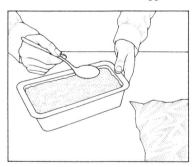

*4* Spoon the mixture into the loaf pan, level the surface and cover tightly with foil. Stand the pan in a roasting pan and pour in water to a depth of 1 inch. Bake in the oven at 350°F for 1½ hours.

*5* Meanwhile, melt the remaining butter in a saucepan. Add the rest of the onion and cook over low heat, stirring occasionally, for 10 minutes until soft but not colored. Add the flour and cook over low heat, stirring, for 2 minutes.

*6* Remove the pan from the heat and gradually blend in the milk, stirring after each addition to prevent lumps forming.

*7* Bring to a boil slowly and continue to cook, stirring all the time, until the sauce comes to a boil and thickens. Simmer very gently for another 2–3 minutes, then add salt and pepper to taste.

*8* To serve, turn out the meat loaf onto a warmed serving plate and peel off the lining paper. Serve immediately, with the hot onion sauce.

**Menu Suggestion**
Serve for a family supper with creamed potatoes and a cucumber and dill salad.

---

**MEAT LOAF**

Meat loaf is a traditional Jewish dish called Klops, and just about every Jewish family has its own favorite version. Some cooks include matzo meal among the ingredients, to bind the mixture and help stretch the meat in the same way as breadcrumbs. Onion sauce is traditional with Meat Loaf, and sometimes mushrooms are added. For this quantity of sauce, use ¼ lb button mushrooms, sliced, and add them to the sauce at the end of step 7.

# LAMB AND PEPPER KABOBS

| 1.00* | 404 cals |

\* plus 4 hours or overnight
marinating; freeze in the marinade

*Serves 4*

1½ lb lamb fillet, trimmed of fat

½ cup dry white wine

½ cup corn oil

¼ cup lemon juice

2 celery sticks, trimmed and very
finely chopped

1 small onion, skinned and grated

2 garlic cloves, skinned and
crushed

1 large tomato, skinned and finely
chopped

4 tsp chopped fresh thyme or 2 tsp
dried thyme

salt and freshly ground pepper

1 medium red pepper

1 medium green pepper

few bay leaves

*1* Cut the lamb into cubes and
place in a bowl. In another
bowl whisk together the wine, oil,
lemon juice, celery, onion, garlic,
tomato, thyme and salt and freshly
ground pepper to taste.

*2* Pour the marinade over the
lamb and turn the meat until
well coated. Cover the bowl and
marinate in the refrigerator for at
least 4 hours, preferably overnight.

*3* When ready to cook, cut the
tops off the peppers and
remove the cores and seeds. Cut
the flesh into squares.

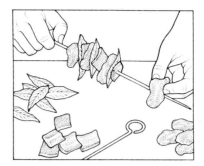

*4* Remove the meat from the
marinade (reserving the
marinade) and thread onto 8 oiled
kabob skewers, alternating with
the squares of pepper and bay
leaves.

*5* Cook over charcoal or under a
preheated moderate broiler for
20–25 minutes until the lamb is
tender. Turn the skewers
frequently during cooking and
brush with the reserved marinade.
Serve hot.

**Menu Suggestion**

For a really quick help-yourself
type of meal, serve these kabobs in
pockets of hot pita bread, and
accompany with bowls of
shredded lettuce or cabbage, sliced
tomato and cucumber.

**LAMB AND PEPPER
KABOBS**

Lamb fillet is from the neck of
the animal. It is an excellent cut
for cutting into cubes for kabobs,
casseroles and curries, because it
is tender without being dry. Leg
of lamb can be boned and cubed,
but it is such a lean cut that it
tends to dry out on cooking.
Shoulder of lamb is also
sometimes boned and cubed, but
this tends to be more fatty and
sinewy. Many large
supermarkets sell lamb fillet, but
if you are buying it from a
butcher, you may have to order
in advance.

# TUNA AND PASTA IN SOUR CREAM

| 0.25 | 780 cals |
|------|----------|

*Serves 4*

**8 oz pasta spirals or shells**
**salt and freshly ground pepper**
**1 tsp vegetable oil**
**7-oz can tuna, drained**
**4 eggs, hard-boiled and shelled**
**2 Tbsp butter**
**⅔ cup sour cream**
**1 tsp anchovy paste**
**2 Tbsp cider vinegar**
**4 Tbsp chopped fresh parsley**

*1* Cook the pasta in plenty of boiling salted water to which the oil has been added, for about 15 minutes until *al dente* (tender but firm to the bite). Drain well.

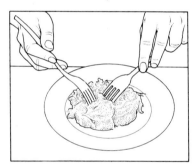

*2* Meanwhile, flake the tuna fish with 2 forks. Chop the hard-boiled eggs finely.

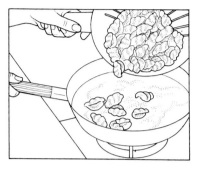

*3* Melt the butter in a deep frying pan and toss in the pasta. Stir in the sour cream, anchovy paste and vinegar.

*4* Add the tuna and egg to the pan with the parsley. Season well and warm through over low heat, stirring occasionally. Serve immediately.

**Menu Suggestion**
This rich and filling pasta dish needs a contrasting accompaniment. Serve with a crisp and crunchy green salad of chopped celery, fennel, cucumber and green pepper.

---

## TUNA AND PASTA IN SOUR CREAM

The type of pasta you use for this dish is really a matter of personal taste, although spirals and shells are specified in the ingredients list. As long as the shapes are small *(pasta corta)*, the sauce will cling to them and not slide off—Italians serve short cut pasta with fairly heavy sauces like this one which have chunks of fish or meat in them. Long pasta *(pasta lunga)* such as spaghetti and tagliatelle are best served with smoother sauces. Italian pasta in the shape of shells is called *conchiglie*, and there are many different sizes to choose from. *Farfalle* is shaped like small bow-ties; *fusilli* is spirals, so too is *spirale ricciolo*; *rotelle* is shaped like wheels. There are also many different types of short pasta shaped like macaroni—*penne* are hollow and shaped like quills with angled ends, *rigatoni* have ridges.

# TAILGATE PARTY

How long *has* it been since you've seen your old buddies? Could a whole year really have passed by? Getting together is reason enough to celebrate, but this tasty meal contributes to the occasion. And it will fortify you and your friends for the rest of the day, no matter how cold the temperature.

Think of a tailgate party as a hot picnic and you've got the idea. The best foods are those that not only pack and travel well, but that are hearty and warming and easy to eat literally out of the trunk of a car.

### Hot and Hearty

Chili is a good bet for your tailgate party because it's warm and spicy—a meal in itself and one that can be kept warm in a wide-mouthed thermos bottle or jug. It's better than soup because its thick and chunky consistency makes it easier to eat without spilling. Ours is an interesting variation on the typical beef and beans. This one is made with turkey and beans. Serve it in large sturdy plastic mugs.

### Toppings

Pack some good-looking plastic containers with garnishes for topping the chili, including any or all of the following: grated Monterey Jack or Cheddar cheese, sour cream, chopped green onions, chopped green peppers, chopped avocado (which has been sprinkled with lemon juice to prevent it from turning brown), chopped tomatoes and/or chopped black olives. Since this chili is not terribly spicy, have on hand a favorite hot sauce, or some Chili Oil or Harissa (Fiery Sauce) for those who can't have it hot enough.

---

### ◆ *MENU* ◆

*warm Brandy Cider Cup (see page 391)*

*Turkey Chili (featured recipe here)*

*tortilla chips*

*French bread*

*hoagies, filled with Coarse Liver Pâté (see page 124) and other flavorful meat mixtures*

*beer*

*a robust red wine*

*Chewy Chocolate Brownies (see page 178)*

*coffee*

---

## Hoagies, Heroes or Subs

Chili with such garnishes, some tortilla chips and slices of French bread is a substantial enough lunch, but since people who go to tailgate parties look forward as much to lots of food and drink as they do to the football game itself, we've got hoagies, otherwise known as hero sandwiches or subs.

Use hoagie or steak rolls, or large slices of French bread and heap on the filling. Don't be skimpy. You can go traditional and make your hoagies from shredded lettuce and onions, tomato slices, sliced cheese and luncheon meats, some oil and vinegar, pepper and salt and dried oregano. Or you can create more unusual fillings: Coarse Liver Pâté with mustard and lettuce; cooked ground or sliced beef with horseradish, lettuce and tomatoes; corned beef with chopped watercress and mustard; ground pork and ham with cranberry sauce; and salami with tomato, lettuce and onions. Make sure there are plenty of napkins handy!

## Drinks and Sweets

A tailgate party isn't a tailgate party without beer. If you really want to bring back memories, bring along the brand you used to drink years ago. A hearty red wine is also good to have for those who prefer not to drink beer. And you can bet that someone is sure to bring along something stronger, too.

Start guests off with a Brandy Cider Cup, heated up (but not boiled) beforehand and kept warm in a thermos. (Don't serve too many of these, they can pack quite a punch!)

Our brownies are chocolately and chewy. Pass them around with the coffee. No one can resist. If people are too stuffed to eat dessert right after the meal—or the game is about to start—save them for half-time.

## TURKEY CHILI

### Serves 8

| |
|---|
| 4 oz butter or margarine |
| 2 medium onions, skinned and roughly chopped |
| 4 Tbsp flour |
| 1 Tbsp chili seasoning |
| 1 lb 12-oz can tomatoes |
| 2 Tbsp Worcestershire sauce |
| 4 Tbsp tomato paste |
| $3\frac{3}{4}$ cups chicken or turkey stock |
| 1 Tbsp sugar |
| 2 bay leaves |
| salt and freshly ground pepper |
| $1\frac{1}{2}$–2 lb cooked turkey meat, cut into large dices |
| 14-oz can sweet red peppers (pimientos), drained |
| $15\frac{1}{4}$-oz can red kidney beans, drained |

1 Melt 2 oz of the butter in a heavy-based saucepan, add the onion and fry for about 5 minutes until golden. Stir in the flour and chili seasoning, then continue frying for 2 minutes.

2 Add the tomatoes with their juice, the Worcestershire sauce, tomato paste, stock, sugar, bay leaves and salt and pepper to taste. Bring to a boil, cover then simmer for 30 minutes.

3 Dice the pimiento. Melt the remaining butter in a frying pan and fry the turkey for 5 minutes.

4 Stir the turkey, diced pimiento and beans into the sauce and simmer for a further 10 minutes.

# LAMB WITH ROSEMARY AND GARLIC

**3.15\*** | $ | 305 cals

\* plus 12 hours standing; freeze after stage 3

*Serves 6*

4¼-lb leg of lamb

2 large garlic cloves, peeled

4 Tbsp butter, softened

1 Tbsp chopped fresh rosemary or 1 tsp dried

salt and freshly ground pepper

2 Tbsp flour

2 cups chicken stock

fresh rosemary sprigs, to garnish

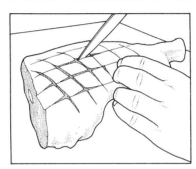

*1* Using a sharp knife, score the surface of the lamb into a diamond pattern to the depth of about ½ inch.

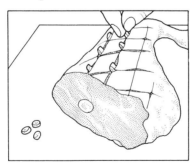

*2* Cut the cloves of garlic into wafer-thin slices. Push the slices into the scored surface of the lamb with your fingers.

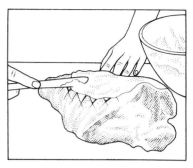

*3* Mix the butter with the rosemary and seasoning and then spread all over the lamb. Place the joint in a shallow dish, cover tightly with plastic and refrigerate for at least 12 hours.

*4* Uncover the lamb and transfer it to a medium roasting pan. Place in the oven and cook at 350°F for about 2¼ hours, basting occasionally as the fat begins to run. Pierce the joint with a fine skewer; when done the juices should run clear at first, then with a hint of red.

*5* Place the joint on a serving plate, cover loosely and keep warm in a low oven. Pour all excess fat out of the roasting pan leaving about 3 Tbsp fat with the meat juices. Sprinkle the flour into the roasting pan and stir until evenly mixed. Cook over a gentle heat for 2–3 minutes until well browned, stirring frequently.

*6* Add the stock and seasoning and bring to the boil, stirring. Simmer for 3–4 minutes, adjust the seasoning. To serve, garnish the lamb with rosemary and serve the gravy separately.

# TRADITIONAL ROAST TURKEY

| 5.30–6.30 | $ | 668–834 cals |
|---|---|---|

*Serves 8–10*

$\frac{1}{4}$ cup butter

3 medium onions, skinned and finely chopped

8 oz lean veal, ground

6 oz lean bacon, chopped fine

3 cups fresh white breadcrumbs

2 large mushrooms, chopped

1 Tbsp chopped fresh parsley or 1 tsp dried

$\frac{1}{2}$ tsp mace or nutmeg

$\frac{1}{4}$ tsp cayenne

salt and freshly ground pepper

1 egg, beaten

$\frac{1}{2}$ cup suet or 4 Tbsp beef dripping

$2\frac{1}{2}$ cups rolled oats

10–12 lb turkey

melted dripping or butter, for brushing

*1* Make the ground veal stuffing. Melt the butter in a small frying pan, add one of the onions and fry gently for 5 minutes.

*2* Meanwhile, put the veal and bacon in a bowl and beat well.

*3* Stir in the fried onions, breadcrumbs, mushrooms, parsley, mace or nutmeg, cayenne and salt and pepper to taste. Bind with the beaten egg; if the mixture is too stiff, add a little milk. Cool for 20 minutes.

*4* Make the oat stuffing. Melt the suet or dripping in a frying pan, add the remaining onions and fry gently for 5 minutes until soft but not colored. Stir in the oats and cook over a gentle heat, stirring, until the mixture is thick and thoroughly cooked. Add plenty of salt and pepper to taste. Turn into a greased $2\frac{1}{2}$-cup pudding mold. Cover with waxed paper and foil.

*5* Remove the giblets and wash the bird. Drain well and pat dry with paper towels.

*6* Stuff the neck end of the turkey with the veal stuffing, taking care not to pack it too tightly. Cover the stuffing smoothly with the neck skin.

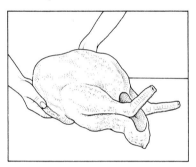

*7* With the bird breast side up, fold the wing tips neatly under the body, catching in the neck skin.

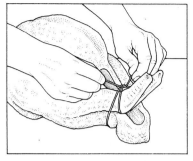

*8* Truss the bird and tie the legs together. Make the body as plump and even in shape as possible.

*9* Weigh the bird and calculate the cooking time, allowing 20 minutes per 1 lb, plus 20 minutes. Put the bird breast side up on a rack in a roasting pan. Brush with melted dripping and sprinkle with plenty of salt and pepper.

*10* Cover the bird loosely with foil. Roast in the oven at 350°F for the calculated cooking time until tender, removing the foil and basting the turkey 30 minutes before the end of cooking time. Turn off the oven and leave the turkey to rest for up to 30 minutes before carving. One hour before the end of cooking the turkey, put the oat stuffing in the oven to steam.

# TURKEY AND BACON KABOBS

| 0.45* | 551 cals |
|---|---|

* plus at least 4 hours marinating; freeze in the marinade

*Serves 4*

2 Tbsp cranberry sauce

6 Tbsp vegetable oil

3 Tbsp freshly squeezed orange juice

1 garlic clove, skinned and crushed

½ tsp ground allspice

salt and freshly ground pepper

1½ lb boneless turkey escalopes

1 small onion, skinned

1 large red pepper, cored, seeded and cut into chunks

6 bacon slices, halved

*1* Put the cranberry sauce, oil and orange juice in a shallow dish with the garlic, allspice and seasoning to taste. Whisk with a fork until well combined.

*2* Cut the turkey into bite-sized pieces and place in the dish. Stir to coat in the oil and orange juice mixture, then cover and leave to marinate for at least 4 hours. Stir the meat in the marinade occasionally during this time.

*3* When ready to cook, cut the onion into squares or even-sized chunks.

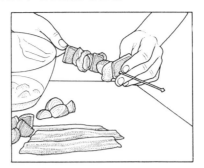

*4* Thread the turkey, onion and red pepper onto oiled skewers with the bacon, dividing the ingredients as evenly as possible.

*5* Broil under a preheated moderate broiler for about 20 minutes, turning the skewers frequently and basting with the remaining marinade. Serve hot.

**Menu Suggestion**

Make a quick, hot sauce to pour over the kabobs by heating together cranberry sauce with orange juice to taste. Serve on a bed of saffron rice with an endive, orange and walnut salad tossed in a sharp oil and vinegar dressing.

---

**TURKEY AND BACON KABOBS**

Turkey is lean and flavorsome, but it has little natural fat, so it can be dry if not prepared and cooked in the correct way. The marinade of oil and orange juice in this recipe is an excellent way of adding moisture to the flesh, and the acid content of the orange helps break down any tough connective tissue. Don't be tempted to omit the marinating time if you are in a hurry; the longer the turkey is marinated the better. If it is more convenient, the turkey can be marinated in the refrigerator overnight, but allow it to come to room temperature before broiling.

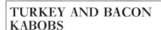

# LAMB AND LENTIL BAKE

| 2.30 | $ | 630 cals |

*Serves 4*

3 Tbsp vegetable oil

8 middle neck lamb chops, total weight about 2½ lb, trimmed of excess fat

2 medium onions, skinned and thinly sliced

1 Tbsp turmeric

1 tsp paprika

1 tsp ground cinnamon

3 oz red lentils

salt and freshly ground pepper

1 lb potatoes, peeled and thinly sliced

1 lb turnip, peeled and thinly sliced

1¼ cups lamb or chicken stock

*1* Heat the oil in a large sauté or frying pan, add the chops and brown well on both sides. Remove from the pan with a slotted spoon.

*2* Add the onions to the pan with the turmeric, paprika, cinnamon and lentils. Fry for 2–3 minutes. Add plenty of salt and pepper and spoon into a shallow 2-quart ovenproof dish.

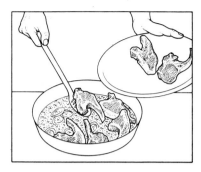

*3* Place the chops on top of the onion and lentil mixture. Arrange the vegetable slices on top of the chops, then season and pour over the stock.

*4* Cover the dish tightly and cook in the oven at 350°F for about 1½ hours, or until the chops are tender. Uncover and cook for another 30 minutes, or until lightly browned on top. Serve hot, straight from the dish.

**Menu Suggestion**
Lamb and Lentil Bake is a complete meal in itself, with lamb chops, lentils, potatoes and turnip baked together in one dish. Serve with a crisp green salad or a seasonal green vegetable.

# VEAL IN CREAM SAUCE

| 1.45 | $ | 469 cals |

*Serves 6*

2 lb stewing veal or braising steak, cubed

1 lb carrots, peeled and cut into fingers

8 oz small white onions, skinned

bouquet garni

$\frac{2}{3}$ cup white wine

$3\frac{3}{4}$ cups water

salt and freshly ground pepper

chicken stock, if necessary

$\frac{1}{4}$ cup butter

6 Tbsp flour

$1\frac{1}{4}$ cups light cream

lemon slices and rolled and broiled bacon slices, to garnish

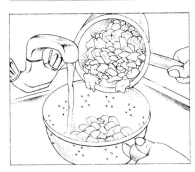

*1* Cover the meat with cold water, bring to a boil and boil for 1 minute. Strain in a colander and rinse under cold running water to remove all scum. Place the meat in a flameproof casserole.

*2* Add the carrots and onions to the casserole with the bouquet garni, wine, water and plenty of salt and pepper. Bring slowly to a boil, cover and simmer gently for about $1\frac{1}{4}$ hours or until the meat is tender.

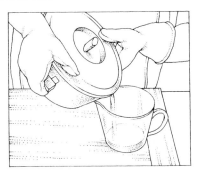

*3* Strain off the cooking liquid, make up to 3 cups with stock if necessary, reserve. Keep the meat and vegetables warm in a covered serving dish.

*4* Melt the butter in a saucepan and stir in the flour, cook gently for 1 minute. Remove from the heat and stir in the strained cooking liquid, season well. Bring to a boil, stirring all the time, and cook gently for 5 minutes.

*5* Take the sauce off the heat and stir in the cream. Warm very gently, without boiling, until the sauce thickens slightly. Adjust the seasoning. Pour the sauce over the meat. Garnish with lemon slices and rolled and broiled bacon.

**Menu Suggestion**

Veal in Cream Sauce is a very rich dinner party dish. Serve with plain boiled rice and a green salad tossed in a vinaigrette dressing.

# STIR-FRIED PORK AND VEGETABLES

| 0.50 | 433 cals |

*Serves 4*

1½ lb pork fillet or tenderloin,
  trimmed of fat

4 Tbsp dry sherry

3 Tbsp soy sauce

2 tsp ground ginger

salt and freshly ground pepper

1 medium cucumber

2 Tbsp vegetable oil

1 bunch of spring onions, trimmed
  and finely chopped

1–2 garlic cloves, skinned and
  crushed (optional)

2 Tbsp cornstarch

1¼ cups chicken stock

6 oz beansprouts

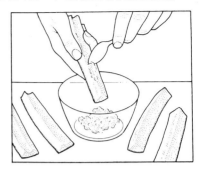

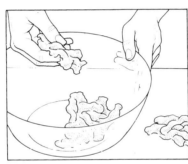

*1* Cut the pork in thin strips and
place in a bowl. Add the
sherry, soy sauce, ginger and salt
and pepper to taste, then stir well
to mix. Set aside.

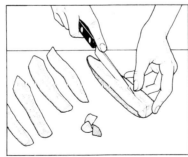

*2* Prepare the cucumber sticks.
Cut the cucumber in half, then
cut into quarters lengthwise,
discarding the rounded ends.
Leave the skin on, to add color.

*3* Using a sharp-edged teaspoon,
scoop out the seeds and
discard. Cut the cucumber
quarters lengthwise again, then
slice across into strips about 1 inch
long.

*4* Heat the oil in a wok or large,
heavy-based frying pan, add
the spring onions and garlic, if
using, and fry gently for about
5 minutes until softened.

*5* Add the pork to the pan,
increase the heat and stir-fry
for 2–3 minutes until lightly
colored, tossing constantly so that
it cooks evenly.

*6* Mix the cornstarch with the
cold chicken stock and set
aside.

*7* Add the cucumber, spring
onions and beansprouts to the
pork, with the cornstarch and
stock. Stir-fry until the juices
thicken and the ingredients are
well combined. Taste and adjust
seasoning, then turn into a
warmed serving dish. Serve
immediately.

**Menu Suggestion**
Both meat and vegetables are
cooked together in this Chinese-
style dish. For a simple meal, serve
on a bed of egg noodles or plain
boiled rice.

# CHICKEN WITH SAFFRON

| 1.15 | $ | 316 cals |

*Serves 6*

| 6 chicken breasts about 6 oz each |
| 2 Tbsp flour |
| salt and freshly ground pepper |
| 3 Tbsp butter |
| 1 cup chicken stock |
| 2 Tbsp dry white wine |
| large pinch of saffron strands |
| 2 egg yolks |
| 4 Tbsp light cream |
| vegetable julienne, to garnish |

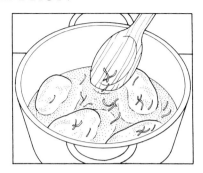

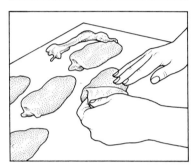

*1* Skin the chicken breasts and remove any fat. Lightly coat the chicken in the flour, seasoned with salt and pepper.

*2* Melt the butter in a medium flameproof casserole. Fry the chicken pieces, half at a time, for 5–10 minutes until golden brown.

*3* Return all the chicken pieces to the pan with any remaining flour and pour in the chicken stock and white wine.

*4* Sprinkle in the saffron, pushing it down under the liquid. Bring up to the boil, cover tightly, and bake in the oven at 350°F for about 50 minutes until cooked.

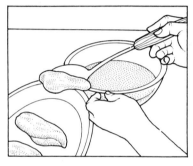

*5* Lift the chicken out of the juices and place in an edged serving dish. Cover and keep warm in a low oven.

*6* Strain the cooking juices into a small saucepan. Mix the egg yolks and cream together and off the heat stir into the cooking juices until evenly mixed.

*7* Cook gently, stirring all the time until the juices thicken slightly. Do not boil. To serve, adjust seasoning, spoon over the chicken and garnish with vegetable julienne. Serve immediately.

# CHICKEN TACOS

| 0.15 | 297 cals |
|------|----------|

| 6 Mexican taco shells |
| 2 Tbsp butter or margarine |
| 1 medium onion, chopped |
| 2 cups diced cooked chicken |
| 4 tomatoes, peeled and chopped |
| salt and freshly ground pepper |
| shredded lettuce |
| $\frac{1}{4}$ lb Cheddar cheese, grated |
| Tabasco sauce |

*1* Put the taco shells in the oven to warm according to the instructions on the package.

*2* Make the filling. Melt the butter in a frying pan and fry the onion until soft but not colored. Stir in the chicken, half the tomatoes and seasoning and heat through.

*3* Spoon 1–2 Tbsp filling into each shell. Add a little lettuce, the remaining tomatoes and the cheese with a few drops of Tabasco sauce; serve the filled tacos immediately.

**Menu Suggestion**
Serve spicy hot tacos as a snack to be eaten with the fingers. Ice-cold beer is the only accompaniment needed, and maybe some fresh fruit such as pineapple to refresh the palate afterwards.

# HALLOWEEN TREATS PARTY

**H**alloween belongs to ghosts and goblins, witches and wizards. When trick or treat is over but before the children exchange their costumes for pajamas, invite them over, along with their parents, for food and drink.

Carve a fat pumpkin, scoop out the pulp (which you can save for baking with butter and spices) ar the seeds (which you can save for roasting) and light up Mr. Jack-O Lantern's frightening scowl with candle. Place him in your front window when trick-or-treaters come to your door. And bring hir to the table later when all the pin sized spooks are finished prowlin the streets and they (and their parents) come to finish up the evening at your Halloween Treat Party (no tricks, please).

**A Party Designed For Childr**
This party is really for children, and the children in us all, so the food should not be so fancy that will be strange and unappealing the little ones. Hot dogs are alwa safe, and if you want to make the more special, buy the little cockt franks and wrap them in small pieces of refrigerated biscuit dough before baking. Place these little biscuit bundles on baking sheets and bake in a preheated 425°F oven for 20 minutes. Have mustard, ketchup and Corn Reli on hand.

Little sandwiches are good, to Keep the fillings simple and everyday enough to please simple palates: sliced cheese, tuna fish, even peanut butter and jelly.

Savory Squares should be different enough to intrigue the

## MENU
◆

hot dogs with mustard, ketchup and
Corn Relish (see page 333)

little sandwiches of cheese, peanut butter
and jelly, and tuna fish

Savory Squares (featured recipe here)

Creamy Ham and Mushroom Puffs
(see page 127)

Hummus (see page 65)

Devil's Food Cake (see page 176)

Doughnuts (see page 361)

Apple Punch (featured recipe here)

— ◆ —

hildren but not so strange that
ey avoid them.

You can supplement the party
enu for the adults on hand with a
uple of more sophisticated
ems, like Creamy Ham and
Mushroom Puffs and Hummus.
The latter served with raw
getables and pita bread.)

And what else but Devil's Food
ake for dessert; everyone will
njoy that. A plate of doughnuts
ay be more suitable for the little
es; they are a lot easier to eat—
d to clean up afterwards—than
ooey cake. Have lots of Apple
unch on hand throughout.

## SAVORY SQUARES

| Makes 10 slices |
| --- |
| $\frac{1}{3}$ cup margarine |
| 2 cups wholewheat flour |
| salt and freshly ground pepper |
| $1\frac{1}{2}$ tsp baking powder |
| 3 Tbsp tomato relish |
| 2 Tbsp water |
| 1 onion |
| 6 oz luncheon meat or ham |
| 1 cup grated Cheddar cheese |
| 1 egg, beaten |
| 2 strips bacon |

In a large bowl, rub margarine
to the flour, salt, and baking
wder. Stir in tomato relish and
e water.

**2** Bind to a smooth manageable
dough. Roll out into a 13 × 9-inch
rectangle. Trim the edges with a
knife.

**3** Finely chop the onion and meat.
Combine with the cheese and stir
in the egg. Season. Cut bacon in
thin strips.

**4** Spread the mixture evenly over
the surface to cover the dough.
Garnish with the bacon strips,
arranged in a pattern.

**5** Bake in the oven at 375°F for
about 30 minutes until the cheese
bubbles up and is golden and the
dough is cooked. Serve hot cut
into squares.

## APPLE PUNCH

| Serves 8–10 |
| --- |
| 2 red-skinned eating apples |
| 2 large oranges |
| 1 cup apple juice |
| 5 cups soda water |
| 5 cups dry ginger ale |

**1** Rub the apples with a clean dry
towel; quarter, core and slice. Slice
the oranges into small pieces,
discarding the seeds.

**2** Place the apple juice and
prepared fruits into a large bowl,

cover and chill for about 2 hours.
Chill the bottles of soda water and
ginger ale.

**3** Just before serving, measure out
the soda water and ginger ale and
combine with the apple juice.
Ladle into glasses for serving.

# HERBY ZUCCHINI FINGERS WITH CREAM

| 0.30* | $ | 147–196 cals |

* plus 1 hour to drain
*Serves 6–8*

2 lb small or medium zucchini
salt and freshly ground pepper
$\frac{1}{4}$ cup butter
1–2 garlic cloves, skinned and crushed
$\frac{2}{3}$ cup vegetable stock or water
4 tsp chopped fresh basil or 2 tsp dried
$\frac{2}{3}$ cup heavy cream

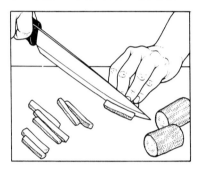

*1* Trim the zucchini, then cut them into neat strips about 2 inches long and $\frac{1}{4}$ inch wide.

*2* Put the zucchini strips in a colander, sprinkling each layer with salt. Cover with a plate, place heavy weights on top and leave to drain for 1 hour.

*3* Rinse the zucchini strips thoroughly under cold running water, then pat dry in a clean dish towel.

*4* Melt half of the butter in a heavy-based saucepan, add the zucchini and garlic and toss over moderate heat for a few minutes.

*5* Pour in the stock, then add half of the basil with salt and pepper to taste. Cover the pan and simmer gently for 5 minutes or until the zucchini are tender but still with some crunch. Transfer the zucchini to a warmed serving dish with a slotted spoon, cover and keep hot.

*6* Increase the heat and boil the liquid to reduce slightly. Add the cream and the remaining butter and basil. Simmer until the sauce is of a coating consistency. Taste and adjust seasoning, then pour over the zucchini. Serve immediately.

---

**HERBY ZUCCHINI FINGERS WITH CREAM**

Zucchini are members of the same cucurbit family as pumpkins, gourds, squashes and cucumbers. They are believed to have been eaten originally by the American Indians, who ground down the seeds of gourds rather than eating the flesh.

It is a good idea to drain zucchini before cooking, as in this recipe. They are a watery vegetable, and can dilute sauces such as this creamy one if they are not drained beforehand. Older zucchini can also be bitter, another reason for extracting the juice before cooking. Always rinse them thoroughly after draining, or the finished dish may be salty.

# POTATO AND CABBAGE BAKE

| 0.35 | 211 cals |

*Serves 6*

1 lb potatoes, peeled and
   quartered
salt and freshly ground pepper
1 lb kale or cabbage, cored and
   shredded
2 small leeks, sliced and washed
$\frac{2}{3}$ cup milk or heavy cream
$\frac{1}{4}$ cup butter or margarine
melted butter, to serve

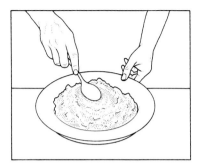

*1* Cook the potatoes in boiling
salted water for 15–20 minutes
until tender. Meanwhile, cook the
kale in a separate saucepan of
boiling salted water for 5–10
minutes until tender. Drain both
potatoes and kale.

*2* Put the leeks and milk or
cream in a saucepan and
simmer gently for 10–15 minutes
until soft.

*3* Put the leeks in a large bowl,
add the potatoes, then the kale,
butter and salt and pepper to taste.
Beat together over gentle heat
until the mixture is thoroughly
blended.

*4* Mound the mixture on a
warmed serving dish and make
a hollow in the top. Pour a little
melted butter into the hollow, to
be mixed in at the last minute.

**Menu Suggestion**
Serve for a mid-week family meal
with chops or sausages.

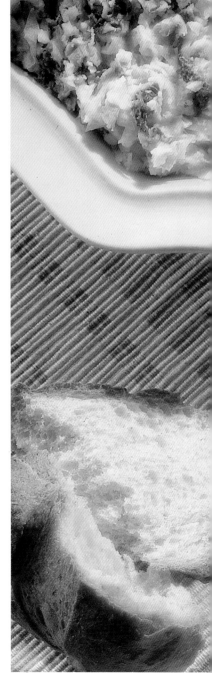

---

### POTATO AND CABBAGE BAKE

In Ireland, this dish, called
Colcannon, is traditionally eaten
on All Hallows' Day, which is
Halloween, October 31. Older
recipes were made with kale,
which was cooked with bacon to
make it really tasty, but
nowadays cabbage is often used
or a mixture of kale and cabbage.
Chopped onion can be
substituted for the leeks, if leeks
are not available. Although
Colcannon is essentially a
homely dish, the addition of
cream and butter makes it quite
rich and special. There is a
superstition surrounding
Colcannon in Ireland, much the
same as the one associated with
plum pudding in Britain. Years
ago, Irish cooks are said to have
hidden gold wedding rings in the
mixture, and it was believed that
the finder would be married
within the year. If the cook hid a
thimble, however, this would
mean the finder would remain
unmarried.

# Bean, Cheese and Avocado Salad

| 2.15* | 613 cals |
|-------|----------|

* plus overnight soaking

*Serves 4*

1 cup dried red kidney beans, soaked in cold water overnight

6 Tbsp olive oil

finely grated rind and juice of 1 lemon

$\frac{1}{4}$ tsp Tabasco sauce

salt and freshly ground pepper

6 oz Edam cheese, rinded and diced

1 small onion, finely chopped

2 celery stalks, trimmed and finely chopped

2 tomatoes, peeled and chopped

1 ripe avocado

celery leaves, to garnish

*1* Drain the kidney beans and rinse under cold running water. Put in a saucepan, cover with fresh cold water and bring to the boil. Boil rapidly for 10 minutes, then simmer for 1–1½ hours until tender.

*2* Drain the beans and put in a bowl. Add the oil, lemon rind and juice, Tabasco and seasoning. Toss well, then leave until cold.

*3* Add the cheese, onion, celery and tomatoes to the beans and toss again to mix the ingredients together. Cover and chill in the refrigerator until serving time.

*4* When ready to serve, peel the avocado, cut in half and remove the pit. Chop the flesh into chunky pieces. Fold the avocado pieces gently into the bean salad and taste and adjust the seasoning. Garnish and serve.

**Menu Suggestion**
Serve with hot wholewheat rolls or baked potatoes.

# TURNIPS IN CURRY CREAM SAUCE

| 0.30 | 270 cals |
|---|---|

*Serves 4*

$1\frac{1}{2}$ lb small turnips

salt

4 Tbsp butter or margarine

1 onion, peeled and finely chopped

4 oz cooking apples

$\frac{1}{2}$ cup light raisins

1 tsp mild curry powder

1 tsp flour

$\frac{2}{3}$ cup hard cider or sparkling wine

$\frac{2}{3}$ cup light cream

2 tsp lemon juice

freshly ground pepper

*1* Peel the turnips, boil in salted water for 10–15 minutes until just tender. Meanwhile, make the sauce. Melt the butter, add the onion, cover and cook gently for 10 minutes until soft and tinged with color. Peel and finely chop the apple and add to the onion, together with the raisins, curry powder and flour. Cook, stirring constantly, for 3–4 minutes.

*2* Pour the cider into the pan, bring to the boil, bubble gently for 2 minutes, stirring. Off the heat stir in the cream, lemon juice and seasoning. Keep warm without boiling.

*3* Drain the turnips in a colander. To serve, place in a heated dish and pour over the curry cream sauce. Serve immediately.

# HOT BEETS WITH HORSERADISH

| 0.20 | $ | 53–80 cals |

*Serves 4–6*

1 lb cooked beets
1 Tbsp sugar
4 Tbsp red wine vinegar
2 Tbsp freshly grated horseradish
salt and freshly ground pepper
1 Tbsp cornstarch

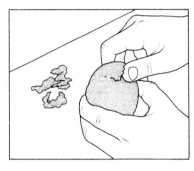

*1* Rub the skins off the beets carefully, using your fingers. Slice the beets neatly into rounds.

*2* Put the beets in a large heavy-based pan, then sprinkle with the sugar. Pour in the wine vinegar and add the horseradish with salt and pepper to taste.

*3* Bring to the boil, without stirring, then lower the heat, cover and simmer gently for 10 minutes.

*4* Transfer the beet slices carefully with a slotted spoon to a warmed serving dish. Mix the cornstarch to a paste with a little cold water, then stir into the cooking liquid in the pan. Boil for 1–2 minutes, stirring vigorously until the liquid thickens. To serve, taste and adjust seasoning, then pour over the beets. Serve immediately.

# THANKSGIVING DINNER

Our Thanksgiving dinner is true to tradition with its roast turkey with stuffing. There are a few surprises, though, that will brighten your dinner table this year with interesting tastes and colors.

Ask just about any American what they have for Thanksgiving and you'll hear, with a few variations, the very same menu. The meal, more than any other of the year, is sacred, etched in tradition. Certainly that's due in a large part to what most people think our ancestors served at those first few Thanksgiving feasts. But it's been preserved by all our families over the years because there is something comforting and reassuring about tradition, at least once a year.

**The First Thanksgiving**

The first Thanksgiving did not look as much like today's feast as we think. Most historians believe that at that first Thanksgiving at Plymouth, Massachusetts in 1621 the 100 or so Indians and their 50-odd Pilgrim hosts and hostesses didn't eat turkey but venison. It most likely was accompanied not by mashed potatoes but johnny cakes, which are cornmeal pancakes. And the pumpkin was boiled, not baked in a pie.

However, wild turkey was a native American fowl, and if it was not served at the very first Thanksgiving, it certainly did show up at later ones. As cooking got more sophisticated, pumpkin, plentiful in the fall and therefore a harvest symbol, became part of more elaborate dishes. Because it

---

## ◆ MENU ◆

*Cream of Carrot with Orange Soup*
*(page 123)*

*Traditional Roast Turkey (page 144)*

*cranberry relish*

*candied sweet potatoes*

*Unpeeled Roast Potatoes (page 289)*

*Herby Zucchini with Cream (page 160)*

*Hot Beets with Horseradish (page 167)*

*Pumpkin Pie with whipped cream*
*(featured recipe here)*

*Almond and Cherry Pie with heavy*
*cream (page 170)*

*apple cider*

*a full-bodied red wine*

---

s a rather bland vegetable, when spices became available in this country it was seasoned and probably first made into soups and puddings and later into breads and pies.

### The Bird

Turkey is not only traditional for Thanksgiving, it's also economical. A big bird feeds a lot of people, and it's as tasty cold as hot.

It is useful to know that a 10-lb turkey yields about $5\frac{1}{2}$ lb meat. As straight roast meat, this will serve 8, plus a further 4 servings as cold cuts, and it should leave you enough meat pickings for a casserole dish as well.

### A Dinner That Matches the Occasion

Our Thanksgiving dinner brings to the table tastes and colors that stretch the imagination and the palate. The deep golden soup that starts the meal is simple to make and light in taste, with a twist of orange to lighten it even more—an appropriate start to a meal that soon picks up speed with a turkey stuffed with a dressing made hearty with oats and spices. A store-bought or family recipe cranberry relish accompanies it.

Instead of mashed potatoes there are roast potatoes. Because you don't peel them first and you certainly won't be mashing them later, they're less bother than mashed potatoes. They're done in the British manner, which means that they come out of the oven crispy and brown and delicious.

Boiled and then sliced sweet potatoes, which are placed in a baking dish and topped with a sprinkling of brown sugar or maple syrup, a little grated lemon or orange rind, a good pinch of ginger and then dots of butter, is the candied sweet potato dish most of us remember well from our own childhoods.

And there are two other vegetable side dishes, one featuring zucchini and the other beets, that bring their distinct flavors and colors to the meal.

### Pies, Pumpkin and Otherwise

Pumpkin pie is a must, and just to be sure no one leaves the table hungry, there's also Almond and Cherry Pie. Have heavy cream flavored with a tsp of vanilla extract ready for spooning on slices of both as they're served.

Fresh apple cider (not the pasteurized kind) is plentiful this time of year and just the thing for everybody. If you want to have wine, choose a full-bodied red one to go nicely with this hearty dinner.

### PUMPKIN PIE

*Serves 6*

| |
| --- |
| 2 eggs, slightly beaten |
| one 16-oz can pumpkin or 2 cups cooked pumpkin |
| $\frac{3}{4}$ cup brown sugar |
| 1 tsp cinnamon |
| $\frac{1}{2}$ tsp ginger |
| $\frac{1}{4}$ tsp ground cloves |
| $\frac{1}{4}$ tsp nutmeg or allspice |
| $1\frac{1}{2}$ cups undiluted evaporated milk or heavy cream |
| one 9-inch uncooked pie shell |
| whole pecans, for garnish |
| heavy cream flavored with 1 tsp vanilla extract, for garnish |

**1** Mix together well the eggs, brown sugar, pumpkin, spices and evaporated milk or cream.

**2** Pour this mixture into the uncooked pie shell.

**3** Bake in the oven at 425°F for 15 minutes. Then reduce the oven temperature to 350°F and continue baking for another 45 minutes, or until a knife inserted into the center of the pie comes out clean.

**4** Garnish the pie by placing whole pecans on the top, around the circumference. Serve with heavy cream.

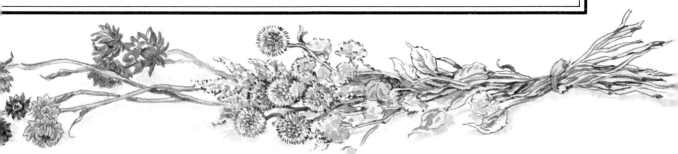

# ALMOND AND CHERRY FLAN

**1.25** | $ | 676 cals

*Serves 6*

1½ cups flour

1 cup butter or margarine

2 eggs, separated

2–3 Tbsp water

12 oz fresh ripe black cherries, pitted

⅓ cup sugar

1 cup ground almonds

1 tsp almond extract

1 Tbsp almond-flavored liqueur (optional)

¼ cup self-rising flour

½ tsp baking powder

2 Tbsp milk

¼ cup sliced almonds

heavy cream, to serve

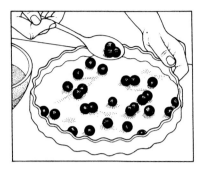

*1* Place the flour in a large mixing bowl. Cut up and rub in 12 Tbsp butter until mixture resembles fine breadcrumbs. Bind to a firm dough with 1 egg yolk mixed with water.

*2* Roll out the pastry, and use to line a 9-inch pie or tart dish. Bake blind in the oven at 400°F for 15–20 minutes until set but not browned; cool slightly.

*3* Scatter the cherries over the pastry. Then cream the remaining butter and sugar well together and beat in ground almonds with the almond extract, liqueur, if using, and the remaining egg yolk. Fold in the self-rising flour and baking powder, sifted together, and lightly stir in the milk.

*4* Whisk the two egg whites until they are stiff, and fold them into the creamed ingredients.

*5* Spread over the cherries in the pan and scatter the flaked almonds on top. Bake in the oven at 350°F for about 30 minutes. Serve warm with cream.

### AMARETTO

Almond-flavored liqueur — *amaretto* — a famous Italian liqueur, which comes from the town of Saronno near Milan in northern Italy, is said to be the best. The Italians are so fond of almonds that they even eat *amaretti* (almond macaroons) with *amaretto* after the coffee at the end of a meal!

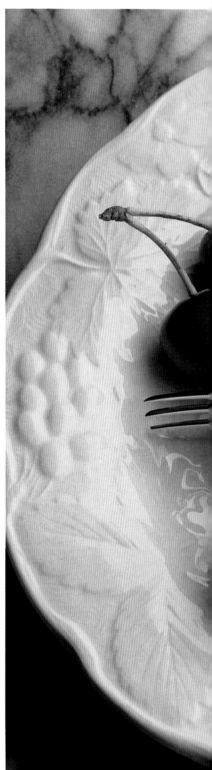

# HOT CHOCOLATE CHEESECAKE

2.45 | $ $ | 377–471 cals

*Serves 8–10*

$\frac{1}{2}$ cup unsalted butter, melted

8 oz chocolate plain crackers, crushed

2 eggs, separated

$\frac{1}{2}$ cup sugar

8 oz cottage cheese

$\frac{1}{2}$ cup ground or very finely chopped hazelnuts

$\frac{2}{3}$ cup heavy cream

$\frac{1}{4}$ cup cocoa powder

2 tsp dark rum

confectioners sugar, to finish

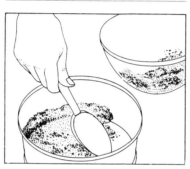

*1* Stir the melted butter into the crushed crackers and mix well, then press into the base and $1\frac{1}{2}$ inches up the sides of an 8-inch loose-bottomed cake pan. Refrigerate for 30 minutes.

*2* Whisk the egg yolks and sugar together until thick enough to leave a trail on the surface when the whisk is lifted.

*3* Whisk in the cheese, nuts, cream, cocoa powder and rum until evenly blended.

*4* Whisk the egg whites until stiff, then fold into the cheese mixture. Pour into the cracker base, then bake in the oven at 325°F for $1\frac{3}{4}$ hours until risen.

*5* Remove carefully from the pan, sift the confectioners sugar over the top to coat lightly and serve immediately while still hot.

# APPLE AND BANANA FRITTERS

| 1.00 | $ | 218–328 cals |

*Serves 4–6*

¾ cup all-purpose flour

pinch of salt

6 Tbsp lukewarm water

4 tsp vegetable oil

2 egg whites

1 large cooking apple

2 bananas

juice of ½ a lemon

vegetable oil, for deep frying

sugar, to serve

*1* Place the flour and salt into a bowl. Make a well in the center. Add the water and oil and beat to form a smooth batter.

*2* Beat the egg whites in a clean dry bowl until they are stiff; then set aside.

*3* Peel, quarter and core the apple. Peel the bananas. Slice the fruit thickly and sprinkle at once with the lemon juice to prevent discoloration.

*4* Fold the beaten egg whites into the batter, then immediately dip in the slices of fruit.

*5* Deep-fry the fritters a few at a time in hot oil until puffed and light golden. Remove with a slotted spoon and pile on to a serving dish lined with paper towels. Serve immediately, sprinkled with sugar.

# CRUNCHY PEARS IN CINNAMON AND HONEY WINE

| 1.00 | 230–344 cals |

*Serves 4–6*

4 Tbsp white wine, vermouth or sherry
4 Tbsp clear honey
1 tsp ground cinnamon
4 Tbsp margarine or butter
1 cup wholewheat breadcrumbs (made from a day-old loaf)
⅓ cup light brown sugar
4 ripe dessert pears

*1* In a bowl, mix together the wine, honey and half of the cinnamon. Set aside.

*2* Melt the margarine in a small pan, add the breadcrumbs, sugar and remaining cinnamon and stir together until evenly mixed. Set aside.

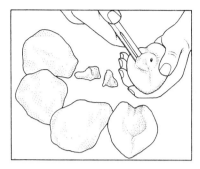

*3* Peel and halve the pears. Remove the cores. Arrange the pear halves, cut side down, in a greased ovenproof dish and pour over the white wine mixture.

*4* Sprinkle the pears evenly with the breadcrumb mixture and bake in the oven at 375°F for 40 minutes. Serve hot.

**Menu Suggestion**
Accompany with yogurt flavored with grated orange rind.

---

**CRUNCHY PEARS IN CINNAMON AND HONEY WINE**

For this recipe you can use Comice dessert pears, but be careful that they are not too ripe—Comice pears very quickly become over-ripe and bruised, and cannot be stored for any length of time. Buy them on the day you intend to cook them and check they are perfect and *just* only ripe before purchase.
Bosc pears are a dual-purpose pear; they are ideal for cooking and eating, so these too can be used for this recipe.

# DEVIL'S FOOD CAKE

| 2.00* | 696 cals |
| --- | --- |

* plus 30 minutes cooling and 1 hour
standing time; freeze after stage 8

*Serves 8*

3 oz semisweet chocolate plus 1 oz
(optional)

$1\frac{3}{4}$ cups light brown sugar

$\frac{3}{4}$ cup milk

$\frac{1}{3}$ cup butter or margarine

2 eggs

$1\frac{1}{4}$ cups all-purpose flour

$\frac{3}{4}$ tsp baking soda

2 cups sugar

8 Tbsp water

2 egg whites

*1* Lightly brush two $7\frac{1}{2}$-inch
layer pans with melted lard.
Base-line with waxed paper and
grease the paper. Leave for 5
minutes to set, then dust with
sugar and flour.

*2* Break 3 oz of the chocolate in
small pieces into a saucepan.
Add $\frac{1}{2}$ cup of the brown sugar
and the milk. Heat very gently,
stirring to dissolve the sugar and
blend the ingredients, then remove
from the heat and leave to cool for
10 minutes.

*3* Put the butter into a bowl and
beat until pale and soft.
Gradually add the remaining
brown sugar and beat until pale
and fluffy.

*4* Lightly whisk the eggs and
gradually beat into the
creamed mixture. Slowly add the
cooled chocolate mixture, beating
until combined.

*5* Sift the flour and baking soda
into the creamed mixture and
gently fold in using a metal
spoon. Turn the mixture into
prepared pans, then tap gently to
level it.

*6* Bake in the oven at 350°F for
about 35 minutes. The cakes
are cooked when they spring back
when pressed lightly with a finger
and have shrunk away a little from
the pans.

*7* Cool in the pans for a couple
of minutes before turning out
onto a wire rack to cool completely. Ease them away from the
pans using a palette knife, taking
care not to break the crust.

*8* Tap the pans on the work surface to loosen the cakes. Gently
pull off the paper and leave to
cool.

*9* Put the sugar for the frosting
in a pan with the water, dissolve over a low heat, then boil
rapidly to 240°F on a sugar thermometer, or until the mixture
reaches the soft ball stage. Check
by plunging a teaspoonful into a
bowl of iced water. It should form
a ball in your fingers.

*10* Meanwhile, whisk the egg
whites in a large bowl until
stiff. Allow the bubbles in the
syrup to settle, then slowly pour
the hot syrup onto the egg whites,
beating constantly. Once all the
sugar syrup is added, continue
beating until the mixture stands in
peaks and just starts to become
matt round the edges. (The icing
sets quickly, so work rapidly.)

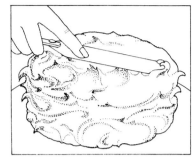

*11* Sandwich the cakes together with a little of the
frosting. Spread the remaining
frosting over the cake with a palette
knife. Pull the icing up into peaks
all over, then leave the cake for
about 30 minutes, to allow the
icing to set slightly.

*12* Break up the chocolate, if
using, and put it in a small
bowl over a pan of hot water. Heat
gently, stirring, until the chocolate
has melted. Dribble the chocolate
over the top of the cake with a
teaspoon to make a swirl pattern.
Leave for 30 minutes before
serving.

# CHEWY CHOCOLATE BROWNIES

| 0.15* | 156 cals |
|-------|----------|

*plus cooling time

*Makes 16*

$\frac{5}{8}$ cup all-purpose flour

$\frac{7}{8}$ cup dark brown sugar

$\frac{1}{4}$ cup cocoa powder

$\frac{1}{4}$ tsp salt

$\frac{1}{2}$ cup butter or margarine

2 eggs, beaten

1 tsp vanilla extract

$\frac{5}{8}$ cup chopped mixed nuts

*1* Put all the ingredients in a bowl and beat thoroughly (preferably with an electric beater) until evenly combined.

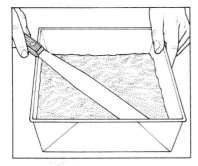

*2* Turn the mixture into a greased 8-inch square cake tin and level the surface with a frosting knife.

*3* Bake in the oven at 350°F for 25 minutes until only just set (the mixture should still wobble slightly in the center). Stand the cake tin on a wire rack and leave until the cake is completely cold. Cut into 16 squares and put in an airtight tin.

**Menu Suggestion**
Moist and munchy Chocolate Brownies are a favorite at any time of day. Try them as a fun dessert for children with scoops of vanilla ice cream and chocolate sauce or chopped nuts.

# W·I·N·T·E·R

*H*oliday time is upon us. Thanksgiving has come and gone, but now there is Christmas and New Year's, and just when winter has dragged on for about as long as we can stand it, there's Valentine's to cheer us up for one brief day.

Many of the dishes that you'll find in this section are fancy foods, some just right for a special family sit-down dinner, others that will beautifully grace a party buffet.

The four menus match the holiday moods. There is a Christmas Eve Open House, with festive dishes that don't demand a great deal of time or skill from you at this very busy time of the year. The menu is designed to accommodate 20, but it's easily expandable.

The Christmas Family Dinner menu will make your Christmas meal very special indeed. And its suggestions for planning and cooking ahead, and soliciting help from the rest of the family, takes the pressure off you, the cook.

The buffet for New Year's Day has lots of fancy finger foods to impress your guests. But there is also a cheese tray that's very easy to put together, so long as you follow our tips for selecting the cheeses and presenting them to their best advantage.

Valentine's Day, the last holiday before spring comes around again, is a quiet supper for two that's designed for what else but—romance.

# GOULASH SOUP WITH CARAWAY DUMPLINGS

2.45 | $ | 515–772 cals

* freeze without dumplings

*Serves 4–6*

1½ lb lean chuck steak

salt and freshly ground pepper

2 Tbsp butter

2 onions, peeled and chopped

1 small green pepper, seeded and chopped

4 tomatoes, peeled and quartered

5-oz can tomato paste

2½ cups rich beef stock

1 Tbsp paprika

1 lb potatoes, peeled

¾ cup self-rising flour

¼ cup shredded suet or lard

1 tsp caraway seeds

chopped fresh parsley, to garnish

⅔ cup sour cream

*1* Remove any excess fat or gristle from the chuck steak and cut the meat into small pieces. Season well.

*2* Melt the butter in a large saucepan, add the onions and green pepper and sauté for 10 minutes until tender.

*3* Add the meat pieces, tomatoes, tomato paste, stock and paprika. Stir well and bring to the boil. Reduce the heat, cover and simmer for 2½ hours, stirring occasionally.

*4* Half an hour before the end of cooking, cut the potatoes into bite-sized pieces, bring to the boil in salted water and simmer until cooked. Drain well and add to the soup while it is simmering.

*5* Make the dumplings. Put the flour, suet, caraway seeds and seasoning in a bowl and add enough cold water to form a firm mixture. Roll into about sixteen small dumplings.

*6* Twenty minutes before end of cooking, drop dumplings into the soup, cover and simmer until the dumplings are cooked.

*7* Garnish with chopped parsley and serve the sour cream separately, for each person to spoon into his or her soup.

**Menu Suggestion**
Serve with fresh French bread and butter and a tossed green salad.

## GOULASH

Goulash soup is simply a more liquid version of goulash, with a similar base of meat and potatoes for easy eating. Both are popular in Austria and Hungary—no one is quite sure in which country the recipe first originated.

Austrian goulash is usually a simple dish made with beef and potatoes, while Hungarian goulash is often made with veal and far more ingredients— usually red and green peppers and mushrooms, sometimes sauerkraut and smoked pork sausage as well. Four ingredients which are common to all goulash recipes are caraway seeds, onions, paprika and tomatoes—the latter giving the dish its characteristic bright red color. Dumplings and sour cream are optional extras.

# SPICED LENTIL AND CARROT SOUP

| 0.35 | $ | 171 cals |

*Serves 4*

$\frac{1}{4}$ cup butter or margarine

7 oz carrots, peeled and grated

1 medium onion, skinned and finely sliced

10 whole green cardamoms

$\frac{1}{3}$ cup lentils

5 cups chicken stock

salt and freshly ground pepper

parsley sprigs, to garnish

*1* Melt the butter in a heavy-based saucepan, add the carrots and onion and cook gently for 4–5 minutes.

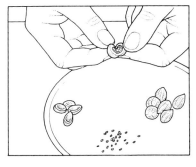

*2* Meanwhile, split each cardamom and remove the black seeds. Crush the seeds with a pestle and mortar, or use the end of a rolling pin on a wooden board.

*3* Add the crushed cardamom seeds to the vegetables with the lentils. Cook, stirring, for a further 1–2 minutes.

*4* Add the chicken stock and bring to a boil. Lower the heat, cover the pan with a lid and simmer gently for about 20 minutes, or until the lentils are just tender. Season to taste with salt and freshly ground pepper. Serve hot, garnished with parsley sprigs.

**Menu Suggestion**
This is a substantial soup for cold, wintry days. Serve for a family supper, with grilled cheese sandwiches.

——————— VARIATION ———————

Use **ham stock** instead of chicken and add a **ham bone** with the stock, removing it before serving. Scrape the ham off the bone and return the meat to the soup.

# SPLIT PEA AND HAM SOUP

| 2.00 | $ | 332 cals |

*Serves 4*

2 pig's trotters (or shanks), split (optional)

1 ham bone

1 cup dried green split peas, soaked overnight in $3\frac{3}{4}$ cups water

8 oz potatoes, peeled and sliced

3 whole leeks, trimmed, sliced and washed

3 celery sticks, sliced, with leaves reserved

salt and freshly ground pepper

2 Tbsp chopped fresh parsley

6 oz cooked ham, diced

*1* Place the pig's trotters (if using) and the ham bone in a large saucepan. Cover with $3\frac{3}{4}$ cups water and bring to a boil. Skim off any scum with a slotted spoon, then lower the heat and simmer for 1 hour.

*2* Add the peas and their soaking water. Continue to cook for about 20 minutes.

*3* Add the sliced potatoes, leeks (including green parts) and celery and continue cooking for another 40 minutes until the peas are soft. Season to taste with salt and freshly ground pepper.

*4* Remove the ham bone and trotters from the pan. Scrape the meat from the bones, discarding fat and gristle. Return the meat to the soup.

*5* Thin the soup, if necessary, with a little extra liquid. Chop most of the reserved celery leaves and add to the soup with the parsley and diced ham. Heat through, then taste and adjust seasoning. Serve hot, garnished with the celery leaves.

**Menu Suggestion**
An old-fashioned soup which is both nutritious and warming. Serve it for a winter lunch or early evening supper, with fresh wholewheat rolls.

> **SPLIT PEA AND HAM SOUP**
> Pig's trotters or shanks are an old-fashioned ingredient which are not always easy to come by. Traditional butchers may sell them, but you may have to order in advance. Although not essential to the soup, they do make a wonderful tasty and gelatinous stock.

# MUSHROOMS IN SOUR CREAM

0.35* | $ | 207 cals

* plus cooling and chilling
*Serves 4*

1 lb button mushrooms
1 bunch of spring onions
4 cardamom pods
2 Tbsp butter
2 Tbsp olive oil
2 garlic cloves, crushed
juice of 1 lemon
⅔ cup sour cream
2 Tbsp chopped fresh coriander
salt and freshly ground pepper
coriander and paprika, to garnish

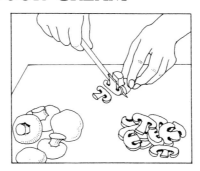

*1* Wipe the mushrooms. Slice them thickly and evenly into "T" shapes. Trim the spring onions and slice finely.

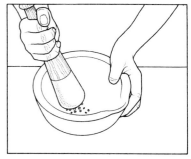

*2* Split open the cardamom pods with your fingernails to release the seeds. Crush the seeds with a mortar and pestle or the end of a rolling pin.

*3* Melt the butter with the oil in a large frying pan. Add the spring onions and garlic and fry gently for 5 minutes until the onions soften slightly.

*4* Add the crushed cardamom seeds to the pan and fry for 1–2 minutes, then increase the heat and add the mushrooms. Cook the mushrooms for a few minutes only until tender, stirring frequently and shaking the pan to ensure even cooking.

*5* Transfer the mushrooms and cooking juices to a bowl. Leave to cool then stir in the lemon juice, sour cream and coriander with salt and pepper to taste. Chill in the refrigerator until serving time. Stir well and garnish with coriander and paprika just before serving.

**Menu Suggestion**
Serve this rich, creamy appetizer with fresh wholewheat or poppyseed rolls. Any light main course such as chicken or fish would be suitable to follow, with a tangy, fresh fruit dessert to finish.

# CRISPY CHICKEN PARCELS

| $0.45$* | $ | 803–857 cals |

* plus 30 minutes chilling; freeze after step 5

*Serves 4*

2 Tbsp butter or margarine

½ cup flour

1 cup milk

2 cups diced cooked chicken

1 Tbsp chopped fresh tarragon or 2 tsp dried tarragon

¾ cup grated Gruyère cheese

good pinch of ground mace

salt and freshly ground pepper

1 Tbsp vegetable oil

8–12 cannelloni tubes

¾ cup dried bread crumbs

¾ cup grated Parmesan cheese

1 egg, beaten

oil, for deep-frying

*1* Melt the fat in a heavy-based saucepan, sprinkle in the flour and cook for 2 minutes, stirring.

*2* Remove from the heat and gradually stir in the milk, then bring to the boil, stirring all the time until very thick. Add the chicken, tarragon, Gruyère, mace and salt and pepper to taste. Stir to mix.

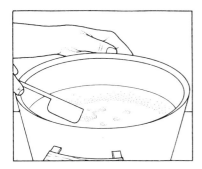

*3* Bring a large pan of salted water to the boil, then swirl in the oil. Drop in the cannelloni. Simmer for 5 minutes, drain.

*4* Using a teaspoon, or a pastry bag fitted with a large plain nozzle, fill each cannelloni tube with the chicken mixture. Pinch the edges to seal.

*5* Mix the bread crumbs and Parmesan in a shallow bowl. Dip the cannelloni tubes first in the beaten egg, then in the bread crumbs mixed with the Parmesan, making sure they are evenly coated. Chill in the refrigerator for 30 minutes.

*6* Heat the oil in a deep-fryer to 350°F. Deep-fry the parcels a few at a time until golden brown and crisp. Drain on absorbent paper towels while frying the remainder. Serve hot.

**Menu Suggestion**

A substantial, hot appetizer which needs no accompaniment other than a dry white wine. Can also be served for a tasty lunchtime snack, with a mixed salad.

187

# CHRISTMAS EVE OPEN HOUSE

**P**lan to get present wrapping and preparations for Christmas Day out of the way early so that you can open your house to friends and neighbors on Christmas Eve with a festive buffet of food, drink and good cheer.

Christmas Eve is a very special time. Most, if not all, of the pre-Christmas preparation rush is over, leaving only the pleasant anticipation of gift-giving and feasting tomorrow. How nice to make the most of the anticipatory mood with a big open house buffet. This is the time to go all out with your decorations, putting wreaths, garlands and other special touches everywhere you know guests will see them, including the bathroom!

**A Buffet Spread For 20**
The buffet spread for this Christmas Eve open house can be as varied as you have the time and energy for it to be. But the way to manage a large spread is to keep to a few dishes that complement each other, that you know are popular and that don't need special attention at the buffet table—just put them out and let guests help themselves. Stick to dishes that can be made in quantity; don't bother with little canapes or other things that must be served hot out of the oven unless you have help during the party.

A baked glazed ham is a very good star attraction, for it looks beautiful and can feed a large crowd. A 12- to 15-lb ham will serve about 20 people. To glaze it lightly spread a Dijon-style mustard all over it and sprinkle

---

### MENU

◆

*baked glazed ham served with Honey Mustard (see page 314)*

*Ratatouille (see page 216)*

*plain baked Brie with French bread slices*

*relish tray, including olives, pickles, celery and carrot sticks*

*Christmas cookies, such as Cherry Garlands (see page 368)*

*Black Bun (featured recipe here)*

*hot cider*

*beer*

*a full-bodied red wine*

———— ◆ ————

about a cup of brown sugar on the top. You can stick the ham with whole cloves if you wish. Pour 2 cups of apple juice in the roasting pan and bake in the oven at 350°F for 1½ hours, basting frequently.

When done, place it on a platter and cut a few slices, to give guests the right idea. Put Honey Mustard and rye bread nearby. Guests can slice off pieces for themselves and make sandwiches. Good accompaniments include some marinated salads that can be made up to a day in advance, like Ratatouille.

A baked wheel of plain Brie is easy and splashy. Take a whole large wheel and place it on an oven-proof platter. A large wheel, usually 5 lb, will serve about 20 people. Don't use a cut wheel because the cheese will ooze and run all over the place as it cooks; the rind of the wheel keeps all under control (until guests start attacking it). Bake in the oven at 350°F for 20–30 minutes. Serve warm with thin slices of French bread.

For dessert, bring out a selection of your family's favorite Christmas cookies, including perhaps a new recipe this year, Cherry Garlands. You might also have a Black Bun, which is a traditional Scottish fruitcake soaked in whisky.

## BLACK BUN

*plus 1–2 hours cooling*
*Serves 12*

| |
|---|
| 3¼ cups flour |
| pinch of salt |
| ¼ cup butter or margarine |
| ¼ cup lard |
| 1 tsp ground cinnamon |
| 1 tsp ground ginger |
| 1 tsp ground allspice |
| 1 tsp cream of tartar |
| 1 tsp baking soda |
| 1 lb seedless raisins |
| 1 lb currants |
| 2 oz chopped mixed peel |
| 1 cup chopped almonds |
| ½ cup dark brown sugar |
| 1 egg, beaten |
| ⅔ cup Scotch whisky |
| 4 Tbsp milk |
| beaten egg, to glaze |

1  Put 1½ cups of the flour and the salt in a bowl. Add the butter and lard and rub in until the mixture resembles breadcrumbs. Add 2–3 Tbsp cold water and stir until mixture begins to stick together. Knead lightly for a few seconds to give a firm, smooth dough.

2  Grease a deep 8-inch round cake tin. Roll out two-thirds of the dough on a lightly floured working surface into a round about 14

inches in diameter. Line the prepared tin with the pastry, making sure it overhangs the sides. Refrigerate while preparing the filling.

3  Sift together the remaining flour, the spices, cream of tartar and baking soda. Mix in the raisins, currants, peel, almonds and sugar.

4  Add the egg, whisky and milk and stir until the mixture is evenly moistened. Pack the filling into the pastry case and fold the top of the pastry over.

5  On a lightly floured surface, roll out the remaining dough to an 8-inch round. Moisten the edges of the pastry case, put the pastry round on top and seal the edges.

6  With a skewer, make four or five holes right down to the bottom of the cake, then prick all over the top with a fork and brush with beaten egg.

7  Bake in the oven at 350°F for 2½–3 hours or until a warmed fine skewer inserted in the center comes out clean. Check near the end of cooking time and cover with several layers of waxed paper if it is overbrowning. Turn out onto a wire rack and leave for 1–2 hours to cool completely.

# FRIED POTATO CAKE

| 0.35 | 566 cals |

*Serves 1*

2 Tbsp butter

2 Tbsp vegetable oil

$\frac{1}{2}$ lb day-old potatoes, peeled

$\frac{1}{2}$ small onion, skinned and finely chopped

salt and freshly ground pepper

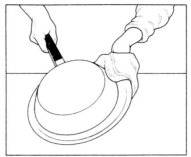

*1* Melt half of the butter with half of the oil in a non-stick frying pan. Grate in the potatoes, then add the onion and salt and pepper to taste. Mix together. Press down well with a spatula.

*2* Cover with a lid and cook over moderate heat for about 12 minutes, or until the potatoes are golden brown underneath.

*3* Turn the potato cake out upside down onto a plate. Melt the remaining butter in the pan with the remaining oil.

*4* Slide the potato cake back into the pan cooked side up and cook for a further 12 minutes or until golden brown underneath. Slide out onto a warmed serving plate and serve immediately.

*5* To serve two: double the quantity of ingredients and follow the recipe above.

**Menu Suggestion**
In Switzerland, these fried potatoes are often eaten as a snack, but they can equally well be served as a vegetable accompaniment to a steak, chop or sausages.

---

**FRIED POTATO CAKE**

These delicious fried potatoes are a simplified version of the famous Swiss dish called *rösti*, which is made with chopped bacon and sometimes Gruyère or Emmental cheese. An alternative method of making this dish, which you might like to try, is to boil the potatoes in their skins for 15 minutes or until they are only just tender, then leave them until completely cold before peeling off the skins with your fingers. Grate the cold potato flesh, then cook as in the recipe above, but reduce the cooking time of the potato cake to about 5 minutes on each side.

Swiss cooks maintain that *rösti* is best made with potatoes that have been cooked the day before.

# CHILI PIZZA FINGERS

| 1.00 | $ | 461 cals |

*Serves 6*

8 oz ground beef

½ tsp chili powder

1 garlic clove, crushed

1 medium onion, chopped

1 small green pepper, cored, seeded and chopped

4 oz mushrooms, wiped and sliced

2 large tomatoes, peeled and chopped

7.51 oz can red kidney beans, drained

¾ cup beef stock

8 oz wholewheat flour

½ cup rolled oats

1 Tbsp baking powder

salt and freshly ground pepper

4 Tbsp margarine or butter

1 egg, beaten

4 Tbsp milk

1 Tbsp tomato paste

6 oz Mozzarella cheese, thinly sliced

basil sprigs, to garnish

*1* First prepare the topping. Place the minced beef, chili powder and garlic in a saucepan and fry for 3–4 minutes, stirring occasionally. Add the onion, green pepper and mushrooms and fry for a further 1–2 minutes. Stir in the tomatoes, red kidney beans and beef stock. Bring to the boil and simmer for about 15 minutes, stirring occasionally until most of the liquid has evaporated.

*2* Meanwhile, combine the flour, oats, baking powder and a pinch of salt in a bowl.

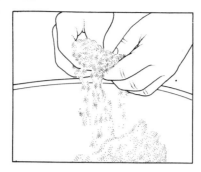

*3* Rub in the margarine until the mixture resembles fine bread-crumbs. Bind to a soft dough with the egg and milk, then turn out on to a floured surface and knead lightly until smooth.

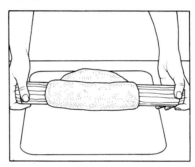

*4* Roll out the dough to a 10 × 7 inch rectangle. Lift on to a baking sheet, then spread carefully with tomato paste. Pile the chili mixture on top and cover with Mozzarella cheese.

*5* Bake in the oven at 400°F for about 30 minutes until golden and bubbling. Cut into fingers for serving, garnished with basil sprigs.

**Menu Suggestion**
Serve as a substantial snack, or an easy supper dish accompanied by a salad of thinly sliced or grated zucchini dressed with a vinaigrette and snipped fresh chives.

# FETA CHEESE PUFFS WITH BASIL

| 0.25 | $ | 274 cals |
|---|---|---|

* freeze after stage 4

*Makes 8*

8 oz Feta cheese, grated

1 cup plain yogurt

2 Tbsp chopped fresh basil or 1 tsp dried

freshly ground pepper

14-oz packet frozen puff pastry, thawed

beaten egg

fresh basil leaves, to garnish

*1* Mix the grated cheese with the yogurt, basil and pepper. (Don't add salt as the cheese adds sufficient.)

*2* Roll out the pastry *thinly* and cut out sixteen 4-inch rounds. Fold and reroll the pastry as necessary.

*3* Place half the rounds on two baking sheets. Spoon the cheese mixture into the center of each one.

*4* Brush the pastry edges with egg. Cover with remaining rounds, knocking up and pressing the pastry edges together to seal. Make a small slit in the top of each pastry puff.

*5* Glaze with beaten egg. Bake in the oven at 425°F for about 15 minutes or until well browned and crisp. Serve warm, garnished with fresh basil leaves.

### FETA CHEESE
Greek Feta cheese can be made from either sheep's or goat's milk. Vacuum packs, which tend to be rather salty, are available at some large supermarkets and good delicatessens, but the best Feta (sold loose in brine) is found in Greek and Middle Eastern stores.

# BLUE CHEESE CROQUETTES

| 1.00* | 416–623 cals |
|---|---|

* plus 2–3 hours chilling, freeze after stage 5

*Serves 4–6*

$\frac{1}{4}$ lb celery

$\frac{1}{4}$ cup plus 2 Tbsp butter or margarine

$\frac{2}{3}$ cup all-purpose flour, plus a little extra for coating

1 cup milk

6 oz Blue Stilton cheese, grated

2 Tbsp snipped fresh chives or 1 Tbsp dried

2 eggs

freshly ground pepper

$\frac{1}{2}$ cup dried white breadcrumbs

vegetable oil, for deep frying

*1* Finely chop the celery; sauté in the butter or margarine for 5–10 minutes until beginning to become brown.

*2* Stir in the flour; cook for 1 minute. Off the heat stir in the milk. Bring to a boil, stirring, then cook for 1 minute—the mixture will be *very* thick.

*3* Remove from the heat and stir in the grated cheese, chives, 1 egg and pepper (the cheese will add sufficient salt).

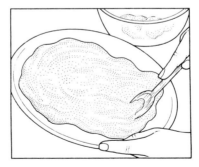

*4* Spread the mixture out in a shallow dish, cover with waxed paper and cool for 30 minutes. Refrigerate for 2–3 hours to firm up.

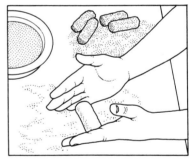

*5* Shape the mixture into 12 croquettes then coat lightly in flour, beaten egg and breadcrumbs.

*6* Deep fry the croquettes at 350°F, a few at a time, for 3–4 minutes until golden brown. Serve hot.

# CHRISTMAS FAMILY DINNER

Let this year's Christmas dinner be a true delight for the *whole* family. Plan a meal that fills the house with delectable aromas all morning long and later graces the table with mouth-watering dishes that were well worth the wait. The secret to creating such a feast without great wear and tear on you, the cook, is to quietly solicit the help of everyone in the house and make pitching in a happy family affair.

Our Christmas dinner takes its main course from the English, who, after all, were celebrating Christmas dinners long before Americans got started. This time it's roast duck, moist on the inside and crispy on the outside and served with variations on traditional side dishes.

Mashed potatoes are subtle enough to allow the spiced stuffing in the duck to take the limelight. And the vegetable casseroles, one of cabbage and apples and another of seasoned carrots, make the most of fresh winter produce.

The appetizer is a light and elegant Fresh Fish Mousse that can be made ahead because it's served cold. Keep the salad simple and green and red for Christmas! Let it be a few favorite green lettuces and a red-leaf like the slightly bitter radicchio and toss it with a flavorful vinaigrette.

The Milk Rolls, shaped into twists or rings and served right from the oven, should be served in a napkin-lined basket so that they stay warm.

Spiced Dried Fruit Compote has a nice Christmasy flavor and aroma. And Viennese Chocolate Fingers are rich and delicious, and a special enough Christmas cookie for the conclusion of this meal.

**Your Christmas Helpers**
Christmas Day should be a merry one for everybody, but too often

## — MENU —
◆

Fresh Fish Mousse *(see page 13)*

Roast Duck with Spice Stuffing
*(featured recipe here)*

mashed potatoes

Red Cabbage and Apple Casserole
*(see page 214)*

Peppered Carrots *(see page 49)*

Shaped Milk Rolls *(see page 386)*

Salad with Vinaigrette *(see page 374)*

Spiced Dried Fruit Compote
*(see page 222)*

Chocolate Viennese Fingers
*(see page 57)*

a full-bodied red wine

— ◆ —

the burden falls on the cook, who looks forward to the holiday with a happy anticipation mixed with not just a little anxiety. You can minimize this if you have in your mind a team of Christmas helpers. They needn't know what you have in store, but if all the family and any visitors do just a little, your day will be easier without spoiling theirs. Then plan ahead, making as much as you can in advance. Most of your last-minute work should be done the day before Christmas, so on Christmas you'll be able to enjoy being with your family.

## ROAST DUCK WITH SPICED STUFFING

*Serves 4*

| |
|---|
| ½ cup Italian risotto rice, boiled and drained |
| 1 cup dried apricots, finely chopped |
| ½ cup pine nuts, roughly chopped |
| ¼ cup seedless raisins |
| 1 onion, peeled and finely chopped |
| ½ tsp ground cinnamon |
| ½ tsp freshly grated nutmeg |
| ½ tsp ground cumin |
| salt and freshly ground pepper |
| 4–4½ lb oven-ready duck |
| 2 Tbsp butter |
| 2 Tbsp light honey |
| watercress sprigs, to garnish |
| canned apricot halves, (optional) |

**1** Make the stuffing. Combine the first eight ingredients together until well mixed, adding salt and pepper to taste.

**2** Wash the inside of the duck and pat dry with paper towels. Put the stuffing inside the neck end of the duck, then truss with string and/or skewers.

**3** Melt the butter and honey together. Stand the duck on a rack in a roasting pan, then prick all over with a fork. Brush all over with the honey and butter and sprinkle liberally with salt and freshly ground pepper.

**4** Roast the duck in the oven at 350°F for 1½–2 hours or until the flesh feels tender when pierced in the thick part of the thigh with a skewer. Serve hot, garnished with watercress sprigs, and warmed apricot halves filled with a little of the stuffing, if you like.

# CHICKEN AND CORN FRITTERS

| 0.30 | 679 cals |

*Serves 4*

3 lb chicken, cut into small
    portions (see page 151)
3 Tbsp flour
salt and freshly ground pepper
1 egg, beaten
1 cup dried bread crumbs
4 Tbsp butter
1–2 Tbsp vegetable oil

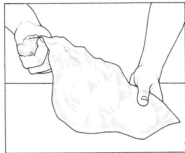

*1* Put the chicken portions in a
large plastic bag with the flour
and salt and pepper to taste. Shake
well to coat the chicken in the
flour.

*2* Dip the chicken first in the
beaten egg and then roll in the
bread crumbs to coat.

*3* Heat the butter and oil together in a large frying pan,
add the coated chicken and fry for
2–3 minutes until lightly
browned on all sides.

*4* Continue frying gently, turning the pieces once, for about
20 minutes, or until tender.
Alternatively, deep-fry the chicken
in hot oil, 325°F, for 5–10
minutes. Serve the chicken hot
and crisp, with fried bananas and
corn fritters (see above right).

*Fried bananas*
Peel and slice 4 bananas lengthways. Fry gently in a little hot
butter or chicken fat for about 3
minutes until lightly browned.

*Corn fritters*
Sift 1 cup flour and a pinch of salt
into a bowl. Add 1 egg and $\frac{1}{2}$ cup
milk and beat until smooth.
Gradually beat in $\frac{1}{4}$ cup more
milk. Fold in an 8-oz can whole-
kernel corn, drained. Fry spoonfuls of the mixture in a little hot

fat for 5 minutes until crisp and
golden, turning once. Drain well
on paper towels.

**Menu Suggestion**
With its own accompaniments of
fried bananas and corn fritters,
this dish needs nothing further to
serve, apart from a crisp green
salad to refresh the palate afterwards. Ice-cold beer is the ideal
drink to offset the richness of this
dish.

# *LAMB KORMA*

| 2.15 | 348 cals |

*Serves 4*

2 onions, skinned and chopped

1-inch piece fresh ginger root,
   peeled

$\frac{1}{3}$ cup blanched almonds

2 garlic cloves, skinned

6 Tbsp water

1 tsp ground cardamom

1 tsp ground cloves

1 tsp ground cinnamon

1 tsp ground cumin

1 tsp ground coriander

$\frac{1}{4}$ tsp cayenne pepper

3 Tbsp vegetable oil or ghee

2 lb boned tender lamb, cubed

$1\frac{1}{4}$ cups yogurt

salt and freshly ground pepper

cucumber and lime slices, to
   garnish

*1* Put the onions, ginger,
almonds and garlic in a
blender or food processor with the
water and blend to a smooth paste.
Add the spices and mix well.

*2* Heat the oil or ghee in a heavy-
based saucepan and fry the
lamb for 5 minutes until browned
on all sides.

*3* Add the paste mixture and fry
for about 10 minutes, stirring,
until the mixture is lightly
browned. Stir in the yogurt
1 Tbsp at a time and season.

*4* Cover with a tight-fitting lid,
reduce the heat and simmer for
$1\frac{1}{4}$–$1\frac{1}{2}$ hours or until the meat is
really tender.

*5* Transfer to a warmed serving
dish and serve garnished with
cucumber and lime slices.

**Menu Suggestion**
Serve with plain boiled or pilau
rice, and perhaps cucumber and
yogurt salad and a spinach and
potato curry.

---

**LAMB KORMA**

Mild in flavor, creamy in texture,
the Indian korma is a very special
dish, which was originally only
served on special occasions such
as feast days and holidays. Our
version is relatively simple
compared with some of the
korma recipes which were
devised for celebrations. These
often contained such luxurious
ingredients as saffron (the most
expensive spice in the world),
cashew nuts and heavy cream. If
you want to make a richer korma
for a dinner party main course,
then add powdered saffron or
infused saffron liquid with the
ground spices in step 1, and stir
in $\frac{1}{2}$ cup chopped unsalted
cashew nuts just before serving.
Substitute heavy cream for the
yogurt and swirl more cream
over the top of the korma before
garnishing.

# TANGY CHOPS

| 0.45 | $ | 526 cals |

*Serves 4*

2 Tbsp vegetable oil

4 lamb loin chops

salt and freshly ground pepper

finely grated rind and juice of
   1 lemon

2 Tbsp chopped fresh parsley or
   2 tsp dried parsley

1 Tbsp chopped fresh mint or 1 tsp
   dried mint

1 tsp sugar

$\frac{2}{3}$ cup beef or chicken stock

*1* Heat the oil in a sauté pan or frying pan, add the chops and fry over brisk heat until browned on both sides. Lower the heat and season the chops with salt and pepper to taste.

*2* Mix the remaining ingredients together. Spoon this mixture over the chops and pour in the stock. Cover the pan tightly and simmer gently for 30 minutes or until the meat is tender. Serve hot on a warmed dish, with the juices poured over.

**Menu Suggestion**
Serve for an informal family meal with broiled or oven-baked tomatoes, potatoes and a seasonal green vegetable.

# GOULASH
## (BEEF STEW WITH PAPRIKA)

| 3.10 | 354 cals |
|------|----------|

*Serves 8*

3 lb stewing veal or braising steak

¼ cup plus 2 Tbsp butter or margarine

1½ lb onions, skinned and thinly sliced

1 lb carrots, peeled and thinly sliced

3–4 Tbsp paprika

2 Tbsp all-purpose flour

3¾ cups chicken stock

4 Tbsp dry white wine

salt and freshly ground pepper

¾ cup sour cream

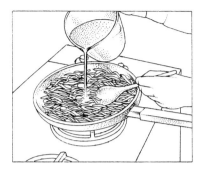

*1* Cut the meat into 1½-inch pieces. Melt the fat in a frying pan and fry the meat, a little at a time, until browned. Drain and place in a shallow ovenproof dish.

*2* Fry the onions and carrots in the fat remaining in the pan for about 5 minutes until lightly browned. Add the paprika and flour and fry for 2 minutes. Gradually stir in the stock, wine and seasoning. Bring to a boil and pour over the meat.

*3* Cover tightly and cook in the oven at 300°F for 2¾ hours until tender. When cooked, pour the sour cream over the goulash and serve.

**Menu Suggestion**
Goulash is traditionally served with dumplings or noodles. An unusual alternative to these accompaniments is a dish of boiled new potatoes and sautéed button mushrooms, tossed together with chopped fresh herbs and some melted butter.

**GOULASH**

This recipe for goulash is simple and straightforward—typical of the kind of goulash to be found in Austria. Hearty and warming, it is the ideal dish to serve in cold weather, especially in the depths of winter when snow is on the ground—the Austrians frequently eat goulash or bowls of goulash soup to keep them warm at lunchtime after a morning's skiing. Goulash is also very popular in Hungary, where it is often made with extra ingredients such as red and green peppers, mushrooms and tomatoes, resulting in a more flamboyant-looking dish with a stronger flavor. When buying paprika to make goulash, look for Hungarian paprika which is labelled *süss* (sweet).

# Sausage and Sweet Pepper Casserole

| 0.45 | 510 cals |

*Serves 4*

**1 lb Italian frying sausages**
  (*salsiccia*)
**3 Tbsp olive oil**
**2 Tbsp butter**
**1 large onion, skinned and**
  **chopped**
**3 peppers (1 green, 1 red, 1 yellow),**
  **cored, seeded and sliced**
**8-oz can tomatoes**
**6 Tbsp chicken or beef stock**
**4 Tbsp dry white wine or water**
**1 tsp dried sage**
**1 tsp dried rosemary**
**salt and freshly ground pepper**
**chopped fresh parsley, to garnish**

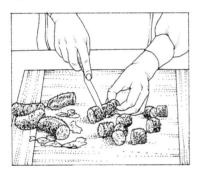

*1* Plunge the sausages into a large pan of boiling water and simmer for 10 minutes. Drain, leave until cool enough to handle, then remove the skin and cut the sausages into bite-sized pieces.

*2* Heat the oil with the butter in a flameproof casserole, add the onion and fry gently for 5 minutes until soft but not colored.

*3* Add the sausage and peppers and fry for a further 5 minutes, stirring constantly.

*4* Mash the tomatoes with their juice in a bowl, then add to the casserole with the stock and wine. Bring slowly to boiling point, then lower the heat, add the herbs and seasoning to taste and simmer uncovered for 10–15 minutes. Taste and adjust seasoning, then garnish with parsley before serving.

**Menu Suggestion**
Serve this colorful Italian dish with risotto rice for an informal supper party. A salad of fennel and cucumber tossed in a minty olive oil and lemon juice dressing may be served afterwards to complete the meal.

---

**ITALIAN SAUSAGES**

Italian frying sausage sold in specialist delicatessens is available as individual sausages, usually called *salamelle*, or in one long piece called *luganega* or *salsiccia a metro*, which is cut and sold by the lb. Both types are suitable for this recipe, but check before buying as some varieties are peppery hot and may not be to your taste. Italians eat a lot of this kind of sausage, which they either fry or broil, or sometimes boil. It is also used frequently in stuffings, and you may like to use it in recipes calling for sausagemeat—with its tasty herbs and spices, it is spicier than most traditional pork or beef sausagemeats.

# TURKEY GROUNDNUT STEW

| 1.15 | 465–698 cals |
| --- | --- |

*Serves 4–6*

2 Tbsp vegetable oil

2 onions, skinned and chopped

1 garlic clove, skinned and crushed

1 large green pepper, cored, seeded and chopped

2 lb boneless turkey, cut into cubes

1 cup shelled peanuts

2½ cups chicken stock

salt and freshly ground pepper

4 Tbsp crunchy peanut butter

2 tsp tomato paste

8 oz tomatoes, skinned and roughly chopped

½–1 tsp cayenne pepper

few drops of Tabasco sauce

chopped green pepper, to garnish

*1* Heat the oil in a flameproof casserole, add the onion, garlic and green pepper and fry gently for 5 minutes until they are soft but not colored.

*2* Add the turkey and fry for a few minutes more, turning constantly until well browned on all sides.

*3* Add the peanuts, stock and salt and pepper to taste and bring slowly to boiling point. Lower the heat, cover and simmer for 45 minutes or until the turkey is tender.

*4* Remove the turkey from the cooking liquid with a slotted spoon and set aside. Leave the cooking liquid to cool for about 5 minutes.

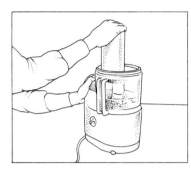

*5* Work the cooking liquid and nuts in an electric blender or food processor, half at a time, until quite smooth. Return to the pan with the remaining ingredients, add the turkey and reheat. Taste and adjust seasoning before serving, adding more cayenne if a hot flavor is desired. Garnish with chopped green pepper.

**Menu Suggestion**
Groundnut stews are traditionally served in the Caribbean with plain boiled rice and a dish of root vegetables such as turnip, rutabaga or parsnip. If desired, hot pepper sauce can also be served as an additional accompaniment.

---

**TURKEY GROUNDNUT STEW**

Groundnut stews originated in West Africa, where groundnuts (or peanuts as we call them) grow in profusion. The cook would buy fresh peanut paste from the market to make groundnut stew, which was a popular Sunday lunch dish—served with ice-cold beer and garnished with fried bananas. Due to the slave trade, groundnut stews spread to the West Indies, becoming an integral part of the local cuisine.

Recipes for groundnut stew vary enormously, some using beef, others chicken, turkey or rabbit. Some recipes use only peanut butter, others like this one, a combination of whole peanuts and peanut butter, which is more authentic. If you like, you can toast or roast the peanuts after shelling, for a darker color.

# SEAFOOD STIR FRY

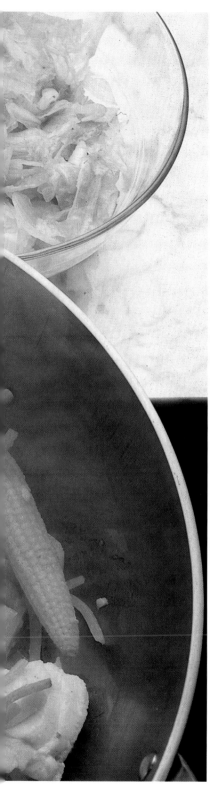

| 0.25 | $ | 288 cals |

*Serves 4*

2 celery sticks, washed and trimmed

1 medium carrot, peeled

12 oz haddock or cod fillet, skinned

12 oz Iceberg or Cos lettuce

about 3 Tbsp peanut oil

1 garlic clove, skinned and crushed

4 oz peeled shrimp

15-oz can whole baby corn, drained

1 tsp anchovy paste

salt and freshly ground pepper

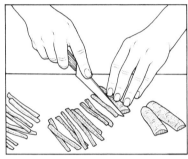

*1* Slice the celery and carrot into thin matchsticks 2 inches long. Cut the fish into 1-inch chunks.

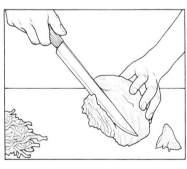

*2* Shred the lettuce finely with a sharp knife, discarding the core and any thick stalks.

*3* Heat 1 Tbsp of the oil in a wok or large frying pan until smoking. Add the lettuce and fry for about 30 seconds until lightly cooked. Transfer to a serving dish with a slotted spoon and keep warm in a low oven.

*4* Heat another 2 Tbsp of oil in the pan until smoking. Add the celery, carrot, fish and garlic and stir-fry over high heat for 2–3 minutes, adding more oil if necessary.

*5* Lower the heat, add the shrimp, baby corn and anchovy paste. Toss well together for 2–3 minutes to heat through and coat all the ingredients in the sauce (the fish will flake apart).

*6* Add seasoning to taste, spoon on top of the lettuce and serve immediately.

**Menu Suggestion**
This stir-fried dish has its own vegetables and therefore needs no further accompaniment other than a dish of plain boiled rice.

---

**SEAFOOD STIR FRY**
It may seem unusual to stir fry lettuce, which is usually only served as a raw salad vegetable, but it is a method often used in Chinese cooking. As long as you use the crisp varieties suggested here—Iceberg or Cos—you will find it gives a fresh, crunchy texture to the dish which contrasts well with the softness of the fish. Avoid using leaf lettuces, which would become limp on cooking, and make sure to time the cooking accurately.

# NEW YEAR'S BUFFET

**D**on't ask your guests to arrive too early. Give them time to sleep in and have a small breakfast at home. And give yourself time to get up leisurely and be relaxed about putting the finishing touches on buffet foods. For while, as host or hostess you want everything to be just right, you don't want to spoil your New Year's Eve worrying about tomorrow.

Since this is an early midday meal it needn't be heavy even though there will be plenty of fancy bite-sized foods. Mushrooms in Sour Cream, Crispy Chicken Parcels, Feta Puffs with Basil and Blue Cheese Croquettes should be enough variety to please everyone.

The time and effort you'll have to give to these canapes can be offset by the cheese tray which can all be bought in advance, so that it's simply a matter of putting it out and slicing the bread when the time comes. So long as you have a good selection of cheeses and the right breads and crackers to go with them, you can't go wrong.

**The Cheese Tray**

A really good cheese tray will contain a generous selection of different cheeses both for visual appeal and in order to cater to a wide range of tastes. Include mild cheeses such as Caerphilly or Gruyere, blue-veined cheeses like Stilton, Roquefort or the milder Gorgonzola, soft and pungent cheese such as Brie or Camembert, a robust Cheddar and perhaps a soft French Boursin. Goat's or sheep's mild cheese can add interest.

To accompany the cheese, serve a selection of crackers, plus some rolls or French bread, since many people prefer these as an accompaniment to strongly

## MENU

◆

*Mushrooms in Sour Cream*
*(see page 186)*

*Crispy Chicken Parcels (see page 187)*

*Feta Puffs with Basil (see page 194)*

*Blue Cheese Croquettes (see page 194)*

*cheese tray*

*Shortbread (featured recipe here)*

*Iced Tutti Fruitti Pudding*
*(see page 110)*

*light red and white wines*

*champagne*

*sparkling water with lemon slices*

—— ◆ ——

flavored cheeses. Butter should also be on the table. Sticks of celery and fresh fruit like grapes can either be arranged on the cheese tray itself or served separately.

Provide at least a few cheese knives so that more than one person can help his or herself at the same time. Have several knives if the tray contains cheeses with very well-defined flavors, like those suggested above.

### The Sweets

Guests are most likely a little tired of Christmas cookies and fruit cake by now. But, after all, it is still the holiday season, so you shouldn't ignore them altogether. A nice compromise is to have variations on the traditional Christmas sweets.

Shortbread is made all year round but it has a particular significance in Scotland at Hogmanay, when it is served to "first footers" who arrive after midnight on New Year's Eve. First footers are thought to bring good luck, so it is the Scottish custom to make them as welcome as possible, and to offer them food and drink—usually shortbread and whisky.

And Iced Tutti Fruitti Pudding is something like a fruitcake but it's actually an ice cream so it's lighter and more refreshing. Sit a

big glass bowl, like a punch bowl, in a tub filled with crushed ice and fill the bowl with scoops of the ice cream.

### Champagne, Wine and Sparkling Water

There should be a nice selection of things to drink: maybe champagne and white and red wines, as well as sparkling water with lemon and lime slices.

### Shortbread

Be sure to use a good-quality butter when making shortbread. The flavor of shortbread relies heavily on the butter in the mixture, and margarine makes a poor substitute.

Traditional Scottish shortbread molds are made with a thistle design in the center. These can be bought at specialist kitchen shops, but they are not essential; an ordinary layer cake tin will do the job just as well.

## SHORTBREAD

| Serves 6–8 |
| --- |
| 1 cup flour |
| 3 Tbsp rice flour |
| $\frac{1}{4}$ cup sugar |
| $\frac{1}{2}$ cup butter |
| sugar, for dredging |

1 Sift the flours into a bowl and add the sugar. Work in the butter with your fingertips—keep it in one piece and gradually work in the dry ingredients. Knead well.

2 Pack into a floured shortbread mold, then turn out onto a baking sheet. Alternatively, pack into a 7-inch layer tin, prick well with a fork and pinch up the edges decoratively with finger and thumb.

3 Bake in the oven at 325°F for about 45 minutes, until firm and pale golden. Mark into 6–8 triangles while still hot. If using a layer tin, cool slightly before turning out onto a wire rack.

4 When cool, dredge with sugar. Serve cut into wedges. Store in an airtight tin. To give as a Christmas present, tie with a piece of red ribbon. Wrap in plastic wrap or foil or pack in a box.

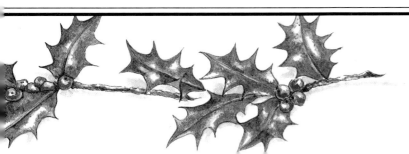

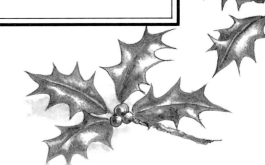

# RED CABBAGE AND APPLE CASSEROLE

| 3.30 | $ | 121–182 cals |

*Serves 4–6*

| 1½ lb red cabbage |
| 2 cooking apples |
| 1 large Spanish onion |
| 1 Tbsp butter or margarine |
| ⅓ cup raisins |
| salt and freshly ground pepper |
| 2 Tbsp granulated sugar |
| 4 Tbsp white wine or wine vinegar |
| 2 Tbsp port (optional) |

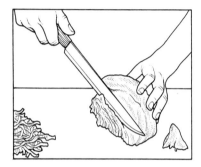

*1* Shred the cabbage finely, discarding the thick central stalk. Peel and core the apples and slice them thinly. Skin the onion and slice thinly.

*2* Brush the inside of a large ovenproof dish with the butter. Put a layer of shredded cabbage in the bottom and cover with a layer of sliced apple and onion. Sprinkle over a few of the raisins and season with salt and pepper to taste.

*3* In a bowl, mix the sugar with the wine, and the port if using. Sprinkle a little of this mixture over the ingredients in the dish.

*4* Continue layering the ingredients in the dish until they are all used up. Cover the dish and bake in the oven at 300°F for 3 hours. Taste and adjust seasoning, then turn into a warmed serving dish. Serve the casserole hot.

## Menu Suggestion

This vegetable casserole has a tangy fruit flavor, which makes it the ideal accompaniment for rich meats. It is especially good with roast pork, duck, pheasant and partridge, and would also go well with the festive turkey at Christmastime.

### RED CABBAGE AND APPLE CASSEROLE

Casseroles of cabbage like this one are popular in northern France, particularly in Ardennes, which borders on Belgium. Both white and red cabbage are used, but with white cabbage dry white wine is usually preferred to the red used here. A spoonful or two of redcurrant jelly is sometimes added to red cabbage casseroles. Substitute this for the port if desired, plus a few crushed juniper berries, which are a favorite flavoring ingredient in northern Europe.

This quantity of cabbage makes enough for 4–6 good helpings; reheat any leftover casserole for another supper as it will have an excellent flavor. If there is any left over, refrigerate it in a covered bowl overnight, then the next day, toss it in a pan with a little butter until hot.

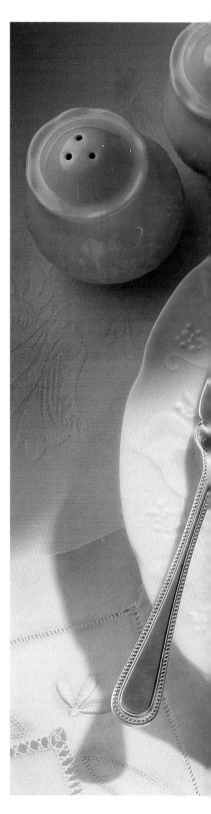

# RATATOUILLE

2.05* | $ | 252 cals

* includes 30 minutes standing time

*Serves 6*

1 lb eggplant

salt

1 lb zucchini

3 red or green peppers

8 Tbsp olive oil

1 lb onions, chopped

1 garlic clove, crushed

1 lb tomatoes, peeled, seeded and chopped, or one 14-oz can tomatoes, drained

2 Tbsp tomato paste

bouquet garni

freshly ground pepper

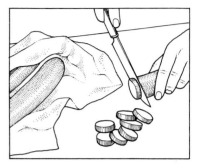

*1* Cut the eggplant into thin slices. Sprinkle liberally with salt and set aside to drain in a sieve or colander for 30 minutes. Rinse under cold running water and pat dry with absorbent paper.

*2* Meanwhile, wash the zucchini and pat dry with absorbent paper. Top and tail them and then cut into thin slices.

*3* Wash the peppers; pat dry with absorbent paper. Slice off the stems and remove the seeds. Cut into thin rings.

*4* Heat the oil in a large saucepan. Add the onions and garlic and cook gently for about 10 minutes until soft and golden.

*5* Add the tomatoes and paste and cook for a few more minutes, then add the eggplant, zucchini, peppers, bouquet garni and salt and pepper. Cover and simmer gently for 1 hour. The vegetables should be soft and well mixed but retain their shape and most of the cooking liquid should have evaporated.

*6* To reduce the liquid, remove the lid and cook gently for another 20 minutes. Check the seasoning and serve hot or cold.

# STUFFED ZUCCHINI WITH WALNUTS AND SAGE

| 1.20 | $ | 422 cals |

*Serves 4*

4 zucchini, total weight about 1½ lb

1 onion, peeled and chopped

7 Tbsp butter or margarine

½ cup walnut pieces, chopped

½ cup fresh white breadcrumbs

2 tsp chopped fresh sage

1 Tbsp tomato paste

1 egg, beaten

salt and freshly ground pepper

2 Tbsp flour

1¼ cups chicken stock

2 Tbsp chopped parsley

walnut halves and fresh sage sprigs, to garnish

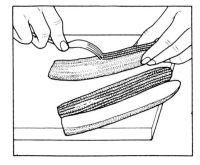

*1* Wipe the zucchini. Using a fork, score down skin at ½-inch intervals, then halve each one lengthwise.

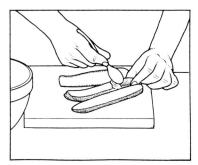

*2* Hollow out the centers of the zucchini using a teaspoon. Blanch in boiling water for 4 minutes, drain, then hold under cold tap. Cool for 15–20 minutes.

*3* Make the stuffing. Fry the onion in 2 Tbsp butter for 5–10 minutes until golden. Remove from heat and stir in half the walnuts, breadcrumbs, half the sage, the tomato paste, beaten egg and plenty of seasoning. Sandwich the zucchini with the stuffing.

*4* Place in a buttered ovenproof dish and dot with a little more butter. Cover and bake in the oven at 375°F for about 30 minutes.

*5* Meanwhile, make the sauce. Melt 4 Tbsp butter in a pan, stir in the flour and cook gently for 1 minute, stirring.

*6* Remove from the heat and gradually stir in the stock. Bring to the boil and continue to cook, stirring until the sauce thickens. Stir in the parsley, seasoning and remaining sage and walnuts. Remove from heat and cover the sauce.

*7* To serve, reheat the sauce. Pour some over the zucchini and serve the rest separately. Garnish with walnut halves and sage sprigs.

217

# GREEK-STYLE NEW POTATOES

| 0.45 | $ | 280 cals |

*Serves 4*

2 lb small new potatoes
1 cup vegetable oil
½ cup white or red wine (see box)
4 Tbsp chopped fresh coriander,
   mint or parsley
salt and freshly ground pepper

*1* Scrub the potatoes clean, leaving them whole. Pat the potatoes thoroughly dry with a clean towel.

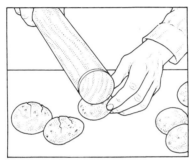

*2* With a meat mallet, hit each potato once or twice so that the flesh breaks slightly. Heat the oil in a heavy-based deep frying pan, skillet or saucepan until a stale bread cube turns golden in 2–3 seconds.

*3* Add the potatoes to the hot oil and fry over moderate heat, turning them frequently, until golden brown on all sides.

*4* Pour off the oil, then pour the wine over the potatoes. Add half of the chopped coriander and a liberal sprinkling of salt and pepper. Shake the pan to combine the ingredients, then cover and simmer for about 15 minutes, until the potatoes are tender.

*5* Turn the potatoes into a warmed serving dish and sprinkle with the remaining coriander. Serve immediately.

**Menu Suggestion**
These tasty potatoes are good with plain roast or broiled lamb; they are also excellent with barbecued meat, especially lamb kabobs.

---

**GREEK-STYLE NEW POTATOES**

For an authentic flavor to these potatoes, cook them in Greek retsina wine. Most retsina is white or red, depending on which is easier to obtain. Retsina, or resinated wine, is something of an acquired taste. It has a strong bouquet and flavor of turpentine, which was discovered almost by mistake.

Originally, some hundreds of years ago, the wine jars or amphorae were sealed with a mixture of resin and plaster, and the flavor of the seal naturally made its way into the wine. The Greeks became so fond of the taste that they began to add pine resin to the must during fermentation, which resulted in a heady wine with a distinctive flavor.

# VALENTINE'S DAY SUPPER

Have you guessed already that this will be a romantic dinner for two? Fill the room with candles everywhere, place a few small red roses in a crystal vase on the table. Put on a long-playing tape of some sentimental music you love. Hide a handmade Valentine under your love's plate. Then sit down to a light, sensuous supper for two.

Make Valentine's Day an intimate celebration. A romantic supper should stimulate the senses and satisfy them, but not so much that you and your companion feel full and heavy after the meal. Choose heavenly foods but prepare them in a simple way so that you can enjoy each other's company, not spend half the evening in the kitchen.

**Start Off Subtlely**
Start with a wonderful combination that marries two different tastes, textures and colors—wedges of sweet, light green honeydew melon wrapped slices of pink prosciutto ham.
    When you go to buy the melon choose one that you like and pick up and smell it. You'll know it's ripe if it has a distinct fruity perfume to it. To prepare it, cut the melon in half and scoop out the seeds. Then slice it into thin wedges and cut the skin away from each. Place it on a salad plate and drape a paper-thin slice of prosciutto over each wedge and serve with a knife and a fork. Alternatively, you can thinly slice the melon and arrange it as a salad interleaved with the ham slices.

**Seafood Stir Fry**
Follow the appetizer with a main course of Seafood Stir Fry. This

---

### MENU
◆

melon with prosciutto
Seafood Stir Fry (see page 211)
plain boiled rice
Piquant Palmiers (see page 386)
Coeurs à la Crème with fresh berries or
Strawberry Sauce, and light cream
(featured recipe here)
a crisp white wine for dinner
a sweet white sparkling wine for dessert
after-dinner chocolates

——— ◆ ———

...ish is lovely to look at: crisp vegetables and tender pieces of fish and shellfish glistening in a light coating of oil and spices.

Stir Fry is always best if it's served immediately, before the vegetables have had a moment to lose any of their crunch. Since everything cooks very quickly, you can step into the kitchen after the first course and then come out again, with finished Stir Fry in hand, in a matter of minutes. The secret is to have everything ready to cook beforehand. Clean and chop the vegetables, prepare the fish and shrimp, crush the garlic, and measure out the oil and spices.

Since this dish contains vegetables and fish, and even lettuce, it needs no side dish other than plain rice and perhaps some light rolls, like elegant Piquant Palmiers, to complete it. Have the cooked rice and the baked rolls warm in a very low oven.

**A Sweetheart of a Dessert**
Coeurs à la Crème, that heavenly rich cheese concoction, is the perfect Valentine dessert. Unmold the hearts onto dessert plates ahead of time and keep them cool in the refrigerator. Just before serving, smother them with fresh strawberries or raspberries, or Strawberry Sauce, and some light cream.

**Wines and Chocolate**
Start with a light white wine for the first and second courses. After the Coeurs à la Crème enjoy a sparkling wine, like Asti Spumante; it's wonderfully fruity and should be served very cold. Then linger over chocolate mints.

## COEURS À LA CRÈME

*plus overnight draining*
*Serves 4–6*

| |
|---|
| 8 oz cottage cheese |
| $\frac{1}{4}$ cup sugar |
| $1\frac{1}{4}$ cups heavy cream |
| 1 tsp lemon juice |
| 2 egg whites, stiffly beaten |
| $\frac{2}{3}$ cup light cream, and fresh raspberries or strawberries, to serve |

**1** Press the cottage cheese through a nylon sieve into a bowl. Add sugar and mix well.

**2** Whip the heavy cream until stiff, then add the lemon juice. Mix into the cheese and sugar mixture.

**3** Line 4 or 6 small heart-shaped molds with muslin (this is unnecessary if serving in the molds). Fold stiffly beaten egg whites into cheese mixture. Spoon mixture into molds. Drain overnight in refrigerator. Serve with cream and fruit.

# SPICED DRIED FRUIT COMPOTE

| 0.50* | $ | 218 cals |

\* plus 1–2 hours cooling and at least
2 hours chilling

*Serves 4*

1 Tbsp jasmine tea
½ tsp ground cinnamon
¼ tsp ground cloves
1¼ cups boiling water
1 cup dried apricots, soaked over-
    night, drained
1 cup dried prunes, soaked over-
    night, drained and pitted
1 cup dried apple rings
⅔ cup dry white wine
⅓ cup sugar
toasted sliced almonds, to
    decorate

*1* Put tea, cinnamon and cloves
in a bowl; pour in boiling
water. Leave for 20 minutes.

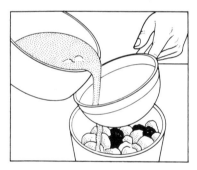

*2* Put dried fruit in a saucepan,
then strain in tea and spice
liquid. Add wine and sugar; heat
gently until sugar has dissolved.

*3* Simmer for 20 minutes until
tender, then cover and leave
for 1–2 hours until cold.

*4* Turn the compote into a
serving bowl and chill for at
least 2 hours. Sprinkle with
almonds just before serving.

# COFFEE-NUT ICE CREAM

| 0.40* | $ $ | 669 cals |

\* plus at least 6 hours freezing and 30 minutes softening

*Serves 4*

| 1 cup shelled hazelnuts |
| 2 Tbsp plus 4 tsp coffee-flavored liqueur |
| 1 Tbsp instant coffee powder |
| 2⅔ cups whipping cream |
| 1 cup confectioners sugar, sifted |

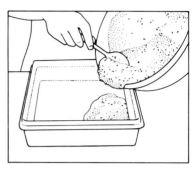

*1* Toast the hazelnuts under the broiler for a few minutes, shaking the pan constantly so that the nuts brown evenly.

*2* Tip the nuts into a clean tea-towel and rub to remove the skins. Chop finely.

*3* Mix 2 Tbsp coffee liqueur and coffee powder together in a bowl. Stir in the chopped nuts, reserving a few for decoration.

*4* In a separate bowl, whip the cream and confectioners sugar together until thick. Fold in the nut mixture, then turn into a shallow freezerproof container. Freeze for 2 hours until ice crystals form around the edge of the ice cream.

*5* Turn the ice cream into a bowl and beat thoroughly for a few minutes to break up the ice crystals. Return to the freezer container, cover and freeze for at least 4 hours, preferably overnight (to allow enough time for the flavors to develop).

*6* To serve, transfer the ice cream to the refrigerator for 30 minutes to soften slightly, then scoop into individual glasses. Spoon 1 tsp coffee liqueur over each serving and sprinkle with the remaining nuts. Serve immediately.

## ICE CREAM MAKERS

It is always satisfying to make your own ice cream, but sometimes the texture is disappointing because large ice crystals have formed in the mixture due to insufficient beating. Electric ice cream makers help enormously with this problem: they are not very expensive and are well worth buying if you like to make ice cream for occasions such as dinner parties when everything needs to be as near perfect as possible. The mixture is placed in the machine, which is then put into the freezer and switched on (the cable is flat so that the freezer door can close safely on it). Paddles churn the mixture continuously until the mixture is thick, creamy and velvety smooth—a consistency that is almost impossible to obtain when beating by hand.

225

# CHOCOLATE COFFEE ICEBOX CAKE

| 1.00* | $ $ | 752–1129 cals |

*plus 3–4 hours chilling; freeze after stage 7

*Serves 4–6*

**2 Tbsp instant coffee granules**
**1 cup boiling water**
**3 Tbsp brandy**
**4 oz semisweet chocolate**
**½ cup unsalted butter, softened**
**½ cup confectioners sugar**
**2 egg yolks**
**1⅓ cups whipping cream**
**½ cup chopped almonds, toasted**
**about 30 ladyfingers**
**candy coffee beans, to decorate**

*1* Grease a 2-quart loaf pan and base-line with waxed paper. Grease the paper.

*2* Make up the coffee granules with the boiling water and stir in the brandy. Set aside to cool for 15 minutes.

*3* Break the chocolate into a small heatproof bowl with 1 Tbsp water and place over simmering water. Stir until the chocolate is melted, then remove from the heat and allow to cool for about 5 minutes.

*4* Sift the confectioners sugar into a bowl. Add the butter and beat them together until pale and fluffy. Add the egg yolks, beating well.

*5* Lightly whip the cream and refrigerate half of it. Stir the remaining cream, the cooled chocolate and the nuts into the butter and egg yolk mixture.

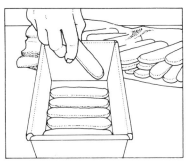

*6* Line the bottom of the prepared loaf pan with ladyfingers, cutting to fit if necessary. Spoon over one third of the coffee and brandy mixture.

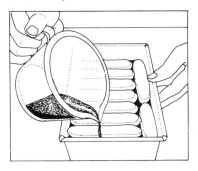

*7* Continue layering the chocolate mixture and ladyfingers into the pan, soaking each layer with coffee and ending with soaked sponge fingers. Weight down lightly and refrigerate for 3–4 hours until set.

*8* Turn out, remove the paper and decorate with the reserved whipped cream and the coffee beans.

227

# PEANUT CRUNCHIES

| 1.00* | 105 cals |
|---|---|

* plus 30 minutes cooling

*Makes about 24*

½ cup butter or margarine

¾ cup soft light brown sugar

3 Tbsp peanut butter

1½ cups all-purpose flour

½ tsp baking soda

½ tsp cream of tartar

2 Tbsp water

beaten egg, to glaze

½ cup salted peanuts

*1* Grease a baking sheet. Put the butter into a bowl and beat until creamy. Add the sugar and peanut butter and beat again until pale and fluffy.

*2* Sift in flour, baking soda and cream of tartar. Using a fork, work dry ingredients in with water to form a soft mixture. Cover; chill for 20 minutes.

*3* Turn out on to a lightly floured surface, knead into a ball and roll out fairly thinly. Cut out about 24 cookies using a 2-inch cutter. Re-knead trimmings as necessary and roll out again.

*4* Place on the prepared baking sheet. Brush with beaten egg and press a few peanuts into the center of each to decorate. Bake in the oven at 375°F for 20 minutes until crisp and golden. Turn out onto a wire rack to cool for 30 minutes.

# WHOLEWHEAT BROWN SUGAR COOKIES

| 1.00* | $ ✳ | 98 cals |
|---|---|---|

* plus 30 minutes cooling

*Makes about 20*

1¼ cups wholewheat flour

¼ tsp baking soda

¼ tsp salt

⅓ cup light brown sugar

⅓ cup butter or margarine, cut into pieces

¾ cup currants

⅓ cup oatflakes

1 egg, beaten

about 1 Tbsp water

*1* Grease two baking sheets. Add the flour, baking soda, salt and sugar into a bowl. Rub in the fat until the mixture resembles fine bread crumbs.

*2* Stir in the currants and oatflakes, then stir in the beaten egg and just enough water to bind the mixture together. Knead in the bowl until smooth. Cover and refrigerate for 20 minutes.

*3* On a lightly floured surface, roll the dough out to about ¼-inch thickness. Cut into rounds with a 2½-inch fluted cutter and remove centers with a 1-inch cutter.

*4* Carefully transfer the rings to the prepared baking sheets. Re-roll trimmings as necessary. Refrigerate for at least 20 minutes.

*5* Bake in the oven at 375°F for about 15 minutes until firm. Transfer to a wire rack to cool for 30 minutes.

*Left to right:*
*Honey Jumbles, Peanut Crunchies,*
*Wholewheat Brown Sugar Cookies*

# HONEY JUMBLES

$\boxed{1.00*}$ $\boxed{\$}$ $\boxed{86\text{ cals}}$

* plus 1½ hours chilling and 30 minutes cooling

*Makes 32*

⅔ **cup soft margarine**

¾ **cup sugar**

**few drops of vanilla extract**

**finely grated rind of 1 lemon**

**1 egg, beaten**

1½ **cups all-purpose flour**

**clear honey, to glaze**

**light brown sugar, to sprinkle**

*1* Put the margarine and sugar into a bowl and beat until pale and fluffy. Beat in the vanilla extract, lemon rind and egg.

*2* Stir in the flour, mix to a firm paste. Knead lightly, cover and chill for 30 minutes.

*3* Roll the dough into a sausage shape—2 inches in diameter, 8 inches long. Wrap in waxed paper. Chill for 30 minutes.

*4* Lightly grease two baking sheets. Cut the chilled dough into ¼-inch rounds. Roll into pencil-thin strips 4 inches long. Twist into "S" shapes and place on the prepared baking sheets. Refrigerate for 30 minutes.

*5* Bake in the oven at 375°F for 12–15 minutes until pale golden.

*6* Remove from the oven and while still warm, brush well with honey, sprinkle with light brown sugar and broil for 1–2 minutes until caramelized.

*7* Transfer to a wire rack to cool for 30 minutes. Wrap and store in an airtight tin for up to 3 weeks.

# LEMON GRANOLA CHEESECAKE

| 0.45* | $ | 317 cals |
|---|---|---|

\* plus at least 4 hours chilling;
freeze without decoration
*Serves 6*

1½ cups granola

6 Tbsp margarine or butter,
   melted

3 lemons

1 envelope unflavored gelatine

8 oz diet cream cheese

⅔ cup plain yogurt

4 Tbsp clear honey

2 egg whites

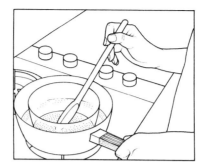

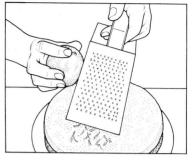

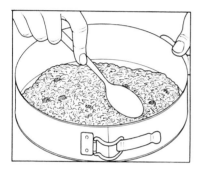

*1* Mix the granola and melted margarine together. With the back of a metal spoon, press the mixture over the base of a greased 8-inch springform cake tin. Chill in the refrigerator to set while making the filling.

*2* Grate the rind of 2 of the lemons on the finest side of a conical or box grater. Set aside. Squeeze the juice from the 2 lemons and make up to ⅔ cup with water. Pour into a heatproof bowl.

*3* Sprinkle the gelatine over the lemon juice and leave to stand for 5 minutes until spongy. Stand the bowl in a pan of hot water and heat gently, stirring occasionally, until dissolved. Remove the bowl from the water and set aside to cool slightly.

*4* Whisk the cheese, yogurt and honey together in a separate bowl. Stir in the grated lemon rind and cooled gelatine until evenly incorporated.

*5* Whisk the egg whites until standing in stiff peaks. Fold into the cheesecake mixture until evenly incorporated.

*6* Spoon the mixture into the springform tin and level the surface. Chill in the refrigerator for at least 4 hours until set.

*7* Coarsely grate the rind from the remaining lemon over the center of the cheesecake, to decorate. Alternatively, slice the lemon thinly and arrange on top of the cheesecake. Serve chilled.

*8* To serve. Remove the cheesecake from the tin and place on a serving plate.

**Menu Suggestion**
A luscious dessert for a special occasion, Lemon Granola Cheesecake is made with more healthful ingredients than other cheesecakes.

---

**LEMON GRANOLA CHEESECAKE**

If you are buying granola specially to make the base for this cheesecake, select a sugar-free variety, or at least one that is low in sugar. Health food shops sell granola loose by the lb, and most stock a sugar-free one. Recipes for granola vary considerably from one brand to another—most health food shops mix their own, but the majority of granola mixtures contain rolled oats, barley or wholewheat flakes and some dried fruit such as raisins. You can of course make up your own granola to suit yourself, or use the recipe on page 10. The addition of chopped hazelnuts gives extra nutritional value, and would be especially good in the base of this cheesecake. As an alternative base, you could use crushed crackers instead. Choose a wholewheat-type, which are not too sweet—ginger biscuits would go well with the flavor of lemon. Put 6 oz biscuits in a bowl and crush them with the end of a rolling pin. Use these crumbs exactly as for the granola in the recipe.

# BASIC INFORMATION

# The Well-Equipped Kitchen

Busy cooks deserve good tools to work with, and pleasant surroundings in which to work. Often having to conjure up meals in minutes, today's cook can turn to many gadgets and appliances which will make life in the kitchen a lot easier. There is no magic about cooking. There is a simple explanation for everything that happens when a food is cooked. The section on cooking techniques will help you understand why you should cook foods in a certain way in order to prepare them with speed and ease.

## KITCHENCRAFT AND COOKING TECHNIQUES

A good cook, like a good craftsman, needs good tools. This does not mean necessarily buying the most expensive equipment and the latest gadgets. It means working out which utensils will be most useful to your style of cooking and eating and making the most of them to save you both time and effort.

The most sophisticated kitchen equipment is of little use if you do not have a well planned kitchen. Kitchens need to have method in the way in which they are laid out; they should save you time and effort in your daily domestic routine; and they should be pleasing places in which to work.

### Ingredients for an easy-to-work-in kitchen

Here are some guidelines for use when planning your kitchen. They are aimed at making your time in the kitchen as pleasant and as efficiently spent as possible.

- Make your kitchen physically comfortable, as well as practical to work in.
- Plan activity centers in your kitchen so that they are well positioned in relation to one another.
- These activity centers need, ideally, to be arranged in the logical order for preparing a meal i.e., storage space, preparation area/work surface, and serving/eating area.
- Wherever possible avoid narrow gaps between work surfaces and appliances.
- Storage closets and cabinets should allow for the storage of all types of food: dry cabinets for canned and packaged goods; ventilated racks for vegetables and firm fruits. You will also need a refrigerator and a freezer.
- For the work surface choose a durable material that will withstand fairly hard wear. There should be a good chopping surface, either separate or inset into the work top—wood or some other non-slip surface. Marble and slate are also good as they can serve the dual purpose of chopping surface and a perfect pastry-making surface.
- If possible, keep all large pieces of equipment on the work surface so that they are at hand when you need them. Keep all small preparation equipment and gadgets close to the work surface.
- Storage of saucepans, baking tins, etc., depends very much on how your cooking facilities are arranged. If you have a built-in range, with a stovetop set into the work surface, then it is advisable to have a cabinet close to the stovetop; most wall-mounted ovens are set into a housing unit, with drawer space underneath for storing pans and tins.

  With a free-standing range, keep all cooking pots and pans, colanders and strainers as close as possible in adjacent cabinets, or hang them on the wall or suspend them from hooks on the ceiling.
- Serving and eating areas should, ideally, be close to one another.
- You will also need good lighting, effective ventilation, and a comfortable floor. You need a good source of light directed on all principal work areas. An exhaust fan or range hood is essential, both to remove excess cooking smells and steam, and to keep the kitchen as cool as possible. The kitchen floor should obviously look nice, but it should also be comfortable to stand on and easy to keep clean. Choose a non-slip surface which is easy on the feet.

# COOKING EQUIPMENT

Choosing the right piece of equipment for a particular job will, in the end, save you time. It pays to invest in good quality equipment as it lasts longer and does the job consistently better than inferior equipment. Here is a guide to the types of equipment you will need to produce delicious food efficiently.

## SAUCEPANS

Good pans are usually expensive, but they last; cheap saucepans do not last and often give off toxic metal substances into the food, which is not desirable.

The best pans to use are those made of metals that conduct heat well: copper, cast iron, or good-quality enamelled steel or stainless steel are good choices. Saucepans with non-stick finish are excellent for boiling milk and making sauces, but they are not such a good choice for some of the "tougher" cooking jobs. Long term they are a bad buy, for the non-stick coating starts to wear off. The heavier the pan, the safer it is to use; solid based pans are also less prone to sticking. Handles are another important aspect to be considered when buying pans. If they are riveted they are much more secure than handles which have been screwed on.

Four saucepans of varying sizes, and one good-sized frying pan is the minimum that you can probably get away with. In addition, most kitchens can make good use of one very large pot, with a handle fixed on either side; it is useful for cooking whole chickens and large pieces of ham and can double as a canning kettle.

## FRYING PANS

Deep frying pans are better than shallow ones; they will hold more food and there is less likelihood of liquids spitting and bubbling over. A lid is essential.

Omelette and pancake pans are by no means musts, but they do make the cooking of both these foods a great deal easier. The sides

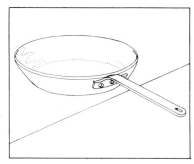

*Omelette pan*

of an omelette pan are curved and not too high, so that the omelette will roll up readily and fall onto the plate without breaking.

## WOKS

A wok is a Chinese cooking utensil which is now very popular in the West as well. It looks like a curve-based large frying pan with two rounded handles and is traditionally made of cast iron, though nowadays you can also buy stainless steel and non-stick ones.

Balance it on a metal collar directly over the heat, so that the wok can be moved backward and forward to ensure even cooking when stir frying. The wok is a very versatile cooking utensil. Food can be deep fried in it, and then drained on a semi-circular rack which clips on to the rim of the wok; this is very useful when you are frying food in batches. A small circular rack can be positioned in the center of the wok and used as a steamer with a domed lid fitted neatly over the top.

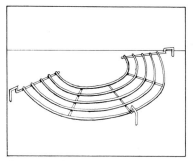

*Semi-circular wok rack for draining*

## FISH KETTLE

A fish kettle is best for poaching whole, large fish. The long oval-shaped pan has handles at either end, and the draining rack that the fish lies on fits neatly inside. The shape of the kettle allows the fish to lie completely flat, without curling; once cooked, the fish can be lifted out easily on the rack, without any danger of it breaking or splitting. If the fish is to be eaten cold it is usually left in the fish kettle in its cooking liquid to cool, and then lifted out.

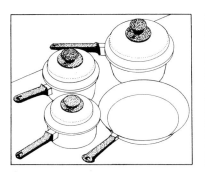

*Choose good quality pans*

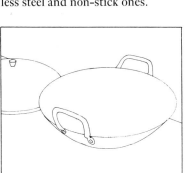

*Cast iron wok*

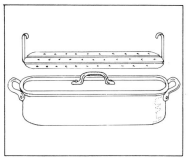

*Fish kettle and rack*

## EGG POACHERS

If you like regular shaped poached eggs, then an egg poacher is the answer. A poacher consists of a base pan (rather like a deep frying pan) which you half fill with water

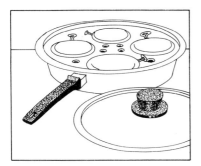

*Egg poacher*

and a tray containing small poaching cups that sits on top (these are often non-stick). A lid goes over the top of the pan while the eggs are poaching gently in the buttered cups.

## BAKING TINS

Baking is a skill; it relies on the precision of the cook, good quality ingredients, and the right shape and size of tin. Even a straightforward packet cake mix can turn out to be a flop if the wrong tin is used. Most recipes specify a particular size of tin, and this should always be used. Rich mixtures should be baked in strong tins; if the tin is too thin then the mixture will burn.

The greatest worry with baking tins is that of sticking; mixtures that are relatively high in fat are usually fairly safe, but those that contain little fat or are high in sugar can be very difficult to turn out of a tin.

To line a tin really neatly takes time and patience. The perfect solution is to use baking tins with a non-stick surface; all the familiar shaped tins that are used in everyday baking are available with a non-stick lining. Here is a list of tins you will need for quick, easy baking:

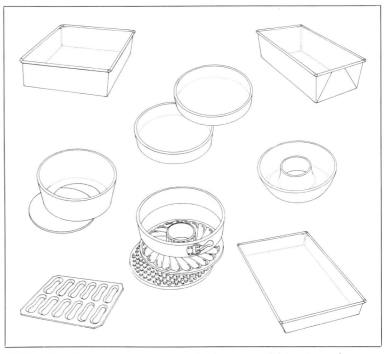

*Baking tins: a layer tin, loaf pan, round cake tins, madeleine tins and a Swiss roll tin*

## BASIC TINS

**Loaf pans**—these come in 1 lb and 2 lb sizes. Use them for cakes and breadmaking.
**Pie pans**—use a round pan with plain or fluted sides and a removable base for tarts.
**Layer tins**—these come in 7–10-inch sizes and are shallow, round tins with straight sides for making layer cakes. (You can also use spring release tins.)
**Swiss roll tins**

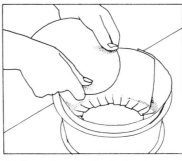

*Lining a deep tin for fruit cake*

**Standard cake tins**—you will need 6-inch, 7-inch and 8-inch tins.

## KNIVES

Good sharp knives are the cook's most important tools. Knives vary enormously in quality, the best ones have taper ground blades—the blade, bolster and tang are forged from one piece of steel, and the handle is fixed securely in place with rivets.
**Cook's knives** are the classic knives used by all top chefs and professional cooks. They have strong, broad and very sharp blades, and the handles are firmly riveted to give added strength while chopping. Classic cook's knives have heavy handles, therefore if they fall they land handle first, avoiding damage to the blade. The larger size cook's knives, those with blades between 6–8 inches long, are extremely versatile—they can be used for chopping, cubing, slicing, mincing

*Two useful sizes of cook's knives*

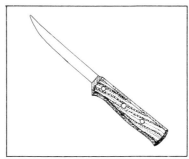

*Boning knife*

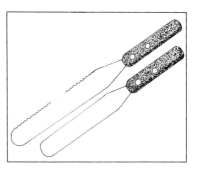

*Two types of frosting knives*

and crushing. Small cook's knives, with blades about 4 inches long are very good for paring vegetables and shaping vegetable garnishes.

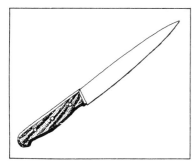

*Filleting knife*

**Filleting knives** have a long, slim, pliable blade. Sharpness and flexibility are essential, as the blade has to follow the bones of the fish very closely. These knives are also useful for skinning.

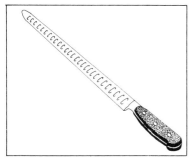

*Fish knife*

**Fish knives** have a strong, rigid, scalloped blade. These are very heavy knives which make them ideal for cutting through the backbones of fish.

**Boning knives** have rigid, narrow, broad-backed blades with very sharp points. They come in different lengths, depending on what they are going to be used to bone. The handles are indented and shaped to prevent your hand from slipping.

**Carving knives** come in many different styles and sizes. Knives suitable for carving large roasts of meat are shaped like an elongated filleting knife; sturdy, but flexible towards the tip of the blade. Serrated knives tend to tear the texture of hot meat and are best reserved for cutting cold roasts.

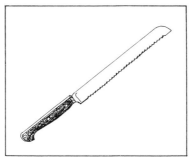

*Bread knife with serrated edge*

**A bread knife** should have a fairly rigid blade, but it should be long enough to slice through the largest of loaves—many bread knives have serrated blades, and they tend to cause less crumbs than a plain-edged knife. Serrated knives can also cope with crisp crusts much better.

**The frosting knife** or spatula has a long evenly wide blade, which is extremely pliable. A frosting knife is used primarily for spreading soft mixtures, such as icings, and for flipping foods such as pancakes.

Serrated frosting knives are very useful for slicing sponges and other cakes into layers.

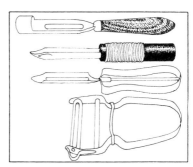

*Variety of potato peelers*

**Potato peelers** are not strictly speaking knives, but they do have a cutting blade and are a must for every kitchen.

237

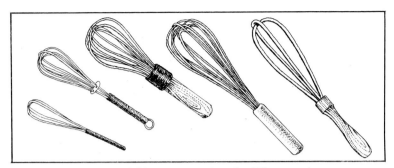

*Balloon whisks are available in varying sizes for different tasks*

## WHISKS

Whisks and beaters cope with a variety of culinary tasks. There are three different kinds of hand whisks: balloon, coiled and rotary beaters.

**Balloon whisks** come in different sizes and weights and they are extremely effective. The large, lightweight, very round whisks are the best for egg whites—they are easy to handle and can be used at quite a speed. Slimmer, thicker ridged, and heavier balloon whisks are better for coping with thick sauces, choux pastry or semi-set ice cream mixtures. They will incorporate more air into a mixture than any other type of whisk, and they are extremely easy to clean.

**Coiled whisks,** which look just as their name suggests, are cheaper than balloon whisks, but nowhere near as effective. You need to use a lot of effort for not much result.

**Rotary beaters** have two four-bladed beaters which are operated by a small handle. Although you need one hand to steady the beater and one to turn the handle, it is a

speedy and efficient way of whisking slack mixtures such as egg whites and thin sauces.

### Electric beaters and whisk attachments

Hand-operated electric beaters, with two beaters like a rotary beater, are very efficient. The

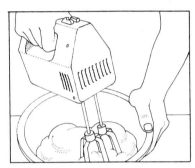

*Hand-operated electric beater*

beaters can be moved around the inside of a bowl or saucepan (non-stick) with relative ease. This is an advantage when making sauces.

The whisk attachment which goes with several food processors

is not that effective; the size of the beaters is relatively small and they cannot move freely through a mixture to incorporate a noticeable amount of air. It is reasonably effective with whisked cake mixtures, but one must not forget that the bowl of most food processors is relatively small. The whisk attachment on large electric mixers is particularly powerful; it is shaped like a squashed balloon whisk and reaches almost every part of the mixing bowl.

## BLENDERS

Electric blenders, also called liquidizers, have become very much an integral part of the kitchen gadget scene. They are extremely labor saving. Some

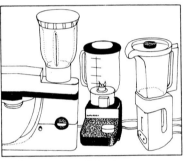

*Different types of blender*

blenders operate freely as a separate gadget, while others fit onto an electric food mixer. The only way in which they differ tends to be as far as capacity and speed are concerned; some are larger and faster than others. The blades in the base of the plastic or glass container rotate at a high speed, pulverising the ingredients inside. It is an invaluable gadget for liquidizing soups, sauces, and fruit and vege-table purées, but it can also chop and grind ingredients to varying degrees. There is a hole in the lid of the blender, so ingredients can be dropped through the top while the blades are whirring.

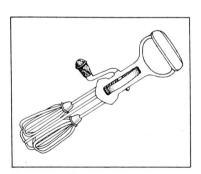

*Rotary egg beater*

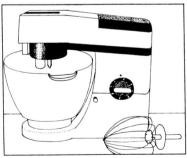

*Electric mixer and whisk attachment*

# CHOPPERS

Choppers have very heavy, deep rectangular blades; they are extremely strong and need to be used with care. They are blade-heavy and tend to drop forward when held. Choppers will cut through most bones, and they are particularly useful for cutting up oxtail. The cleaver is the Chinese equivalent of the chopper, but it is much more versatile; the blade is finer and sharper and can be used for chopping, slicing, mincing and scraping, and for making vegetable garnishes.

# SCISSORS

All-purpose kitchen scissors can be used for removing chicken skin; splitting bread dough decoratively; roughly cutting parsley, chives and other herbs; removing the cores from kidneys.

**Fish scissors** have serrated blades, with one slightly longer than the other. Use for trimming fins and tails, and cutting through bones.

**Poultry shears** have a strong spring between the two blades, which makes them extremely robust. They are excellent for cutting through the bones and carcass of all poultry.

# KITCHEN SCALES

There are basically two different types of kitchen scales: balance (the traditional variety) and spring balance. Long term, balance scales are a better buy as there is less that can go wrong; unlike spring balance scales they are not dependent on a spring.

Spring balance scales are extremely easy to use and fairly accurate. However, the needle on the dial occasionally gets knocked out of position, so it should be reset each time the scales are used. Some spring balance scales are designed to sit on the work surface, while others can be mounted on the kitchen wall. Unless you have very smooth and level kitchen walls, it is better to buy free-standing scales for accuracy.

*Manual juice extractors*

# SQUEEZERS
## Juicers

Juicers or citrus presses come in different shapes and sizes; some are manual and others are operated electrically. The basic principle behind all of them is exactly the same. A rigid dome of glass or plastic presses into the center of the halved fruit, thus squeezing out the juice. Some of the juicers are hand held, which means that you hold them over a bowl; others have a container beneath the juicer which collects the juice. Apart from those juicers which will take halved grapefruits and oranges, there are also smaller ones.

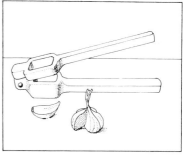

*Garlic press*

## Garlic presses

These are the smallest squeezers of all. They look like small potato ricers and work in a similar manner. Put the peeled clove of garlic into the press and squeeze down gently—if you squeeze very gently you just get the juice of the garlic—harder, you get the flesh.

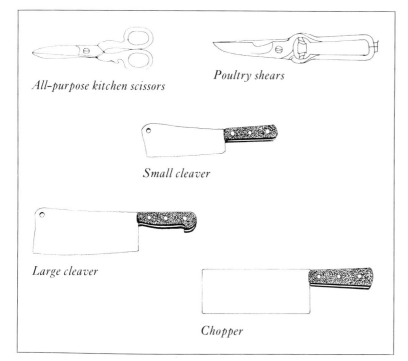

*All-purpose kitchen scissors*

*Poultry shears*

*Small cleaver*

*Large cleaver*

*Chopper*

239

## ELECTRIC MIXERS AND FOOD PROCESSORS

Electric mixers and food processors can tackle most of the day-to-day culinary tasks, and they are great labor-saving devices for those who are pushed for time and/or have a large family to feed.

### The electric mixer

The large size electric mixers, or table mixers as they are often called, have very powerful motors which can drive a variety of attachments such as: potato peelers, bean shredders and cream makers. The main disadvantage with the table mixer is that it is so bulky, and consequently takes up a lot of space, either on the work surface or in a cabinet. The bowl of the standard table mixer is very capacious and will hold twice as much as most food processors.

### The food processor

The food processor is a compact machine which is primarily used for chopping, mincing, grinding and blending. It is simple to use, strong and comparatively quiet. The plastic processor bowl fits over a spindle; the cutting, shredding and whisking attachments in turn fit over the spindle.

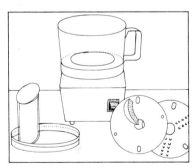

*Food processor showing blades*

The lid that fits over the bowl has a funnel through which food or liquid can be fed. When the machine is turned on, the cutting blade or other attachments move very fast—vegetables are chopped in 10 seconds, minced in 15

seconds, and puréed in 20 seconds. Food processors have revolutionized some of our methods of preparation; for example, they are a great help when making pastry and bread doughs, soups, pâtés and terrines.

A word of warning: even though you can buy whisking attachments for food processors, they are not as effective as the beaters on a traditional electric table mixer.

## GRINDERS

This useful gadget quickly turns cooked or raw meat, fish and vegetables into tiny particles. It is an asset when using up leftover cooked food and is also excellent for preparing your own freshly ground meat at home.

Hand grinders are usually made from cast iron or a strong plastic. They fit firmly onto the work surface, either by means of small rubber suction pads or a screw clamp; the latter is the most secure, and the larger grinders are always fitted with a clamp. The handle on the grinder turns a "screw" which pushes the food to be ground towards small cutting blades or extruding disks. The size of the perforations in the metal disks dictates the final texture of the ground food, which will either be fine, medium or coarse.

Grinder attachments can also be bought to fit into many table electric mixers.

## PRESSURE COOKERS

Pressure cookers can save you a great deal of time. There are many different models available, but basically a pressure cooker looks like a heavy-duty saucepan, with a domed lid. It has a weight on it which helps determine the level of pressure at which the food will cook and it also has a safety valve for steam to escape. It works on the principle of increasing the boiling temperature of water and then trapping the resultant steam. (This is achieved by means of added pressure.) Some models of pressure cooker only operate

under one pressure; however, the more recent models operate under three; so you can choose which pressure to use according to the type of food you are cooking.

The food is put into the base of the cooker with the appropriate amount of liquid; the lid is then firmly closed and the pan placed over the heat until steam comes through the vents. The necessary pressure weight is then added until a hissing noise is emitted; at this point the heat is turned down for the remainder of the cooking time. (This is always indicated in individual recipes.) After cooking, the pressure has to be released, either slowly or quickly, depending on the food inside. Most recent pressure cookers have an automatic setting on the lid, complete with a timer; this enables you to set both the cooking time and the speed at which pressure should be released.

The pressure cooker is particularly good for cooking the following types of foods:

**Stocks and Soups**
**Meat**—the less expensive, tougher cuts
**Poultry and game** (especially boiling fowl and casserole game)
**Firm textured fish** (pressure cooking eliminates the fishy smell)
**Root vegetables**, such as turnips
**Beans**
**Grain**—brown rice
**Steamed puddings**—both sweet and savory

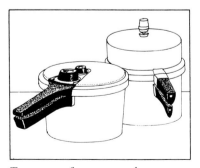

*Two types of pressure cooker*

**Preserves**—jams, marmalade, canned fruits and chutney

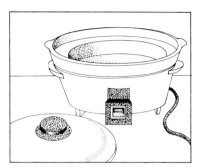

*Crockpot or slow cooker*

# CROCKPOTS

Cooking in a crockpot (or slow-cooker) is an up-dated version of a traditional method of cooking: our great-grandmothers would leave casseroles cooking gently all day in the very coolest part of the kitchen range.

The crockpot consists of an earthenware bowl which sits neatly inside an outer casing. An electric element is fixed between the base of the bowl and the casing, and it operates on two settings—low (75 watts) and high (130 watts). When plugged in it only uses about the same amount of power as a light bulb.

As the name suggests, a crockpot or slow-cooker cooks foods very slowly; so slowly that it can cook food while you are out of the house. It saves time, money and fuel. With most recipes, all the ingredients can be put into the crockpot at once and then left to cook for several hours. The steam which condenses on the crockpot lid returns to the pot, thus keeping the food moist. Subtle, rich flavors develop during long, slow cooking, and it is ideal for the tougher and cheaper cuts of meat. The crockpot heats very gently so there is no risk of burning, sticking or boiling over; consequently it is very easy to clean. Food does not need to be stirred during cooking, and it is important to resist the temptation to remove the lid while cooking. If it is removed, heat is lost from the crockpot and it takes a long time for the original temperature to be regained.

### General guidelines

- The crockpot needs pre-heating before food is added.
- Meat has a better appearance and flavor if it is lightly browned before it goes into the crockpot.
- Always bring stock and other liquids to a boil before adding them to the crockpot.
- Most foods should be started off on the High setting, and then reduced to Slow for the remainder of the time; chicken and pork to be "roasted" should be cooked on High for the whole cooking time.
- Always follow the given quantities of liquid in a recipe accurately; too much liquid can result in overcooking.
- Meats with a high fat content should be trimmed very well before being put into the crock-pot; fats do not bake off as they do in a conventional oven.
- A crockpot should not be used for re-heating any cooked frozen food.
- Leftovers from food that has been cooked in a crockpot must be brought to boiling point in a saucepan before being eaten.

A crockpot is suitable for cooking most foods, as long as recipes are adapted accordingly. It is, however, particularly successful when preparing the following:

**Soups**
**Cooked pâtés**
**Root vegetables**
**Meat and poultry**—casseroles and "roasts"
**Fish casseroles**
**Cheese fondue**
**Steamed puddings**
**Rice pudding** (and other grain puddings)
**Lemon curd**

# COOKING BRICKS

Cooking bricks are simplicity itself to use and always produce delicious-tasting, moist and tender

*Unglazed, earthenware cooking bricks*

food. They come in a variety of shapes and sizes and can be used for cooking most meats, fish and even potatoes, although they always tend to be referred to as "chicken bricks". Made of porous, unglazed earthenware, with close-fitting lids, these bricks are very similar in concept to the clay pots used in Greek and Roman times. Before using a brick, always give it a preliminary soaking in cold water each time that you use it in order for it to impart moisture to the food being cooked.

After draining, place the seasoned food into the cooking brick with herbs, chopped vegetables, and any other flavorings or seasonings that you like, and put the lid on top. Put the brick into a cold oven, and then turn it on. As the oven heats up, condensation forms on the lid of the brick, and trickles back onto the food; this acts as a baste and keeps the food moist. All the flavor, juices and aroma of the food are conserved naturally, and the food is far less fatty than it is when cooked by many other more conventional methods, such as roasting or frying.

Cooking bricks should never be washed with detergent as this will taint the food. Just wipe out well with a clean damp cloth or wash in water to which a little vinegar has been added. The bricks do darken with use, but this does not mean that they are dirty, just discolored.

# Ingredients

The best dishes, be they simple or complex, have one thing in common: they all depend upon fresh, good-quality ingredients. In this chapter you will read about buying meats, poultry and fish and how to prepare them for cooking. You'll learn about special techniques for preparing particular vegetables. And you'll find a chart that quickly shows you the best ways to wrap and store your foods in the refrigerator.

## BUYING BEEF

Beef is available all year round, and offers a variety of cuts to suit all cooking methods and occasions, from large roasts to economical braising and stewing cuts. When buying fresh beef look for a fresh, slightly moist appearance. The redness of the meat will vary after cutting and exposure to air, but this need not affect your choice. The lean meat roasts should be smooth and velvety in texture. Coarse-textured lean beef is usually an indication that the meat is suitable only for braising and stewing. Beef that is very coarse will almost certainly need slow cooking to tenderize it.

The lean meat should be surrounded by a layer of creamy-white fat. The color of the fat may vary for a number of reasons, none of which will affect the taste. The fat should, however, always be firm and dry. Marbling, or flecks of fat in the meat, will help to keep

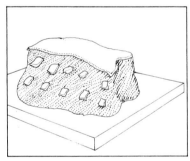

*A lean larded roast*

the meat moist during the cooking and often gives it a better flavor. Very lean roasts are sometimes sold larded with fat to help keep them moist.

## CUTS OF BEEF

**1 Flank** This is a lean cut that is often sold sliced ready for frying or braising. Roasts need a slow moist cooking method such as pot roasting.

**2 Brisket** An economical and tasty roast sold on the bone or boned and rolled. It has a high percentage of fat and needs a slow moist cooking method, such as pot roasting or braising, to prevent shrinkage and to tenderize it. If roasting, wrap it in foil to seal in the juices. It is often salted or pickled, in which case it should be boiled.

**3 Rump** The traditional roast used for pot roast. It contains no bone and is very lean. This roast is also pickled ready for boiling.

**4 Shank** An excellent cut for stews and soups. Meat and bone are cooked together to give a jellied stock. Beef shanks are very nutritious and make richly flavored stews and casseroles.

**5 Round** Similar to shank; makes excellent soups and stews. Cubed, shank and round are often sold together as stewing steak.

**6, 7 Chuck and Shank** Two economical cuts, and a good choice for stews as the rich juices make superb gravy. Also used for ground beef.

**8 Short plate** An inexpensive cut which deserves wider recognition. It is ideal for pot roasting on the bone, and for stews. Not suitable for dry heat cooking methods.

**9, 10 Chuck and Blade** Lean meat from the shoulder which is removed from the bone and used for braising and stewing. Also called shoulder.

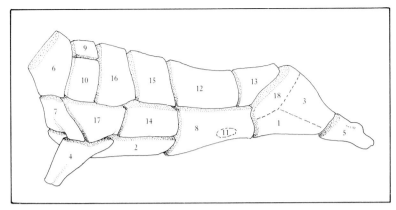

*Major cuts of beef to be found at your butcher*

# BUYING VEAL

The color and quality of veal depends greatly on the age at the time of slaughter, and the method of rearing. Milk-fed calves have very pale flesh that is highly valued. The best veal comes from calves that are fed on a rich milk diet and, as this method of rearing is expensive, the price of veal is high. As the calf is weaned from milk and starts to eat grass, the flesh tends to become darker. When buying veal the flesh should be pinkish beige, with no dark or discolored particles. It should be very lean and moist with no juice running from it.

# CUTS OF VEAL

**1 Shoulder** A large roast, usually boned, rolled and tied, then cut into various sized roasts. It can be stuffed, then pot roasted or braised. The meat can be cubed for casseroles and pies.

**2 Fillet** Thin slices cut from the leg. They are very lean and usually flattened before cooking. Can be fried or stuffed as for beef roulades.

**3 Cutlet** Thin slices cut across the grain from the topside. They are very lean and usually flattened before cooking. Shallow frying is the best cooking method.

**11 Skirt** A tasty economical stewing meat that comes from inside the ribs and the flank.

**12 Sirloin** A tender and delicious prime cut. Can be roasted in the piece or broiled as steaks. The fillet is found on the inside of the sirloin bone, and the fillet and sirloin together provide an ideal roast. T-bone, sirloin and porterhouse steaks come from the sirloin. The roasts can be bone-in or boneless. The fillet can also be separated from the sirloin for roasting in one piece or sliced into fillet steaks—the most tender for broiling or frying.

**13 Rump Steak** The perfect steak for broiling or frying. Although not as tender as fillet, it is preferred by many as it has a fuller flavor. The lean meat should be velvety, close grained and bright red in color, with a moderate amount of fat.
**Ribs** May be bone-in or boned and rolled. Rib roasts should have a layer of firm dry fat and marbling in the lean meat.

**14 Short Ribs** A popular roast, but also cut into steaks for broiling and frying.

**15 Standing Ribs** The traditional cut for English roast beef.

**16, 17 Back and Top Ribs** Less expensive than standing ribs and ideal for pot roasting and braising. The rib eye is a boneless piece.

**18 Topside** A lean cut, usually sold with a layer of fat wrapped around it. Roast slowly and keep well basted. Usually more tender when served slightly underdone. Makes a perfect pot roast.

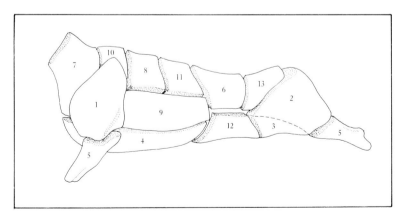

*Major cuts of veal to be found at your butcher*

**4 Breast** Usually sold boned, this cheaper cut can be rolled and tied, and stuffed if desired. It can be pot roasted or braised.

**Pie Veal** Shin, leg and neck cut into small pieces for use in pies, blanquettes and casseroles.

**5 Knuckle** Cut into rounds, with the marrow bone in the center. Traditional cut for Osso Bucco.

**6 Loin** A succulent roast. Veal chops are cut from the loin.

**Leg, Shoulder or Breast** Small boneless roasts wrapped in a thin covering of pork fat for slow cooking, or pot roasting.

**7 Neck** A stewing cut which needs slow moist cooking. It can be cut into small pieces for pies.

**Ground Veal** Very lean meat, useful for patties, particularly when mixed with ground pork to keep the mixture succulent.

**8 Best Neck** An economical cut. It can be chined and roasted on the bone, or boned, stuffed and rolled for roasting. Also suitable for braising and stewing. Cutlets can be cut if the "eye" muscle is large.

**9 Ribs** when boned are sliced and braised or casseroled.

**10 Middle Neck** is usually sliced into cutlets for braising.

**11 Cutlets** are trimmed neatly of most fat and used for broiling or frying.

**12 Flank** is a tough cut that can be stewed or ground and cooked slowly for a long time.

**13 Rump** is a tender cut usually sliced into cutlets or medallions to be fried or broiled.

## HOW MUCH MEAT TO BUY

Although servings vary according to the age, taste and appetite of the people being served, as a guide allow 4–6 oz raw meat without bone and 6–12 oz with bone, per person.

## STORING FRESH BEEF AND VEAL

Freshly cut meat should be stored in a cool place, preferably a refrigerator. Unwrap the meat and

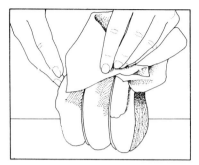

*Wiping meat with absorbent paper*

wipe the surface with paper towels, then wrap in foil or plastic wrap to prevent the surface drying out. Place the meat in the coldest part of the refrigerator, away from cooked meats and other foods. Fresh meat can be kept for 3–5 days in the refrigerator, although it is advisable to cook smaller cuts within 1–2 days.

## STORING COOKED BEEF AND VEAL

Cooked meats should be wrapped or covered to prevent them drying out before they are put in the refrigerator. Leftover stews and casseroles should first be allowed to cool and then put in the refrigerator or a cool place in a covered dish. They should be used within 2 days and reheated thoroughly before they are eaten. Bring the dish to boiling point and simmer for at least 10 minutes.

# TECHNIQUES WITH BEEF AND VEAL

## HOW TO BONE A BREAST OF VEAL

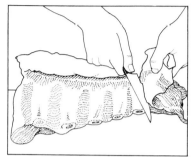

*1* Place the breast of veal, skin side down, on a board. Cut along the flap of the meat over the bones and pull back to reveal the bones.

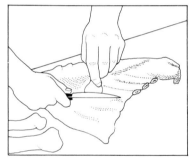

*2* Carefully cut around each bone with a small sharp knife. Working from one end, scrape each bone away from the meat, then lift the bones from the meat. Any meat left on the bones can be scraped off and placed on the boned meat.

*3* Trim off excess fat and skin. Turn the meat over and remove the skin by cutting between the skin and the fat, pulling skin away with other hand.

*4* Turn the meat over and spread stuffing evenly over it. Roll up from one long edge. Tie neatly at regular intervals.

## HOW TO TIE UP A ROAST

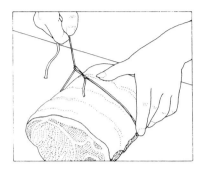

*1* Gather or roll the meat to the required shape. Slide a piece of uncolored string under the roast and make a loop with one end.

*2* Thread the other end of the string through the loop, then pull the end to tighten. Tie a knot and cut off the ends of the string.

*3* Repeat at 1–2-inch intervals, depending on how firm the roast is.

## HOW TO LARD A ROAST

Strips of fresh pork fat, called lardons, are threaded through the meat before cooking to help keep the meat moist and baste it from within. The easiest way to thread the lardons into the meat is with a special larding needle.

*1* Cut the pork fat into long strips about $\frac{1}{4}$ inch wide. You will need 1–1$\frac{1}{2}$ oz fat per 1 lb of meat.

*2* Using a hinged larding needle, close the toothed clip securely over the end of a strip of pork fat.

*3* Push the point of the needle under the surface of the meat and draw it through the meat. Release the clip and trim off excess fat, leaving a short length.

*4* Repeat at 1–2 inch intervals until the surface of the meat is evenly larded.

# *PREPARING POULTRY*

To get the best out of poultry prepare it carefully before cooking. If any quills have been left behind after plucking (this is most likely with the large birds such as goose and turkey) remove them carefully with tweezers. Rinse all birds well, inside and out, in cold water and dry thoroughly with paper towels.

### TRUSSING

Trussing keeps poultry in a good shape for roasting, making it more attractive on the table and easier to carve. Always remove the butcher's or packager's trussing so that you can wash and dry the bird, then truss it again yourself. A *trussing needle* (a long needle with a large eye) is useful, but failing this, use a skewer and fine string to truss the bird.

First fold the neck skin under the body and fold the tips of the wings back toward the backbone so that they hold the skin in position; set the bird on its back and press the legs well into the sides, raising and plumping the breast. Make a slit in the skin above the vent and put the tail through.

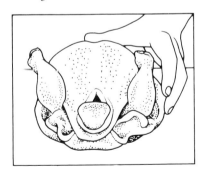

*Tail end of chicken*

Thread the needle with fine string and insert it close to the second joint of the right wing; push it right through the body, passing it out so as to catch the

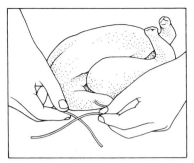

*Tying the ends of string*

corresponding joint on the left side. Insert the needle again in the first joint of the left wing, pass it through the flesh at the back of the body, catching the tips of the wings and the neck skin, and pass it out through the first joint of the wing on the right side. Tie the ends of the string in a bow.

To truss the legs, re-thread the needle and insert it through the gristle at the right side of the tail. Pass the string over the right leg, under the back and over the left leg, through the gristle at the left side of the tail. Carry it behind the

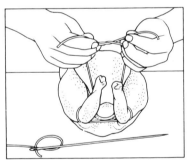

*Trussing the legs*

tail and tie the ends firmly together.

If using a skewer, insert it right through the body of the bird just below the thigh bone and turn the bird over on its breast. First,

245

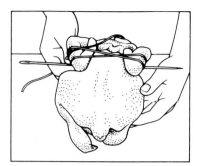

*Using a skewer to truss*

catching in the wing tips, pass the string under the ends of the skewer and cross it over the back. Turn the bird over and tie the ends of the string together round the tail, securing the drumsticks.

## CUTTING

Although poultry pieces are readily available, cutting up a bird yourself is cheaper and leaves you with bones and giblets for stock. Cut a chicken several hours before starting to cook a casserole so that you can make stock first. Or, if you have to use water for cooking, add the backbone to it.

Use a sharp, heavy knife or *poultry shears*. Start by trimming off the excess skin at the neck end and removing any chunks of fat from inside the body cavity. Cut off the knuckle ends from the legs, and the wing tips; use for stock.

With the bird breast side up, neck towards you, cut straight along one side of the breast bone from the vent to the neck. Spread open and cut along one side of the backbone to divide it in half. If your knife is not sharp enough, lay

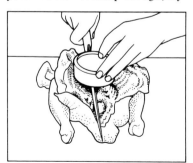

*Breaking the bones with a weight*

it along the cutting line and give the back of the knife a firm bang with a heavy weight to break the bones first. Then cut along the other side of the backbone and remove to use in the stock.

To quarter a chicken or game hen cut each half in half again crossways between the breast and

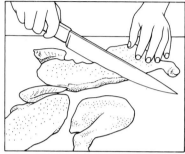

*Quartering poultry*

the leg. To quarter a duck, leave plenty of breast meat with the leg portion as there is very little meat on the leg. For duck recipes using breast only, use all the breast and save the thin legs for pâté.

Large birds may require dividing again. The leg can be divided in two through the center of the joint to give a thigh and a drumstick portion. The wing quarter can be divided to give a wing and a breast portion.

### Alternative method

If you prefer to take the meat off the carcass rather than cutting right through the bones you will need a small sharp knife, sometimes known as a *filleting knife*.

Start with the chicken breast side up with the neck end towards you. Gently pull the leg away from the body and cut through the skin between the thigh and the breast; repeat on the other side of the bird. Turn the bird over and continue cutting through the skin around the legs, following the natural line of the thighs down towards the backbone. You will find a tiny succulent portion of meat where the backbone joins the thigh—the oyster. Loosen the oysters but don't detach yet. With

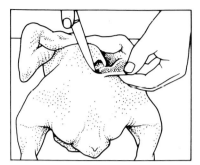

*Loosening the oyster*

bird on its back, push the legs outwards until the joints release. Turn the bird over, slip knife into joint and ease the legs away from the backbone, making sure oyster is still attached. Set aside.

Turn bird over, wings towards you. Cut through the skin and

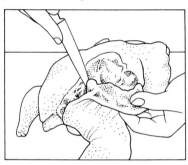

*Working breast meat from bones*

flesh along one side of the breast bone. With knife flat against rib cage, work breast from the bones, keeping the meat in one piece.

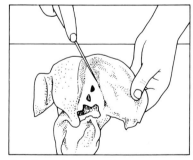

*Bending wing away from carcass*

Then grasp the wing firmly and bend it away from the carcass until

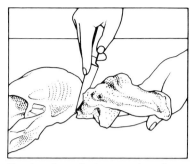

*Cutting through sinews and tendons*

the joint releases. Cut through any sinews and tendons and set the breast aside. Repeat on the other side. You are now left with a bare carcass that can be used for stock.

To make a *chicken supreme* take the breast portion only, with no wing attached and remove the skin. With a sharp knife, cut and scrape the meat from the bones, gently pulling back the meat in one piece as you cut. Underneath the main breast meat is a thin fillet of meat only loosely attached to the rest; try not to separate this. Discard bones and cut out the white tendon that remains.

## BUTTERFLYING
Butterflying is a way of preparing a small whole bird for broiling. The bones are left in but the body is opened flat. Use for small chickens and game hens. You will need poultry shears or a sharp, heavy knife.

The easiest method is to lay the bird on its breast and cut along the center of the backbone with shears. With a knife, work from inside

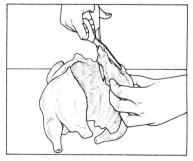

*Cutting along the backbone*

the cavity; insert the knife through the vent, put as much weight on it as you can and press down to break your way through the bone. The skin should remain attached to the bone on either side.

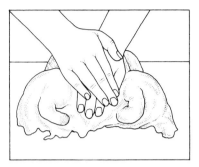

*Flattening the bird with the hands*

Force the two halves of the bird open with your hands, turn it over and lay it as flat as you can on a board. Then, with the heel of your hand, bang the center of the bird firmly to break the breast bone, collar bones and wishbone. With a slightly bigger bird you may find this easier with the flat of a meat mallet or a rolling pin.

Although the body now seems quite flat, it will start to curl back into its natural shape as soon as the heat gets to it. To prevent this happening thread skewers across the body to hold it flat during cooking. Use two long skewers, one from leg to leg, the other from wing to wing and remove them before serving.

## SKINNING
One of the joys of roast poultry is the crisp brown skin. But for recipes in which the skin is not crisped it is often nicer to remove the skin before cooking.

For a breast portion with no wing attached this is a simple matter, the skin will peel away easily. But wing and leg portions are not so easy as the skin is very firmly attached at the thin ends of the joints.

To help you keep a grip on the meat use a clean damp cloth and grasp the joint firmly. For a leg portion, first slip your fingers under the skin at the thigh end and loosen it all round. Grasp the

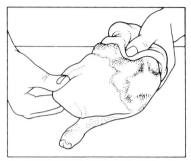

*Peeling the skin*

meaty part firmly with a cloth in one hand and peel the skin off the joint so that it is inside out. When you reach the point where it is bonded to the bone take a small sharp knife and slip it between skin and bone to cut the skin away cleanly.

On a wing portion, lift the skin away from the breast where it is loose and gently peel it away along the first wing bone as far as it will go. Then hold the meaty part firmly with a cloth in one hand, take your small sharp knife and, working with the tip, ease the skin away from the joint. There is very little meat on the second wing bone so the skin clings tightly. Slit the skin on the inside of the wing and gently peel it away all round. Cut off the wing tip just above the joint, taking all the skin with it.

## BONING
With the bones removed, a chicken or duck makes a lovely meaty casing for stuffing and the resulting roast is easy to carve. A classic galantine or ballotine is made this way. The stuffed bird is shaped into a neat roll, stitched up securely with fine string and either roasted or poached. After cooking it is chilled and usually finished with a glaze of aspic or a creamy sauce.

Sometimes a ballotine is served hot with a rich accompanying sauce—very impressive for a party dish and much easier to carve in front of guests than a whole bird. Usually the stuffing is rich so that one bird will serve up to twice as many prepared this way rather than simply roasted.

Even more dramatic is the traditional quail inside a chicken, inside a goose—rarely served these days but a delight to imagine.

Another approach is to bone only the breast, leaving the leg and wing bones intact. This way the cavity can be generously filled with stuffing and the breast re-formed to its natural shape. This gives a finished dish that looks like the conventional roast poultry, but with an amount of stuffing that makes it go much further. The savory flavors of the stuffing will permeate right through the breast flesh as it cooks.

Individual portions with the bones removed also make attractive casings for savory fillings. *Chicken Kiev* is the example most people know—a boneless chicken breast with the wing bone attached; the breast meat is wrapped round a portion of garlic butter, and the whole thing is dipped in egg and bread crumbs and deep-fried.

A leg portion with the bone removed can be filled in the same way; the end of the knuckle bone is usually left in place to give the joint shape and keep the end firmly closed.

### Boning a whole bird

The secret of success is a sharp knife; a boning knife with a blade about 5–6 inches long would be a good one to choose. The procedure is the same for all birds even though the carcass shapes differ somewhat.

Lay the bird on a board breast side up. Cut off the wings at the second joint and the legs at the first. Turn the bird breast down.

Cut cleanly through the skin and flesh down the center of the

back from vent to neck. Keeping the knife close to the carcass and slightly flattened to avoid damaging the flesh, carefully work

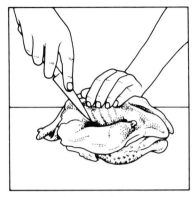

*Exposing the wing joint*

the flesh off the rib cage on one side of the bird until the wing joint is exposed; repeat on the other side to expose the other wing joint.

Take hold of the severed end of one wing joint. Scrape the knife over the bone backwards and forwards, working the flesh from the bone; try not to damage the

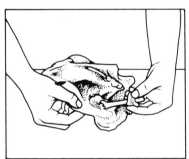

*Drawing out the bone*

skin. When the wing and socket are exposed, sever the ligaments with the point of the knife and draw out the bone. Repeat with the second wing.

Continue working the flesh off the main frame until the leg joint is exposed. Sever the ligaments attaching the bone to the body

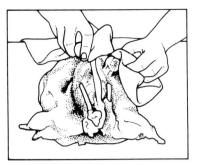

*Breaking the leg joint*

flesh and break the leg joint by twisting it firmly (use a cloth to get a good grip). Working from the body end of the leg, hold the end of the bone firmly and scrape away all the flesh from the thigh. Cut carefully round the joint with the point of the knife and scrape the drumstick clean in the same way. Pull the bone free. Repeat with the other leg.

Now go on to work the flesh from the rest of the main frame. Take care not to cut the skin over the breast bone, where the flesh becomes very thin, as the two halves of the breast must remain attached to each other.

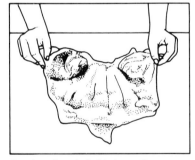

*Laying the whole bird out flat*

You can now lay the whole bird out flat ready to spread the stuffing over the cut surface.

### Leaving the limbs on

If you want to leave the bones in the wings and legs, sever the appropriate joints with a knife as you reach them and continue round the carcass as before.

## Boning a leg

With the point of a sharp knife cut round the end of the bone at the thigh end of the leg to free the

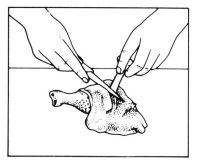

*Scraping the flesh off the bone*

flesh. Then grasp the end firmly and scrape the flesh carefully off the bone, taking care that you do not cut through the flesh. When you reach the joint use the point again to sever the ligaments all round. Scrape and work your way down the drumstick until you reach the knuckle. Cut off the bone joint above the knuckle and remove it.

## CARVING

For perfect carving you need a long, sharp knife and a long-handled fork with two long prongs and a finger-guard. Place the bird on a flat carving dish or board — sides higher than about $\frac{1}{2}$ inch will get in your way. Some carving dishes have spikes to hold the meat in place; some have a channel round the edge to drain the juices away from the standing bird.

If you garnish the bird with vegetables or other trimmings to take it to the table, remove these before you start to carve so that you have room to work. If you have a large carving dish you can arrange the carved meat along the edge of the dish ready for serving; if using a smaller dish have another hot dish ready to take the slices as they are prepared. Carving onto individual plates is not ideal as you will not be able to mix dark and light meats in each serving.

## Carving chicken and turkey

Place the bird on the dish so that one wing is towards your left hand with the breast diagonally towards

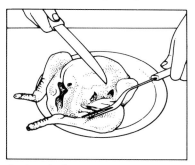

*Prying the leg outwards with fork*

you. Steadying the bird with the flat of the knife, pry the leg outwards with the fork, exposing the thigh joint. Cut through the joint to sever the leg. On a turkey or large chicken hold the end of the drumstick in one hand and cut slices from the leg in a downward slant away from you, turning the leg to get slices from all round the joint. When the bone is bare set it to one end of the dish. For a medium-sized chicken the leg will not have enough meat for carving but can be divided into two at the joint, giving a thigh and a drumstick portion. If the chicken is small the leg may be served as a single portion.

Next remove the wing that is facing you. Hold the wing with the fork and cut through the outer layer of the breast into the joint. Ease the wing from the body and cut through the gristle. A turkey wing may be divided again; a chicken wing is too small and is served in one piece.

Carve the breast in thin slices parallel with the breast bone. If the bird is stuffed, the outer slices of meat and stuffing will carve together; the rest of the stuffing will have to be scooped out with a spoon. Carve one side of the carcass clean before turning the dish round and starting the process again on the other side of the bird.

# PREPARATION OF FISH AND SHELLFISH

Fish make delicious and versatile casserole dishes, encompassing both fish soups and stews. They differ from meat casseroles in that they are not designed to make the fish tender by long, slow cooking but they ensure that the fish is moist and absorbs other flavors. This is very useful for making bland fish into exotic dishes.

## BUYING

There is a wide variety of fish available, both at fish stores and supermarkets, fresh or frozen.

Depending on the type of fish and individual recipes, fish may be bought in many different forms. It can be a whole fish including the head and tail; a piece of a whole, large fish; fish steaks (on the bone) and fish fillets (boned and sometimes skinned).

Fish is usually sold by weight but some shellfish such as scallops are sold individually. Whole fish is considerably cheaper per pound but do not forget that you are also paying for the wasted parts and the more expensive fillets may work out cheaper.

Buy fish when it is in season and therefore at its best and cheapest. Always buy fish which is absolutely fresh—look for a bright color with shiny, silvery scales, firm flesh, bright, bulging eyes and a clean, fresh smell.

Allow 4–12 oz of fish per person, depending on the type of fish and whether it includes bones, heads, guts, etc. A medium-sized whole fish of about 8 oz will serve one person. If there are lots of other ingredients in the casserole less fish will be necessary. Oily fish is more rich and filling than white fish.

For most fish casseroles, the fish specified in the recipe can usually be substituted by another fish of a similar type.

## TYPES OF FISH

**Flatfish** (*sole, halibut, flounder, turbot*): have white fine flesh with a delicate flavor. Sole and flounder are available whole or as fillets. Turbot is prized for its firm flesh, and is usually sold in steaks. Halibut makes a cheaper substitute for turbot.

**Round White Fish** (*bass, bream, cod, conger eel, dog fish, haddock, hake, monkfish, mullet (red and grey), snapper, skate, whiting*): bass, bream, mullet and snapper are usually cooked whole. Cod, sold as steaks or fillets, is a good choice for casseroles, fried fish and fish cakes; whiting is a cheaper substitute. Conger eel and monkfish both have firm flesh very suitable for many types of preparation.

**Oily Fish** (*herring, mackerel, tuna*): herring and mackerel are usually cooked whole. Tuna is often sold in steaks, and fresh grilled or broiled tuna is delicious. Because it is oily, it needs little or no additional butter or oil during cooking. Canned tuna's firm texture is suitable for casseroles.

**Freshwater Fish** (*eel, salmon, sea trout, trout*): eels have a rich meaty texture, ideal for casseroles. Salmon is a prized fish, in season during the summer months. It can be dry, and moist methods of cooking like poaching, are therefore recommended. Grilled or broiled salmon is a wonderful dish, but coat it with a little butter or oil first. Sea trout is a smaller, less expensive substitute for salmon.

**Shellfish** (*crab, crawfish, crayfish, hard-shell and soft-shell clams, lobster, mussels, octopus and squid, oysters, shrimp, scallops*): may be cooked on their own, but are often added to other fish dishes for their color and flavor. Mussels and octopus are both popular in Mediterranean dishes. Crayfish, shrimp and scallops all make colorful, flavorsome additions to

baked and broiled dishes. Oysters are usually made into a stew, fried or eaten raw.

## STORAGE

In theory fish should never be stored, as it should be cooked and eaten as soon as it is purchased. However, if fish has to be stored it should be covered in the coldest part of the refrigerator, or surrounded by ice. Ideally, fish should be cooked on the same day as purchased, but if it has to be kept overnight, remove the guts and clean the fish well before wrapping in clean paper or film.

If fish has been cooked and made up into a casserole it may be cooled quickly and stored in the refrigerator, covered overnight and reheated before serving.

Ideally, frozen fish should be defrosted before cooking and this can be done in the refrigerator or more quickly at room temperature.

## PREPARATION

Most fish stores will prepare the fish for you or you may do it yourself. This involves cleaning the fish, which may then be left whole or skinned and filleted or cut into steaks.

## CLEANING

**Scaling**: Some fish have scales which should be removed before cooking. Scrape the blunt edge of

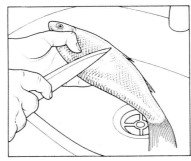

*Scaling round fish*

a knife along the fish from tail to head (this can be very messy so do it over the sink or sheets of paper). Rinse off the scales under the tap.

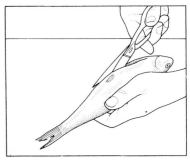

*Slitting belly of round fish*

**Gutting**: Round fish: using a sharp knife or scissors make a slit along the belly from the gills towards the tail (if the fish is to be left whole make as small a slit as possible). Pull out innards with your fingers. Rinse the fish under

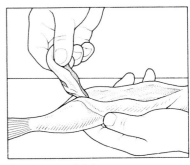

*Gutting round fish*

cold, running water until completely clean. Flat fish: make a slit just behind the head under the gills and clean in the same way.

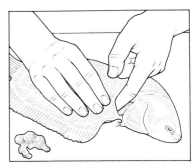

*Gutting flat fish*

Cut off the fins and gills. If the fish is to be cooked whole the head and tail may be left on or off. Rinse in cold water then dry.

## SKINNING

Round fish are usually cooked with their skin on but it is also possible to skin them raw: with a sharp knife, slit the skin down the backbone, loosen the skin around the head and peel it off towards the tail. Turn over and repeat.

*Skinning whole round fish*

For whole flat fish: cut the skin across above the tail on the dark skin side. Slip your thumb in the slit just under the skin and carefully loosen the skin around the sides of the fish.

Hold the fish firmly by the tail and pull the skin off quickly towards the head in one piece.

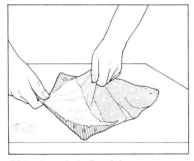

*Skinning whole flat fish*

(Salt on your fingers will prevent them from slipping.) Usually only the dark skin is removed but the process may be repeated with the other side.

Fillets of fish may be skinned by placing on a board, skin side down. Hold the tail firmly and with a sharp knife cut just above the skin, sawing from side to side and pressing the flat of the blade against the flesh. Work towards

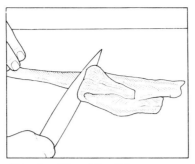

*Skinning fillet of flat fish*

the head end until the skin is removed—it should come off in one piece.

## FILLETING

Round fish are usually filleted before skinning. Cut off the head. Cut along the center of the back through the flesh to the bone, from the head to the tail, and cut along the belly of the fish. Remove the

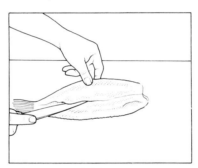

*Filleting round fish*

fillet working from the head down, pressing the knife against the bones and using short, slicing movements. Remove the fillet from the other side in the same way. Small round fish such as herring may be boned but with the head and tail left intact; or with the head and tail removed to give one fillet: slit the fish open along the belly and remove the innards. Open out the fish so that all the skin is facing upwards. Press firmly with fingers along the center of the back to loosen the backbone. Turn the fish over and ease up the

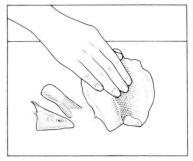

*Loosening backbone of round fish*

backbone in one piece. Reshape the fish if it is to be left whole, or roll up towards the tail, or cut into two fillets.

Flat fish are usually cut into four fillets, two from each side. Lay the unskinned fish flat on a board and cut through the flesh to the backbone along the length of the fish. Cut away a fillet from one

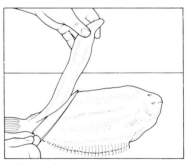

*Filleting flat fish*

side of the backbone with a sharp knife using short, sharp movements and repeat with the other side. Turn fish over and repeat.

## SHELLFISH

All shellfish needs very careful cleaning and preparation and this is often done at the store.

All live shellfish must be boiled before using in a recipe: boil in salted water for 5–30 minutes depending on type of fish.

Most shellfish have indigestible or inedible parts such as "beards," gills, intestines and stomach which must be removed. Shells must also be removed to expose the meat.

# VEGETABLE PREPARATION TECHNIQUES

Whether they are to be served raw or cooked, most vegetables need very simple preparation: after thorough cleaning they can be cut to the desired shape and size. However, some vegetables need special attention or a special technique for a particular effect.

## CHOPPING
To chop an onion, cut in half lengthwise and place on a board with the cut side down. With a very sharp, pointed knife, make horizontal cuts not quite through the length of the onion. Cut down

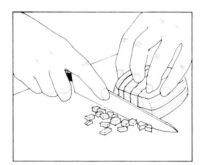

*Cut across onions to make cubes*

the length of the onion, then follow with downward cuts across the onion to make cubes. The number of cuts made each way will determine how coarsely or finely chopped the onion will be.

Large, firm vegetables such as cabbages are easier to chop if they

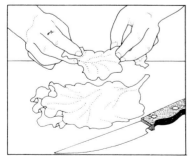

*Chop leafy vegetables in layers*

are first cut in halves or wedges before cutting lengthwise and then across.

Large leafy vegetables can be chopped by placing several leaves on top of each other before cutting.

To chop small leafy vegetables and herbs very finely, first chop or shred the leaves on a large board. With a large, sharp knife, hold down the point with your other hand while chopping quickly with a pivotal action across the

*Chopping fresh herbs finely*

vegetable. Turn the board at right angles and chop in the same way, repeating until the leaves are finely chopped.

## DRAINING
This technique removes the juices from watery vegetables which may be bitter (e.g., eggplant and cucumbers).

*1* Cut the vegetables into slices about $\frac{1}{4}$ inch thick, or according to the recipe. Place in a colander, sprinkling each layer with salt.

*2* Cover the slices with a plate, place heavy weights on top and leave to drain for 30 minutes, until the juices have seeped out of the vegetable. Rinse well to remove the salt and bitter juices, then dry with paper towels.

## DICING
*1* Cut slices either lengthwise or across the vegetable to the same thickness as the desired cube, which may be large or small. Cut each slice into sticks.

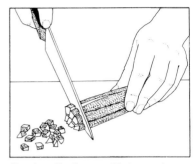

*Cutting sliced vegetable into cubes*

*2* Cut across the sticks to make cubes (some smaller vegetables may be kept whole by careful handling until the final cuts into cubes).

## GRATING
Vegetables can be grated finely or coarsely, depending on the grating blade used. Usually used for salads and in some oriental dishes.

## JULIENNE
These are strips of vegetable that are matchstick shape and size. Cut the vegetable into thin slices the

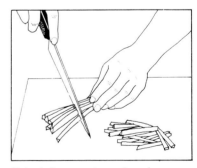

*Trim julienne strips to length*

size of a matchstick. Cut the slices into thin sticks, then trim to the desired length.

## PREVENTING DISCOLORATION

Some vegetables such as avocados and Jerusalem artichokes turn an unpleasant brown color on contact with the air once they have been peeled or prepared. Acid in the form of lemon juice will prevent them from browning if sprinkled or brushed over the cut surfaces immediately after cutting.

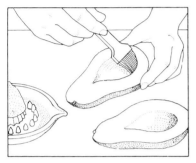

*Brush lemon juice over cut avocados*

Covering the cut vegetable immediately with plastic wrap will also help prevent browning. If the vegetable is to be served in a salad it may be tossed in a dressing made with lemon juice or vinegar. Vegetables that are going to be cooked may be immersed in water that has been acidulated with a little lemon juice or vinegar.

## SHREDDING

A large, firm vegetable like a cabbage should first be cut in half, quarters or wedges. Slice across or lengthwise down the vegetable to shave off thin slivers.

For leafy vegetables, place several on top of each other and roll up lengthwise. Hold firmly and cut across the roll into very thin slices which will unfurl into long, thin shreds.

# STORAGE OF FRESH FOODS

A well-stocked refrigerator will put variety in your cooking. Most foods will keep between three days and a week if bought really fresh and stored properly.

Perishable foods such as meat, fish, dairy products, salads and leafy green vegetables are best kept in the refrigerator. The

*Keep perishable food in the fridge*

stronger greens will survive quite well in a cool closet if there is no space in the fridge, along with root vegetables and fruits. For cool storage, choose somewhere where the temperature will not rise above 50°F, and put them in a well-ventilated box or basket.

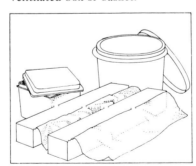

*Always cover or wrap foods*

Cover or wrap all foods before you put them in the refrigerator, and allow cooked foods to cool first. Warm or uncovered foods cause the frozen food compartment to become frosted up, which will prevent the refrigerator operating efficiently.

Keep raw meat, bacon, poultry

and fish in the coldest part of the refrigerator which, if you have a frozen food compartment, will be directly under that. If you have a refrigerator with no frozen food compartment, check the manufacturer's booklet for the coldest area. Keep cooked meats and prepared dishes in the middle shelves and vegetables and salad greens at the bottom—in the special box if there is one. The refrigerator door is less cold than the main body of the cabinet and there is usually specially designed storage there for milk, cheese, butter and eggs.

Most foods, especially cheese and cooked meats, will taste better if removed from the refrigerator about 30 minutes before serving. This takes the chill off and allows the flavor to come through.

If you spill anything in the refrigerator, wipe it up immediately before it has time to solidify. Remember this is supposed to be a hygienic storage area—stale spilled food is a perfect breeding ground for bacteria. And keep an eye out for oddments tucked away in corners and see that they are either eaten quickly or thrown out if necessary.

Defrost the fridge regularly unless it does this automatically— it works more efficiently when frost free. Clean it with a weak

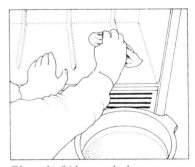

*Clean the fridge regularly*

solution of baking soda in warm water, using a clean cloth. Ordinary soap or detergent tends to leave a penetrating smell which may be absorbed by the stored foods.

## REFRIGERATOR STORAGE

| Food | How to Store | Number of days |
|---|---|---|
| **Cheese** | | |
| Cream or cottage | Original pack, plastic wrap or foil | 7–14 |
| cheese | Covered container, plastic wrap or foil | 2–3 |
| | | |
| **Eggs** | | |
| Fresh in shell | Small end down | 14 |
| Hard-boiled in shell | Uncovered | up to 7 |
| Whites | Covered container | 3–4 |
| Yolks | Covered with water if whole | 2–3 |
| | | |
| **Fats** | Original wrapper, in door compartments | 14–28 |
| | | |
| **Fish** | | |
| Cooked | Covered loosely in plastic wrap or foil. Or place in covered container | 2 |
| Raw | Covered loosely in plastic wrap or foil | 1–2 |
| | | |
| **Fruit and vegetables** | | |
| Hard and pit | | |
| fruits | Lightly wrapped or in the crisper | 3–7 |
| Salad vegetables | Clean and drain, store in crisper or lightly wrapped in plastic wrap or in | |
| | a plastic container | 4–6 |
| Soft fruits | Clean and refrigerate in a covered container | 1–3 |
| Greens | Prepare ready for use. Wrap lightly or place in the crisper | 3–7 |
| | | |
| **Milk** | | |
| Fresh milk | In original container or covered jar | 3–4 |
| Milk puddings, | | |
| custards, etc. | In covered dishes | 2 |
| Cultured milk | In original container | 7 |
| | | |
| **Yeast, fresh** | In loosely tied plastic bag | up to 28 |
| | | |
| **Cooked meats** | | |
| Casseroles | Wrap in foil or plastic wrap or leave in the covered dish they were cooked in | |
| with bacon | or any other covered container | 2 |
| Casseroles | | |
| without bacon | | 3 |
| Roasts | | 2 |
| Ham | | 2–3 |
| Meat pies | | 1 |
| Pâté | | 2 |
| Sliced meat with gravy | | 2–3 |
| Sliced meat without gravy | | 2–4 |
| Stock | | 4 |
| | | |
| **Meat** | | |
| **Uncooked** | | |
| Baked ham: smoked | Wipe surface with clean damp cloth. Cover lightly with plastic wrap or foil. | |
| and unsmoked | Refrigerate right away | 7 |
| vacuum packed | | 10 |
| Bacon slices | Wrap tightly in foil or plastic wrap | |
| Cured pork chops | | |
| and steaks: | | |
| smoked and | | |
| unsmoked | | 10 |
| vacuum packed | | 7 |
| Beef | | 3–5 |
| Ground | | 1–2 |
| Variety meats | | 1–2 |
| Pork, fresh | | 2–4 |
| Sausages | | 3 |
| | | |
| **Poultry** | | |
| Whole fresh | Draw, wash, dry and wrap in plastic wrap or foil. Remove | |
| poultry | wrappings from ready-to-cook birds | 2–3 |
| Cooked poultry | Remove stuffing. Wrap or cover with plastic wrap or foil. | |
| | Refrigerate right away | 2–3 |

# Cooking Techniques

Here are some quick and easy techniques—including broiling and frying—as well as a number of longer cooking methods, like casseroling. Once you have grasped the basics of these you will find them extraordinarily straightforward.

## *A WIDE VARIETY OF TECHNIQUES TO CHOOSE FROM*

When cooking you can use a variety of different techniques from broiling to frying and roasting to poaching. As well as understanding all the techniques you must also bear in mind the type of food that you are going to cook and the time you have to cook it in. Under each technique you will find guidelines as to which foods are best suited to this particular method of preparation, from meats, poultry and fish, to vegetables, grains and beans.

## QUICK AND EASY COOKING METHODS
### BROILING
Broiling is one of the simplest and quickest methods of cooking. It simply involves placing the food under the heat source, turning it and then removing it when cooked. Generally, small pieces of food are broiled like chicken portions, sausages or fish fillets, all of which cook relatively quickly.

To perfect the technique always preheat the broiler before using it. The high temperature sears the surface of the food, sealing in all the juices, before cooking continues. With thick pieces of food, such as steaks or chops, sear both sides, but you do not need to do this with finer foods such as thin cutlet or fillets of fish, ideal foods when you are in a hurry. To speed up cooking time place foods to be seared near the source of heat, then lower the broiler pan for the remainder of the cooking time.

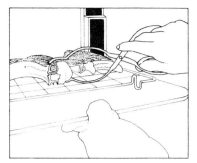

*Turning meat under the broiler*

To make the food taste its best keep it moist throughout broiling; brush it from time to time with oil, melted butter or a marinade. However, do not be tempted to season meat with salt until after it has been cooked as this can toughen it. Test the food while it is cooking to see if it is done.

When broiling chicken and pork, always broil them very thoroughly to ensure that they are cooked through. Steak and lamb, however, can be cooked according to personal preference and to the amount of time available.

Use tongs for turning the food during broiling, and never pierce it with a fork or skewer or you may get hot fat sprayed at you. Always serve broiled foods immediately as they dry out quickly and toughen if kept warm.

*Brushing meat with marinade*

## IDEAL BROILING FOODS
**Beef**—steaks (fillet, rump, sirloin, sirloin strip and T-bone), sausages and beefburgers
**Lamb**—loin chops, cutlets, leg steaks (cut from fillet end), liver and kidneys
**Pork**—tenderloin, spareribs, loin chops, sausages, liver and kidney
**Bacon and Ham**—slices and steaks
**Veal**—fillet (as kabobs), cutlets, loin chops, liver
**Chicken**—breasts, drumsticks, thighs
**Fish**—thick fillets, steaks, small whole fish
**Mushrooms**
**Tomatoes**

## FRYING
Foods can be deep fried, shallow fried or stir fried. It is useful to have all these ways of cooking at your fingertips since they all give quick results and are easy to do once you have mastered the technique. Basically they all depend on two simple principles, which are that you use relatively small pieces of food and that you use hot fat to cook them in.

## DEEP FRYING
A variety of foods can be successfully deep fried from potatoes to cheese, chicken and fish. Indeed, entire meals can be deep fried.

The technique involves heating a large amount of oil, usually vegetable oil, in a solid-based pan or deep-fat fryer, lowering food into it, letting it cook for a few minutes and then taking it out. Here are some steps to deep frying.

### Steps to deep frying
Fill a heavy-based pan no more than two-thirds full of oil. Start heating the oil very gently at first, and then raise the heat. Check the temperature of the oil carefully, either by using a frying thermometer, or test with a cube of stale bread (see below).
- Coat the foods for deep frying with breadcrumbs or batter; this

protects them while being cooked and also prevents moisture from the food leaking into the oil.

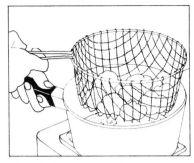

*Deep frying small portions*

- When cooking small portions or pieces of food, lower them into the fat in a wire frying basket; this makes it easier to remove them from the hot fat.
- Always lower the food into the hot oil slowly.
- Once the food is cooked, remove it carefully using a wire basket or a perforated spoon, and drain on paper towels.
- Remove all crumbs and remnants of fried food with a perforated spoon, otherwise they will burn and taint the flavor of the oil. Do not allow water or liquids to get into the fat or it will "spit".
- Turn the heat off as soon as you

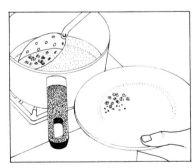

*Removing crumbs after frying*

have finished deep frying, and leave the pan to cool without moving it.
- Once the oil is quite cool, strain it thoroughly, and store in a clean bottle for future use.

*Straining cooled oil for storage*

### Deep frying temperatures
The temperature of hot oil for deep frying varies considerably according to the type of food and on whether it is raw or has already been cooked. Raw food is cooked at a lower temperature than cooked. A frying thermometer is the most accurate method of gauging the heat of the oil; alternatively, use a cube of day-old bread.

### The bread cube method
- If the bread cube sinks to the bottom of the pan of oil and does not frizzle at all, then the oil is not yet hot enough.
- If the bread cube frizzles gently, then the oil has reached about 350°F and you can fry pastry dough and do the first frying of sliced potatoes.
- If a light blue haze rises from the oil and the bread cube browns in 1 minute then the oil has reached about 375°F and is at the right temperature for frying coated fish fillets, croquettes and fruit fritters.
- If a noticeable blue haze rises from the oil and the bread cube browns in 30 seconds, then the oil has reached about 400°F and it is ready for frying small fritters, croûtons, coated cooked foods (such as fish cakes), and the second frying of sliced potatoes.

## SHALLOW FRYING

Shallow frying is another quick and easy method of cooking, although not quite as quick as deep frying. It is ideal for cooking chops, steaks, cutlets, liver, sausages, bacon, eggs and fish. All you need to do is fry the food in a shallow amount of hot fat (about $\frac{1}{2}$–1 inch) over moderate heat. Turn the food once during cooking. You can use a variety of fats from cooking oil, vegetable oil, olive oil, white cooking fat, lard, margarine, butter, or a mixture. If you want to use butter don't use it on its own as it burns at a relatively low temperature. It is advisable to mix it with oil or margarine.

It is best to coat the food before shallow frying it; this helps to protect it from the temperature of the fat and also prevents fragile items, such as fish fillets, from collapsing.

The guidelines for safe and successful shallow frying are very similar to those for deep fat frying, although there are distinct differences. The fat must be heated gently at all times, even during the actual cooking; there is no need to use a fat thermometer to test the heat of the oil, just drop a small piece of stale bread into the hot fat and it should sizzle steadily without spitting. Lower the coated food into the hot fat gently, and turn it during frying with a per-

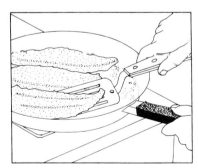

*Turning food during frying*

forated spoon or spatula. (Scoop off any crumbs or remnants of food from the surface of the cooking fat so they don't burn.)

Remove the cooked food with a perforated spoon or spatula and drain thoroughly.

## STIR FRYING

Stir frying is a traditional Chinese method of cooking which has gained tremendous popularity throughout Europe in recent years. It is a quick and versatile technique that can be used for vegetables, meat, fish, rice and noodles. The secret of the technique lies in cutting up the food into uniformly sized small pieces and then cooking them very quickly in oil. The beauty of this method of cooking is that the food retains its shape, texture and taste.

A wok, the traditional Chinese cooking utensil, is the best receptacle to use for stir frying. It is a large, deep metal pan with a completely spherical base and two looped handles.

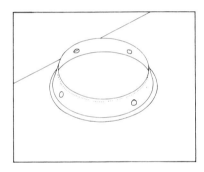

*Metal collar to support wok on ring*

Place the wok directly on the gas or electric ring. (It works better on gas.) You can buy a metal collar which you fit around your cooking ring; it acts as a support for the wok. This makes it easier to move the wok around as the food is cooking, ensuring that each surface of the wok comes in contact with an even temperature; an all-essential fact in stir frying.

When you stir fry foods you'll find that they cook very quickly, so it's important to have everything well prepared in advance. Chop your food up into evenly sized small pieces and, if using meat or fish, coat it in flour. Place the wok

over the heat, preferably standing on a metal collar, and add a few spoonfuls of oil to it. Once the oil is hot, add the finely cut ingredients, either all at once or in stages, depending on the recipe. Garlic, ginger root and other highly flavored ingredients are often used. These should be fried first and then the other ingredients should be added. Tilt the wok backward and forward over the

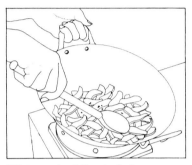

*Tilting wok while stir-frying*

heat while you stir and turn the ingredients with a long-handled spatula until cooked.

## POACHING

This is a subtle cooking technique used for preparing delicate foods which cook quickly. Poaching describes the gentle agitation of a hot liquid by natural movement of the liquid. Odd bubbles occur, but not the steady bubbling that one associates with simmering. The choice of cooking liquid depends

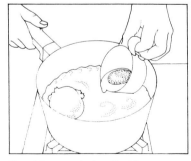

*Poaching eggs in hot liquid*

to a large extent on what you are poaching; for fish, a court bouillon or wine would be most

257

appropriate; for meat, a vegetable or meat stock or wine; for eggs, water.

When poaching eggs and quenelles, add them to the liquid, once it is hot and quivering. Fish fillets, on the other hand, should be put into the pan with cold liquid and then brought to the correct temperature for poaching. Fish is usually poached covered, but many other foods are poached without a lid.

**Suitable poaching foods**
Boned and skinned chicken breasts
Meat and fish quenelles
Fish fillets and thin fish cutlets
Shellfish, such as scallops
Eggs
Gnocchi
Soft fruits, such as peaches

## STEAMING
This is a quick and nutritious way of cooking food and is generally applied to vegetables. All you need is a simple metal steamer which you place in a saucepan. Pour in

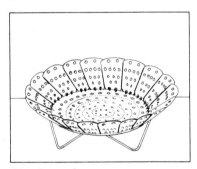

*Simple metal steamer*

boiling water to just beneath the steamer, add the vegetables and cover with a lid. The vegetables will cook in the steam and, unlike when they are cooked in water, very little nutritious value will be lost. Steaming is also an excellent way of reheating food.

## SLOW BUT EASY
There are a number of cooking techniques that fall under this heading: roasting, barbecuing, pot roasting, casseroling, boiling, poaching and steaming. They are

all easy and once the cooking is underway require little supervision.

## ROASTING
Roasting is certainly a very effortless way of cooking. Once the food is in the oven, you can virtually forget about it, apart from giving it the occasional baste. However, roasting is only suitable for prime, tender cuts of meat, and for poultry and most game.

Roasting is a direct heat method of cooking, and the food needs to be kept moist throughout cooking. Before putting the roast or bird into the oven spread it with fat (duck is the only exception to this rule—it is naturally fatty and should be pricked with a skewer before roasting). With meat, poultry or game that dries out quickly, like chicken, veal, venison, pheasant and grouse, it is advisable to cover it with strips of

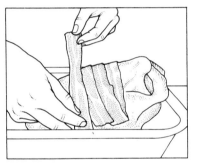

*Adding moisture with strips of bacon*

bacon. This gives added moisture.

Veal, lamb and pork can be boned, stuffed and rolled before roasting as can poultry and game. Use a well-flavored stuffing which will moisten and enhance the flavor of the meat during cooking. Stuffing makes the meat go further, but it takes longer to cook.

Another way of keeping the food moist during roasting is to cover it with cooking foil, dull side up; the foil can be removed either for the first or last part of cooking time to allow the food to brown. When using foil, add on an extra few minutes cooking time.

Place your meat, poultry or feathered game on a grid or rack in a roasting tin. This is important since it makes it easy to baste the food during cooking and to roast vegetables under it.

Roast in a preheated oven for the given time, basting with the

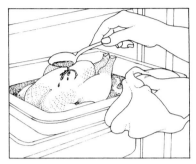

*Basting poultry during cooking*

juices and fat in the roasting pan from time to time. Test to see whether the meat is done. Push a skewer right into the meat, take it out and feel it; when it is hot to the touch the meat is done. Beef, lamb and game are often served underdone, but chicken, turkey and pork should always be well cooked. If you are using a meat thermometer, insert the thermometer in the thickest part of the meat before it goes into the oven, making sure that it does not touch the bone. All roast meats are

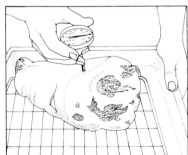

*Inserting a meat thermometer*

much easier to carve or cut if they are first allowed to "settle" after cooking. Remove from the oven and keep warm for about 15 minutes until ready to serve.

**What to roast**
**Beef**—whole fillet, standing or rolled rib, sirloin tip, eye of round or rolled rump
**Lamb**—leg, best end of neck, breast, shoulder, loin
**Pork**—tenderloin, shoulder, loin, ham
**Veal**—loin, leg, shoulder, breast, best end of neck
**Poultry**—chicken, Cornish hen, turkey, duck, guinea fowl
**Game** (young)—wild duck, pheasant, pigeon, grouse, venison.

**Roasting times and methods**
There are three basic methods of roasting (see chart for methods and timing).

**Method A**
The meat is first roasted at 450°F for 15 minutes, and the heat is then reduced to 350°F for the remainder of the cooking time.

**Method B**
The meat is roasted at 375°F for the whole cooking time.

**Method C**
The meat is roasted at 325°F for the whole cooking time. This long slow method of roasting is most suitable for large turkeys, and for roasts which are not considered prime roasts like, for example, rump roast, picnic shoulder of pork and breast of lamb.

Remember to allow extra roasting time if foil and/or stuffing are used, and to weigh roasts and birds *after* stuffing in order to calculate accurate cooking time.

# BARBECUING

Barbecuing is a wonderfully easy way of cooking food out-of-doors. It lends itself perfectly to entertaining, since you can get delicious results with the minimum of effort.

A barbecue is like an outdoor broiler, depending on charcoal for its fuel. The grill needs to be heated first and then the meat or fish which is to be cooked is placed either directly on the grill or first in foil and then on the grill.

**Preparing food for barbecuing**
- Always use good-quality meat; poor quality meat does not cook very well on a barbecue
- Marinate the food for at least 1 hour before barbecuing it. This enhances its flavor and ensures moistness
- Allow chilled foods to come to room temperature before putting them on the barbecue; chilled foods give off moisture which can cause spitting
- Brush foods with oil to prevent them from sticking to the barbecue grill
- Season meat and poultry with salt after cooking as salt draws off the meat juices
- Watch food carefully once it is on the barbecue, and test from time to time
- As well as barbecuing directly on the barbecue grill, food can also be wrapped in foil and cooked either on the grill or in the coals

**Good foods for barbecues**
**Beef**—lean steaks, good stewing (kabobs)
**Lamb**—chops, leg steaks, fillet (kabobs)
**Pork**—chops, spareribs, tenderloin (kabobs)
**Bacon and sausages**
**Veal**—chops, leg fillet (kabobs)
**Chicken**—drumsticks, thighs, split breasts
**Variety meats**—kidneys
**Fish**—firm-textured fish such as swordfish, salmon, halibut, monkfish and cod; whole fish such

| | Methods A & B | Method C |
|---|---|---|
| **Beef** (whole fillet, rump, sirloin, standing or rolled ribs, eye of round) | 15–20 minutes for every 1 lb plus 20 minutes | 30 minutes for every 1 lb plus 30 minutes |
| **Lamb** (leg, shoulder, loin, best end of neck, breast) | 20–25 minutes for every 1 lb plus 25 minutes | 35–40 minutes for every 1 lb plus 40 minutes |
| **Pork** (shoulder, ham, loin) | 30 minutes for every 1 lb plus 30 minutes | 40–45 minutes for every 1 lb plus 45 minutes |
| **Veal** (loin, leg, shoulder, breast, best end of neck) | 25–30 minutes for every 1 lb plus 30 minutes | 35–40 minutes for every 1 lb plus 40 minutes |
| **Chicken** (whole bird) | 20 minutes for every 1 lb plus 20 minutes | 30 minutes for every 1 lb plus 30 minutes |
| **Turkey** 5–8 lb | 20 minutes for every 1 lb plus 20 minutes | 30 minutes for every 1 lb plus 30 minutes |
| 8–14 lb | — | 20 minutes for every 1 lb plus 20 minutes |
| Over 14 lb | — | 15 minutes for every 1 lb plus 15 minutes |
| **Duck** | 15 minutes for every 1 lb plus 15 minutes | 20 minutes for every 1 lb plus 20 minutes |

as bass, trout, mackerel and sardines
**Shellfish**—split lobster, large shrimp and scallops
**Vegetables**—corn on the cob is particularly good
**Fruit**—particularly bananas, cubes or slices threaded on skewers, in their skins or skinned and wrapped in foil

## POT ROASTING

This is a one-pot method of cooking larger pieces of meat, whole birds and fish. It involves the minimum of preparation and long, slow cooking. Simply brown the meat all over in hot fat in a heavy pan, remove from the pan while browning vegetables in the fat. Place the meat on top of the vegetables; add a little liquid, cover and cook in a moderate oven.

For an even quicker pot roast use the cold start method and simply put all the ingredients in the pot at once and place in the oven. The cooking time will be longer.

**Good foods to pot roast**
Brisket or chuck of beef; boned, stuffed and rolled breast of lamb or veal; stuffed hearts; rolled shoulder of venison; and chicken.

## CASSEROLING

With very little preparation and long, slow cooking you have a dish that can be prepared in advance and then reheated as required. Casseroles freeze very well and can be brought to the table in their casserole dish. In short, they save you a great deal of time.

There are two types of casseroles—brown (fry start) and white (cold start). To make a brown casserole, fry small chunks of meat in fat until browned all over. Remove and drain on paper towels. Add vegetables to the pan and fry until well coated. Add seasoning, stir in some flour, put back the meat and add some liquid. Cover tightly and simmer either on top of the stove or in a slow to medium oven until tender.

A white casserole is quicker to prepare. Simply layer the same ingredients as for a brown casserole into your dish and place in a slow to moderate oven, cooking until tender.

## GOOD FOODS FOR CASSEROLING

**Beef**—shoulder, chuck, blade, rump, brisket, round
**Lamb**—breast, middle or best end of neck, loin. Shoulder and leg may be cooked as roasts or boned and cubed
**Pork**—spareribs, loin and shoulder chops and tenderloin. Ham steaks and roasts and cooked, cubed ham
**Veal**—breast, neck, shoulder, shin, leg, knuckle
**Variety meats**—ox and sheep's kidneys; calves' and sheep hearts; lambs' and sheep's tongues; oxtail
**Poultry**—roasts
**Game**—grouse, rabbit
**Beans**

## BOILING

Boiling is an easy technique that involves covering the food in a liquid, heating it until it comes to the boiling point and then, more often than not, lowering the heat and simmering it. The cooking time will depend on what type of food is being cooked as well as its size. You can boil meat, fish, grains, beans and vegetables.

**Boiling meat and poultry**
Tie or truss joints and poultry carefully with string, so that they retain their shape during cooking. Smoked and salty ham should be soaked in cold water beforehand and the soaking water should be discarded. This gets rid of some of the saltiness. Place the meat or poultry in a large pan with enough cold water to cover. Bring to a boil. Lower the heat and remove any surface scum with a slotted spoon. Add chopped onion, some chopped peeled root vegetables, a bay leaf, a small bunch of parsley and a few peppercorns. (Add salt at the end of the cooking time or

*Removing surface scum*

the meat will toughen; but don't add it to pickled or cured meat.) Cover the pan tightly and simmer very gently. The exact time depends on the type of meat; with boiling fowl it depends on age. As an approximate guide, allow 30 minutes for every 1 lb, plus an extra 30 minutes.

**Suitable meats for boiling**
**Beef**—brisket or rump
**Lamb**—leg of mutton
**Pork**—ham hocks, spareribs, neck bones, side of bacon, shoulder butt
**Poultry**—boiling fowl
**Grains**
**Beans**
**Vegetables**

# How to Cook Vegetables For Maximum Goodness

The nutritive value of vegetables is greatly reduced by storage, preservation, preparation and cooking, and therefore all vegetables should be prepared carefully to ensure that they retain as much goodness as possible.

Choose fresh vegetables which are in season and therefore at their best (and least expensive). Frozen and canned vegetables can be used, but try and avoid canned vegetables. These have often been canned and left in salty water for so long that they have lost their nutritional value.

The first essential is that vegetables should be as fresh as possible and used as soon as possible. If they must be stored for a short while, keep them correctly to prevent nutrient loss. For example, store potatoes and root vegetables in paper in a cool dark place, salad greens and other vegetables in the refrigerator.

Vegetables contain more nutrients when they are raw than they do after cooking, so try to eat as many raw vegetables as possible. However, a more varied diet is possible with cooked vegetables, and some vegetables need to be cooked to make them edible and make the nutrients available, such as globe artichokes and asparagus. The main purpose of cooking vegetables is to soften the cellular tissue and to gelatinize any starch so that it can be more easily digested.

Often the tastiest and most nutritious parts of the vegetable are thrown away during preparation. The most obvious example of this wastage is the peeling of potatoes and root vegetables, as most of the nutrients are concentrated just below the skin and peeling removes a high

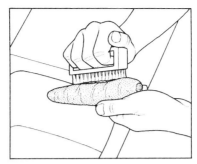
*Scrub root vegetables rather than peel*

proportion of the goodness. Instead of peeling, they can be well washed and scrubbed. Many other vegetables are also trimmed unnecessarily—only damaged parts, roots and tough ends need be removed. For instance, the stalks of green vegetables can be chopped and cooked with the leaves; the green tops of leeks are just as tasty as the white stems; the leaves from a cauliflower can be cooked as well as the head; and mushrooms may be wiped instead of peeled. Very young peas and broad beans can be cooked in their pods, like snow peas. Always keep the cooking liquid from vegetables, as it is the most nutritious part. A lot of the vitamins from the vegetables will have been leeched out into it. Use if for soups, stews or just drink it.

After peeling or shredding, vitamin C is rapidly destroyed by oxidation, either directly or by the action of an enzyme present in the plant tissues. This loss can be kept to a minimum by preparing vegetables immediately before use and by plunging them into boiling water at the start of the cooking process—this will destroy the enzyme. If vegetables must be prepared in advance, they should be covered immediately and kept in the refrigerator until required. Root vegetables that have been prepared can be immersed in a saucepan of cold water to prevent the air turning them brown.

During cooking, nutrients are destroyed mainly by the passage of

soluble minerals and vitamins from the tissues into the cooking water, and the destruction of some vitamins by heat. Thus, some vitamin B and C are lost into the water, as they are heat sensitive and water soluble. Therefore vegetables should be cooked in the

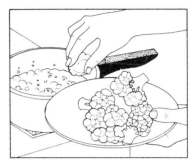
*Plunge vegetables into boiling water*

minimum amount of boiling water, or steamed, and the cooking water should be used, so that nutrients are not wasted. Cover the pan so that the vegetables will cook more quickly, and the ones at the top will cook in the steam. Cook vegetables for the minimum amount of time so that they are only just tender, still a bright color and slightly crisp.

Overcooked vegetables will have less nutrients as well as being dull and soggy, and the amount of fiber will be reduced. Never add baking soda to improve the color, as this destroys vitamin C.

Vegetables should always be served as soon as possible; keeping them warm destroys the vitamin C as well as the bright color.

# TRICKS OF THE TRADE

Food should look as good as it tastes, and vice versa. Presentation is very much part of the art of cooking, and it is eye appeal which first sets the taste buds working. Some garnishes and decorations are very time-consuming to prepare, but many are both quick and easy. Ideally the garnish or decoration on any dish should be edible, and echo the ingredients in that particular dish. Garnishes and decorations can also help to balance texture and color; you would use crisp garnishes with smooth, otherwise soft foods, and rich greens or reds to offset cream-colored sauces. Keep these finishing touches as simple and uncluttered as possible; the food should never look fussy or contrived.

## FINISHING TOUCHES

- If a colorful ingredient is used in a dish, keep a little back before cooking to use as a garnish—a ring or two of green or red pepper, a few peas, feathery tops from fresh carrots, celery leaves or fennel
- Leave the small fresh green leaves on cauliflower when cooking it; it looks much more attractive
- Browned sliced almonds add a crunch to cooked white fish, and a pleasing contrast to broiled whole fish, such as trout

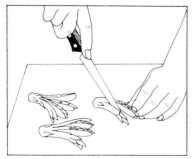

*Fanning out asparagus tips*

- Use asparagus tips fanned out on top of a cooked chicken breast or lamb cutlet
- Finely snipped crisp bacon adds a pleasing savory crunch on top of creamed potato
- Sprinkle a mixture of oven-dried breadcrumbs and finely grated lemon rind over cooked green vegetables, such as broccoli
- Give a mimosa garnish to pale vegetables such as cauliflower or Jerusalem artichokes. Chop the whites of hard-boiled eggs finely and sieve the yolks. Sprinkle the white over first of all, and then the sieved yolk
- Black lumpfish roe looks stunning on yellow or cream-colored dishes, such as egg salad or noodles in a cream sauce
- Chop set aspic jelly with a wet knife; use to garnish roasts of cold meat or cold fish such as salmon
- If a dish is to be served with a side-serving of mayonnaise or hollandaise sauce, fill a large hollowed out tomato or half a lemon with the chosen sauce

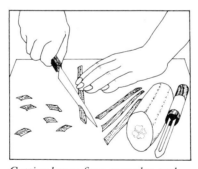

*Cutting leaves from cucumber peel*

- Cut leaves from cucumber peel to garnish fish mousses and pâtés
- Peel carrots. Using a potato peeler, cut thin spirals of carrot; plunge into a bowl of iced water. Use to garnish portions of pâté and terrines
- Put orange and lemon rind into the blender with granulated sugar; blend until smooth. Use

for sprinkling over the top of fruit pies and crumbles

*Cutting angelica with dampened scissors*

- When using angelica and glacé cherries for decoration, you will obtain a neater finish if you chop both of them with dampened kitchen scissors
- Use mint sprigs for garnishing portions of melon or grapefruit. For a truly sparkling finish, dip the mint sprigs in beaten egg white and then in sugar
- A little meringue shell filled with a whirl of cream makes a pretty garnish for a fruit mousse or fool
- Try a curl of semisweet chocolate for a special ice cream

*Cutting curls of semisweet chocolate*

or mousse; use chocolate that is firm but not chilled, and form the curls using a potato peeler
- Sandwich vanilla wafers together with plain chocolate and leave until set. Use to decorate trifles and large mousses

● Clever doiley-dusting looks most effective on plain sponge cakes. Use confectioner's sugar

*Dusting confectioner's sugar over a doiley*

to dust over a doiley; and then dust cocoa or chocolate powder over another doiley.

## ADD A DASH OF FLAVOR
● For a strong orange flavor, use frozen concentrated orange juice rather than freshly squeezed orange juice
● Add an extra piquant flavor to canned soups: a dash of white wine to fish or chicken soups, and a dash of sherry to oxtail and other rich brown soups
● If you are making up a salad which contains quite a sizeable quantity of fruit, use orange juice in the dressing rather than white wine vinegar—it is less harsh
● Use chopped fresh coriander as a garnish for soups which respond to a spicy addition; it is good with carrot, mushroom and Jerusalem artichoke
● For potato salad, pour the prepared dressing over the potatoes while they are still warm—for an unusual flavor add a dash of Pernod
● Cook vegetables in real chicken stock for a really rich flavor

## PRESENTATION
Here are some garnishes and decorations which have that extra panache; they are simple to make but ultra effective.

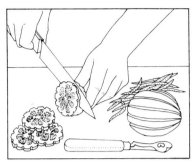

*Slicing oranges into cartwheels*

### Orange or lemon cartwheels
Using a canapé cutter, cut down the length of the lemon or orange, taking strips out of the rind. Cut the fruit into slices. Use to decorate desserts or drinks.

### Stuffed cucumber rings
Cut thickish slices of cucumber and hollow out the centers. Fill with cream cheese, finely chopped red pepper and chopped spring onion. Chill and then cut into thinner slices. An attractive garnish for Parma ham and salami.

---

### CRAFTY TRICKS
● Not enough cream to go around? Fold whisked egg whites into heavy cream.
● If a soup is too salty, add a peeled potato or a good slice of French bread; simmer for a few minutes to allow some of the salt to be absorbed.
● To mend a cracked pie crust, brush all over the cracks with beaten egg white. Return to the oven for a few minutes until the egg white has sealed the cracks.
● If you want to make mayonnaise or white sauce go further, thin it with light cream, yogurt or sour cream.

---

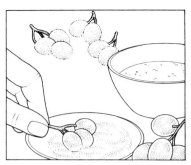

*Dipping fruit in frosting mixture*

### Frosted fruits
They can be used as a most attractive garnish for both sweet and savory dishes. You simply dip the fruits in a mixture of egg white and confectioner's sugar. Grapes and strawberries look particularly attractive frosted. Use them on platters of cold meat or as a border garnish for elaborate cakes.

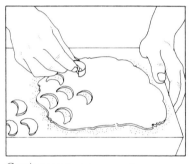

*Cutting out pastry crescents*

### Pastry crescents
Roll out puff pastry trimmings and cut out small crescent shapes. Glaze with beaten egg and bake until golden. Use to garnish fish dishes.

### Gherkin fans
Hold the gherkin firmly on a chopping board at one end. Using a small sharp knife cut a series of tongue-shaped slices along the length of the gherkin; do not cut right through the stem end. Fan out each pickle fan. Use to garnish platters of cold meat and savory mousses.

263

# MAKING THE MOST OF LEFTOVERS

Leftovers are bonus foods. All the hard work of selecting, doing the basic preparation and cooking have already been taken care of. Some dishes actually taste better on the second day. This is particularly true of soups, casseroles like lasagna and chili, and very spicy foods. The extra day gives the ingredients and spices more time to blend and mellow together.

But plainer foods, like roast beef, chicken, lamb, pork and cooked vegetables that wind up as leftovers may need a little help. The challenge is to make such leftovers taste like dishes in their own right, not merely a repeat of yesterday's repast.

What follows are some interesting ideas for making the most of those plainer leftovers, suggestions for dishes that actually call for precooked meats and vegetables.

## MEAT
So many delicious dishes can be made with a small amount of leftover roast meat or poultry that it is worth cooking a roast or whole chicken just for a few.

**Beef** The best beef for leftovers is that which has been roasted rare, leaving the cold meat pink and juicy. Take it off the bone for storage, removing any excess fat as you work. Fat is never tasty reheated, however much you like it on the outside of a roast. When grinding cooked beef, use the coarsest blade you can, or preferably chop the meat finely with knives; finely ground cooked beef is inclined to turn into a paste.

When it comes to using up cooked beef, few people will say no to a simple plate of cold sliced meat. But if you are bored with that, or there are only messy ends

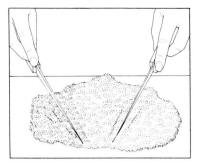
*Chopping meat finely with knives*

left, try what the British call "bubble and squeak". You can use leftover cabbage, but it is best made with freshly cooked cabbage that is still crisp. Fry the roughly chopped cooked cabbage lightly in butter, add small slices of beef and heat through with some of the leftover gravy and some seasonings like Worcestershire sauce and perhaps sliced pickles or pickled onions. It will squeak and bubble as it cooks, and will taste delicious.

*Use leftovers as a stuffing*

Alternatively use the beef to stuff green peppers or giant tomatoes, onions or baked potatoes. Mixed with a spicy tomato sauce and rice, or the middle of the potato, it is almost worth cooking beef especially to have some left over.

**Chicken** The best chicken meat for reheated dishes comes from a boiled chicken, as it remains moister than a roast bird, but cold chicken is always acceptable in a new dish. A chicken pie, with a little ham or bacon and a puff pastry top gives no hint that it is

leftover meat. A savory chicken pancake, the filling made with a good béchamel sauce and perhaps a few mushrooms and herbs to add flavor to a small amount of meat, makes a perfect evening snack. Chicken does not grind up well, the flesh is too fine and turns paste-like in a grinder, so always chop or shred the meat for reheating.

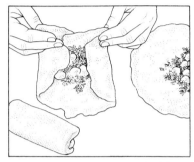
*Leftovers make good pancake fillings*

Never throw away the carcass and giblets from a chicken. They make excellent stock or soup, especially if there is a little meat left on the bones. Add some finely chopped vegetables or rice to bulk out the soup.

**Ham** Is perfect reheated. A small ham, boiled or baked for one meal, leaves ideal amounts of meat to put with chicken in a pie, to make a sauce for tagliatelle with cream and herbs or to chop for an omelette. Thickly sliced boiled ham is also good lightly fried and served with a fruit glaze.

**Lamb** Take care not to overcook lamb the first time around. As long as it is young and tender, lamb is best served when still lightly pink in the center, and cooking it like this will mean that it does not become hard and chewy when reheated. If you are not planning to eat it right away, the leftover meat will keep best if removed from the bone. Cut it off the bone in the largest chunks possible, wrap tightly in foil and keep in the refrigerator for up to four days.

Do not grind, slice or cube it until you are ready to use it; the more cut surfaces there are exposed to the air, the more quickly it will go bad.

For grinding, the leaner leg is best, although the shoulder meat is sometimes sweeter and many people prefer it. Cut most of the fat off shoulder meat before grinding or slicing for reheating. Shepherd's pie is the traditional English way of using up roast lamb, and there are many exciting dishes from Greece and the eastern end of the Mediterranean based on lamb. Moussaka is the classic, while stuffed eggplant is a delicious variation. In the North African tradition, you could try meatballs seasoned with garlic and coriander—make tiny ones to serve as an unusual snack with drinks. Apart from mint, the traditional herbs to put with lamb are garlic, rosemary and thyme, while ground coriander and a good garam masala powder will spice it appropriately.

**Pork** leftover pork is more limited in use, as it should always be thoroughly cooked in the first place and reheating is inclined to harden it. It is best combined with other meats in a meat loaf or meatballs, or layered up with cabbage leaves and tomato sauce to make a Dutch-style stuffed cabbage dish.

# VEGETABLES

Large whole vegetables that cannot be bought divided sometimes pose problems in a small household, but there are many ways of getting around them.

**Avocado** Will go black if cut and left, so if you eat one half with vinaigrette, you must do something with the other half right away to keep it in good condition. Puréed, seasoned with a little lemon juice and covered with

$\frac{1}{4}$ inch of oil, it will keep in the refrigerator for a few days. Mix the purée with cream cheese or sour cream and seasonings for a dip to serve with snacks and drinks, or a Mexican-style meal.

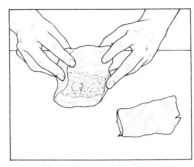

*Use cabbage leaves for wrapping*

**Cabbage** When you have eaten half a Savoy-type cabbage as a vegetable, use the other half layered up with sausagemeat and tomato sauce in a stuffed cabbage dish, or to make cabbage rolls (*dolmas*). White cabbage keeps extremely well in a cool place and makes excellent coleslaw.

**Celery** A whole head of celery can go on forever for one or two people, so just use the inside stalks for salad. The outer stalks are good braised, or for soup or chopped in a stew. Chop the leaves for garnishes.

**Eggplant** Is good sliced and broiled or fried, in a ratatouille or a moussaka. A half eggplant also forms the base for a main meal if stuffed with a good meaty filling.

**Lettuce** The crisp varieties keep best, even if they do look bigger than the traditional roundhead soft-leaved variety. Iceberg lettuce keeps particularly well—you can just slice off what is needed for any meal and pop the rest back in the refrigerator.

**Peppers** Green, red and yellow peppers are excellent cooked, in casseroles, and in salads. Half a pepper or some leftover chopped

pepper will keep in the refrigerator for several days.

**Pumpkin** May not be something you want to eat every day, but it is fun to have once in a season. You can use it as a vegetable, baked with the roast or fried in butter. It can also be used to make a sweet pie, puréed and spiced.

**Zucchini** A large zucchini may look a giant if you face it on your own, but you can use it in many different ways. Peel and bake some of it with a roast for a really tasty, seasonal vegetable, then stuff the rest with ground leftovers later in the week. Cover the cut surface tightly with plastic wrap and it will keep for several days. For a change, blanch it and use in a salad.

# Eat Well, Eat Wisely

Some people already eat healthfully but most of us could improve our diet by aiming to eat less fat, particularly saturated fats, sugar and salt and consume more dietary fiber. There is such a wide variety of natural ingredients to choose from for a healthful diet, that eating well and wisely will always be interesting and exciting.

## *INGREDIENTS FOR HEALTHFUL EATING*

### *MEAT*

In order to maintain a healthful, balanced diet, there is no need to become a complete vegetarian. There is, however, no need to eat meat every day. Three to four times a week should be enough, and then only at one meal during the day.

Meat is an excellent source of first-class protein, which means that it does not have to be combined with any other ingredient in order to give you the right type of protein that your body needs.

Meat, and especially liver, is a rich source of B vitamins, in particular vitamin B12 which is essential for healthy red blood cells. Red meats and variety cuts are rich in iron and the lighter meats in potassium.

Containing no carbohydrate or dietary fiber, all meats, even the leanest looking, do contain some fat. The fat in meats like lamb, pork and beef is mostly the saturated type, so try to eat less of these; choose lean cuts and eat more poultry and game, which are relatively low in fat.

Try to eat liver or kidneys once every two weeks so that you benefit from their high iron content.

If possible, avoid all types of processed meats. These have a high salt, and very often high fat, content and most contain preservatives and other artificial ingredients.

Too many salty or smoked foods are not to be recommended, but a little ham or bacon occasionally will do no harm. Buy the leaner cuts and, for the best flavor and texture, cook them yourself.

Many people buy sausages for a quick and easy meal. Before buying, check the meat content on the label, or ask your butcher exactly what his recipe for sausages contains. Avoid the pink colored, smooth textured varieties. Look, instead, for the natural colored, herb-flecked types. Most sausages contain preservative.

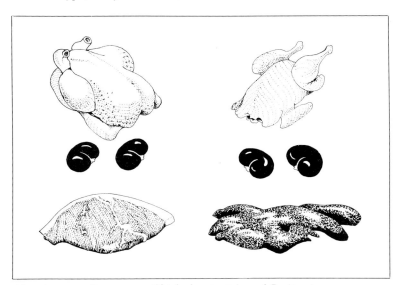

*Meat is an excellent source of high class protein and B vitamins*

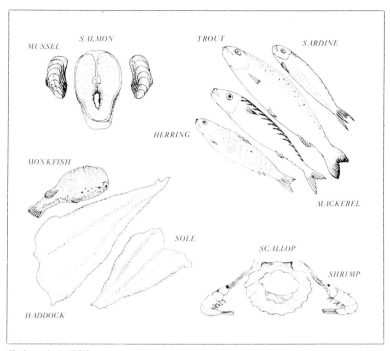

*Fish and shellfish are protein-packed, and white fish is very low in fat*

# VEGETABLES

Fresh vegetables have a large part to play in a healthful diet. The different types provide a wide variety of vitamins and minerals, and all provide significant amounts of dietary fiber. If a selection are served at each meal, sometimes raw in a salad and sometimes cooked, you will obtain the best possible range of nutrients.

The vitamin most associated with vegetables is vitamin C, and this is found in the largest amounts in the green, leafy types.

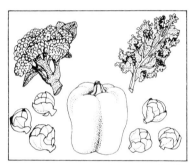

*Green vegetables, rich in vitamin C*

Broccoli, Brussels sprouts, kale and green peppers contain the most, closely followed by cabbage,

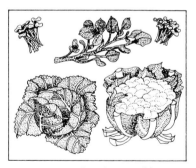

*More vitamin C rich vegetables*

cauliflower, mustard and cress and watercress. Potatoes are another good source and other types of vegetables contain smaller amounts.

Carotene, which is converted by the body into vitamin A, is to be found most often in vegetables

Most packaged meat dinners also contain a lot of fat. They are made with white flour and fillings may contain coloring and almost certainly preservatives and artificial flavorings. It is best to make them yourself.

Some butchers make their own pâtés from only natural ingredients. Other bought pâtés are not so nutritious. Read the labels and, if in doubt, make your own.

## FISH

Fish and shellfish are a superb source of high quality, first-class protein and, like meat, need not be combined with other foods in order to supply the body with exactly the right type of protein that it needs.

There are basically two types of fish—white and oily. Both contain little or no carbohydrate and no fiber.

White fish are one of the few foods that contain iodine. They have an exceptionally low fat content since their natural oils are contained only in the liver.

The fat in oily fish is distributed throughout the flesh. It has a high proportion of poly-unsaturated fat and contains valuable amounts of vitamins A and D.

Most fish also contain small amounts of B vitamins, and varying amounts of the mineral zinc, which is found in only a few foods. Many shellfish are a good source of iron.

Fish products such as batter or bread-coated fish tend to be expensive; their coating is made from refined crumbs and often contains artificial coloring and in some cases preservative. It is better to coat and cook fresh fish fillets yourself, which is healthier and more economical.

Smoked fish should be eaten only occasionally. Not only does it have a high salt content, but some varieties such as mackerel and kippers are often artificially colored.

267

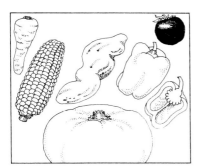

*Vegetables high in carotene*

that are red or orange colored. Carrots in particular, are a good source, as are red peppers, pumpkin, tomatoes, corn and sweet potatoes. Green vegetables which also supply significant amounts include broccoli, chicory,

*Green vegetables high in carotene*

kale, spinach, mustard, watercress and avocados.

The B vitamins are also found in vegetables. Important amounts of vitamin B1 (thiamin) are contained in avocados, globe and Jerusalem artichokes, asparagus, broccoli, kale, mushrooms,

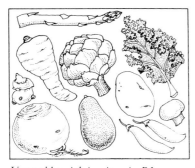

*Vegetables rich in vitamin B1*

parsnips, peas, potatoes and turnips.

Vitamin B2 (riboflavin) can be found in asparagus, French beans,

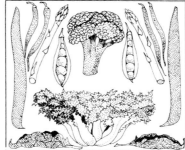

*Vegetables rich in vitamin B2*

broccoli, chicory, peas and spinach.

There is no vitamin D in any vegetable only tiny amounts if any, of vitamin E.

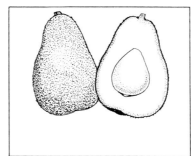

*Avocados contain vitamin E*

Vitamin K is found in varying amounts in all green vegetables.

The main mineral to be found in vegetables is calcium. There are

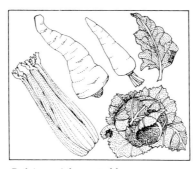

*Calcium-rich vegetables*

large amounts in cabbage and all leafy green vegetables, carrots, celery, spinach and parsnips. Iron is also to be found in green vegetables, in particular spinach and watercress. Mushrooms and peas are also good sources.

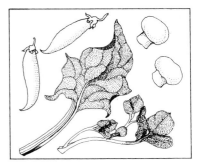

*Vegetables high in iron*

Most vegetables contain potassium, zinc and other minerals.

Carbohydrate is present in all vegetables, but the amounts vary widely. It is lowest in the leafy types and the seed-filled vegetables, such as cucumber and squash. There are moderate amounts of carbohydrate in

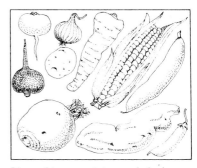

*Vegetables containing carbohydrate*

turnips and onions, and large amounts in potatoes, sweet potatoes, parsnips, beets, peas, broad beans and corn.

The only vegetable to contain more than a trace of fat is the avocado, and this fat is unsaturated. All vegetables, therefore, can be included in large amounts in a healthful diet.

Of the processed vegetables that

are available, frozen are more nutritious than canned. They have been quickly blanched and frozen, thus preserving as much of the vitamin content as possible.

Canned vegetables have often been cooked for a longer time and, in many cases, they are put into salted and sugared water. Their nutritional content can be lower than that of fresh vegetables. (However, if you feel that your store cupboard would be incomplete without a few cans of vegetables for emergency use, read the labels when buying.) Some are now packed without added salt and sugar.

# DRIED BEANS

Dried beans have been used throughout the world for many centuries, but it is only recently that they have become an alternative protein food in the West.

In a vegetarian diet, beans are an important source of protein, but to make the most of this they must be eaten with grain products. Proteins are made up of chains of substances known as amino acids. The amino acid chains in animal proteins (meat, fish, eggs, dairy products) are similar to those in our own bodies. When they are eaten alone, they provide all the amino acids that we need. The

proteins found in beans are lacking in certain amino acids. These, however, are to be found in grain products. Therefore, a meal containing both beans and grains will provide protein that is just as good as a meat or fish meal.

Grain products to serve with beans include wholewheat bread pasta, bulgur wheat, buckwheat, oats and cornmeal.

Because of their need to be

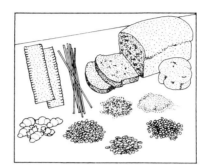

*Grains and beans to serve together*

eaten with other ingredients in a meal, beans are referred to as a "second-class" protein food, but this should not be considered in any way to their detriment.

The one exception to this rule is the soybean, which contains the right type of protein in order to be served alone.

All beans contain the B group vitamins, thiamin, riboflavin and niacin. Most contain significant amounts of iron, potassium and calcium.

All but soybeans are fairly high

in carbohydrates; and where the others contain only a trace of fat, soybeans contain 18–22% but this fat is mostly the unsaturated type.

There are many different types of beans available at the moment and they can be bought from health food shops, ethnic shops and supermarkets. They include the large white butter beans, small white haricot beans and the pale green flageolets. There are four types of kidney bean: red, brown, black and the white kidney or cannellini beans. Black-eyed peas are small, kidney shaped and ivory with a black spot. Chick peas are round, with a slight point at one end and are usually cream colored, although red and black varieties can be found.

The two smallest varieties are the maroon colored aduki beans and green mung (or moong) beans.

Pinto beans are a speckly grey-pink color and kidney shaped.

Soybeans are round and ivory or black colored, becoming peanut shaped on soaking.

Split red lentils are still the most popular. There are also tiny brown Indian lentils, tiny grey ones, sometimes called puy, and slightly larger green or Egyptian lentils. All these types are sold whole and are eliptical in shape. Some Indian shops also sell white lentils.

All beans should be stored in airtight containers, preferably in a

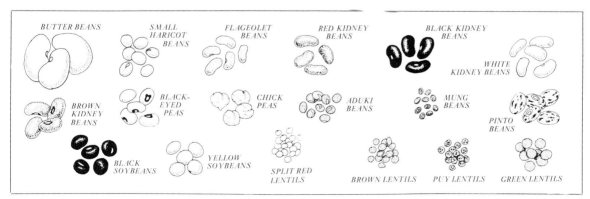

*Beans are an important source of protein in a vegetarian diet*

cool, dark cupboard. They will keep for up to six months, after which, their skins toughen.

Apart from variations of timing, the cooking process for all beans is the same. First of all, they must be soaked, either overnight or by the quick-soak method.

If certain types of beans are not properly cooked they can cause stomach upsets. These include all types of kidney beans, pinto beans, flageolets, haricot and aduki beans. To render them harmless, they must at some time during their cooking process be boiled vigorously for at least 10 minutes. It is a good idea to build this into the soaking method when cooking any beans, so that it becomes an unforgettable habit.

To soak overnight, simply cover the beans with cold water. The next morning, drain them, bring to the boil in fresh water and boil for 10 minutes. Drain. Cook with fresh water.

For the quick-soak method, put the beans into a saucepan and cover with cold water. Bring to the boil and boil for 10 minutes. Cover the pan tightly and leave the beans in the same water for 2 hours. Drain and cook in fresh water for the specified time.

After soaking, simmer the beans in fresh water until they are tender. Mung and aduki beans need 45 minutes to 1 hour. Black-eyed peas need 1 hour. Kidney beans, haricot beans and flageolet need 2 hours and chick peas and soybeans up to 3 hours.

These times can be speeded up by using a pressure cooker.

Lentils and split peas need no soaking. (Red lentils and green and yellow split peas will cook to a purée in about 45 minutes. Whole lentils need 45 minutes to 1 hour to become soft.)

# SOY PRODUCTS

The versatile soybean forms the base for many products which help to add protein to vegetarian and vegan (non-dairy) diets.

## TAMARI SAUCE

This is a natural soy sauce made only from fermented soybeans and sea salt. (The cheaper kinds of soy sauce are made from soybean extracts and contain caramel.) Tamari sauce can be used to flavor Chinese and Japanese dishes, salad dressings, barbecue sauces and many other vegetarian and non-vegetarian dishes. Buy it from health food shops and oriental grocers.

## SHOYU SAUCE

This is another natural soy sauce. It is made from fermented soybeans, bulgur and sea salt. It, too, is available from health food shops.

## MISO

This is a thick, dark brown paste, made from soybeans and grains such as whole barley or brown rice. It is high in protein and B vitamins with a flavor in many ways similar to beef extract.

Miso is used to enrich vegetable soups and stews, to which it must be added only for the last few minutes of cooking. The types of miso that you find are:
Hacho miso, made only from soybeans.
Mugi miso, made from soybeans and barley, and lighter in color with a slightly less salty flavor.
Kome miso, made from soybeans and white rice, and salty.
Genmai, made from soybeans and brown rice, and slightly sweet.

## TOFU

This is also known as soybean curd and has always been an important ingredient in Chinese cooking. Recently it has become much more readily available in the West and is constantly being used in new and exciting dishes, both sweet and savory.

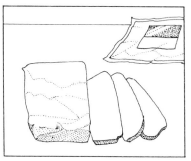

*Tofu provides first-class protein*

Tofu looks rather like cheese in the early stages of making before the whey has been completely drained off. It is off-white in color and is formed into soft blocks. Tofu can be bought by weight from Chinese stores or conveniently packaged into cartons from the health food shop.

Tofu provides a first-class protein. It has relatively low carbohydrate and fat contents and is a good source of calcium, iron and the B vitamins, thiamin and riboflavin.

## SOY MILK

Soy milk is a substitute milk made from soybeans. It is sold in cartons and cans. Soy milk can be used and drunk in exactly the same ways as ordinary milk.

It contains protein, B vitamins, and some calcium, with no lactose or saturated fats. If possible, look out for the types of soy milk that do not contain added sugar.

## SOY FLOUR

This is made from ground, dried soybeans. It is a creamy yellow color with a nutty flavor. It does not possess the rising properties of grain flours but up to 25% can be used in bread or pastry recipes to add extra protein without changing the original flavor. You must, if using soy flour, bake at a slightly lower temperature, since soy flour has a tendency to burn in a hot oven.

For those allergic to milk, soy flour and water can be made into a substitute white sauce.

# THE BENEFITS OF VITAMINS

Vitamin A: For healthy skin and good eyesight.

Vitamin B group — main vitamins: Vitamin B1 (Thiamin), Vitamin B2 (Riboflavin), Niacin, Vitamin B12: Important for healthy blood and nervous system. They act as a catalyst, releasing energy from starch and sugar foods thus allowing full use of protein intake.

Vitamin C: As this vitamin is not stored by the body, we need to eat fruit and vegetables each day. Essential for healthy skin and body tissues.

Vitamin D: In most cases our requirement of this vitamin is manufactured in our bodies by the effect of sunlight on the skin. Calcium and phosphorus should be in the diet with Vitamin D. It is required for the growth and strength of bones and teeth, therefore particularly important for children, pregnant women and nursing mothers. Cod liver oil, halibut oil and vitamin preparations can be used in the correct dosage to supplement the diet.

Vitamin E: The need for this vitamin (in most foods) is not yet properly understood.

Vitamin K: This is made in the body and is present in many foods. Needed for blood clotting.

## OTHER NUTRIENTS

**Proteins** Repair and renewal of tissue in adults; growth in children.

**Fats** Needed in small amounts for normal health. Vitamins A and D are fat soluble and are found in most foods with a fat content.

**Carbohydrates** Produce energy and heat. Small quantities needed for most people; more for those leading very active lives.

## MINERALS

Calcium: Needed for healthy bones and teeth, as well as blood clotting and muscle functions. Vitamin D must be present for absorption of calcium.

Iron: Forms part of the red pigment of the blood which carries oxygen around the body. Also present in muscles. Important for women, since deficiency may cause anaemia.

---

## TEXTURED VEGETABLE PROTEIN (TVP)

This is a highly processed product of the soybean which is used as a meat extender or substitute. TVP is sold in dried form and reconstituted immediately when boiling water is poured over it.

Although it provides protein, TVP often contains artificial colorings and flavorings, and the cooked texture is not good. It is not necessary in a wholefood diet.

## SOY GRITS

Also called soy splits, these are made from cooked, cracked soybeans. In appearance, they look like small pieces of chopped soybean. Soy grits need no soaking and will cook in 45 minutes, while providing the same nutrients as whole soybeans.

# *FRUIT*

The wide variety of fruits that are available all the year round provide a healthy and natural sweetness. Both fresh and dried fruits can be included in a wholefood eating program every day, and at any meal.

## FRESH FRUITS

Fresh fruits are an excellent source of dietary fiber and none contains more than a trace of fat.

Most fresh fruit contains significant amounts of vitamin C. Fruits with large amounts are strawberries, citrus fruit, red

*Vitamin C rich fruits*

currants, gooseberries, raspberries and kiwi fruit.

The amount of vitamin C is far greater when the fruit is eaten fresh. Cooking can destroy up to 50 per cent.

Carotene, which is converted to vitamin A in the body, is found in

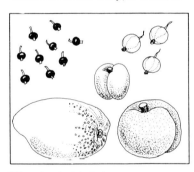

*Vitamin A rich fruits*

yellow-colored fruit such as apricots (which have the highest count), mangoes, peaches and yellow melons. There is also a little vitamin A in gooseberries and some other fruits.

271

Small amounts of B vitamins can be found in fresh fruit. Citrus fruits, plums, pineapple, melon and bananas are the best sources of thiamin. Other B vitamins

*Fruits containing thiamin*

found in fruits include riboflavin, nicotinic acid, pyridoxine, pantothenic acid and folic acid.

No fruits contain vitamin D. Vitamin K is present in some fresh fruit, in particular the pith and white fiber of citrus fruit.

All fresh fruits contain carbohydrate in varying amounts. Those with a high carbohydrate count (over 10 g per 100 g) are fresh dates, bananas, grapes, apples, nectarines, cherries, greengage plums and pineapple. Those with 6–10 g per 100 g are cooking apples, damson plums, fresh figs, plums, peaches, pears, mulberries,

*Fruits high in carbohydrate*

oranges, tangerines, passion fruit and kiwi fruit.

Those fruits with 5 g carbohydrate per 100 g or less include grapefruit, melons, cranberries,

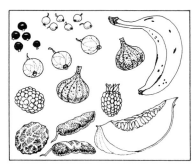

*Fruits containing protein*

red currants, lemons, gooseberries and loganberries.

Protein is found in only tiny amounts in most fruits. Those fresh fruits which contain slightly higher amounts than others include fresh dates, passion fruit, bananas, blackberries, red currants, figs, gooseberries, loganberries, melons and mulberries.

## DRIED FRUITS
Dried fruits are full of concentrated goodness. Since most of the water content has been taken away, the amount of nutrients per 100 g (4 oz) is far greater than that of fresh fruits.

All dried fruits are an excellent source of dietary fiber and all contain only a trace of fat. Because of the drying process, none contains more than a trace of vitamin C.

All dried fruits, except peaches and apricots, contain large amounts of thiamin (vitamin B1). Peaches and apricots, on the other hand, contain large amounts of carotene (which is converted to vitamin A). Prunes contain some but other dried fruit contain very little.

One of the values of dried fruits is their high mineral content. Potassium, calcium and phosphorus contents of most varieties are particularly high.

The carbohydrate content of all dried fruits is high. Unsoaked, it varies from 43–63 g per 100 g (about 2 oz per 4 oz).

All dried fruits contain small amounts of protein.

If possible, when buying dried fruits, choose the duller, stickier kinds that are usually sold in health food shops. The shiny fruits in sealed plastic packs, which are sold by supermarkets, are sometimes coated with a mineral oil.

Do not buy more than one month's supply of dried fruit at a time. If stored for any longer, it may become dry looking and develop a sugary coating. This dried fruit can still be used successfully for cakes, but is not quite so effective for serving unsoaked or for making fruit compotes.

Store dried fruits in airtight containers in a cool, dark cupboard.

Dried fruits can be eaten raw as snacks and chopped into salads. They can also be reconstituted and used in desserts and other dishes. Since boiling them destroys large amounts of the B vitamins (in particular thiamin), it is best to soak dried fruits in water or natural fruit juices for six hours or until they are soft. Use just enough liquid to cover them and either use the liquid in the final dish or save it for drinking.

# DAIRY PRODUCTS

## MILK

Milk contains large amounts of calcium, plus other minerals including potassium, zinc and phosphorus. It is a good source of vitamin A, thiamin, riboflavin and other B vitamins. There is also some vitamin C. A useful amount of protein is present in milk and the amounts of fats and carbohydrate vary according to the type that you use. Ordinary whole milk contains 11 g fat and 14 g carbohydrate per 275 ml ($\frac{1}{2}$ pint). The fats are 55% saturated fats and, therefore, if you have to follow a low-cholesterol diet, whole milk should be used in moderation.

## RAW MILK

This is whole milk that has not been subjected to any heat treatment. It is the most nutritious milk, since no vitamins have been destroyed by pasteurization or heat treating. The fat and carbohydrate counts are the same as for ordinary whole milk. The availability of this milk depends on where you live, and whether selling raw milk is allowed.

## WHOLE PASTEURIZED MILK

The majority of the milk available is whole and pasteurized. Pasteurizing kills off bacteria; it involves the milk being heated to around 161°F, held for 15 seconds, rapidly cooled and then bottled. The process destroys some of the thiamin and a proportion of the vitamin C. The level of vitamin C in pasteurized milk further falls by 50% after 12 hours.

## HOMOGENIZED MILK

Homogenized milk is heat treated in a similar way to ordinary pasteurized milk. It is then further processed in order to break up the fat globules which then stay evenly distributed throughout the milk. Homogenized milk can therefore be frozen, but once thawed it should be used quickly and not refrozen.

## ULTRA HEAT TREATED (UHT) MILK

This is homogenized milk which has been heated to a temperature of 275–300°F. Consequently, it will keep for up to six months. The heat treatment reduces the vitamin content and affects the flavor. UHT milk is a good standby to have for emergency use, but it is not the best quality milk to use regularly.

## SKIM MILK

Probably the best to choose for a healthful diet, skim milk is pasteurized or UHT milk that has had virtually all its fat content removed, making the finished product lower in cholesterol and containing only half the calories of ordinary pasteurized milk.

## PART SKIM MILK

This is pasteurized milk with most of the fat content removed. It contains 1 or 2% fat for added flavor.

## FORTIFIED SKIM MILK POWDER

This is spray dried skim milk, enriched with vitamins A and D. When reconstituted, it has a similar vitamin content to ordinary skim milk.

## EVAPORATED MILK

This has had its water content reduced from around 86% to 68%. Unless it has been skimmed before evaporation, it will have a higher fat and carbohydrate content than ordinary milk. The vitamin content will have been lowered and the flavor changed. Evaporated milk should not feature often in a healthful diet.

## CONDENSED MILK

This is a considerably concentrated milk product with a high proportion of sugar. It should not be included in a healthful diet.

## GOAT'S MILK

Goat's milk is becoming increasingly popular and easier to obtain. Compared to ordinary pasteurized milk, it has almost equal protein and carbohydrate counts but slightly more fat. The mineral content is higher, it has slightly more vitamin A and twice the vitamin D. The amount of vitamin C is about the same although, since the milk is not usually pasteurized, this does not diminish so rapidly.

The fat globules in goat's milk are smaller than in cow's and are evenly distributed throughout the milk, making it more easily digestible. This, and the fact that in constitution goats milk is nearer to human milk than cow's milk, makes it more suitable for babies of six months and onwards, and for anyone who may have a cows' milk allergy.

## STORING MILK

Untreated and pasteurized milks should be kept in the refrigerator or a very cool larder. In the refrigerator they will keep for up to three days, in a larder for up to two.

UHT milk will keep in a cool place for up to six months, but it is wise to check the date stamp. Once opened it should be treated like fresh milk.

Skim milk powder should be kept in a cool cupboard and used within three months once opened.

## YOGURT

Yogurt is made by introducing two harmless bacteria, Lactobacillus bulgaricus and Streptococcus thermophilus, into either whole or skim milk. These bacteria feed on the milk sugars and produce an acid which coagulates the protein, resulting in the thick consistency of yogurt.

Vitamins and minerals remain similar in proportion to those in whole or part-skim milk.

Yogurt is higher in protein than milk, but contains less vitamin A, unless this vitamin has been added artificially. It is richer in B vitamins and minerals and, since the milk sugars have been partially fermented, contains fewer carbohydrates.

Most plain or unflavored yogurts on the market are alive to the extent that they all contain the two types of introduced bacteria and no pasteurization or sterilization has taken place. You will find sugar, which is used mostly as a sweetener, on the ingredients lists of some brands.

Smaller brands of yogurt, that are more often to be found in health food shops, are also made from whole or skim milk. Different brands vary in texture and flavor because of the different methods of manufacture.

Some fruit yogurts have been pasteurized or sterilized after they are made. This prevents the fruit from fermenting but unfortunately it also removes 95% or more of the beneficial bacteria. Some smaller manufacturers sell live fruit yogurts. These obviously will have a shorter shelf life.

Many fruit yogurts also contain coloring and preservative, and most contain sugar.

If you wish to eat fruit yogurts it is best to make your own by mixing fruit purées into plain yogurts. To make your own yogurt see page 152.

## USING YOGURT

Yogurt can be eaten at any time of the day and can be used in either sweet or savory dishes.

It is particularly delicious served with breakfast cereal or granola, and can make a refreshing summer drink as well as a convenient picnic food. As a dessert, serve it mixed with fruit purées, nuts, honey or sugar-free jam. Use instead of cream to top fruit salads and other desserts; or make light textured mousses, ice-creams and fruit fools.

Yogurt makes a perfect, low-fat salad dressing and is an excellent meat tenderizer when used in a marinade. Swirl it into soups, make into a sauce for broiled meats, use to top casseroles and stews or pour over white fish before baking.

When cooking with yogurt, care should be taken not to heat it too vigorously as it will curdle. Let the yogurt come to room temperature before adding to a hot dish and, if adding to a soup or sauce, whisk it into the hot liquid just before serving.

## BUTTERMILK

Cultured buttermilk is made in a similar way to yogurt. It is more liquid than yogurt and is generally sold in 1-quart cartons. Buttermilk makes a refreshing drink, either straight from the carton or diluted with mineral water. Mixed into cakes and biscuits instead of milk, it makes them extremely light textured.

## CHEESE

Most cheese is made by adding rennet or a similar substance and starter cultures to milk, which then separates into curds and whey. The whey is drained off and the further processing of the curds determines the final character of the cheese. The many different types of hard and soft cheeses available can all be included in a healthful eating pattern.

All cheeses are excellent sources of calcium. The other mineral present in significant amounts is phosphorus.

Vitamins A and D are present in all cheeses, but in greater amounts in the full fat types. Cheese is also an important source of the B vitamins, riboflavin, biotin and B12.

Most cheeses contain no carbohydrate at all. Cottage cheese contains a very small amount.

The fat content of cheese varies widely, depending on the manufacturing process and on whether whole or skim milk has been used. Hard cheeses, such as Cheddar, have a high fat content, as does cream cheese. There are medium fat cheeses such as Edam and low fat varieties including cottage cheese.

The fat contained in cheese is 50–60% saturated and so consumption of the high fat types has to be watched carefully if you are following a low cholesterol diet.

The protein provided by cheese is a first-class protein. This means that cheese does not have to be combined with any other ingredient in order to supply the body with every amino acid that it needs for healthy growth and repair. Weight for weight, cheese supplies more of this protein than meat or fish, so only small amounts, particularly of the hard types, are needed to make a nutritious meal.

Mature Cheddar will cost slightly more, but it has a stronger flavor and so only small amounts will make a dish that is both substantial and full of flavor. This will be better for your budget and better for your health.

When you buy hard cheese, it should look fresh with no dried areas or beads of fat on the surface. If it is pre-wrapped, it should not look moist or greasy or have any trace of mold.

If mature hard cheese is in good condition when it is bought and is securely wrapped in plastic or foil, it should keep for up to one month in a refrigerator. Stilton should be eaten within a week. If you have no refrigerator, keep cheese in the coolest place possible, again wrapped in plastic or foil. It should keep for up to a week, depending on the outside temperature. Hard cheeses have a better flavor and texture if they are brought to room temperature before being eaten.

Hard cheese is one of the most useful and versatile ingredients in the kitchen. Use as a filling in wholewheat sandwiches or on top of wholewheat toast. Make cheese into salads, stir it into sauces, sprinkle over soups, casseroles and bean and pasta dishes, and make a meal of lightly cooked vegetables by scattering them with grated cheese and chopped nuts

### HARD CHEESES
Hard cheeses include Cheddar, Cheshire, Caerphilly and Stilton — plus others such as Gruyère, Parmesan, Pecorino, Emmenthal, Gouda, Edam and Jarlsberg.

Vegetarian cheeses are made

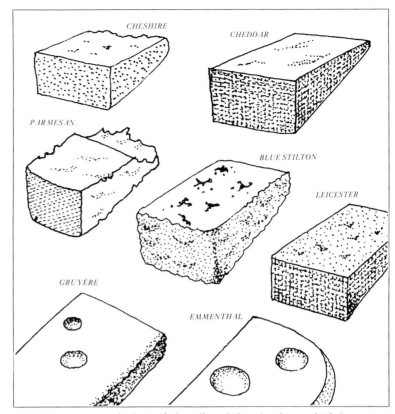

*Hard cheeses are made from whole milk and therefore have a high fat content*

with non-animal rennet. There are Cheddar and Cheshire types available in some health food shops and some supermarkets.

Most of the hard cheeses are made from whole milk and therefore have a high fat content.

Stilton has the highest fat count with 40 g fat per 100 g. Cheddar and Gruyère around 34 g and the

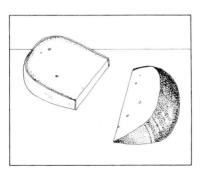

*Gouda and Edam; medium fat cheeses*

other hard cheeses around 30 g. Gouda has 26 g fat and Edam 22 g.

If you plan to cook with hard cheese and would rather buy the traditional product, it is best to buy the farmhouse or matured varieties. Hard cheese can also be added to breads, pastries and pancakes and stirred into egg custards or fillings for quiches.

### SOFT CHEESES
Soft cheeses include not only the creamy textured types that are sold in packages, but the softer molded cheeses such as Camembert. Like the hard cheeses, their fat content varies widely.

Camembert and Brie have a fat count of around 23 g per 100 g.

Cream cheese contains a staggering 47 g fat per 100 g, and so should only be eaten occasionally.

Cottage cheese is often made from skim milk. It is therefore low in both fat and calories. Many varieties now contain preservative, so if you do not like your food to contain any artificial ingredients, it is best to always read the label.

To make a homemade curd, or cottage, cheese stir 2 Tbsp plain yogurt into 5 cups whole milk. Cover and leave in a warm place for 12 hours. Pour the curds and whey into a scalded dish cloth. Bring up the sides to make a bag. Hang it up to drip for 24 hours.

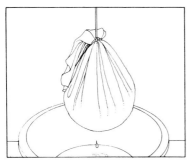

*Making cheese*

Unwrap the cheese, turn it into a bowl and mix with a fork.

Fromage blanc is a European cheese which has become very popular over the last few years. It is a low fat cheese with a rich, creamy flavor but a thin texture.

All soft cheeses should be stored in the refrigerator and ideally eaten within three days of purchase.

Use them for dips, spreads and pâtés, beat them with eggs to make quiche fillings, use them to make

*Spoon soft cheese over fruit*

low fat mousses and sweet molds; spoon them over fresh or stewed fruit.

### VEGAN CHEESES
See under Nuts and Seeds (page 142).

### EGGS
Eggs are an excellent source of first-class protein, containing a perfect balance of amino acids for growth and repair of body tissue. One egg will supply one tenth of the average adult daily protein needs.

Vitamins A and D are to be found in eggs, as are the B vitamins thiamin, riboflavin, biotin and B12 in significant amounts, and other B vitamins in smaller amounts. There is also a small amount of vitamin E.

The minerals contained in eggs include iron, calcium, potassium and magnesium.

Eggs contain only a trace of carbohydrate and 10.9 g fat per 100 g. Egg yolks are the single most concentrated source of cholesterol in our diet and most experts advise eating no more than 3–5 egg yolks (including those in made up dishes) a week. The fact that eggs are easy to eat and that so much goodness is packed into one small shell, they make an excellent food for children, invalids and the elderly.

Store eggs, pointed end down, in a cool place or refrigerator and use them within one month of purchase.

# NUTS AND SEEDS

Nuts and seeds, when mixed with whole grain ingredients, will provide a high protein meal.

They contain significant amounts of fiber while all but chestnuts have a low carbohydrate content.

All nuts and seeds are rich in minerals, particularly phosphorus, potassium, iron and calcium. In varying quantities, they also contain B vitamins and vitamin E.

With the exception of chestnuts, nuts and seeds have a high fat content. In some the fats are mainly polyunsaturated, in others they are monounsaturated (which seem to have little effect one way or the other on blood cholesterol) but in some, especially coconut, the fats are mainly saturated.

Most nuts and seeds are high in calories, but since only small amounts are usually mixed with grains to make vegetarian dishes, nut based meals need not be fattening.

All nuts and seeds should be sold when they are ripe and fully mature, and at the peak of their nutritional value. Shelled nuts may soon start to deteriorate after this, so never buy more than one month's supply at a time.

Store nuts in airtight containers in a cool, dark cupboard and chop or grind them as needed.

## ALMONDS
Almonds are available in their skins, blanched, sliced, slivered and ground. If possible, always buy them with skins as once almonds have been processed they

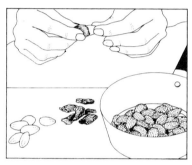

*Peeling blanched almonds*

may lose some of their oils and natural flavors.

To blanch almonds, put them into a shallow pan and cover with cold water. Bring to the boil and remove immediately from the heat. Leave the almonds in the water, taking each one out separately and squeezing it out of its skin.

The fats contained in almonds are mostly monounsaturated. Their potassium, calcium, iron and magnesium content is high. They contain vitamin E and their carbohydrate count is low.

## BRAZIL NUTS
Brazil nuts can be bought whole or in pieces. They contain large and almost equal proportions of saturated, polyunsaturated and monounsaturated fats.

The potassium, calcium, magnesium and iron counts are high, and they contain small amounts of vitamin E.

## CASHEW NUTS
Cashew nuts are low in most minerals apart from potassium. Their fat content is over 50% monounsaturated, the rest being made up of both saturated and polyunsaturated fats.

## CHESTNUTS
Chestnuts can be bought fresh, dried or canned. To peel fresh chestnuts, slit the tops. Put them

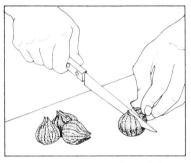

*Preparing chestnuts to be peeled*

into a saucepan of cold water and bring to the boil. Remove from the heat and leave the chestnuts in the water, taking each one out separately and peeling away the outer and inner skins.

To reconstitute dried chestnuts, soak them in cold water for 3 hours and then simmer in the soaking water for 30 minutes. Where a recipe calls for 1 lb fresh, unpeeled chestnuts, use 8 oz dried.

Canned chestnuts and unsweetened chestnut purée are useful storecupboard ingredients.

Unlike most other nuts, chestnuts are low in fats but high in carbohydrates. They are also lower in calories than other nuts. They are high in potassium and contain small amounts of B vitamins.

## COCONUT
The fats in coconuts are almost all saturated fats. The protein content

is high. So, too, is the amount of potassium and iron. There are small amounts of calcium, magnesium and only traces of some B vitamins.

To check that a coconut is fresh when bought, shake it to make sure it contains plenty of liquid.

Shredded coconut can be bought in most supermarkets. These have a higher food and calorie value by weight than fresh coconut.

## HAZELNUTS
Hazelnuts are rich in both calcium and vitamin E, and the B vitamins, folic acid and pantothenic acid.

Approximately 75% of the oil content is monounsaturated.

Toasted chopped hazelnuts can be bought in health shops and some supermarkets. These are useful for sprinkling over cakes and desserts as they have a slightly sweet flavor.

## PEANUTS
Peanuts are technically not nuts at all but members of the legume family. As they resemble nuts in flavor, they are classed with nuts.

Peanuts are high in protein, but like the other beans, must be served with a whole grain product.

Their fat content is 49 g/100 g and made up of about 50% monounsaturated, 35% polyunsaturated and the rest saturated.

They are high in potassium and iron, contain small amounts of most of the B vitamins (with the exception of B12) and some vitamin E.

## PEANUT BUTTER
This is made from ground roasted peanuts. Spread on wholewheat bread, it can provide a first class protein meal. If possible, buy the types that contain no salt or preservatives.

## PECANS

These are similar in shape to walnuts, only more elongated. The shells are a smooth, speckled tan.

Pecans are high in potassium, calcium, magnesium and iron, and also contain significant amounts of zinc. They contain traces of B vitamins and carotene and a small amount of vitamin C. The larger proportion of their oil is mono-unsaturated and the rest mostly polyunsaturated.

## PINE NUTS

Pine nuts are high in protein, calcium, iron and the B vitamin niacin. The larger proportion of their fats is monounsaturated, while most of the remainder is polyunsaturated.

## PISTACHIO NUTS

Pistachio nuts are exceptionally high in protein, iron and potassium, and contain small amounts of most B vitamins. The larger proportion of their fats is monounsaturated.

## WALNUTS

Walnuts are high in potassium, calcium, magnesium, iron and zinc. They contain small amounts of B vitamins, a trace of vitamin E, and are high in protein. Walnut oil is the highest in polyunsaturates of all nuts.

## PUMPKIN SEEDS

White, grey and green varieties of pumpkin seeds are available. They are exceptionally rich in iron and calcium, and their protein content is high. They contain large amounts of the B vitamin niacin and small amounts of other B vitamins. Their fats are mostly polyunsaturated.

## SESAME SEEDS

These are tiny, flat, tear-drop shaped seeds and vary from a pale cream color to black. They are often sprinkled over breads and salads. Sesame seeds can be used as they are or toasted until golden

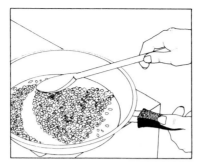

*Toasting sesame seeds*

in a dry frying pan over a medium heat.

These seeds are exceptionally high in protein, potassium, calcium and the B vitamin niacin, and contain significant amounts of the other B vitamins. The larger proportion of their fats are poly-unsaturated and they are rich in lecithin.

## TAHINI

This is a paste made from ground sesame seeds. There are pale brown and dark brown varieties, the paler one having the finer flavor.

Use tahini for salad dressings, sauces and sandwich fillings, and for making bean pâtés and dips such as hummus.

## SUNFLOWER SEEDS

Sunflower seeds are small, pale grey colored, tear-drop shaped seeds with a creamy flavor.

They are exceptionally high in protein, calcium, magnesium, iron and potassium. These seeds contain significant amounts of most B vitamins and a large amount of vitamin E. The larger proportion of their fats is polyunsaturated.

## NUT CHEESE

An imitation hard cheese can be made from ground nuts and hard vegetable margarine with a little yeast extract for seasoning.

It can be eaten with fruit, bread or biscuits and in cold dishes and salads. It is not suitable for cooking as it does not have the melting qualities of dairy cheese.

# GRAINS AND GRAIN PRODUCTS

All grains contain protein and, when mixed with other second class protein ingredients such as nuts or beans, will provide good quality protein for healthy growth and repair of body tissue.

The B vitamins and minerals such as calcium, iron and copper are to be found in all grains and some contain vitamin E.

One important constituent of grains and grain products is dietary fiber. This is only present in useful amounts when the grains are unrefined, that is, when their outer coating, or bran, is left intact.

## WHEAT

Wheat is one of the most used grain in the Western world. The whole wheat grain is made up of

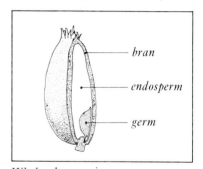

*Whole wheat grain*

the bran, the endosperm, or starchy part, and the germ, which is the most nutritious but which makes up only 2% of the grain.

Contained in the germ are most of the vitamins of the B group, a large amount of vitamin E, and minerals such as calcium, potassium, iron, copper and magnesium.

**Wholewheat berries** These can be cooked to make an accompaniment to a main meal or as part of bread loaves.

Sprouting wheat grains will lessen the carbohydrate content but will provide vitamin C.

**Wheat bran** This is the outer coating of the wheat grain. Adding extra bran to bread mixtures, sprinkling it over cereals and into drinks will greatly increase your fiber intake. However, it is far healthier if you can obtain all your fiber from wholemeal bread and other wholegrain products and from fruits, vegetables and beans.

**Wheat germ** Wheat germ is the tiny nutritious part that has been separated from the main grain. It is consequently a highly concentrated source of B vitamins, vitamin E and minerals. If untreated, store in the refrigerator to prevent rancidity. Treated or stabilized wheat germ has been processed to prevent this.

Wheat germ can be sprinkled over sweet dishes and cereals, and used in crumble toppings, coatings and gratin dishes. It can also be added to pastry, cake and bread mixes.

**Wheat flour** Wheat flour is produced by grinding the wheat grain. Wholewheat flour contains the whole (100%) of the wheat grain, with nothing added and nothing taken away. It therefore contains all the nutritious substances of the wheat germ and all the bran.

White flour is a 70% extraction of the wheat grain. It consists mostly of the endosperm or starch and contains very little bran. Certain B vitamins and calcium have by law to be added back, but they are not in the original proportions. Most white flour has also been chemically bleached to make it a pure white color.

Unbleached white flour is a 70% extraction flour that has not been chemically bleached.

Bread flour is flour produced from hard wheat, giving it superior bread making qualities. Some wholewheat flours contain a proportion of hard wheat, making them suitable for both bread and other baking purposes.

---

**THE FIBER FACTOR**

Dietary fiber (roughage) is found only in plant foods. It is indigestible and remains in our intestine after other nutrients have been absorbed. While it seems odd that something of no nutritional value should be so important, fiber plays a vital role in keeping our bodies healthy. It prevents constipation and may also prevent certain disorders like cancer of the colon and diverticulosis. Fiber works by holding a lot of water so eating enough results in soft, bulky waste matter which is easy for the intestine to push along without pressure or straining. Potentially harmful substances are also diluted and eliminated quickly from the body so spend less time in contact with the wall of the intestine. The fiber in cereals is particularly good at holding moisture but that in other vegetable foods has its own protective effect and it is sensible to eat fiber from a variety of different sources. There is no recommended daily intake for dietary fiber but most experts agree that a healthy diet should contain at least 1 oz a day.

However, there's no need to add bran to everything, simply eat more foods that are naturally high in fiber like wholegrain cereals (including wholemeal and some brown breads), breakfast cereals like Shredded Wheat, Weetabix and some granolas), wholewheat pasta, brown rice, fresh fruit and vegetables and beans.

---

Stone ground flour has been ground slowly between old fashioned mill stones. Slow grinding produces less heat and therefore destroys fewer vitamins. Most other flours are ground very fast on a roller mill. It is also possible to buy flour which has been slowly ground on rollers in order to maintain goodness.

**Wheat breads** Wholewheat bread is made with wholewheat flour. Brands sold by large commercial companies may contain preservatives and stabilizers. It may also include some white flour.

Wheat germ breads are usually made from an 81% or 85% extraction flour with added wheat germ.

**Bulgur wheat** This is made from whole wheat grains that have been soaked and then baked until they crack into small yellow particles.

To use, soak the wheat in warm water for 20 minutes. Drain and squeeze dry. Mix the wheat with an oil and vinegar dressing and add other ingredients such as parsley, olives and tomatoes to make a salad.

*Preparing bulgur wheat*

Bulgar can also be cooked. Allow 2½ cups liquid to 2 cups wheat and cook until it has all been absorbed.

**Wholewheat pasta** All pasta is made from a special hard, high-protein wheat called durum wheat. Wholewheat pasta is made from the whole part of the wheat grains. Many different types are now available. Cook wholewheat pasta in the same ways and for the same amount of time as white pasta.

**Wholewheat semolina** Semolina is a coarsely ground flour produced from durum wheat. The wholewheat variety makes tasty puddings. It can also be soaked and served as a salad in the same way as bulgur. After adding the salad dressing, leave 30 minutes.

**Storing wheat products** Whole-wheat grains will keep for up to a year but once ground should not be kept for longer than one month if the full vitamin E value is to be maintained.

The exceptions are pasta and bulgur which will keep for up to 3 months.

Store all wheat products in a cool dark place in airtight containers, or in the freezer or refrigerator.

## OATS

Oats are high in protein, potassium, calcium, magnesium, iron and zinc, and contain small amounts of most B vitamins.

**Oat groats** These are whole oat grains. They can be cooked in a similar way to rice.

**Rolled oats** These are used mainly for oatmeal. They are produced by steaming and rolling either whole or pin-head oats. Use them also in granola and crumble toppings.

**Storing oat products** Whole oat grains should keep for up to a year. Oat products quickly become rancid and should not be kept for longer than one month. Store them in a cool, dark place in air-tight containers.

## BARLEY

Barley contains large amounts of calcium, potassium and magnesium, and a certain amount of iron. It is high in the B vitamin niacin and contains small amounts of other B vitamins.

**Scotch barley** This is the barley grain with only the rough outer husk removed. It can be bought in some health food shops. Cook in the same way as brown rice and use to enrich casseroles.

**Pearl barley** This has both outer layers removed and so does not have the fiber content of scotch barley.

**Barley flakes** These are made in the same way as rolled oats and are sold separately besides being included in some granola mixtures.

**Barley flour** Unrefined barley flour can be bought from some health shops. Use it to make light pastries or to replace up to half the flour in bread and cakes.

## RYE

Rye is rich in potassium, calcium, magnesium, iron and zinc, and contains small amounts of B vitamins.

**Rye groats** These or whole rye grains are found in some health food shops. They can be cooked as a single grain but need a long cooking time.

**Rye flour** Dark and light rye flours are available, the dark containing more bran. Rye flour has a delicious nutty flavor but contains only a small proportion of gluten. It should therefore be mixed half and half with whole-wheat flour when making bread.

## RICE

Whole-grain rice, known as brown rice, has its outer coating of bran intact. Both long and short grain types are available.

Brown rice is rich in fiber and contains more iron, calcium, protein, niacin and thiamin than the white varieties.

The cooking time is longer than for white rice, usually 40–45 minutes. The methods of cooking are the same, although brown rice cannot be cooked in a steamer in the Chinese manner.

**Rice flour** 100% whole brown rice flour is available from some health food shops.

## BUCKWHEAT

Buckwheat consists of tiny, brown heart-shaped seeds. They are high in protein, phosphorus and potassium, and contain most of the B vitamins. The grains are gluten free and so useful in a gluten restricted diet.

Buckwheat is usually lightly toasted and cooked to make the dish called kasha which has a pungent, nutty flavor.
**Buckwheat flour** This is a fine and grey colored flour. It is used for making pancakes. In a gluten-free diet, buckwheat flour can be used for bread and cakes although these will not rise in the same way as those made with wheat flour.
**Buckwheat spaghetti** This is made from a mixture of buckwheat and wholewheat flours giving a pleasing nutty flavor. Buckwheat spaghetti cooks more quickly than wholewheat or white spaghetti.

## MILLET

Millet takes the form of tiny, round, pale yellow seeds. It is rich in protein, calcium, iron and the B vitamins thiamin, riboflavin and nicotinic acid. It is very quickly cooked and can be served as an accompaniment or stuffing. Millet can also be mixed with nuts and beans to make a main protein meal.

## CORN

Corn consists mainly of carbo-hydrate and contains more carotene than any other grain. It also contains significant amounts of potassium, calcium and iron, niacin and traces of other B vitamins.
**Popcorn** Dried corn which expands and softens when heated.
**Cornmeal** Coarse yellow or white flour made from a 95% extraction of the corn and therefore high in nutrients and fiber. Use it to make corn bread or Italian polenta. Masa harina is cornmeal made from hulled corn. It is not as nutritious, but is used to make tortillas.

**Cornstarch** This is made from the starch of the corn kernels. It is a useful thickening agent but contains virtually no fiber or important nutrients.

## TRITICALE

This is a cross between wheat and rye. The whole grains are sold mainly for sprouting.

Triticale flour is also available for bread baking.

# *FATS AND OILS*

For a healthy diet, it is best to east less of all fats and oils. In particular, eat less butter, block margarine, lard, suet and other shortenings. Switch to soft margarines with a low saturated fat content, and pure vegetable oils, but try to cut down on these too.
**Butter** Butter is an animal product and therefore contains a high pro-portion of saturated fats. However, it is made simply by churning cream and then usually adding a little salt. There are no artificial additives or chemical processes involved.

Butter also contains vitamins A and D, calcium and small amounts of iron and magnesium. There is only a trace of carbohydrate.
**Margarine** All margarines are 80% fat and contain about the same calories as butter.

Margarines are made from animal, fish or vegetable oils either combined or singly.

If edible oils appears on an ingredients list, the margarine probably contains a mixture of animal and vegetable fats.

Generally the harder the margarine, the greater the pro-portion of saturated fats it contains. These need not neces-sarily be animal fats but vegetable fats that have been artificially saturated. Margarines with a high proportion of polyunsaturated fats are very soft.

Most margarines also contain whey solids, a little salt, water, lecithin, emulsifiers which help the oils mix with the water (these may be chemical or of natural origin), coloring, flavoring and vitamins A and D which must be added by law.

The best margarine for health is a soft margarine (low in saturated fat) made solely from vegetable oils.
**Low-fat spreads** These are made with similar ingredients to those of margarine, with extra water added. They are lower in fats and calories than ordinary margarine or butter.
**Lard** Lard, including the soft types, has a high proportion of saturated fats and should be used in moderation, if at all.
**Vegetable shortenings** These are a mixture of different types of fats that have been chemically re-fined and whipped. They are highly saturated, contain little goodness and should not be included in a healthy diet.
**Cream of coconut** Cream of coconut is pure coconut oil which is sold in the form of a white block. It can be used for frying, for enriching vegetable curries and as a cream substitute in sweet dishes.

Although cream of coconut is a pure vegetable product, it has a high proportion of saturated fats and should only be used in moderation.
**Vegetable oils** Most vegetable oils are high in polyunsaturated fats and low in saturated fat, making them ideal for cooking and for salad dressings. Safflower and sunflower oils contain the most polyunsaturated fats. Olive oil contains mostly monounsaturated fats and coconut oil is the only one high in saturated fats. Other oils to buy are corn, soy and peanut. Walnut and sesame oils are excellent but more expensive.

Oils labelled simply "vegetable" or "cooking" oil contain a mixture of oil, including rape seed oil, can be quite high in saturated fat, and have a poor flavor.

Cold pressed oils are produced by pressing the nuts or seeds to extract their oils. They are deep amber colored with strong, nutty flavors.

Store in a cool, dark place and once opened, all oils should be used within one month.

# Sugars and Sweeteners

Manufactured sugar is the one ingredient that is totally unnecessary in a healthful diet. It is high in calories and although these calories are no more fattening than those from other foods, sugar has very little bulk so it is easy to eat a lot. Sugar also contains no other nutrients (some brown sugars contain tiny amounts of certain vitamins and minerals but the quantities are insignificant) and it is far better to get energy from foods that supply a range of nutrients and are bulky enough to satisfy hunger. Sugar is also bad for teeth, particularly when eaten in sticky forms like cakes, biscuits and sweets; the more frequently sugar is eaten the more harm it does.

**White sugar** White sugar is virtually 100% sucrose, contains no minerals and should be avoided whenever possible.

**Confectioners sugar** This is a highly refined form of white sugar, and should be avoided whenever possible.

## BROWN SUGARS

**Raw sugar** The granules are small and the overall sugar soft and sticky. Raw sugar is produced from the sugar cane which has been less refined than in the production of white or brown sugars. It contains traces of B vitamins and minerals.

**Brown sugar** This is often bought in mistake for raw sugar. It is in fact made from fine grain white sugar and sugar syrups, and contains no useful nutrients. There should be a list of ingredients on the pack.

## SUGAR SUBSTITUTES

**Molasses** Molasses contains all the goodness of the sugar cane that is discarded in the production of white sugar. It includes minerals, B vitamins and about two thirds the calories of white sugar. It is a thick syrup with a strong flavor and so a little goes a long way. It is available in sulphured and unsulphured forms.

**Honey** Honey has been credited with many properties, but even so it does contain about 80% sugars and so should be eaten in moderation. Its flavor is richer and sweeter than that of sugar so you do not need to use so much.

Honey consists of 80% sugars, (mainly in the form of fructose and glucose), 20% water and the small amounts of some vitamins.

Honey also contains just over two-thirds the calories of sugar.

**Maple syrup** This is produced by tapping the sap of maple trees and considerably reducing it. It therefore contains a high proportion of sugar, but is also a rich source of minerals such as calcium, phosphorus, potassium and sodium.

Maple syrup is a fairly thin, dark red-brown syrup and, once opened, is best kept in the refrigerator.

**Malt extract** This thick, sticky, brown syrup produced from germinated barley grains consists mainly of maltose. It also contains small amounts of protein, B vitamins and minerals.

**Sugar-free jam** This is made from fruits, fruit juices and natural pectin, and comes in a variety of different fruit mixtures It can be used in the same way as ordinary jam since it is just as sweet but most are much lower in calories.

**Fructose** Fructose resembles fine confectioners sugar. It is far sweeter than normal sugars, so less can be used, thus reducing the calorie levels of anything made from it. Fructose contains little goodness and should not be necessary in a healthful diet.

**Artificial sweeteners** Artificial sweeteners are man made. Weight for weight, most are many times sweeter than sugar with no or few calories. Artificial sweeteners include saccharine, aspartame and acesulfame K.

Sorbitol, the artificial sweetener produced for diabetics, is made from glucose and so supplies calories. Eating too much (more than about 2 oz a day) may have a laxative effect.

# SALT AND SALT SUBSTITUTES

A small amount of salt (sodium chloride) is essential for maintaining bodily health. However, too much salt (or rather the sodium part of salt) is thought to lead to high blood pressure in certain individuals with an inherited tendency to develop this disorder. So it is advisable to eat less salt by using less in cooking and at the table as well as eating fewer salty foods.

**Rock salt** This is salt taken from underground deposits. It has fairly large granules which, when roughly crushed and sold for use in salt mills and for cooking, tend to compress together.

**Table salt** Most table salts are produced from rock salts that have been finely ground and mixed with a small proportion of magnesium carbonate to make them run freely.

**Iodized salt** This has iodine salts added and is recommended in areas with a natural iodine deficiency.

**Sea salt** This is produced by the evaporation of sea water. It may be fine or coarse crystals or in flakes. Some fine varieties have magnesium carbonate added.

**Salt substitutes** These are mostly produced from potassium salts and are useful in some cases of high blood pressure but check with your doctor first.

**Sesame salt (gomasio)** This is a useful substitute for ordinary salt. It is made by grinding together five parts roasted sesame seeds to one of either pure rock salt or sea salt.

# CHOCOLATE AND CAROB

**Cocoa powder** Cocoa powder is made from the cocoa bean. It is rich in iron but contains caffeine and has a bitter flavor which needs to be tempered by a sweetener.

**Chocolate** Chocolate is cocoa powder and cocoa butter. It must contain at least 35% dry cocoa solids and a minimum of 18% cocoa butter. Chocolate is high in fats and contains traces of carotene and of some B vitamins and minerals. Unsweetened chocolate contains no sugar. Semisweet and sweet chocolate has sugar added. Milk chocolate also includes milk solids.

**Carob powder** This is produced from the carob bean (also known as the locust bean) and is naturally sweet. It contains vitamins A and D, some B vitamins and minerals such as calcium and magnesium. It also includes protein and a small amount of fiber. Carob powder contains less fat and sodium than cocoa, fewer calories and no caffeine. Because of its sweet flavor, you need less sugar or other sweetener in order to make it taste pleasant.

**Carob bars** These are made in a similar way to chocolate bars. Most contain sugar but sugar-free brands are available.

# CONVENIENCE FOODS

Using the occasional package of frozen vegetables or fruit or can of corn will do no harm if, for most of the time, your diet is based on fresh products. Other products which may help out in emergencies are the cans of fruit in natural juices without sugar, but it is best not to use them regularly.

Manufactured goods such as pies, instant desserts and even batter-coated fish all contain preservatives, and in many cases artificial flavorings. Their fat, sugar and salt content is also often high. Manufactured goods of this type should feature only occasionally in a healthful diet.

283

# HEALTHFUL COOKING

Buying fresh and wholesome ingredients is just the beginning to eating healthier. How you prepare and cook those foods once you're in the kitchen can make all the difference. There are a number of very good cooking methods, including broiling, steaming, poaching and stir-frying and others, that use little fat. And while they might artfully use blends of herbs and spices; marinades made from fruit juices, wine and vinegars; and fresh fruit and vegetable garnishes; there are no rich sauces that can often overwhelm delicate foods and add extra fat and calories.

The finished dishes that use such healthful cooking methods are lighter in fat and often more delicate in texture without being bland.

## COOKING METHODS

### BROILING
Broiling is a cooking method which is suitable for meat and fish, and also some vegetables.

### MEAT
As it is a fairly quick way of cooking, you need only the best quality meats such as steaks and chops. Variety meats can also be broiled.

*Trimming fat from steak*

Trim all but a very thin rim of fat from the meat and on steaks, slash the rest at 1-inch intervals to prevent the meat from curling. Before broiling, all meat should be lightly brushed with oil to prevent sticking. The oil can be flavored with wine or cider, chopped herbs or spices such as paprika, cumin and coriander. Season with pepper but not salt as this draws out the juices.

If you have time, marinate the meat in a flavored mixture to improve taste and tenderness.

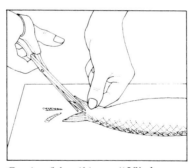
*Cutting fish tail into a "V" shape*

### FISH
You can broil whole small fish or fish fillets. Small fish should be properly cleaned with fins removed. The heads can be left on if wished and the tails should be rimmed in a neat V-shape.

Fish also benefits from being brushed with oil and seasoned.

### VEGETABLES
Types which can be broiled include mushrooms, zucchini,

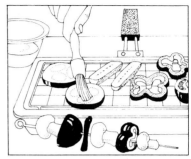
*Broiling vegetables*

eggplants, peppers and tomatoes. Brush them with a flavored oil and either lay the vegetables directly on the rack or put on to kabob skewers.

### METHOD
If you have an open, wire rack under a conventional broiler, first cover it with perforated foil. Turn the broiler to high and get the foil hot.

For meat, lay it on the hot rack. Broil one side until done, turn over and cook the other side. Lamb and beef can be rare, medium or well done. Pork must be well done.

For whole fish, cook the same as for meat. Fillets of oily fish should be laid, cut side up, on the rack and cooked only on that side. White fish fillets are best placed in a shallow, heatproof dish. Steaks can be cooked like whole fish.

Instead of serving broiled foods with the usual savory butters, make yogurt sauces by beating plain yogurt with herbs, spices, lemon juice and tomato paste etc.

## DRY-FRYING

Dry-frying, or pan frying, is particularly suited to all types of good quality meats.

If possible, use a ridged cast-iron pan. This enables much of the fat to drain from the meat, besides giving it an attractive ridged pattern.

### METHOD

Prepare the meat as for broiling. Lightly oil the pan and place on a high heat until the oil sizzles. Lay

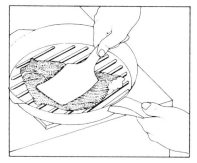

*Dry-frying meat*

the meat in the hot pan and cook for 1 minute, pressing down against the ridges. Turn and cook the second side in the same way. Lower the heat to medium. If possible, turn the meat at right angles to its original position. Cook for the remaining time on that side. Turn again and complete cooking.

As with conventionally broiled meats, garnish with flavored yogurt.

## STIR-FRYING

Stir-frying, a method of cooking taken from the Chinese, can be used for meat, fish, vegetables or nuts. The cooking process is extremely quick, which preserves vitamins and also prevents the ingredients from soaking up too much oil.

All ingredients for stir-frying must be cut into small, thin slices before cooking begins.

Use a lightly flavored oil such as peanut, sunflower or safflower. Choose flavorers such as garlic

and ground ginger. Try small amounts of liquid such as sherry or soy sauce for adding at the end if wished.

You will need a large, heavy frying pan or a wok. Those with electric stoves may well find a flat based wok more effective than one that is round based. A wooden or perforated spoon or fish-slice is necessary for moving the ingredients around.

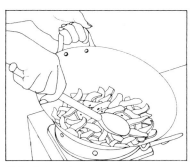

*Stir-frying thinly sliced food*

### METHOD

Heat the oil in the wok on a high heat. Add those ingredients that need a longer cooking time, plus the dry flavorers. Stir-fry for about 2 minutes. Add other ingredients and continue to stir until all are done (the process is rarely longer than about 6 minutes and the vegetables should still be crisp). Add liquid ingredients if using and serve as soon as possible.

## STEAMING

Steaming is a light method of cooking which involves no fats and

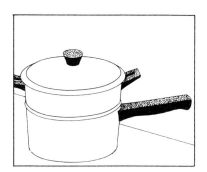

*A large steamer for fatless cooking*

preserves both nutrients and flavor. It is particularly suited to vegetables and fish. Chicken also steams effectively.

A large steamer is a useful piece of equipment in any kitchen. It consists of a saucepan with a perforated container that sits inside it and a well-fitting lid.

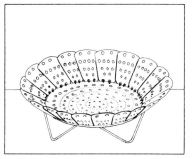

*Small steamers fit into saucepans*

You can also buy small steamers which open up rather like a flower and can be fitted into any sized saucepan. Failing this, use a steamproof colander that can sit neatly in a saucepan and be covered with foil.

### VEGETABLES

Cut them into fairly small, even sized pieces. If mixing vegetables, make sure that they have similar cooking times.

### METHOD

Put the prepared vegetables into the steamer. Bring the water to the boil in the saucepan. Lower in the steamer. The water must not bubble up and touch the vegetables. If there is too much water, pour some away. Cover the pan and cook until the vegetables are just tender. They will take about half as long again as boiled vegetables, and when done should still be slightly crisp. Serve as soon as possible.

### FISH

Use white fish fillets, cut into portions, fish cutlets, small whole fish such as whiting, or thin flat-fish fillets which should be rolled or folded. Season well with pepper, spices and herbs.

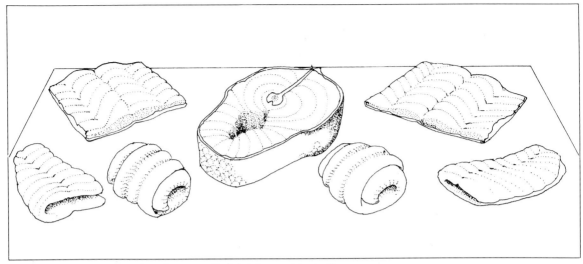

*Fish responds well to steaming. Season well with spices and herbs first*

Fish must always be steamed in a closed container in order to keep flavor and juices. Large enamel plates which fit inside the steamer are ideal since they conduct heat efficiently. Foil can also be used.

### METHOD
Lightly grease the plates or foil. Put the fish on one plate and cover

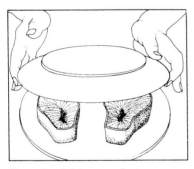

*Steaming fish between 2 plates*

with the other. Or line the steamer with foil. Put on the fish. Cover completely with the sides of the foil. Fish portions can also be individually wrapped in foil parcels.
Bring a saucepan of water to the boil. Lay the plates on top or lower in the steamer. The water must not touch the container. Steam until the fish is done. Steamed fish cooks extremely

quickly—thin fillets need about 8 minutes, thick cutlets about 20 minutes.

### CHICKEN
Flavor pieces with ingredients such as soy or Worcestershire sauce. Wrap in parcels of oiled foil. Place in the steamer for about 45 minutes.

## BOILING AND POACHING
Both meat and fish can be simmered gently in a flavored liquid until they are tender, moist and full of flavor. With meat, the process is usually called boiling. When a similar method is used for fish, it is called poaching.

### MEAT AND POULTRY
Lean beef roasts, lean pork, leg or

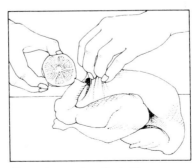

*Preparing poultry for boiling*

rolled breast of lamb and whole chickens can all be boiled.
Salted meats such as tongue should be soaked for 8 hours in cold water and drained. All meats should be securely tied. Chickens can be rubbed with spices such as paprika or curry spices and bunches of herbs, or a half lemon can be put inside the body cavity.

### METHOD
Put the meat or poultry into a large saucepan and add enough water to just cover meat and to come just over the legs of the chicken. Add a large onion, carrot and celery stalk, a bouquet garni and 1 tsp black peppercorns, plus 1 tsp whole cloves for salt meats. A little cider, wine or beer can also be added if wished. Bring the liquid to just below boiling point. Cover and simmer gently until tender. Meats need about 25 minutes per 1 lb, chicken 20 minutes.
Vegetables can be cooked with boiled meats. Add them towards the end of the cooking time, so that when the meat is tender the vegetables are cooked too. Suitable vegetables include carrots, celery, wedges of firm cabbage, whole small onions, and broad beans and peas tied loosely in muslin bags.
Boiled meat and poultry can be

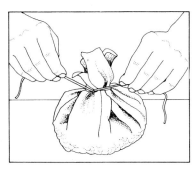

*Tie beans in muslin for boiling*

served hot or cold. The stock produced when boiling unsalted meats may be used as a thin gravy or can be made into a sauce by stirring 1¼ cups into 1 Tbsp melted margarine or butter and 1 Tbsp wholewheat flour. Chopped herbs and pickles, such as capers or gherkins, can be added for flavor. The stock from salted meats is too salty to make a pleasant sauce. Salted meats are best served plainly with their vegetable accompaniments.

If the meat is to be served cold, cool it in the stock to room temperature and, if possible, leave in a cool place for at least 2 hours after removing from the stock.

Pickles are a favorite accompaniment for boiled meats. They can also be diced and mixed into salads, with flavored oil and vinegar or yogurt based dressings.

### FISH
Fish is poached in a flavored liquid often known as a court bouillon.

Use absolutely fresh fish as the method brings out the natural flavor. Use whole small or large fish, both round or flat, thick fish fillets or steaks, and smoked fish such as kippers and smoked cod or haddock fillets.

### METHOD
Use a large pan, big enough to take the fish without bending (an oval one is ideal). It is a good idea to put a trivet or small rack in the base of the pan. If you use a purpose-made fish poacher, it will have a built-in plate. Place a piece of muslin under both this and the fish so that the fish can be lifted out easily. A clean linen towel or foil can also be used.

For fresh fish, put a glass of dry white wine into the pan and enough water to just cover the fish. Add 1 tsp black peppercorns, a bouquet garni and an onion, carrot and celery stalk, roughly chopped. A pinch of mace will give an additional pleasant flavor.

Smoked fish can be poached in plain water with the same flavorings or in a mixture of half water and half milk.

For water-based mixtures, bring them to the boil, cover and simmer for 10 minutes. Cool to just below simmering and carefully lower in the fish. Cook until the flesh flakes easily when tested with a fork.

Small fillets take about 5 minutes, smoked about 5 minutes, fillets 6–10 minutes depending on thickness, whole fish from 15–30 minutes depending on size.

Milk-based liquids should be infused with the flavorings on a low heat for 5 minutes before the fish is added and cooked as before.

### BRAISING
When meat is braised, it is generally first browned in butter or oil, after which vegetables are softened in the same fat. This gives an added richness to the final flavor. This effect can be achieved without fat.

### METHOD
Put ⅔ cup stock into a flameproof casserole, bring to the boil and add the braising vegetables (usually chopped onion, carrot and/or celery). Cook over a medium heat until beginning to soften and the stock has reduced to about 3 Tbsp. Raise the heat, put in the meat and sear it on all sides. Add any remaining stock or flavoring ingredients, cover and cook in the oven for the required amount of time.

### COLD START CASSEROLES
Many casseroles can be successfully made without involving the initial searing process.

### METHOD
Dice lean meat and any vegetable ingredients. Layer these in a flameproof casserole with seasonings and other dry flavoring ingredients (herbs, spices). Pour in enough liquid to just cover. This can be water or stock or a mixture. Up to ¾ cup can be replaced by wine or cider, up to 1¼ cups by beer. Add other flavorings such as tomato paste or Worcestershire sauce.

Place the casserole on top of the stove over a moderate heat. Bring the liquid to the boil. Cover and cook in the oven for the required amount of time.

### SAUTÉ DISHES
Sauté dishes also usually involve an initial frying process. As with braising, there is an alternative.

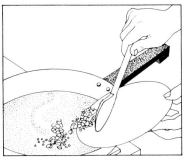

*Sautéing without fat*

### METHOD
Bring ⅔ cup stock to the boil in a deep frying pan or sauté pan. Put in one chopped onion and a chopped garlic clove. Boil until the liquid is reduced to about 2 Tbsp. Put in the meat and sear it.

Stir in wholewheat flour to thicken if necessary. Stir in stock or a mixture of wine or stock. Add herbs if using. Cover and cook gently for the required amount of time.

# SAUCES, DRESSINGS AND SPREADS

A good sauce or dressing can transform everyday food into something special, but they are all too often fattening and unhealthy! These recipes have been specially chosen to include in a healthful diet to add interest and flavor without being too calorie-laden.

## BLENDER TOMATO DRESSING

*Makes about ⅔ cup*

| |
|---|
| 2 Tbsp tomato juice |
| 2 Tbsp cider vinegar |
| 2 Tbsp clear honey |
| 1 egg yolk |
| salt and freshly ground pepper |
| 2 Tbsp chopped fresh chives |
| sprig of parsley |
| 4 Tbsp sunflower oil |

*1* Put the tomato juice, vinegar, honey, egg yolk, seasoning, chives and parsley in a blender or food processor and blend for 30 seconds.

*2* Gradually add the sunflower oil and blend until smooth. Use as a dressing for crisp mixed vegetable salads.

## YOGURT DRESSING

*Makes ⅔ cup*

| |
|---|
| ⅔ cup plain yogurt |
| ¼ tsp mustard powder |
| salt and freshly ground pepper |
| 1 Tbsp lemon juice |
| 1 Tbsp chopped fresh parsley |

*1* Place the yogurt, mustard, seasoning, lemon juice and parsley in a bowl.

*2* Mix well together. Serve with crunchy vegetable salads such as shredded cabbage, cauliflower and Chinese leaves.

## SOUR CREAM AND WATERCRESS DRESSING

This dressing is better made at least 30 minutes before serving.

*Serves 4*

| |
|---|
| ½ bunch of watercress |
| ⅔ cup sour cream |
| ½ tsp lemon juice |
| salt and freshly ground pepper |
| a little milk |

*1* Remove and discard the coarse stalks, then chop the watercress finely.

*2* Mix with the sour cream and lemon juice and season to taste.

*3* Add enough milk to give a pouring consistency.

*4* Good with beans and bean salads. Also goes well with cold fish dishes and baked potatoes.

## PLAIN YOGURT

*Makes about 2½ cups*

| |
|---|
| 2½ cups milk |
| 1½ Tbsp plain yogurt |
| 2 Tbsp skim milk powder (optional) |

*1* Use absolutely clean, well rinsed containers and utensils. Warm an insulated jar. Pour the milk into a saucepan and bring to the boil. (If you want a thick yogurt, keep the pan on a very low heat after this for 15 minutes.) Remove from the heat and allow to cool to 113°F.

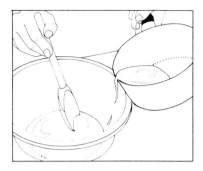

*2* Spoon the plain yogurt into a bowl and stir in a little of the cooled milk. Add the skim milk powder, if used, to make a smooth paste. Stir in the remaining milk.

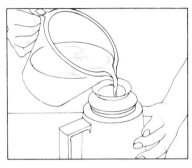

*3* Pour into the warmed insulated jar. Cover and leave for 8–9 hours, undisturbed.

*4* Transfer the yogurt into small pots or cartons and place in the refrigerator immediately. It will keep for up to 10 days.

## WHOLEWHEAT BREAD SAUCE

*Makes about 1¼ cups*

3 cloves

1 small onion

1¼ cups milk

½ bay leaf

pinch of mace

½ cup wholewheat breadcrumbs

salt and freshly ground pepper

1 Tbsp margarine or butter (optional)

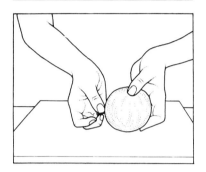

*1* Push the cloves into the onion. Put the milk into a saucepan with the onion, bay leaf and mace.

*2* Bring gently to the boil, remove from the heat and leave to stand for 15 minutes.

*3* Strain the milk and return to the pan with the breadcrumbs. Season the mixture and heat gently, stirring, until boiling.

*4* Beat in the margarine, if using, and serve the sauce hot as an accompaniment to poultry.

# *VEGETABLE DISHES*

Vegetables play an important part in a healthful diet. Raw vegetables are particularly good, losing none of their goodness in the cooking process. But if you want some variations with cooked vegetables, try these recipes for a tasty alternative to the usual method of plain boiling.

## UNPEELED ROAST POTATOES

*Serves 4*

2 lb small or medium old potatoes

4 Tbsp margarine or butter, or 2 Tbsp vegetable oil

*1* Scrub the potatoes and cut them into 1-inch cubes.

*2* Place the margarine in a large shallow roasting tin and put in the oven at 425°F until the fat is melted and hot.

*3* Mix the potatoes into the margarine and bake in the oven for 1 hour, stirring occasionally, until really crisp and golden brown.

## CAULIFLOWER NIÇOISE

*Serves 4*

1 cauliflower

salt

1 Tbsp vegetable oil

1 small onion, chopped

1–2 garlic cloves, crushed

3 tomatoes, peeled and quartered

finely grated rind and juice of 1 lemon

*1* Break the cauliflower into florets, place in a saucepan of boiling salted water and cook for 5 minutes. Drain and place in a warmed serving dish. Keep hot.

*2* Heat the oil in a pan, add the onion and garlic and fry for 3 minutes. Add the tomatoes and cook for 3 minutes. Add the lemon juice and cook for a further 2 minutes.

*3* Pour over the cauliflower and serve sprinkled with finely grated lemon rind.

## STEAMED SNOW PEAS

*Serves 6*

1½ lb snow peas

salt and freshly ground pepper

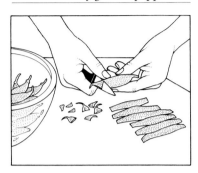

*1* Tip and tail the pods and remove any side strings. Place in a colander or steamer over a pan of boiling, salted water (see page 149).

*2* Cover and steam gently for about 5 minutes or until just tender. Do not overcook. Spoon into a warmed serving dish, toss gently with seasoning.

## DHAL (LENTIL PURÉE)

*Serves 4*

½ cup red lentils

1¼ cups cold water

2 Tbsp sunflower oil

1 medium onion, finely chopped

2 Tbsp margarine or butter

salt and freshly ground pepper

*1* Rinse the lentils and put in a saucepan with the cold water. Bring to the boil and simmer for about 1 hour until tender, adding more water if they get too dry.

*2* Meanwhile, heat the oil in a pan, add the onion and fry for 5 minutes until soft.

*3* When the lentils are tender, remove from the heat and stir vigorously to form a purée. Add the margarine and fried onion and stir over the heat. Season.

# *BREADS*

Bread-making need not be limited to the usual yeasted loaf alone. You can try your hand at making your own more exotic breads such as puris, chappattis and parathas from India, and pita, the popular Greek bread, all made with wholewheat flour for extra flavor and goodness.

## WHOLEWHEAT BREAD

*Makes two 2 lb or four 1 lb loaves*

2 oz fresh yeast or 2 Tbsp active dry yeast and 1 tsp honey

3¾ cups tepid water

3 lb plain wholewheat flour

2 Tbsp light brown sugar

4 tsp salt

2 Tbsp margarine or butter

*1* Grease two 2 lb or four 1 lb loaf tins. Blend the fresh yeast with 1¼ cups of the water. If using dried yeast, dissolve the honey in 1¼ cups of the water and sprinkle over the yeast. Leave the fresh or dry yeast liquid in a warm place for 15 minutes until frothy.

*2* Mix the flour, sugar and salt together in a large bowl. Rub in the margarine. Stir in the yeast liquid, adding enough of the remaining water to make a firm dough that leaves the bowl clean.

*3* Turn out on to a lightly floured surface and knead the dough until firm, elastic and no longer sticky. Shape into a ball, cover with a clean cloth and leave to rise in a warm place for about 1 hour until doubled in size.

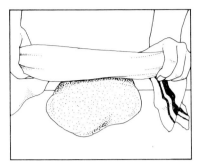

*4* Turn the dough onto a floured surface and knead again until firm. Divide into 2 or 4 pieces and flatten firmly with the knuckles to knock out any air bubbles. Knead well until firm.

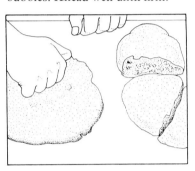

*5* Shape the dough into the tins. Brush with salted water. Cover with a cloth and leave to prove for 1 hour at room temperature until the dough rises to the tops of the tins.

*6* Bake in the oven at 450°F for 30–40 minutes until well risen and firm. Cool on a wire rack.

# CHAPPATTIS

*Makes about 6*

| |
|---|
| $\frac{3}{4}$ cup wholewheat flour |
| $\frac{1}{4}$ tsp salt |
| 1 tsp baking powder |
| 1 Tbsp margarine or butter |
| 6 Tbsp water |
| vegetable oil for frying |

*1* Mix together the flour, salt and baking powder in a bowl. Rub in the margarine and add enough water to mix to a stiff dough. Turn on to a floured surface and knead well for 10 minutes.

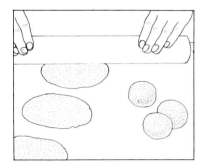

*2* Divide the dough into 6–8 pieces and shape each into a small ball. Roll each ball into a 4-inch round.

*3* Heat the oil in a frying pan and fry the chappattis one at a time until they puff up, turning once. Drain on absorbent paper and serve while still warm as an accompaniment to a curry.

# PARATHAS

*Makes 12*

| |
|---|
| $2\frac{1}{2}$ cups wholewheat flour |
| 1 tsp salt |
| $1\frac{1}{4}$ cups water |
| $\frac{1}{2}$ cup ghee or clarified butter, melted |

*1* Mix the flour and salt together in a bowl. Add the water and bind to a soft pliable dough—it may be slightly sticky. Knead lightly, using a little flour if necessary. Cover and leave to rest for about 15 minutes.

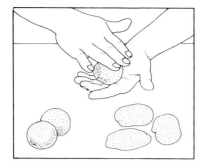

*2* Divide the dough into 12 and roll each piece into a smooth ball using the palms of your hands.

*3* On a lightly floured surface, roll each ball out into a 6-inch round.

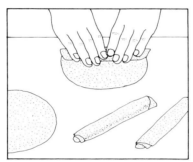

*4* Smear a little cooled but not set ghee over each one and roll up like cigars.

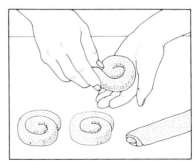

*5* Lift up the roll and place one end in the center of your hand. Carefully wind the rest of the roll around the center point to form a disc. Press lightly together.

*6* Roll out each round on a floured surface to a 5–6 inch circle.

*7* Heat a frying pan. When really hot, cook a paratha until bubbles appear. Flip over.

*8* Cook the underside for about 30 seconds while smearing the top with ghee.

*9* Turn over the paratha twice more, smearing the second side with ghee. When browned, remove from pan. Wipe pan between frying parathas.

# PITA BREAD

*Makes 8*

| |
|---|
| $\frac{1}{2}$ oz fresh yeast or $1\frac{1}{2}$ tsp active dry yeast and 1 tsp raw sugar |
| about $1\frac{1}{4}$ cups tepid water |
| $3\frac{3}{4}$ cups wholewheat flour |
| $\frac{1}{2}$ tsp salt |

*1* Grease a baking sheet. Blend the yeast with a little of the water. If using dried yeast, dissolve the sugar in the water and sprinkle over the yeast. Leave the fresh or dried yeast in a warm place for 15 minutes until frothy.

*2* Sift the flour and salt into a bowl and make a well in the centre. Add the yeast liquid and remaining water. Mix to a dough.

*3* Turn out onto a floured surface and knead for about 10 minutes. Place in a bowl, cover with lightly oiled plastic and leave to rise in a warm place for 2 hours until doubled in size.

*4* Knead on a floured surface for 2–3 minutes. Divide the dough into 8 even pieces, knead each into a ball and flatten to about $\frac{1}{4}$ inch thick.

*5* Place on the baking sheet, cover with lightly oiled plastic and leave to prove in a warm place until doubled in size.

*6* Bake in the oven at 450°F for about 10 minutes. Cool on a wire rack.

## PURIS
## (INDIAN WAFERS)

*Makes 8*

¾ **cup wholewheat flour**

**1 Tbsp margarine or butter**

**salt and freshly ground pepper**

**about 4 Tbsp water**

**sunflower oil, for frying**

*1* Put the flour in a bowl and rub in the margarine. Season. Gradually work in just enough water to give a pliable dough and knead well. If time permits, cover and leave the dough for 1 hour.

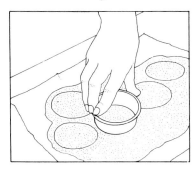

*2* Roll out the dough wafer-thin between sheets of non-stick paper, then cut out rounds about 3 inches in diameter. If they are not to be fried at once, cover the rounds with a damp cloth.

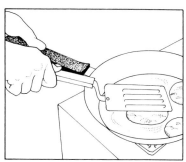

*3* Heat the oil in a frying pan and fry the rounds one or two at a time: slide each raw puri into the oil and hold it down with a slotted spatula, pressing lightly to distribute the air.

*4* Turn once, then drain on absorbent paper. Serve as an accompaniment to a curry.

# PASTRY, PASTA AND PIZZA

There is no need to rule out pastries, pastas and pizzas when following a healthful eating plan. They are more nutritious when made with wholewheat flour rather than white, and a fresh pizza or bowl of pasta need not be laden with calories as long as you choose toppings and fillings carefully.

## WHOLEWHEAT PASTRY

For wholewheat pastry the proportion of flour to fat is two to one. Therefore, for a recipe requiring ½ pound pastry, make up the pastry using 2 cups flour and ½ cup fat.

*Makes 2 crusts*

1½ **cups wholewheat flour**

**pinch of salt**

**6 Tbsp margarine or butter**

*1* Mix the flour and salt together in a bowl and add the margarine in small pieces. Using both hands, rub the margarine into the flour between finger and thumb tips until there are no lumps of margarine left and the mixture resembles fine breadcrumbs.

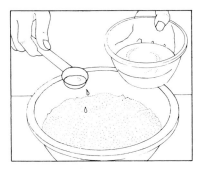

*2* Add 2 Tbsp water all at once, sprinkling it evenly over the surface.

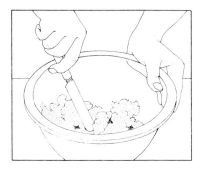

*3* Stir the water in with a round-bladed knife until the mixture begins to stick together in large lumps.

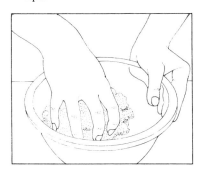

*4* With one hand, collect the mixture together and knead lightly for a few seconds, to give a firm smooth dough. The pastry can be used straight away, but is better allowed to "rest" for 15 minutes. It can also be wrapped in polythene and kept in the refrigerator for 1–2 days.

*5* When the pastry is required, sprinkle a very little flour on the working surface and on the rolling pin, not on the pastry, and roll out the dough evenly in one direction only, turning occasionally. The usual thickness is about ⅛ inch. Do not pull or stretch the dough. Use as required. The usual oven temperature for wholewheat pastry is 400–425°F.

# Herbs, Spices and Other Flavorings

The term *herb* applies when leaves, flowers and sometimes the stem of a non-woody plant are used, either fresh or dried. A spice, on the other hand, refers to parts of an aromatic, often woody plant and may include the seeds, bark or roots. It is usually dried and then used either whole or ground. Herbs and spices can be used either individually or in combinations.

## A–Z OF HERBS

### ANGELICA

A tall plant that can be grown as a perennial or biennial. The bright green leaves are divided into large leaflets and the small yellow flowers grow in a ball-like cluster. The thick, hollow stems of angelica are candied and used to decorate desserts. The leaves can be used fresh in savory dishes and both stems and leaves are used for herb teas.

### BASIL

Basil is a delicate annual plant that survives only during the summer months. It has small, soft, oval leaves and tiny white flowers. It can be used fresh or dried, in most savory dishes and is particularly good in those that contain tomatoes. It is also an essential ingredient in the famous Italian pesto sauce. Try it in soups, sauces and dressings, stuffings and casseroles.

### BAY

Bay laurel leaves come from an evergreen tree that can be kept small in pots or allowed to grow to full height in the open. The leaves are large, flat, oval and glossy. Used fresh but most often dried (the fresh leaves can sometimes taste rather bitter), bay leaves are tied into bouquets garnis; they can also be used alone (both whole and crumbled) to flavor sauces, soups and casserole dishes. Always discard the whole bay leaves before serving.

### BERGAMOT

Bergamot, or bee's balm, is a perennial plant, bushy and about 12 inches high. The leaves are broad and oval and the flowers large, red and shaggy. Bergamot is mostly used to make a herbal tea known as oswego tea, but it can also add a fresh flavor to summer drinks.

### BORAGE

Borage is an annual plant with large, fleshy, hairy leaves and small blue flowers. The leaves have a delicate, cucumber-like flavor and, when young, can be added to summer salads. They can also be candied. Both flowers and leaves can be added to summer drinks, and the flowers are used to decorate fruit salads.

### CHAMOMILE

Chamomile is an annual plant with feathery leaves and white, daisy-like flowers. Rarely used in cooking, chamomile's chief use is in making a delicate-flavored, soothing tea (for which the dried flower-heads are used).

### CHERVIL

Chervil is an annual plant, closely related to parsley. It has very delicate, lacy leaves with a hint of licorice about their flavor. Because they are so delicate, large amounts of the fresh herb must be used. Chervil can be used in fish dishes and herb butters, and is particularly good with eggs and with vegetables such as carrots. It also brings out the flavor of other herbs, and is used in *fines herbes* mixtures.

## CHIVES

Chives are a perennial member of the onion family. The thin, almost grass-like leaves grow in clumps and have a deli-cate, onion

flavor. Snip them away with scissors and more will grow. Chives are often added to egg salads and omelettes and they are good with oily fish, in green summer salads and in herb butters. The tufted purple flowers are edible and make a pretty garnish.

## COMFREY

Comfrey is a tall, perennial plant with clusters of purple, bell-like flowers and large, fleshy, hairy leaves. It is often used medicinally, but the fresh leaves can be cooked in butter or deep-fried and eaten as a vegetable. They can also be used (dried and powdered) in herbal teas and, when young, can be added to salads. In addition, the dried root is sometimes used to flavor country wines.

## CORIANDER

Coriander is a highly aromatic annual plant, re-lated to parsley. The fresh leaves are often used, scattered over Middle Eastern dishes and curries. They can also be used sparingly in salads and stuffings, and look good sprinkled over summer soups. It is also known as cilantro.

## CURRY PLANT

The curry plant is a shrubby peren-nial plant that grows into a low spreading bush with green, spiky leaves. Although it is not used in authentic Indian curries, the leaves do have a strong curry-like flavor. Add them sparingly to winter soups and stews, to stuff-ings for game and to veal dishes. They can be used fresh or dried.

## DILL WEED

Dill is an annual plant, related to parsley and grow-ing quite tall with feathery leaves. These are re-ferred to as dill weed so as to dis-tinguish them from the seed (see spices). Dill is often used in cucumber salads and pickles. It is good with fish and summer vege-tables, and in Scandinavia is an essential ingredient in the dish of salted raw salmon known as Gravlax. It is also macerated in wine vinegar to make dill vinegar

## FENNEL

Not to be con-fused with the bulbous stem vegetable, Florence fennel, the herb fennel is a very tall, peren-nial plant with large, feathery leaves and clusters of tiny yellow flowers. It has a fresh flavor reminiscent of licorice and is most often used with fish. It is also very good in green and potato salads, and goes well with pork. The stems may be dried, broken into short lengths and placed under meat which is to be barbecued.

## LAVENDER

Lavender is a well-loved, sweetly scented perennial plant with long, spear-like, gray-green leaves and spikes of purple flowers.

Lavender is usually grown for its aromatic properties, but it can be added to mixtures of herbs for stews, casseroles and marinades for game. The flowers can be crystal-lized, used to make conserves or made into jelly.

## LEMON BALM

This perennial plant has pale green, heart-shaped leaves which have a distinct lemony flavor. Use them in fish and poultry

dishes, in sauces, marinades and stuffings. They can be added to salads, cream cheese, fruit salads and milk puddings, and will make a refreshing addition to summer fruit cups as well as a soothing tea.

## LEMON VERBENA

Lemon verbena is a perennial plant that likes a warm, sunny situation. It is a tall shrub with long, pale green, pointed, lemon-

scented leaves, which can be used in stuffings (sparingly) and to flavor fish and poultry. Add them to fruit salads and puddings, or use them to flavor wine cups and to make a refreshing tea.

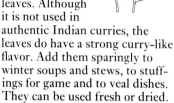

## LOVAGE

A medicinal as well as a culinary herb, lovage grows very tall, with dark, shiny leaves and clusters of yellow flowers. It has a  celery-like flavor, which adds a sharp spiciness to casseroles and soups, as well as green salads and omelettes.

## MARJORAM

Although there are two varieties of marjoram (sweet and wild), the name marjoram is usually applied to the sweet—the  wild being more commonly referred to as oregano (see right). Sweet marjoram is a low-growing perennial plant with small, oval leaves. It has a spicy, slightly sweet flavor that will enhance rather than mask delicate flavors. Marjoram is often tied into bouquets garnis, and is used to flavor soups and stews. It is good with pork, veal and poultry, eggs and vegetables.

## MINT

There are many different varieties of this perennial, oval-leaved plant. The one most used is *spearmint*. It is a favorite accompaniment to lamb, and is made into mint jelly and a mint sauce with vinegar. Add a sprig to new potatoes and green peas as they cook and scatter chopped fresh mint over them for serving. Add chopped mint to salads (both sweet and savory) and to Middle Eastern tabbouleh. *Applemint* has rounded slightly furry leaves. As its name implies, it has a slight

apple flavor. It makes delicious mint sauce and jelly and a sprig added to apple jelly as it cooks will improve the flavor. Chopped applemint leaves can be added to fresh fruit salads or sprinkled over cut grapefruit. *Peppermint* has dark green, shiny leaves with a hint of purple. Oil distilled from them contains menthol and is used to flavor candy, liqueurs and toothpaste. The chopped leaves can be added to fruit salads and made jellies, sauces and peppermint tea.

## OREGANO

Also known as wild marjoram, oregano is a perennial plant. It has a more pungent, spicy flavor than sweet marjoram (see left) and it 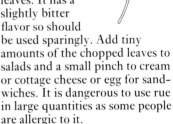 is much used in Italian cooking, adding interest to pasta dishes and pizzas. It also makes a good addition to vegetable dishes, particularly those containing tomatoes, egg plant, zucchini and sweet peppers. It is nearly always used dried.

## PARSLEY

Parsley is probably the most used of all herbs. It is a biennial plant with bright green leaves which can either be curled or flat 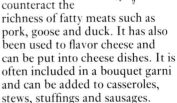 (Italian parsley). It is always included in bouquets garnis and *fines herbes*. It can be used too as a garnish for all savory dishes and can be chopped into salads and herb butters. It can also be used to make parsley sauce, and tartare and Ravigote sauce and is excellent with fish and seafood, with veal, poultry, eggs and vegetables.

## ROSEMARY

Rosemary is a perennial, shrubby bush, the leaves of which can be picked all through the year. They are small and spiked, dark green on one side and gray-green on the other. Rosemary has a strong, pungent flavor. It may overpower other herbs, so is best used on its own to flavor lamb, pork and poultry, root vegetables and fish. In small quantities it can also be used to flavor bread rolls. It is available fresh, as dried leaves or in powder form.

## RUE

Rue is a perennial herb with a woody stem and small, blue-green, irregularly cut leaves. It has a slightly bitter flavor so should be used sparingly. Add tiny amounts of the chopped leaves to salads and a small pinch to cream or cottage cheese or egg for sandwiches. It is dangerous to use rue in large quantities as some people are allergic to it.

## SAGE

Sage is a perennial herb with gray-green, oval leaves. It has been used for centuries to flavor and counteract the richness of fatty meats such as pork, goose and duck. It has also been used to flavor cheese and can be put into cheese dishes. It is often included in a bouquet garni and can be added to casseroles, stews, stuffings and sausages.

### SALAD BURNET

Salad burnet is a perennial herb, its leaves grow in a fountain-shaped clump. Each has a red stem with six or more pairs of round leaflets on either side. Salad burnet has a slightly bitter, cucumber-like flavor and the young leaves can be added to salads and used to flavor vinegar. It can also be added to vegetable dishes and soups and stuffings.

### SAVORY

There are two types of savory, the perennial winter and the annual summer savory. They look similar with small, spiky dull-green leaves. Both have a peppery flavor, but that of summer savory is fresher. Both types are good with pork and can be added to beef casseroles, egg dishes, tomato-flavored sauces and veal stews. Summer savory is known as "the bean herb." Add it to both broad and snap beans when cooking.

### SORREL

For flavor and delicacy of texture, choose French sorrel with its shiny, large, spear-shaped leaves. It is a perennial plant and can be picked for most of the year. It can be used to make the delicately flavored sorrel soup and also in omelettes, sauces and stuffings (particularly with fish). The raw leaves can be chopped and added to salads and can also be cooked alone as a vegetable.

### SWEET CICELY

Sweet cicely is a tall, attractive perennial plant with ferny leaves and clusters of tiny white flowers. The leaves have a sweet, aniseed-like flavor. Add them to green salads and salad dressings, omelettes and pancakes. They are also delicious sprinkled into fruit salads, and act as both sweetener and flavoring when cooked with tart fruits. Sweet cicely is often used as a flavoring for liqueurs.

### TANSY

A tall perennial plant with ferny, dark-green leaves and button-like yellow flowers. Use the youngest leaves as they are the most tender. Traditionally, chopped tansy has been added to omelettes, but it can also be put into stuffings, casseroles and sausages. With the chopped leaves of sage and mint, it makes a delicious herb butter.

### TARRAGON

The culinary variety is French tarragon. It is a perennial which dies down in autumn and has narrow, green shiny leaves and a  spicy flavor. Tarragon is often used in chicken dishes and is an essential ingredient in Béarnaise, Tartare and Hollandaise sauces and in *fines herbes*. It can also be used to make herb butter and added to salads.

### THYME

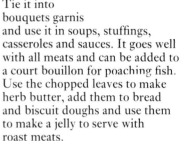

The low-growing, perennial thyme with its tiny, dull green leaves is a favorite in most herb gardens. Tie it into bouquets garnis and use it in soups, stuffings, casseroles and sauces. It goes well with all meats and can be added to a court bouillon for poaching fish. Use the chopped leaves to make herb butter, add them to bread and biscuit doughs and use them to make a jelly to serve with roast meats.
*Lemon thyme* is a variety of thyme. A low-growing perennial with tiny, shiny leaves on woody stems, its flavor is that of lemon with strong undertones of thyme. Use it with fish dishes, and also with lamb and veal. Add the leaves to fruit salads and put a sprig into the pan when scalding milk or cream for sweet dishes.

### WOODRUFF

Woodruff is a delicate, perennial plant with small, spiked leaves growing in whirls around the deli-  cate stems. The white star-like flowers grow on the top ruff of leaves. Woodruff has a vanilla-like scent and can be used like a vanilla pod. Steep the leaves in milk before making custard or pastry cream, or add it to the saucepan while you are scalding cream to make ice cream.

# A–Z OF SPICES

## AJOWAN

Small, light brown, slightly elongated seeds which have a rather coarse flavor of thyme, ajowan is a spice related to caraway and cumin. It is used most often in Indian cookery, both to flavor food and to counteract the effect of ingredients such as beans which can cause flatulence. It is also used medicinally to relieve stomach upsets.

## ALLSPICE

Also known as Jamaica pepper, the seeds of all-spice are just slightly larger than peppercorns and dark brown in color. Despite its alternative name it is not peppery in flavor, but delicately spicy with a tinge of cloves, cinnamon and nutmeg. Allspice can be bought whole or ground and it can be added to both sweet and savory dishes. Add ground all-spice to ginger cakes and scald whole seeds in milk for making puddings and custards. It is also an ingredient in pickling spice and is used in salting meats.

## ANISEED

The tiny, purse-shaped seeds of anise have a warm, sweet, pungent flavor and can be used in sweet and savory dishes. Add them to cakes, biscuits and candy, to the syrups of fruit salads and to creams and custards. Their flavor also goes well with fish and pork, vegetables and cream cheese.

## CARAWAY

The small, elongated, dark brown seeds of caraway have a warming but slightly sharp flavor. Their valuable digestive properties make them particularly suitable for eating with rich, fatty foods such as pork, but they are also excellent added to cabbage dishes and sauerkraut. Most often, however, they are added to cakes and pastries and baked apples. In Germany they are used to flavor cheese and are an ingredient in some liqueurs.

## CARDAMOM

Available as pods and seeds, cardamom comes from a perennial plant related to ginger. The pods (which contain the seeds) can be either green or white. Cardamom seeds should always be bought inside their pods, removed by crushing and discarding the pods, and ground at home as, once ground, their light, sweet, sherbety flavor is quickly lost. Green cardamom has the finer flavor and is added to both sweet and savory dishes, particularly in Indian cooking. Use it with meat, poultry and rice; add it to Turkish coffee and hot punches. White cardamom has a slightly coarser flavor but may be used in the same ways.

## CASSIA

Related to cinnamon. The dried bark, the dried unripe seeds and the dried leaves are all used in cookery. The bark has a similar flavor to cinnamon but is not as strong; it may be used in the same way as cinnamon sticks. The seeds, sometimes known as Chinese cassia buds, are used in drinks and candy and are added to pots pourris.

## CAYENNE PEPPER

Derived from a hot, red variety of the capsicum family. The pods are small, long and narrow and, when picked and dried, both pods and seeds are ground together. Cayenne pepper has a clean, sharp flavor and is used for flavoring seafood in many parts of the world. It is also added to Indian curries and the spiced stews of the Middle East, as well as the classic brown and Hollandaise sauces in Western cooking.

## CELERY SEEDS

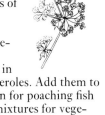

The tiny, light brown, slightly elongated seeds of celery have a bitter, celery flavor and therefore should be used sparingly in soups and casseroles. Add them to a court bouillon for poaching fish and to pickle mixtures for vegetables and seafood. A small pinch will enliven a salad dressing; they can also be added to bread rolls.

## CHILIES

Small varieties of capsicum with a specially hot flavor. *Whole dried chilies* are added to pickling spice and are used for flavoring spiced vinegars. They can be finely chopped and added to hot spiced dishes when fresh chilies are not available. The seeds are the hottest part, so if you want a less fiery flavoring, omit these. Always wash your hands thoroughly after handling chilies. Pure *chili powder* is made by grinding dried red chilies and has a clean, fresh, hot taste. It is added to Indian curries, spiced Middle Eastern dishes and used in Caribbean and Creole cookery. It is good with seafood and in sauces. Commercial *chili powder* consists of chili powder that has been mixed with oregano, chocolate, cumin and other flavorings. It is often used in Mexican dishes. *Fresh chilies* are small and tapering and should look smooth and shiny. They are sold either unripe (green) or ripe (red). They have a hot flavor and are used in curries and other hot dishes; they can also be added very sparingly to salads made from dried beans. Core and seed them before use, although a few seeds can be left in if a very hot, pungent effect is needed for a particular recipe.

## CINNAMON

Native to Ceylon, cinnamon is the bark of a tree which is a member of the laurel family. The bark is peeled from the young shoots of the tree, then left to dry in the sun so that it curls into quills, known as cinnamon sticks. The bark of the cassia tree is often sold as cinnamon, which it resembles closely, both in flavor and appearance. Known for centuries for its fragrant and therapeutic qualities, cinnamon has many uses in cooking. Use the sticks to infuse flavor into drinks, pickles, fruit compotes, milk puddings and casseroles. Ground cinnamon is best for cakes and puddings — it has a special affinity with chocolate.

## CLOVES

The name *clove* comes from the Latin word for nail, *clavus*, which the spice resembles in appearance. Cloves are in fact the flower buds of an evergreen shrub native to the Moluccas or Spice Islands, but nowadays the majority are imported from Zanzibar

and Madagascar. The volatile oil of cloves is a powerful antiseptic (it is a standard remedy for toothache) and cloves are also used in the making of pomanders. In cooking, cloves are used both in their whole and ground form. Whole cloves are most often used in marinades for meat and fish, and for infusing pickles and hot drinks; they are also used for studding whole onions and hams. Use ground cloves in baking and puddings, particularly with apples.

## CORIANDER

Round, light brown seeds with a fresh, spicy flavor. They can be bought whole or ground and are used in many Indian and Pakistani dishes. Their flavor is improved if they are gently dry-roasted before grinding. Use coriander in curries and put the whole seeds into vegetables à la grecque. Ground coriander can be added to bread and cakes. The spice is an ingredient in liqueurs and vermouths.

## CUMIN

Small, dark brown, elongated seeds with a rich, dry flavor. Cumin is frequently used in Indian and Middle Eastern dishes. In European cooking the whole seeds are sometimes used in pickling. A sweet, spicy drink is made with cumin, ginger and tamarind, but apart from this cumin is not used in sweet dishes.

## DILL

The oval, flattened seeds of the dill plant are dried and used whole as a spice. Use them in pickles and sprinkle them sparingly into salads. They can be added to cabbage and to dishes of braised root vegetables. Like caraway seeds, they can be added to cake mixtures, buns and candy.

## FENNEL SEEDS

The tiny, purse-like seeds of fennel have a warm, slightly bitter, aniseed flavor. They have strong digestive qualities and so are often used with rich meats and oily fish. Sprinkle them over mackerel or herrings before broiling. Add them to pork and creamy sauces. They can also be used to flavor pickles and added to bread and cakes. Fennel is also used occasionally to flavor curries.

## FENUGREEK

Small, hard, yellow-brown seeds. To remove their slightly bitter taste, fry them in hot oil before using until they brown. Whole or ground fenugreek is used in the cooking of Mediterranean countries, but is most often used in Indian curries. The whole, untreated seeds can be used to flavor pickles; they can also be sprouted and used in salads, providing an excellent source of vitamin E.

## GINGER

*Fresh ginger root* can be bought whole, in chunks or ground in the form of a light, beige-colored powder. The whole pieces 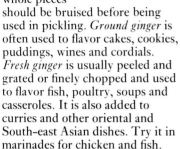 should be bruised before being used in pickling. *Ground ginger* is often used to flavor cakes, cookies, puddings, wines and cordials. *Fresh ginger* is usually peeled and grated or finely chopped and used to flavor fish, poultry, soups and casseroles. It is also added to curries and other oriental and South-east Asian dishes. Try it in marinades for chicken and fish.

## JUNIPER

Round, purple-brown berries, about twice the size of pepper-corns with smooth skins. They are always bought whole and are easy to grind as they are soft. Juniper berries are often included in spice mixtures for meat and are excellent with pork and game. They can be added to casseroles and pâtés, and are also good with cabbage. Juniper berries are an important flavoring ingredient in gin.

## LAOS POWDER

Closely related to ginger and is similar in that the root is the part used. It has a peppery ginger taste and is used 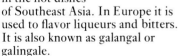 in the hot dishes of Southeast Asia. In Europe it is used to flavor liqueurs and bitters. It is also known as galangal or galingale.

## MACE

Mace blades form the outer casing of the nutmeg (see right). They are bright red when harvested and dry to a deep orange. Mace can be bought ground to powder. The flavor is similar to nutmeg, but more delicate. Mace is often used to flavor sauces, or added to stuffings, pâtés, soups, stews, cheese sauces and cakes.

## MUSTARD SEED

There are three types of mustard seed: black, brown and white. *Black mustard* is grown in only a few areas in Europe. *Brown mustard* has a similar flavor and is used in most English mustard mixes. *White mustard* is used mostly in American mixed mustards. Whole mustard seeds are used in pickling and can also be used in stuffings, sausages and certain curried dishes—particularly those containing spinach. They are increasingly being used in spiced grainy mustards. *English Dry Powder* was once made from ground black mustard seeds, but since these have become more scarce it is made from brown mustard with a little white mustard added. Also added are ground turmeric and wheat flour. To mix, add warm water to make a fine paste and leave for 10 minutes. Mustard powder has numerous uses in cooking, wherever a hot flavor is called for.

## NUTMEG

Bought whole, as a small, oval, shiny nut, or ground. If bought whole, grate it only as you need it using a special nutmeg grater or other fine grater.

Nutmeg can be used in sweet and savory dishes. Add it to puddings, cakes and cookies and grate it over puddings. Use it with vegetables (particularly spinach); in sausages and stuffings and Middle Eastern spiced dishes; and in punches and night-time drinks.

## PEPPER

Available whole or ground. Black and white peppercorns come from a tropical vine. To produce *black pepper* the  berries are picked when green and dried whole. For *white pepper*, they are allowed to ripen and turn red and the skin is removed before drying. White pepper has a milder flavor than black. It is used in delicately flavored dishes and light-colored sauces and mayonnaise. Black pepper is used in most savory dishes and can also be used in desserts. *Green peppercorns*: Some peppercorns are picked when still green and pickled in brine or vinegar or in their own juices.

These can be used whole or coarsely crushed, and give a hot "pickle" taste to recipes. They are used to flavor most meats and game (but particularly steak and duck) pâtés and sausages and savory butters. Green peppercorns also go well with fresh strawberries.

*Pink peppercorns* are totally unrelated to the black peppercorn family, but come from a completely different plant, sometimes known as Brazilian pepper. Although they enjoyed some popularity a few years ago, this was short-lived as it was discovered that they can cause an allergic reaction.

## POPPY SEED

Sometimes called maw seeds, these are derived from the opium poppy. The most common type in Europe is called black poppy seed, although in color the tiny round seeds are blue-gray. The type used in India has a smaller, creamy-yellow seed. Both have a distinct nutty flavor.

Poppy seed is used in curries, but most often is sprinkled over breads and used as a filling in cakes and pastries.

## SAFFRON

The tiny dried stigmas of the saffron crocus, this is the most expensive spice in the world. The stigmas or strands of saffron should be a brilliant orange color and have a pungent, bitter taste.

Ground saffron is usually cheaper, but does not have such a good flavor and varies enormously in quality.

Saffron is used extensively in Indian and Mediterranean cooking and to flavor many rice dishes such as pilafs and paella, soups and fish dishes.

## SESAME

Tiny, flat, oval seeds which may be red, light brown or black. They have a rich, nutty flavor and are often sprinkled over breads. They can also be toasted and used in salads and sprinkled over hot spiced dishes. A nutty flavored edible oil is derived from sesame seeds. They are also ground to produce a rich gray paste known as tahini, which is used for dips, a dip of chick peas called hummus.

## STAR ANISE

The star-shaped fruit of an evergreen tree native to southwest China. When dried it is a red-brown color and the flavor is one of pungent aniseed.

In China, star anise is used to flavor stewed and simmered dishes, particularly those of duck, beef, chicken and lamb. It is also placed under whole fish for steaming. It is used whole and one star is quite sufficient to flavor a large dish. Star anise is one of the ingredients of five-spice powder.

## SZECHUAN PEPPERCORN

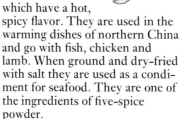

Used mainly in Chinese cookery, Szechuan peppercorns consist of small, round red-brown, rough-coated berries which have a hot, spicy flavor. They are used in the warming dishes of northern China and go with fish, chicken and lamb. When ground and dry-fried with salt they are used as a condiment for seafood. They are one of the ingredients of five-spice powder.

## TURMERIC

Related to ginger and the part used is the knobbly rhizome, which is bright orange inside the peel. Whole pieces of turmeric can be bought, but this is one spice that is most frequently bought ground.

Use it quickly as its flavor deteriorates on keeping. Turmeric is used in curries and curry powder and is added to mustards and pickles. Its bright color makes it useful for coloring rice and sweet Indian dishes.

## VANILLA

The pod of a type of orchid, yellow-green when picked and dark brown after curing and drying. The pod can be re-used several times provided it is dried well and stored in a plastic bag.

Vanilla is essentially a flavoring for sweet dishes particularly ice creams, custards and pastry cream. Use it to flavor hot chocolate or coffee drinks and infuse it in wine cups. Keep it permanently in a jar of sugar to make your own vanilla sugar.

## GRINDING YOUR OWN SPICES

Spices taste better when freshly ground. Peppercorns and allspice berries can have their own peppermills. Small amounts of spice can be crushed with a pestle and mortar or with a rolling pin. Grind large amounts in a coffee grinder, remembering to wipe it out well each time with paper towels, so that no cross flavoring occurs. Most spices benefit from being gently dry-fried for a few minutes before being ground. This releases extra flavor, especially with spices such as cumin and coriander.

# OTHER FLAVORINGS

## ASAFOETIDA

This is not a true spice but is derived from the resin of a plant native to Afghanistan and Iran. It can be bought in solid form but as it is very hard is best bought ground, in powder form. The flavor is pungent, a little like spicy garlic. Like ajowan, it is used to counteract flatulence. Asafoetida is used in very small quantities, mainly in Indian cooking for pickles, fish and vegetables. In India, it is often used as a substitute for salt.

## CAPERS

The pickled buds of the caper bush that grows wild around the Mediterranean. Capers are dull green, pointed at one end and with a  pungent pickle flavor. They are used with fish and in sauces such as Tartare, Remoulade and Ravigote. They can also be used to flavor butter and as a garnish, sprinkled over salads and seafood.

## COCONUT MILK

The coconut milk referred to in many recipes has nothing to do with the natural "milk" or juice in the center of the coconut, but is actually made using either fresh coconut or creamed coconut (sold in cans in supermarkets and delicatessens). In Indian and Southeast Asian dishes, it gives a subtle, creamy flavor and takes the harsh "edge" off hot, fiery spices.

## GARLIC

Garlic is a perennial plant that is more often grown as an annual. It is a member of the onion family and has small, white, oval-shaped bulbs  or cloves held together in a cluster by a white outer skin. Garlic will enhance most savory dishes: add it to salads, soups, casseroles, pâtés, sauté dishes and roasts.

Garlic is readily available dried and powdered, and is a convenient substitute for fresh garlic in soups and savory dishes.

## GERANIUM

The geraniums most used for culinary purposes are the rose-scented, mint-scented and lemon-scented varieties. Put  leaves into the base of a cake tin when making a sponge cake and remove them when the cake is cooked. When making custard add them to the pan when scalding the milk. They can also be used to flavor milk puddings, sweet sauces, sorbets, jellies, jams and herb teas.

## HORSERADISH

The grated root of the horseradish plant is available dried in jars. Use it as for fresh. Horseradish, related to mustard, is a perennial plant, of which the long tapering, creamy colored root is used. Lift the roots in Autumn, scrub and grate them and preserve them in jars, covered with wine vinegar. Use horseradish to make a creamy sauce for roast beef. Add it to beets or cucumber salads and to vinaigrette dressings. Sprinkle it over mackerel fillets before broiling.

## LEMON GRASS

Lemon grass is grown mostly in tropical and sub-tropical countries but is imported to the West, in fresh and dried forms. It has thick, grass-like leaves which smell and taste strongly of lemon. It is most often used in the cooking of Sri Lanka and Southeast Asia to flavor curry and meat dishes. It can also be used with fish and to flavor sweet puddings.

## ROSE

Both the petals and hips of sweet scented roses can be used for culinary purposes. The petals can be crystallized and  made into jam. Rose vinegar (made from rose petals infused in wine vinegar) adds a delicate flavor to salads and you can make rose petal wine. Rose hips are an excellent source of vitamin C. Make them into syrup or rose hip jelly. Probably the most common use of roses in cooking, however, is in rosewater, used to flavor and perfume many Middle Eastern sweets and confections.

## TAMARIND

Tamarind is the large pod that grows on the Indian tamarind tree. After picking, it is seeded, peeled and pressed into a dark-brown pulp.

It is used to add a sour flavor to chutneys, sauces and curries, to which it is added in the form of tamarind juice.

## VIOLET

Sweet violets grow wild and can also be cultivated. The violet is a tiny perennial plant with heart-shaped leaves and sweet-scented mauve or white flowers. The petals can be crystallized and used to decorate desserts. They can also be used to make an unusual vinegar to flavor all kinds of sauces and stews. The petals are placed in a glass bottle to about one-third full and then topped up with red or white wine vinegar. The bottle is sealed and left in a warm place for two to three weeks before straining for use. The petals are also steeped in white wine cups.

---

### DRY-FRYING SPICES

Dry-frying will mellow the flavor of spices. They can be dried singly or in mixtures. If mixing the spices, put the hardest ones such as fenugreek into the pan first and add softer ones such as coriander and cumin after a few minutes.

Heat a heavy frying pan over moderate heat. Put in the spices and stir them constantly until they are an even brown (do not allow them to burn). Tip the spices out to cool and then grind them in an electric grinder.

In China, a mixture of anise pepper and salt is roasted in this way to be used as a condiment for seafood and poultry.

---

# HERB AND SPICE MIXTURES

## BOUQUET GARNI

This is a small bunch of herbs, tied together with string so it can be suspended in soups, casseroles and sauté dishes and removed before serving. The classic ingredients are bay, parsley and thyme, but other herbs can be added to suit a particular dish. When dried herbs are used for a bouquet garni they are tied in a small muslin bag.

## CURRY POWDER

The flavorings for authentic Indian curries are made up of different mixtures of ground spices which include cumin, coriander, chili powder and other aromatics.

You can mix your own, but for speed, bought curry powders are available. Besides using it in ethnic dishes, curry powder can add spice to many other types of dishes.

Add it to salad dressings, sprinkle it into sauces and casseroles, and rub it into chicken skin before poaching.

## FINES HERBES

This is a mixture of the finely chopped or dried leaves of parsley, chervil, chives and tarragon.

## FIVE-SPICE POWDER

A ground mixture of star anise, Szechuan peppercorns, fennel seed, cloves and cinnamon or cassia. Five-spice powder is used in authentic Chinese cookery. It is beige colored and very pungent and should be used sparingly. Five-spice powder is used to season Chinese red-cooked meats (meats simmered in soy sauce) and roast meats and poultry. It can also be added to marinades and sprinkled over whole steamed fish and vegetable dishes.

## GARAM MASALA

A mixture of spices used in Indian cookery. It most frequently contains black pepper, cumin, cinnamon, black or green cardamoms, cloves and bay leaves.

## HARISSA

Harissa is a hot mixture of chili and other spices that is used in Middle Eastern cooking. It can be bought in powder and paste form and may contain up to twenty spices. It is often served with couscous and other North African dishes: it is put into a separate bowl, stock from the main dish is poured in to dilute it and it is spooned back over the dish to taste.

## MIXED SPICES

These are mixtures of sweet-flavored ground spices. The main ingredient is nutmeg and included in smaller amounts are cinnamon, cloves, ginger, cardamom, vanilla, allspice and sometimes fennel seed.

Mixed spice is most often used in sweet dishes, cakes, cookies and candy, but it can be added sparingly to curries and spiced Middle Eastern dishes.

## PICKLING SPICE

Pickling spice is a pungent mixture of varying spices, usually based on black peppercorns, red chilies and varying proportions of mustard seed, allspice, cloves, ginger, mace and coriander seed.

| NAME | STARTERS AND SOUPS | MAIN COURSES AND VEGETABLES | DESSERTS AND BAKING |
|---|---|---|---|
| AJOWAN | Curry-flavored soups | Curries containing beans, meat, vegetables | None |
| ALLSPICE | Beef and minestrone soups; pickles | Baked ham; beef stews; carrots; creamed potatoes; meat loaves; spiced meats | Apple pies and crumbles; cakes; fruit salads; puddings; stewed fruits |
| ANGELICA | Seafood salads | Baked or grilled fish; carrot, pea, and potato salads; use leaves as vegetables | Candied stems for decoration; cheesecake; cooked with sharp fruits; fruit salads; preserves |
| ANISEED | Cheese dips; cream soups; seafood | Carrots; zucchini; cucumber and green salads; fish; pork; poultry | Cookies; cakes; candy; fresh fruit, especially figs; syrup for fruit salads |
| ASAFOETIDA | Fish; pickles | Indian curries containing beans | None |
| BASIL | Bouillabaisse and other fish soups; gazpacho; seafood; pesto sauce; tomato soup | Fish dishes; herb butter; meat casseroles; pasta; stuffings for poultry; tomato and green salads | Chop and add to flour for pastry for sweet pies |
| BAY | Aspics; soups; stocks | Meat, fish and vegetable dishes | Flavor milk for rice puddings |
| BERGAMOT | Flavor cream cheese; summer drinks | Salads; stuffings | Apple jelly; crystallize; herbal tea; sweet batters |
| BORAGE | Deep-fried in batter | Green salads | Herbal teas; summer drinks |
| BOUQUET GARNI | Aspics; meat and vegetable soups; stocks | Braised vegetables; casseroles; most meats, poultry and game; poached fish; sauces; stews | None |
| CARAWAY | Cream cheese; dips; seafood, pickles; vegetable soups | Beets; cabbage dishes; coleslaw and other salads; offal, pork; potatoes; tomatoes; veal | Cookies; bread; cakes; pastries |
| CARDAMOM | Green pea soups; melon; pickling; spiced and curried soups | Curries and spiced dishes; rice | Bread; buns; custards; fruit salads; stewed and baked fruit; yeast cakes |
| CASSIA | Pickles; spiced drinks | Chinese dishes; curries; ground sprinkled over vegetables; rice | Poached fruits; stewed fruits |
| CAYENNE PEPPER | Fish soups and chowders; seafood salads; tomato soup | Curried vegetables; curries and other spiced meat dishes; egg dishes; fish dishes; salad dressings | None |
| CELERY SEED | Fish and meat soups; pickle mixtures; seafood | Casseroles; coleslaw; fish; salad dressings; sauces; stews | Bread; savory biscuits |
| CHAMOMILE | Flavor sherry | None | Herbal tea |
| CHERVIL | Fish; fish soups; herb butters; seafood; vegetable soups | Chicken; cucumber; egg and cheese dishes; fish; meat sauces and casseroles; root vegetables; salads | Breads and savory biscuits |
| CHILI: fresh | Hot, spiced soups; seafood | Curries and hot, spiced dishes; egg dishes; beans; salads | None |
| dried | Pickles | Curries and hot dishes; vinegar for salads | None |
| powder | Dips; fish soups and chowders; pickles; seafood | Barbecue sauce; curries and hot spiced dishes; eggs; fish; Creole dishes; poultry; salad dressings; veal | None |
| CHIVES | Chilled soups; dips | Egg, cheese and fish dishes; garnish for potato dishes; herb butters; salads; stuffings for poultry | None |
| COMFREY | Fritters | Cooked as vegetable; salads | Herbal tea |
| CORIANDER leaf | Dips; pickles; seafood; sprinkle over chilled soups | Salads; scattered over curries and Middle Eastern dishes; stuffings | None |
| seed | Seafood; spiced and chilled soups; yogurt dips | Curried vegetables; curries and mild spiced meat dishes; beans; rubbed over pork or poultry before roasting; salad dressings; stuffings | Cookies; cakes; fruit salads; stewed fruits |
| CUMIN SEED | Chutneys; pickles; spiced soup | Beef; cabbage; carrots; chicken; curries; kabobs; lamb; marinades; beans; rice dishes | None |
| CURRY PLANT | Fish soups; seafood; spiced soups | Casseroles and stews; stuffings for veal and game | None |
| CURRY POWDER | Cream and cottage cheese; dips; seafood | Curried dishes; hot sauces; rice; salad dressings; sauces for eggs; white fish | Savory bread and biscuits |
| DILL SEED | Light vegetable soups; pickles | Cabbage; carrots; casseroles of lamb and pork; cucumber; marrow; poached and baked fish; salad dressings; turnips | Biscuits; sprinkle over bread and buns |
| DILL WEED | Cheese dips; seafood; summer soups | Cauliflower; cucumber; kidneys; salads; salmon and other fish; sauces for fish; veal, pork | None |
| FENNEL leaf | Fish soups; seafood; summer soups | Chicken; eggs; fish; pork; salads and dressings; stuffings | None |
| seed | Pickles; seafood | Casseroles; chicken; herrings; mackerel; potatoes; salad dressings; sauces for fish | Cookies; cakes; cooked apple dishes |
| FENUGREEK | Pickles | Indian and Middle Eastern dishes; sprouted in salads | None |
| FINES HERBES | All meat soups; dips | Butters; casseroles; egg dishes; stuffings | None |
| FIVE SPICE POWDER | Marinades; steamed fish | Chinese simmered meat dishes; Chinese stir-fried vegetables; roast meats and poultry | None |
| GARAM MASALA | Seafood | Indian dishes | None |
| GARLIC | Cream cheese dips; vegetable and meat soups | All meats and poultry; casseroles and stews; marinades; salad dressings; sautéed dishes | None |
| GERANIUM, SCENTED | Cream cheese dips | Vinegars for salads | Cakes; jams; jellies; puddings; sauces; sugar; syrup for fruit salads; teas |
| GINGER, FRESH | Seafood | Chicken; curries; fish; marinades | None |
| GINGER, DRIED | None | Baked ham; fish; pot roasts; beans; rice | Cakes and cookies; fruit pies; puddings; spiced drinks; stewed fruit |
| HORSERADISH | Sauce with smoked mackerel and trout | Salad dressings for potatoes and beets; sauce with beef; sauce with fish and hot beetroot | None |
| JUNIPER BERRIES | Pâtés; pickles; seafood | Baked ham; cabbage; casseroles; game; pork; pot roasts; poultry; salted meats | Spiced drinks containing gin; stewed apples |

303

| NAME | STARTERS AND SOUPS | MAIN COURSES AND VEGETABLES | DESSERTS AND BAKING |
|---|---|---|---|
| LAOS POWDER | Seafood | Southeast Asian dishes | None |
| LAVENDER | Game soup | Casseroles, particularly beef, game and poultry; marinades for game; stews | Conserves; crystallized flowers; jellies |
| LEMON BALM | Cream cheese dips; fish soups; seafood | Fish; green salads; marinades; poultry; sauces; stuffings; veal | Flavor sugar; fruit salads; herbal tea; puddings; summer drinks |
| LEMON GRASS | Seafood | Curried dishes; fish; salads | Puddings; syrup for fruit salads |
| LEMON THYME | Cream cheese dips; seafood | Casseroles; chicken; fish; grills; herb butters; lamb; marinades; salads; sauté dishes; veal | Fruit salads; milk for custards and puddings |
| LEMON VERBENA | Seafood | Fish; green and rice salads; poultry; stuffings and sauces; veal | Flavor sugar; fruit salads; herbal tea; sweet puddings; wine cup |
| LOVAGE | Dips; pickles; seafood; vegetable and meat soups | Casseroles; green salads; poultry; stuffings | None |
| MACE | Pickles; seafood | Beef; chicken; meatballs; meat loaves; pâtés; pork; sauces; stuffings; veal | Cookies; cakes; whipped cream |
| MARJORAM | Vegetable and meat soups | Casseroles; grilled meats; herb butters; sauces; stuffings; tomatoes | Flavor sugar; herbal teas |
| MINT (SPEARMINT) | Cream cheese dips; grapefruit; sprinkled over melon; summer soups; yogurt drinks | Lamb roasts and grills; mackerel, mint sauce; new carrots; peas; potatoes; salads; stuffings; trout | Fruit salads; ice creams; summer drinks |
| MIXED SPICE | Melon | Curries and spiced dishes; beans | Cookies; cakes; drinks; fruit salads; stewed fruits |
| MUSTARD powder | Leek and celery soups | Braised celery and leeks; grilled meats; herrings; casseroles; salad dressings; stuffings | Cookies; bread; scones |
| seed | Pickles | Cabbage; celery; curries; oily fish; pork; rabbit; stuffings; veal | None |
| NUTMEG | Cream soups | Fish; cabbage; chicken; egg and cheese dishes; meat loaves; pasta; pâtés; root vegetables | Cookies; cakes; dried fruits; fruit salads; puddings; pastries; stewed fruits; sweet breads |
| OREGANO | Minestrone; pâtés; tomato soup | Egg dishes; green peppers; Italian dishes and pasta; onions; potatoes; quiches; stuffings | None |
| PAPRIKA | Dips; seafood; soups | Beef; curries; goulash; pork; beans; rice; spiced meat dishes; veal; white fish | None |
| PARSLEY | All soups; fish and seafood | Baked and grilled fish; casseroles; egg and cheese dishes; herb butters; meats; most salads; sauces for poached fish; sauté dishes; vegetables | Savory breads |
| PEPPER black | Clear soups; cream cheese dips; pickles | Most savory dishes | Sweet cakes and cookies |
| white | Cream soups; pickles; seafood | Casseroles; chicken; eggs; fish; mayonnaise; veal; white sauces | None |
| PEPPERCORNS, green | Cream cheese dips; seafood | All meat, poultry and game; herb butters; pâtés; sauces; sausages | With fresh strawberries |
| POPPY SEEDS | Dips; onion soup; spreads; sprinkled over chilled soups | Carrots; curries; peas; potatoes; salads; scattered over savory pie crusts | Sprinkled over baked goods |
| ROSE | None | Rose petal vinegar for salads | Crystallized petals; rose hip syrup; rose hip tea; rose petal and hip wine; rose petal jam and jelly; rose petal tea; rose water |
| ROSEMARY | Chicken and tomato soups | Grills; lamb; pork; roasts; root vegetables; sauté dishes; some egg dishes; sparingly in salads | Flavor sugar; syrup for fruit salad |
| RUE | Cream and cottage cheese dips; egg spreads | Very sparingly in salads | None |
| SAFFRON | Soups (especially fish); cream cheese | Chicken; fish dishes; paella; pilaf and other savory rice dishes; some egg dishes; turkey | Cookies; bread; buns; cakes |
| SAGE | Cream and cottage cheese dips; tomato, celery, leek and lentil soups | Casseroles; cheese and egg dishes; herb butters; meat loaves; pâtés; pork; beans; salads; sausages; stuffings for pork and poultry; veal | Herbal teas; savory breads and biscuits |
| SALAD BURNET | Summer soups | Salads; stuffings; vinegar | None |
| SAVORY | Vegetable soups | Beef casseroles; broad and French beans; egg and cheese dishes; pork; pork pies and sausages; beans; stuffings for pork and veal | None |
| SESAME SEEDS | In *hummus* (chick-pea dip); other dips | Dry-fried in salads; in salads; over vegetables *au gratin*, or fish and chicken dishes | Made into candy; scattered over bread, rolls, biscuits and pies |
| SORREL | Soup alone or with other vegetables | Egg dishes (especially omelettes); sauce for fish, chicken and veal; spinach; spring greens; stuffings for chicken, veal and lamb | Layer with brown sugar, raisins, and mixed spice to make sweet pie |
| STAR ANISE | Pickles | Chinese steamed fish; flavoring for Chinese boiled eggs; meats simmered in soy sauce | None |
| SWEET CICELY | Cream cheese dips | Green salads; omelettes; salad dressings | Fruit salads; pancakes |
| SZECHUAN PEPPERCORN | Fish and seafood | Steamed fish and chicken; Chinese dishes | None |
| TANSY | Cream cheese dips | Beef casseroles; butters; omelettes and other egg dishes; stuffings | Apple pudding; flavor sugar |
| TARRAGON | Aspics; clear soups; tomato soups | Butters; carrots; chicken; fish; mushrooms; salads and dressings; some egg dishes; sauces; stuffings | Flavor sugar |
| THYME | Cream cheese; pâtés; vegetable and meat soups | Meat, lamb and chicken casseroles; meat loaves; pasta; stuffings; vegetables | Flavor sugar; herbal teas |
| TURMERIC | Curried and spiced soups; seafood | Curries; egg dishes; fish; rice | Coloring for bread and cakes |
| VANILLA POD | None | None | Custards and creams; drinks; ice-cream; puddings; sugar; wine cups |
| VIOLET | None | Vinegar for salads | Crystallized petals; white wine cups |

# GROWING AND PRESERVING HERBS

While bunches and sprigs of fresh herbs can be bought at supermarkets and greengrocers, for flavor and convenience, the best supply of herbs you can have is fresh ones that you have grown yourself.

Herbs take up very little growing space and will fit in almost anywhere. You can create a separate plot in your garden for them, or you can tuck them in between your vegetables, or create a herb border in front of your flowers. If you haven't even this amount of space, you will be happy to know that many herbs grow well in window boxes, in tubs on balconies, and in pots on sunny windowsills.

The advantage of growing them in pots and tubs is that you can extend their growing season by sheltering them on the warm side of your house or by bringing them indoors when the weather starts to dip in autumn. While they may not continue to grow all winter long this way, you'll most likely get a few extra weeks or maybe even months out of them, which means you'll have the extended pleasure of using fresh herbs rather than dried or frozen ones.

## SITING THE HERB GARDEN

A herb garden should be as close as possible to the kitchen. If possible the plot should be south-facing, but if not, at least make sure that it is sheltered and catches as much sun as possible. Herbs like light, dry, well-drained soil. It does not have to be particularly rich, but if you can dig in some rotted manure or compost before you begin you will make growing conditions ideal. If the soil is rather acid, it is advisable to add lime to it.

## LAYING OUT THE HERB GARDEN

Herbs are attractive plants and so it is easy to make the herb garden pretty as well as useful.

If the herbs are to grow in a border, make sure you know their full growing height and put the tallest at the back.

Some herbs, such as mint and lemon balm, spread rapidly. If you are growing them in an open bed it is best to control them so they do not take over.

If you have plenty of room and a square or wide oblong plot, you can lay out your herbs in the fashion of an Elizabethan knot garden, where small, intricate patterns of different herbs were grown individually, surrounded by hedges of lavender, rosemary or low-growing boxwood.

Another good idea is to make a checkerboard pattern with paving stones, so you have small, square beds of different herbs (see below).

If you have only limited space you can still achieve an attractive pattern by growing your herbs within the spoke patterns of an old cart wheel (see below).

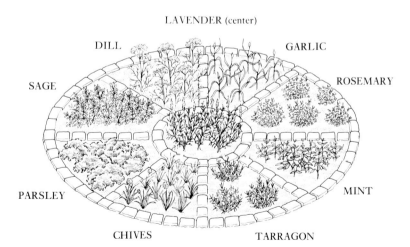

LAVENDER (center)

DILL

GARLIC

SAGE

ROSEMARY

PARSLEY

MINT

CHIVES

TARRAGON

*A variety of containers for growing herbs.*

Of course, you do not have to set aside a special plot for herbs. They can be grown very successfully among vegetables and can even protect the vegetables from insect pests. Try growing sweet basil next to tomatoes, summer savory by beans; sage will protect carrots and thyme keeps away cabbage maggot.

In other parts of the garden herbs such as lavender and rosemary can make attractive, low hedges between flower beds. Bay trees can be decorative where climate is right, whether in tubs or in open, sheltered ground. Chives make pretty edging plants.

## CARING FOR THE HERB GARDEN

Herbs will give you little trouble and need the minimum of attention. Keep the ground weed free, clear out and replant the annuals every year and cut back the perennials in autumn or spring. If possible, dig in a little well-rotted manure or compost every autumn or spring.

## PROPAGATING HERBS

You can collect seed in the autumn from most annual plants and sow it in the prepared bed the following spring.

When perennial plants get old and woody, you can take cuttings from them or divide the roots. Make sure that your new plants are growing well before taking out the old ones.

## GROWING HERBS IN TUBS

Herbs grown in tubs on balconies or patios can be made into an attractive feature. You can use wooden barrels cut in half and treated with wood preservative, stone tubs, or the largest flower pots that you can find. Mount the tubs on bricks and fill them where they are to stand, because they will be too heavy to carry.

Fill and plant the tubs in spring. Put broken crockery or pieces of brick in the bottom, half fill the tubs with soil and top with growing compost or soil.

Plant several herbs such as thyme, marjoram and parsley in one tub and make sure that they are watered regularly.

## HERBS IN WINDOWBOXES

What could be more convenient than a windowbox of herbs growing outside the kitchen window? It is best if it is a window which gets plenty of sun and is sheltered from the strongest winds.

Make the box fit to the size of the window and make sure that you can reach it easily and open the window without the box falling off!

Put wire mesh in the bottom, then broken crockery or stones and top with compost.

Water the plants whenever they look dry and cut them regularly.

## GROWING HERBS INDOORS

Herbs thrive well if they are grown in small pots indoors. Parsley, chives, thyme, sage, rosemary and marjoram are most suitable, and basil will last longer indoors than out.

Choose 6-inch diameter pots and put them in a position where they will get plenty of light but will not get too hot. Water them regularly.

A charming Elizabethan custom was to grow herbs in hanging baskets, and these are useful when there is little space elsewhere. Make them in the spring. Line the baskets with moss and fill them with a mixture of good quality compost and soil.
They are best planted with low-growing, compact culinary herbs such as parsley, chives, thyme, marjoram and winter savory.

The baskets can be hung indoors or out. If putting them outside, hang them in the shed or greenhouse for a week first to harden them off. Make sure the baskets are watered regularly to prevent them drying out.

# PRESERVING HERBS

It is a good idea to preserve all the herbs that you cannot pick during the winter. This will include all the annuals (e.g. chervil, basil) and those perennial plants that die right back such as lovage and fennel.

If you have large bushes of other perennials, such as thyme, sage and marjoram, you may not need to preserve them, but if your bushes are small and woody your winter supply of leaves will be sparse, so you will be wise to build up a winter store.

## HARVESTING

Herbs contain volatile, or essential oils, which give the characteristic flavor and smell to different varieties. The content of these oils is greatest just before the herbs flower and at the start of the flowering period. It is at this time, therefore, that herbs should be cut for preserving.

Cut herbs on a dry, warm day, after the dew has dried but before the sun has become really hot. Handle them carefully and use good sharp scissors as bruising could cause loss of oils or discoloration.

You can safely take away about one third of perennial herbs such as sage and thyme. Try to shape the plants attractively as you do so. Annual plants such as sweet basil or summer savory can be cut to 3–4 inches from the ground. If you take out the center spikes you will encourage the side shoots to grow thickly.

Cut only as many herbs as you can deal with in one day. Discard any blemished or discolored twigs and take the herbs indoors and away from the sun immediately after cutting.

## DRYING

Small quantities of herbs are best dried in bunches. Tie about ten sprigs together with strong thread

or fine cotton string. Hang them in a warm, dry, airy place, away from the light, such as in a well-ventilated attic, over a central heating boiler or in a not too hot airing cupboard. The temperature should not exceed 90°F. Larger

quantities of herbs are best dried on racks. These can be improvised by covering cake cooling racks with muslin or with brown paper into which you have punched holes with a skewer.

If you dry herbs frequently, make special stacking racks. Construct oblong frames of light wood, strengthened with diagonal cross pieces and with muslin stretched over them.

Stack the frames one above the other. These work best if they are all filled at once so the humidity remains the same. Put any new fresh herbs at the top as moisture rises.

Whether in bunches or on racks, most herbs will dry in 4 to 5 days. They should still be a bright, fresh color and both twigs and leaves should snap crisply. If they are not completely dry, leave them a while longer, otherwise they may become musty.

## DRYING HERBS IN A MICROWAVE OVEN

Finely chop the herbs and spread them out on a double layer of kitchen paper. Microwave on High for $1\frac{1}{2}$ minutes. Take them out and stir them about with your fingers to check if they are dry.

Delicate herbs, such as fresh coriander, will be dried after this time. Others need longer. Microwave on High again, checking and stirring after each minute. When done, the herbs will be dry, crisp and bright green.

## DRYING HERB SEEDS

When the seeds are full but not quite brown, cut off the flower heads, together with about 6 inches of the stalk. Put the heads upside down in brown paper bags and hang them up to dry in the same way as bunches of herbs. After about 5 days, give the bags a shake and the seeds will drop down inside.

## STORING DRIED HERBS

Strip the leaves carefully from the stems and leave them whole. This will preserve more flavor than crumbling them.

Dried herbs keep best in airtight jars away from the light. Choose wood, earthenware or dark-colored glass. See-through glass jars should be covered with paper or adhesive plastic covering.

In a cool larder, dried herbs will keep their flavor for 6–8 months. After that, any left can be scattered around the herb garden or sprinkled round pot plants to keep away insect pests.

## USING DRIED HERBS

The flavor of dried herbs is very concentrated and consequently you will need much less than fresh herbs in any dish. Use the following equivalents:

| Fresh | Dried |
| --- | --- |
| 1 tsp | $\frac{1}{2}$ tsp |
| 1 Tbsp | 1 tsp |
| 3 Tbsp | 1 Tbsp |

Dried herbs tend to be tougher than fresh ones, so are best used in cooked dishes. If adding them to a salad, soak them for 30 minutes in the dressing first.

It is a good idea to keep some of your favorite dried herbs or herb mixtures in separate herb mills for ease of use.

You can also make your own bouquets garnis by tying small amounts of dried herb mixtures in circles of muslin.

### FREEZING HERBS
Herbs with large fleshy leaves, such as basil, mint and parsley tend to freeze better than the delicate ones like fennel and dill. You can freeze herbs in plastic bags, in

ice cubes or chopped and spread out on trays. There is no need to blanch them first.

Whole leaves can be put in usable amounts in small plastic bags. Make sure they overlap as little as possible and freeze them flat. They can be chopped or crumbled and used when still frozen.

Sprigs of herbs can also be frozen in bags as can collections of sprigs tied together to make bouquets garnis. They can be taken straight from the freezer and popped into a casserole.

Plastic wrap may be used instead of bags but make sure it is sealed securely.

Pack the bags of frozen herbs, each type separately, in labelled boxes. The herbs will keep for up to 4 months.

To freeze herbs in ice cubes, finely chop them and pack them

into ice-cubes trays so the compartments are two-thirds full. Top them with cold water and open freeze them until solid. Take them out of the trays, then store them together in labelled plastic bags. These herb cubes can be added directly to sauces, soups, sautéed dishes and casseroles. You can make them with single herbs or bouquet garnis mixtures.

To freeze herbs on trays, chop them and spread them out on the tray. Freeze them until they are hard and then pack them into tubs. They should stay loose and you can simply spoon them into whatever dish you are making. They are also suitable for adding to salads and sprinkling over foods before serving.

## CANDYING FRUIT OR HERBS

### SPICY CANDIED PEEL

| 6 oranges, lemons or grapefruit |
| --- |
| 2 cups granulated sugar |
| 5 whole cloves |

Wash or scrub the fruit thoroughly, halve or quarter it and remove the pulp. Simmer the peel in a little water for 1–2 hours until tender. (Change the water 2–3 times when cooking grapefruit peel.) Remove peel. Make the liquid up to $1\frac{1}{4}$ cups with water. Add $1\frac{1}{4}$ cups of the sugar and the cloves, dissolve over a low heat, then bring to the boil. Add the peel, remove from the heat, cover and leave for 2 days.

Strain off the syrup, discarding the cloves. Dissolve another $\frac{3}{4}$ cup sugar in it and simmer the peel in this syrup until semi-transparent. The peel can be left in this thick syrup for 2–3 weeks. Drain off the syrup and place the peel on a wire rack to dry.

Put the rack in a warm place such as an airing cupboard, in the oven at the lowest setting with the door slightly ajar, or in the residual heat of the oven after cooking. The temperature should not exceed 120°F or the fruit may brown and the flavor spoil. The drying will take several hours and is completed when the peel is no longer sticky. Store in airtight jars or containers.

### CANDIED ANGELICA

| angelica shoots |
| --- |
| salt |
| granulated sugar |

Drop the angelica shoots immediately into brine—1 Tbsp salt to 5 cups water—and leave for 10 minutes. Rinse in cold water. Boil the angelica for about 5 minutes until tender. Drain, retaining the liquid and scrape to remove the outer skin.

Using the angelica cooking liquid, make a syrup of 1 cup sugar to $1\frac{1}{4}$ cups of the liquid. Place the angelica in a bowl, add the syrup, cover and leave for 24 hours. Drain off the syrup, add $\frac{1}{3}$ cup sugar to every $1\frac{1}{4}$ cups and bring to the boil. Pour back into the bowl over the angelica, cover and leave for 24 hours. Repeat this process a further five times until the syrup is of the consistency of runny honey. Boil the angelica for 2–3 minutes at the last addition of the sugar, then leave for 2 days. Dry off on a wire rack in a warm place or in the oven at 225°F. Store in screw-topped jars.

# POT POURRIS

A bowl or jar of pot pourri will scent a room delicately and naturally. Pots pourris were first made in Elizabethan times to disguise the odor of old damp buildings. They were also believed to have curative properties, particularly where living conditions were insanitary. If you have fragrant flowers and herbs in the garden and are able to buy spices and essential oils, making a pot pourri should be easy.

There are four main types of ingredients in a pot pourri: those giving the predominant perfume; more subtly perfumed ones, to give an underlying scent; fixatives; and preservatives.

## PREDOMINANT PERFUMES

These usually come mainly from sweet scented rose petals and lavender, but other strongly scented flowers and leaves can also be added. These include carnations, lilac, heliotrope, jonquil, jasmine, wallflower, magnolia and hyacinth. In the herb garden, find mints of all varieties: rosemary, woodruff, penny royal, pineapple sage and the many varieties of thyme, basil and lemon verbena. The scented leaves of geraniums and pelargoniums can also be added.

Strongly scented spices such as aniseed, coriander and fennel can be added to this mixture, together with the roots of ginger, sweet flag and angelica and dried orange and lemon peel.

## UNDERLYING PERFUMES

These are added in smaller amounts to make a full-bodied scent. They come mainly from scented leaves such as thyme, marjoram, sage, bay, tansy, the scented geraniums, lemon balm and tarragon.

Sweet spices, either ground or whole, can also be added. These include cinnamon, nutmeg, allspice, cardamom and coriander.

Essential oils of herbs, which can be bought at druggists and herbalists, are further suggestions for improving the scent of a pot pourri. Add them only a drop at a time, stirring after each addition. They are very strong and too much would spoil the final result.

## FIXATIVES

Adding a fixative will help to preserve the scent of a pot pourri. Dried, powdered orris root is the most common. Violet-scented, it is the root of *Iris germanica* and you can either grow and dry it yourself or buy it from herbalists.

Other plant fixatives include the dried powdered root of calamus (sweet flag); the dried pods of tonquin bean; the essential oil of sandalwood; and powdered resins such as gum benzoin and frankincense.

## PRESERVATIVES

The preservatives prevent the ingredients of a pot pourri from decaying. Sea salt or another non-iodized salt is best for this purpose. Dry it in a low oven for several hours before use. Borax can also be used.

To keep the pot pourri dry, bury in it a small cotton bag of silica gel (available at chemists) which you can dry out occasionally in a low oven.

# BASIC POT POURRI MIXTURE

| |
|---|
| 6 cups predominant perfume mixture |
| 2 cups underlying perfume mixture |
| up to 3 drops strongly perfumed essential oil or up to 10 drops milder oil |
| fixative: 1½ oz orris root or 3 oz other |
| up to 1¼ cups preservative |

## DRY METHOD

Dry all the ingredients on racks as for herbs. As they dry, mix them with the appropriate amount of fixative and store them in air-tight jars until you have enough to make up the mixture. Continue to dry herbs and flowers throughout the summer.

When all the flowers and herbs are dried and fixed, mix them with the preservative and a chosen mixture of spices, oils and a few pieces of citrus peels. Put them into a jar with a cotton bag containing about 4 oz silica gel. Cover tightly and leave for 6–8 weeks. The pot pourri is then ready for use.

A mixture of dried flowers can be added to a dry-method pot pourri purely for their color to add to the final appearance. These can include borage, delphinium, feverfew, heather, marigold, mullein, pansy and tansy.

## MOIST METHOD

Making a pot pourri by the moist method preserves the scent for a longer time, but the color will not be as good.

Half dry the petals and leaves until they have a leathery texture. Then mix them together and layer them in a large jar with half their volume of preservative. If this does not fill the jar, more can be added over a period of 3 days. Stir before adding more layers. When the jar is full, cover tightly and leave it in a dark place for 2 weeks.

Take out the solid mass which has formed and break it up. Add fixative and oils as required, a drop at a time.

## KEEPING THE POT POURRI

If a pot pourri is kept in an open bowl it will perfume the room strongly for a few weeks but after that will lose its scent. It is best kept in a closed container and uncovered and stirred periodically. "Refresher oils" are available. Use these from time to time.

Choose glass containers for pot pourri made by the dry method, and earthenware or pottery for that made by the moist method.

# HERBAL RINSES

Dried rosemary makes a refreshing hair rinse for medium to dark hair; dried chamomile brings out the highlights of fair hair. It's best to make several rinse sachets at a time, storing them in any attractive jar that has an air-tight lid.

Make some sachets by cutting 2-inch squares of muslin or cheesecloth. Put a teaspoonful of dried rosemary or chamomile in the center of each square, and tie the squares into a bundle with a piece of cotton. When you need a hair rinse, place one of the sachets in $2\frac{1}{2}$ cups of already boiling water, remove from the heat, and leave to cool.

## MAKING A SCENTED BATH BAG

These little lavender bags are meant for hanging on a ribbon from a bath tap, so the hot water flows through them and becomes permeated with fragrance. Of course, you can use other ingredients if you want a different scent — perhaps a mixture of orange blossom, lime blossom and eau de cologne mint — but really anything with a good smell will fit the bill.

The bags themselves are very easy to make. Cut two small squares from scraps of tiny-printed fabric, using pinking shears to give a decorative edge. Stitch wrong sides together along three sides.

Buy a 28-inch length of narrow ribbon, and about $\frac{5}{8}$ inch down from the top of the bag, stitch the ribbon to both sides of the bag, about 5 inch in from each end of ribbon.

Fill the bag with dried lavender, then tie the 5-inch ribbon-ends tightly to one side of the bag with a single knot. This will close the neck of the bag securely. Then tie the ribbon-ends to the other side and finish with a bow. The central portion of ribbon will form a loop for tap-hanging.

## MAKING A POMANDER

The original pomander of Elizabethan times consisted of a strongly scented pot pourri, formed into a ball with fragrant gum or wax and worn round the neck or waist in a small, perforated container. It was thought to ward off diseases.

Another type, more frequently carried by doctors and court officials, consisted of an orange or lemon stuck with cloves. This orange pomander is easy to make. It can be hung in the wardrobe, put into a linen drawer or, alternatively, placed in a pot pourri jar.

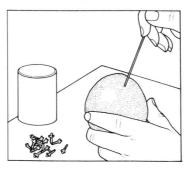

Choose a small, thin-skinned orange, free from blemishes. Prick holes in the peel with a darning needle or fine skewer, leaving a cross pattern round

which you will eventually tie a ribbon. Make the holes fairly close together, and do not go so deep as to let the juice run out.

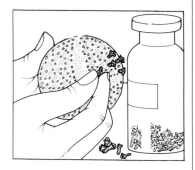

Stick cloves in the holes so the spaces between the cross are covered completely. Mix equal parts of ground cinnamon and orris root. Roll the orange in the mixture, rubbing and patting the powder well in. A little freshly grated nutmeg and ground ginger may also be added.

Wrap the orange in waxed paper or put it into a brown paper bag. Leave it in a cool, dark place for 5–6 weeks or until it is hard and dry. Shake off any loose powder and tie the pomander round with ribbon. It should keep its scent for several years.

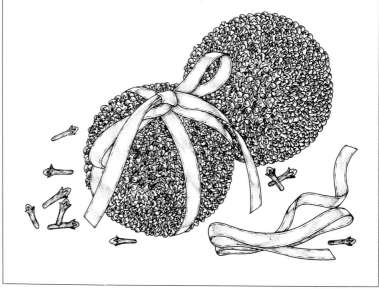

# BÉARNAISE SAUCE

*Makes about $\frac{2}{3}$ cup*

3 Tbsp white wine vinegar

6 black peppercorns

$\frac{1}{2}$ bay leaf

$\frac{1}{2}$ tsp mace

1 slice onion

2 tarragon leaves

2 egg yolks

salt and freshly ground pepper

7 Tbsp unsalted butter

2 tsp glaze or jelly at base of beef dripping (optional)

1 tsp mixed chopped tarragon, parsley and chervil

1 tsp snipped fresh chives

*1* Put the vinegar, peppercorns, bay leaf, mace, onion and tarragon leaves into a small saucepan. Bring the vinegar to the boil and boil until it is reduced to 1 Tbsp. Remove from the heat.

*2* Cream the egg yolks in a bowl with 1 Tbsp butter and a pinch of salt. Strain in the vinegar and beat well.

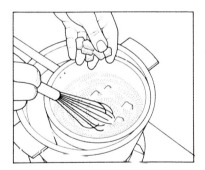

*3* Put the bowl into a saucepan of boiling water and turn off the heat. Stir until the mixture begins to thicken. Beat in the butter in small pieces. Beat in the meat glaze if using. Season to taste and add the herbs. Serve warm.

# HOLLANDAISE SAUCE

*Makes about $\frac{2}{3}$ cup*

4 Tbsp white wine vinegar

6 black peppercorns

$\frac{1}{2}$ tsp mace

1 slice onion

1 bay leaf

3 egg yolks

10 Tbsp unsalted butter

salt and freshly ground pepper

2 tsp lemon juice

2 Tbsp light cream

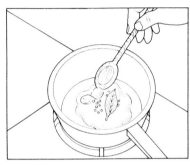

*1* Put the vinegar into a small saucepan with the peppercorns, mace, onion and bay leaf. Boil to reduce to 1 Tbsp. Set aside.

*2* Beat the egg yolks in a bowl with 1 Tbsp butter and a pinch of salt. Strain in the vinegar. Put the bowl into a saucepan of boiling water. Turn off the heat and beat in the remaining butter, in small pieces. Beat until thick. Remove from pan. Season to taste and beat in lemon juice and cream. Serve immediately.

# HORSERADISH SAUCE

*Makes about 1 cup*

$\frac{3}{4}$ cup grated horseradish

1 tsp mustard powder

1 tsp sugar

2 tsp white wine vinegar

$\frac{2}{3}$ cup heavy cream, lightly whipped

Mix all the ingredients together and leave the sauce to stand for 20 minutes before serving.

# *FLAVORED SALT AND SUGAR*

Herb or spice salts can be added to salad dressings and soups. Use them to season vegetables and to rub sparingly over meat before roasting or grilling.

Herb sugars are delicious in custards or sweet soufflés, or sprinkled onto cakes, cookies or sweet pastries. Suitable herbs include rosemary, thyme and lemon thyme, angelica, sweet cicely, marjoram and scented geraniums. Peppermint and lemon balm sugars are delicious sprinkled over fruit salads.

*To make herb sugar*: put a sprig of the fresh herb into a jar of granulated sugar. Seal it and leave the herb to scent and flavor the sugar for about three weeks. It can be left in the jar while the sugar is in use. For a continual supply of herb sugar, the jar can be topped up with more sugar and the old sprig replaced with a fresh one.

## VANILLA SUGAR

Make as herb sugar, using a vanilla pod instead of fresh herbs.

## CINNAMON SUGAR

Make as vanilla sugar, using a cinnamon stick instead of the vanilla pod.

## HERB SALTS

To make a herb salt: mix **equal volume** of the chosen **herbs** and **non-iodized salt**. Spread the mixture on a baking sheet and put it in a very low oven with the door left slightly ajar for 30 minutes. (The warmth releases essential oils of the herbs which are absorbed by the salt). Cool and store in a screw-topped jar.

## SPICED SALTS

Spiced salt is used in the same ways as herb salt. Pound **non-iodized salt** with equal quantities of spices such as **cumin**, **celery** or **fennel** seeds or **allspice** and **juniper** berries.

# STUFFINGS

## THYME STUFFING

*Makes about 2 cups*

4 Tbsp butter
1 small onion, peeled and finely
    chopped
1½ cups fresh white or wholemeal
    breadcrumbs
1 Tbsp chopped fresh thyme
1 Tbsp chopped fresh parsley
2 tsp chopped fresh marjoram
finely grated rind and juice of 1
    lemon
1 egg, beaten
salt and freshly ground pepper

Melt the butter in a frying pan on
a low heat. Add the onion and
fry for 5 minutes until soft.
Remove the pan from the heat and
stir in the remaining ingredients.
    Use for stuffing lamb or poultry.

## MINT AND ROSEMARY STUFFING

*Enough stuffing for one end of a
10–12 lb turkey*

2 onions
2 celery stalks
2½ cups fresh white or wholemeal
    breadcrumbs
2 Tbsp mint sauce (page 150)
2 tsp chopped fresh rosemary
finely grated rind of 1 lemon
salt and freshly ground pepper
1 egg, beaten

Finely chop the onion and celery
and soften them in the butter. In a
large bowl, mix together the
breadcrumbs, mint sauce, rosemary and lemon rind. Stir in the
celery and onion. Mix well and
bind together with the egg.

## LEMON BALM STUFFING

*Makes about 1 lb*

2 cups dried prunes
2 cups cooking apples
½ cup fresh lemon balm leaves,
    finely chopped
1 egg yolk

Stone and chop the prunes. Peel,
core and chop the apples. Mix
them with the lemon balm leaves
and bind the mixture with the egg
yolk. Use for stuffing duck.

## SAGE AND ONION STUFFING

*Makes about 2 cups*

2 large onions, peeled and chopped
1 Tbsp butter, melted
1½ cups fresh white or wholewheat
    breadcrumbs
2 Tbsp chopped fresh sage or 2 tsp
    dried sage
salt and freshly ground pepper

Put the onions in a saucepan of
cold water. Bring to the boil and
simmer them until tender, about
10 minutes. Drain well and mix
with the remaining ingredients.
Use for stuffing pork or poultry.

## PARSLEY STUFFING

*Makes about 1 cup*

2 Tbsp butter
1 onion, finely chopped
1 cup fresh white or wholemeal
    breadcrumbs
4 Tbsp chopped parsley
finely grated rind of 1 lemon
juice of ½ lemon
4 Tbsp dry white wine

Melt the butter in a frying pan,
add the onion and fry gently for 5
minutes until soft. Take pan from
heat and mix in remaining ingredients. Use for stuffing poultry.

## SPICY APRICOT STUFFING

*Makes about 1½ cups*

¾ cup dried apricots
1 cup fresh breadcrumbs
¼ tsp ground mixed spice
1 Tbsp chopped fresh parsley
salt and black pepper
1 Tbsp lemon juice
2 Tbsp butter, melted
1 egg, beaten

Soak the apricots overnight in
cold water. Drain and chop them.
Mix them with all the remaining
ingredients. Use for stuffing pork,
lamb or chicken.

## APRICOT-CURRY STUFFING

*Makes about 2 cups*

2 cups fresh breadcrumbs
1 cup dried apricots, finely
    chopped
1 Tbsp chopped fresh parsley
4 Tbsp butter
1 onion, peeled and finely chopped
juice and grated rind of 1 orange
1½ level tsp curry powder
salt and pepper
1 egg, beaten

*1* Place the breadcrumbs in a
bowl and add the apricots and
parsley. Melt the butter in a small
saucepan, add the onion and
orange rind; cook until soft.

*2* Remove from the pan and add
to the breadcrumbs. Sprinkle
in the curry powder and cook
gently for 1 minute. Pour 3 Tbsp
orange juice over and bubble
gently for 30 seconds.

*3* Blend the curried orange juice
into the breadcrumbs. Season
and bind with egg.

# FLAVORED VINEGARS AND OILS

Herb and spice vinegars and oils will give a subtle flavor to dressings, marinades and sauces.

## MAKING HERB OIL

Herb oils can also be brushed over meat and fish before grilling. To make a herb oil, choose a bland oil such as sunflower, peanut or safflower oil, or a mild olive oil.

Most culinary herbs are suitable. Choose from rosemary, thyme, tarragon, marjoram, fennel, savory, sage and basil. They should all be used fresh. Lightly bruise enough herb sprigs to half-fill a glass bottle or jar. Cover them with oil and seal with non-corrosive tops.

Leave the oil for 2 weeks in a warm place. Shake once a day.

Strain the oil, pressing down hard on the herbs. Taste. If the flavor is not strong enough, repeat the process. When the oil is ready, decant into bottles and seal.

## MAKING HERB VINEGAR

A good-quality white or red wine vinegar is the best for making most herb vinegars. Most fresh herbs can be used as a flavoring (never use dried ones).

Chop enough fresh herbs to half fill a bottle. Warm double their volume of wine vinegar and pour it over the herbs. Cover tightly

and leave in a cool, dry place for about 6 weeks.

Strain the vinegar through muslin. Taste and add more vinegar if the flavor is too strong. Pour into bottles and seal with air-tight, corrosion-proof tops.

## CHILI VINEGAR

Make as for Herb Vinegar, using $\frac{1}{2}$ **cup crushed, dried red chilies** to every **$2\frac{1}{2}$ cups wine vinegar** instead of herbs.

## GARLIC VINEGAR

| |
|---|
| 3 garlic cloves, peeled and coarsely chopped |
| $2\frac{1}{2}$ cups distilled vinegar |

*1* Place the garlic in a warmed jar. Bring the vinegar to the boil and pour it onto the garlic.

*2* Allow to cool and cover with a non-corrosive seal. Leave in a cool place for 1 week. Taste.

*3* If the flavor is strong enough, strain the vinegar and bottle. If you prefer a stronger flavor, leave vinegar for a few days more.

## HORSERADISH VINEGAR

Make as for Herb Vinegar, using $\frac{1}{2}$ **cup grated fresh horseradish** to every **$2\frac{1}{2}$ cups wine vinegar** instead of herbs.

## SPICED VINEGAR FOR PICKLES

| |
|---|
| 5 cups distilled vinegar |
| 2 Tbsp white mustard seeds |
| $\frac{1}{2}$ tsp black peppercorns |
| 1 tsp cloves |
| 1 tsp allspice berries |
| 4 dried red chilies |
| 1 piece cinnamon stick or cassia bark |

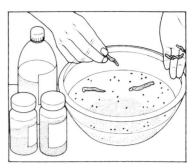

*1* Put the vinegar and spices in a large bowl or earthenware casserole. Cover tightly.

*2* Stand container in a saucepan of water. Bring water to boil and remove from heat. Leave container in pan for 2 hours. Strain. Use immediately or bottle tightly.

## CHILI OIL

The use of chili oil will give an underlying hot flavor. Bottled chili oil can be bought in oriental stores, but to make it yourself, bruise six dried red chilies, put them into a jar with $2\frac{1}{2}$ cups sunflower or peanut oil and leave them to infuse on a sunny windowsill for 2–3 weeks. It will keep indefinitely.

## HARISSA (FIERY SAUCE)

| |
|---|
| $\frac{1}{2}$ cup dried red chilies |
| 1 garlic clove, peeled and chopped |
| 1 tsp caraway seed |
| 1 tsp cumin seed |
| 1 tsp coriander seed |
| pinch of salt |
| olive oil |

*1* Soak chilies in hot water for 1 hour. Drain well, then grind into a paste in a pestle and mortar or in an electric mill together with the garlic clove and spices. Add a pinch of salt.

*2* Put into a jar, cover with olive oil and seal. It will keep in the refrigerator for up to 2 months. The oil can be used in salad dressings.

313

# JELLIES AND RELISHES

Herb jellies are traditionally served with roast meats. Rosemary or mint will go with roast lamb; parsley with ham; sage with pork; and thyme with poultry.

## HERB JELLY

5 lb cooking apples

5 cups water

few sprigs of chosen fresh herb

5 cups distilled vinegar

sugar

6–8 Tbsp chopped fresh mint, parsley or thyme; or 6 Tbsp chopped fresh sage; or 4 Tbsp chopped fresh rosemary

*1* Remove any bruised or damaged parts from the apples. Roughly chop them without peeling or coring.

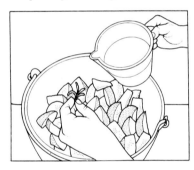

*2* Put them into a large saucepan with the water and herb sprigs. Bring to the boil and simmer gently for 4–5 minutes or until soft and pulpy, stirring from time to time to prevent sticking. Add the vinegar and boil for a further 5 minutes.

*3* Spoon the apple pulp into a jelly bag and leave it to strain into a large bowl for at least 12 hours.

*4* Discard the pulp. Measure the liquid and put it into a preserving pan with 1 lb sugar for each 2½ cups liquid. Heat gently, stirring, until the sugar has dissolved. Boil rapidly for 10 minutes.

*5* Test for setting. When the setting point is reached, take the pan from the heat and remove any scum with a slotted spoon. Stir in the chopped herbs.
　　Cool slightly. Stir again to distribute the herb. Place in canning jars and process.

## SWEET CIDER JELLY

5 cups sweet apple cider

thinly pared rind 2 oranges

1 Tbsp chopped fresh rosemary

3 lb sugar

1 bottle liquid pectin

Put the cider, orange rind and rosemary into a large saucepan. Bring slowly to the boil and reduce the heat. Add the sugar and stir to dissolve it, without boiling. Add the pectin and bring to a fast rolling boil. Boil hard for 1 minute. Strain into warm jars and process.
　　Serve with pork and bacon roasts.

## APPLE AND MINT RELISH

10 oz cooking apples

⅔ cup plain yogurt

2 Tbsp chopped fresh mint

salt and freshly ground black pepper

Peel and coarsely grate the apple. Stir it into the yogurt together with the mint and seasoning.
　　Spoon into a serving dish. Cover with plastic and chill for 30 minutes before serving.
　　Serve with roast meats.

# MUSTARDS

## HONEY MUSTARD

*Makes about 4 Tbsp*

2 Tbsp mustard powder

1 tsp honey

2 Tbsp dry white wine or cider

warm water (optional)

Put the mustard into a pot. Add the honey and wine or cider and mix well. Add warm water if needed for right consistency.

## TARRAGON MUSTARD

*Makes about 3 Tbsp*

2 Tbsp mustard powder

2 tsp chopped tarragon

1 Tbsp tarragon vinegar

warm water

Put the mustard powder and tarragon into a bowl. Mix in vinegar and then enough warm water to make it the right consistency.

## WHOLEGRAIN MUSTARD

*Makes about 1 cup*

½ cup black mustard seeds

½ cup white mustard seeds

½ tsp salt

¼ tsp freshly ground black pepper

2 Tbsp dark soft brown Barbados sugar

cider vinegar or herb vinegar

*1* Put the mustards, salt, pepper and sugar into a bowl. Just cover them with the vinegar. Leave them for 24 hours.

*2* Lightly blend in an electric blender or food processor. As the mixture thickens in the blender you may need to add more vinegar or, if cider vinegar has been used, dry cider. Put into a jar and cover with a non-corrosive lid.

# HERB AND SPICE MIXTURES

## BOUQUET GARNI

A bouquet garni is the French term for a small bunch of herbs and spices which is used to add flavor to stews, casseroles, soups etc. Bouquets garnis can be bought ready made, though the flavor of a freshly made bouquet is far superior.

For the basic bouquet garni, tie together 2 sprigs parsley, 1 of thyme and 1 bay leaf.

If using dried herbs, tie together in a muslin bag 1 tsp dried parsley, $\frac{1}{2}$ tsp dried thyme and $\frac{1}{2}$ bay leaf, crumbled.

● If liked, 1 sprig of fresh marjoram can be added with the thyme; or $\frac{1}{2}$ tsp dried.

● To go with lamb, add 1 rosemary sprig to the basic bunch of fresh herbs; $\frac{1}{4}$ tsp dried crumbled rosemary to muslin bag.

● To go with pork, add 1 sprig each of sage and savory; or $\frac{1}{4}$ tsp each of dried.

● To go with beef, add 1 thinly pared strip orange rind and 1 sprig of celery leaves; or $\frac{1}{4}$ tsp dried grated orange rind.

● To go with chicken, use lemon thyme instead of thyme and tie in 1 strip lemon rind; or add $\frac{1}{2}$ tsp dried lemon thyme.

● To go with fish, replace the thyme with lemon thyme and add a sprig of fresh fennel; or add $\frac{1}{2}$ tsp dried lemon thyme and $\frac{1}{4}$ tsp dried fennel.

## FINES HERBES

| |
|---|
| 1 cup chopped fresh parsley |
| $\frac{1}{2}$ cup chopped fresh chervil |
| $\frac{1}{2}$ cup chopped fresh chives |
| 2 Tbsp chopped fresh tarragon |

Mix the herbs together and use to flavor omelettes and other egg dishes, fish, poultry and salads.

## FIVE-SPICE POWDER

This is the mixture of spices used in authentic Chinese cookery.

| |
|---|
| 2 Tbsp Szechuan peppercorn |
| 2 Tbsp star anise |
| 2 Tbsp cassia bark or cinnamon stick |
| 2 Tbsp whole cloves |
| 2 Tbsp fennel seed |

Grind together all the spices. Store in an airtight jar. Keeps for up to one month.

## PICKLING SPICE

This is a basic mixture for pickles and chutneys. Different spices can be added according to taste and availability. For example, some contain whole chilies, giving a hotter flavor. Coriander seeds, juniper berries and mustard seeds can also be added.

| |
|---|
| 1 Tbsp mace |
| 1 Tbsp allspice berries |
| 1 Tbsp whole cloves |
| 7-inch cinnamon stick |
| 6 black peppercorns |
| 1 bay leaf, crumbled |

Mix all the ingredients together well. Store in an airtight, screw-topped jar. Keeps well for up to 1 month. Tie in a muslin bag to use.

## GARAM MASALA

This is a basic recipe for the mixture of ground spices which is frequently used in Indian cookery; the amounts can be increased or decreased according to taste and spices such as dried red chilies or whole coriander may be added.

| |
|---|
| 4 white cardamoms or 10 green cardamoms |
| 1 Tbsp black peppercorns |
| 2 tsp cumin seeds |

## MIXED SPICE

| |
|---|
| 2 Tbsp whole cloves |
| 2 Tbsp ground ginger |
| 2 Tbsp whole allspice berries |
| 5 inch stick cinnamon |
| $\frac{1}{4}$ tsp black peppercorns |
| 2 Tbsp freshly grated nutmeg |

Grind the whole spices together and mix with the nutmeg and ginger. Store in an airtight, screw-topped jar. Keeps well for up to 1 month. Use for baking.

## CURRY POWDER

| |
|---|
| 2 Tbsp cumin seeds |
| 2 Tbsp whole fenugreek |
| $1\frac{1}{4}$ tsp mustard seed |
| 1 Tbsp black peppercorns |
| 8 Tbsp coriander seeds |
| 1 Tbsp poppy seeds |
| 1 Tbsp ground ginger |
| 1 tsp chili powder |
| 4 Tbsp ground turmeric |

Combine all the ingredients in an electric blender or coffee grinder and blend to a fine powder. Store in an airtight container. Will keep for up to 3 months.

# Plan and Cook Ahead

In this chapter you will find tips on how to cope with everyday cooking, as well as more special occasions, including Christmas. When time permits, preserves can be made for year-round use, and when you are in a hurry, the freezer can be used as a reliable standby.

## PLANNING AHEAD

Although preparing and cooking meals can be a real pleasure, if it is your responsibility day after day it can easily become a chore. But with a little foresight and imagination you can find ways to do it when the mood strikes, or when you have spare time and are not rushed. In other words, cook ahead, and ensure that feeding your family always remains an enjoyable task.

### PLANNING MEALS
There's a lot to be said for writing down your weekly menu plans. It helps you to think of ways to keep within the family budget and to make best use of your time. You can plan to cook extra meat on one

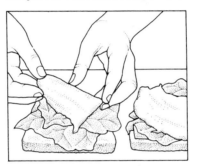

*Serve leftover cold meat in sandwiches*

night for serving later in the week or if you are having a family outing you could include pot-roasted meat for one meal and have leftover for serving cold in sandwiches. Plan different types of meals—not ones that all have to be started at the same time, or that all require last-minute attention.

Each meal should be nutritionally balanced and also include a variety of textures and colors as well as flavors. Avoid a sequence of rich sauces or too many pale-colored dishes. You wouldn't want to serve a creamy soup followed by a fish pie with a custard for dessert. On the other hand a creamy soup is an excellent choice if the main course consists of grilled lamb chops and some brightly colored vegetables. Make sure that the family is not begging for something crunchy to eat by the end of the meal. Offset a spicy meat dish with plain boiled rice or mashed potatoes.

### SHOPPING
After noting what you have in store make out your shopping list. To save time always shop for several meals at a time. Most packaged foods are date stamped to tell you the minimum keeping time, after which flavor is impaired. Take advantage of fruit and vegetables when they are in season and combine low prices with best flavor.

Don't be too rigid about your list. An impulse buy may be a bargain, provided it doesn't mean having to juggle the entire meal plan. Also, you can't count on finding a certain ingredient, especially if it is fairly unusual. Have an alternative cut of meat or a different vegetable in mind in case what you originally planned turns out to be unavailable or exorbitantly priced.

### COOKING A MEAL
To make life easier in the kitchen look at your chosen recipes and see how much can be made in advance. Does the recipe include a sauce (those without eggs or cream) which can be reheated without risk of curdling? Or you could make the stuffing before breakfast, or the dessert the night before?

Calculate the timing of each dish so that you can be sure you start cooking the one which takes longest first, and that all are ready together, or in the order required.

# EASY ENTERTAINING

A successful dinner party starts with guests being greeted by a confident and calm host. Being organized is the key to success. Start by planning your menu well in advance and get as much as possible out of the way before guests arrive. Practical considerations like seating, table linen, flowers and fresh towels in the bathroom must be taken into account too. Buy your wine and any spirits well in advance, not forgetting garnishes like cocktail olives or onions.

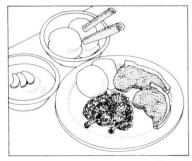

*A traditional three-course meal*

For easy entertaining, stick to a traditional three-course meal. Any extras can consist of fruit and cheese *Never experiment*: always select dishes that you have made before. (To broaden your repertoire try out new dishes on your family first.)

Plan dishes which require only last-minute assembling, brief cooking or reheating. Start by choosing your main course, then pick a first and last course which balance it.

## APPETIZERS

One certain way to make your entertaining easy is to avoid a hot first course altogether and serve something cold before guests assemble at the table. In this way you can easily slip off to the kitchen to do last-minute work on the main course. Crudités served

with a spicy mayonnaise are always popular; also good for serving informally are stuffed mushrooms, a pâté or a mousse with toast.

Soups are also good first courses as they can be prepared in advance and simply reheated if they are to be served hot. Add any milk, yogurt or cream when reheating to avoid curdling.

## MAIN COURSES

Select a casserole or stew which can be made in advance and served with vegetables which are cooked at the last minute. Conversely, serve broiled or fried foods, and have a vegetable casserole or ragout ready-prepared. If you plan to pan-fry escalopes or steaks, then make sure you have enough frying pans to cope with all the frying at the

*Equipment for deep-fat frying*

same time. For deep-fat frying have everything ready beforehand, together with any last-minute garnishes.

## DESSERTS

Most cold desserts can easily be made in advance. Gelatine-based desserts like cheesecakes and cold mousses only become firm after at least 4 hours in the refrigerator.

Serve light simple desserts after a substantial main course and rich luxurious ones after a light meal.

# MEAT AND POULTRY

Meat and poultry, especially chicken, continue to be a favorite choice for many family meals. It's important for the busy cook to find a good friendly butcher and stick to him. If he appreciates your business he will be more likely to do some of the more fiddly and time-consuming tasks such as boning a shoulder of lamb and chopping or grinding meat to the size you require for a particular dish.

Plan to buy enough meat to allow for leftovers which can be made into another main course. You may wish to buy enough meat at one time for the whole week and do most of your meat cooking on the weekend when you have time. Allow 4–5 oz boneless meat per serving and 5–12 oz meat on the bone per serving (depending on how much bone).

Bear in mind that the larger a piece of meat the longer it will keep: for example, ground meat should be used on the day of purchase, whereas a large roast will keep for up to 5 days in the coldest part of the refrigerator. If you do buy your meat all at once you may wish to cut it yourself, and for this you must have a good sharp kitchen knife. The food processor is a great time saver for grinding meat, but remember that ground meat should not be

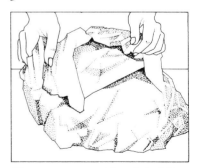

*Keep meat wrapped loosely in foil*

317

prepared more than 12 hours in advance or blood will ooze out and the meat become dry. Wrap meat loosely with foil to allow air to circulate, otherwise it will deteriorate rapidly. (Never leave meat in sealed plastic bags.)

Poultry should be used within 24 hours of purchase; frozen birds *must* be completely thawed before cooking. When preparing a bird for roasting, never place warm stuffing in a cold bird unless you are about to put it straight into a hot oven, otherwise dangerous bacteria may develop. Prepare stuffing in advance, but refrigerate it separately until just before roasting.

Although chops and steaks are always popular and take very little time to cook, they are expensive. To add variety to meals, choose from the more economical cuts and cook stews and casseroles.

## STEWS, CASSEROLES AND BRAISED DISHES

Almost all stews and casseroles improve in flavor if made at least

*Removing solid fat from stew*

24 hours ahead. Allow them to cool, then cover and refrigerate. The fat will rise to the surface and become solid, making it easy to degrease the dish—especially important for oxtail and other fatty meats. They will keep covered in the refrigerator for up to 3 days.

Beef is the favorite meat for this long, slow and moist form of cooking, which tenderizes the tougher cuts. Most cuts of pork and lamb are tender and so long

slow cooking is not so often used, but some cuts can make excellent casseroles. Boiling fowls are very good value, but tough and require slow cooking. When cooking stews and casseroles on the stove they must be very slowly simmered—if allowed to boil the meat will toughen. Stir occasionally to prevent sticking and check to see if more liquid is needed. Cooking these dishes in a casserole in the oven is easier, as no attention should be required provided that the temperature is sufficiently low, but unless other items can be cooked at the same time it is less economical. Single

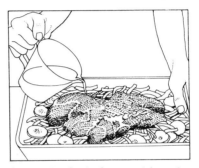

*Moistening braised meat with stock*

large pieces of beef are excellent braised in the oven on a bed of chopped vegetables moistened with stock.

If you plan to reheat a stew or casserole, undercook vegetables, particularly root vegetables which will crumble if overcooked, either by cutting in larger-than-usual pieces, or adding halfway through. Add green vegetables and any chopped fresh herbs when reheating. Enrich fricassees and blanquettes with egg and/or cream when reheating to avoid curdling. Reheat in a 350°F oven. Sliced meats are best reheated with a little gravy added to keep them moist.

## MARINADES

A marinade is a great way to prepare meats in advance. Flavored with herbs and spices, a marinade will add flavor to meat and also help tenderize it.

Marinades also help prevent meat from spoiling and in some cases it may be left to marinate for several days. Immerse the meat in the

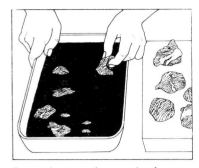

*Immersing meat in a marinade*

marinade, cover and refrigerate until ready for cooking. With poultry, flavor will penetrate better if it is skinned first.

# FISH

Fish requires very little cooking time, making it a good choice for midweek family meals when you are on a tight schedule and have little time to spend in the kitchen. But it can be a fiddly task to prepare fish for cooking, so patronize a fishmonger who will clean and fillet fish for you. Otherwise, you can prepare fish up to 12 hours before cooking, but make sure you use a good sharp knife. Keep the fish in the refrigerator, loosely wrapped to prevent the flesh from drying out. The fish can then be broiled or fried. *Avoid overcooking*—most fish needs as little as 5 minutes on each side.

Allow 6–8 oz of fish per serving, depending on whether it is a fillet or whole fish. Fresh fish should be cooked on the same day; smoked fish can be kept for 2–3 days in the refrigerator.

Fish needs to be kept moist as it easily dries out. Fish casseroles can be made in advance and re-heated just before serving, but make sure that the fish is sub-merged in liquid. With white fish like cod and haddock, cook extra and use the leftovers for fish pies, fish cakes or croquettes, or to serve cold in a salad. To pre-cook fish for pies etc, cover with cold water and bring to the boil. Turn off the heat and leave for 5 minutes, then drain. With frozen fish, leave for 10–15 minutes. Do not be tempted to leave any longer as it will become soggy. The cooking liquid can be set aside as the basis for a sauce. Leave the fish to cool, then fork into flakes, removing the skin and bones.

Marinating is a good way to keep fish moist during storage.

Ceviche, a Mexican dish using raw fish, makes an excellent

*Turning fish chunks in a marinade*

dinner-party starter. Use firm white fish chunks and marinate in lemon juice for up to 12 hours, though 1 hour is all that is needed; turn the fish once during marinating. Salmon marinated in lime juice is also delicious. Toss the fish with chopped sweet peppers in a garlicky vinaigrette.

Once shellfish are removed from their shells they very quickly dry out. This is especially so with molluscs like mussels, oysters and scallops. Avoid preparing these in advance unless you wish to incorporate them in a cold fish salad or in a soup or sauce. Have ready pancakes or vol-au-vent cases to make a lunch dish which needs only last-minute assembling and reheating.

Remember that canned fish is a useful standby. Use canned tuna or salmon for mixing with rice or pasta for a quick midweek meal, or for making a party mousse.

# COOK-AHEAD FISH DISHES

## FISH CAKES

*Makes 10*

1 lb mealy potatoes (peeled weight), cooked
12 oz leftover cooked cod or haddock fillet, flaked
2 Tbsp butter or margarine
4 Tbsp chopped fresh parsley
finely grated rind of $\frac{1}{2}$ lemon
salt and freshly ground pepper
flour
2 eggs, beaten
1$\frac{1}{2}$ cups fresh breadcrumbs
vegetable oil, for shallow frying

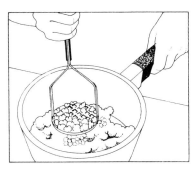

*1* Mash the potatoes and stir in the fish, butter, parsley, lemon rind and seasoning to taste.

*2* When the mixture is cool but not cold, turn out on to a lightly floured surface.

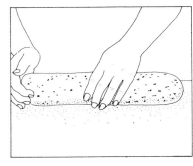

*3* With floured hands, shape into a sausage about 15 inches long. Make sure that the surface is free from cracks.

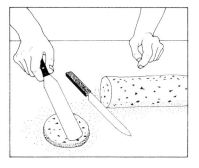

*4* Cut the roll into ten 1$\frac{1}{2}$-inch slices. One at a time, place the slices on a floured surface and pat with a palette knife to level the surface and reduce the thickness to about $\frac{3}{4}$ inch.

*5* Coat the fish cakes one at a time in the beaten eggs, then in the breadcrumbs. Chill in the refrigerator for at least 30 minutes or until required.

*6* When ready to serve, put enough oil in a frying pan to come about halfway up the fish cakes. Heat until a cube of bread turns golden brown in 50–60 seconds. Lower in a few cakes and fry until golden brown. Turn over and cook for a further 5–10 minutes.

*7* Drain well on absorbent paper while frying the remainder.

**FREEZING INSTRUCTIONS**
Prepare the fish cakes to the end of step 5. Open freeze on baking sheets until firm. Pack into rigid containers and return to freezer. Thaw for 2 hours only and complete as in steps 6 and 7.

## FISH CROQUETTES

*Makes 12*

4 Tbsp butter or margarine

¾ cup flour

1¼ cups milk

12 oz leftover, cooked white fish, flaked

2 Tbsp finely chopped parsley

1 Tbsp capers, roughly chopped

1 tsp lemon juice

salt and freshly ground pepper

cayenne pepper

1 egg, beaten

¾ cup dried breadcrumbs

vegetable oil, for deep-frying

*1* Melt the butter in a saucepan, add half the flour and cook over low heat, stirring with a wooden spoon, for 2 minutes.

*2* Remove the pan from the heat and gradually blend in the milk, stirring after each addition to prevent lumps forming. Bring to the boil slowly, then simmer for 2–3 minutes, stirring. Cover and leave for at least 30 minutes until cold.

*3* Stir the fish into the sauce, beating until smooth. Stir in the parsley, capers and lemon juice, mixing well. Season with salt, pepper and cayenne.

*4* Turn the mixture onto a board, divide in half, then into 12 fingers. With *lightly* floured hands, roll each portion into a sausage about 3 inches long.

*6* When ready to serve, heat the oil in a deep-fryer to 350°F. Place a few croquettes at a time into a frying basket and lower gently into the hot oil. Deep-fry for 2–3 minutes or until golden brown. Drain on absorbent paper while deep-frying the remainder.

### FREEZING INSTRUCTIONS

Prepare the croquettes to the end of step 5. Open freeze on baking

sheets until firm. Pack into a rigid container and return to the freezer. Thaw for 2 hours only; complete as in step 6.

## MARINADE FOR RAW FISH

*Serves 4*

1 tsp coriander seeds

1 dried red chili, seeded and roughly chopped

juice of 4 limes

juice of 2 lemons

2 Tbsp olive oil

freshly ground black pepper

1 medium onion, finely sliced

1 lb fish fillets (monkfish, flounder, sole)

*1* Crush the coriander seeds and chili to a fine powder in a mortar. Mix with the lime juice, lemon juice, olive oil, pepper and onion rings. (Do not add salt as this draws the juices out of the fish making the dish very watery.)

*2* Pour over the fish, mix well, cover and chill in the refrigerator for at least 6 hours or until the fish turns opaque or white.

# FRUIT

A bowl of fruit saves many busy cooks from the time and trouble of making a dessert. The various textures, colors and flavors of fruit make it a good choice to finish off any meal, especially a substantial one where the refreshing taste of fruit is welcome.

Choose fruit which is slightly underripe for serving several days after buying. Store underripe fruit at room temperature, to speed up

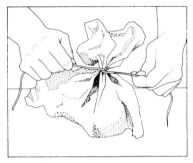

*Ripen fruit in a brown paper bag*

ripening, place the fruit in a brown paper bag and tie tightly. Store ripe fruit in the refrigerator. Pick over and wipe soft berry fruits, discarding any damaged ones. Other fruits can be washed in advance and given a good polish with absorbent paper. Grapes, however, should be washed just before serving to keep their bloom.

Gluts and other fruit bargains usually mean that the fruit is ripe and must be used very soon. Make sure that you have the time to prepare the fruit either for the freezer or for making preserves. Adding sugar to fruit will help keep it for longer in the refrigerator. Make fruit purées and freeze for 6–8 months, or store in the refrigerator for 2–3 days; use to make fools and fruit mousses or serve as a sauce for ice cream.

If you are after a trouble-free impressive dessert select exotic (though expensive) fruits such as mangoes, kiwi fruits and papayas

to add to a fruit salad. When serving cut-up fruit remember that bananas, apples and peaches should be left until the last moment and sprinkled with lemon juice to prevent discoloration. Lemon juice also heightens the flavor of a fruit salad. Keep cut fruit in the refrigerator, tightly wrapped with plastic.

Fruit puddings like crumbles and fruit pies can be made up to the baking stage in advance, or pre-baked, then warmed through just before serving. Meringue shells and pie cases can be made several days ahead of time and filled with fruit, cream or ice cream just before serving.

# CHEESE

Whether you serve cheese on its own or with fruit, it makes an interesting and satisfying conclusion to a meal. Always keep cheeses well covered before serving, otherwise they will dry out around the edges very quickly. Wrap them individually to prevent flavors from mingling. They are best stored in an airtight container in the larder; if kept in the bottom of the refrigerator take out 30 minutes before serving. Soft cheeses will keep for up to 10 days and hard cheeses for up to 1 month.

Fresh cheeses like *fromage blanc* and *petits suisses* are ideal for serving with soft berry fruits. Cheddar and other hard cheeses are good companions to apples and pears as well as nuts. Soft cheeses like Brie and Camembert go well with grapes.

# VEGETABLES

Vegetables are a vital part of most meals because they add valuable nutrients and fiber and help to balance them. But it is important that they be prepared and cooked properly. It is all too easy to sacrifice vegetable texture, nutrition and flavor in the name of expediency.

Most vegetables can be prepared up to 12 hours before serving (but remember that there will be a nutrient loss); after that flavor is slightly impaired. They should be tightly covered with plastic and stored in the refrigerator until ready for cooking. Root vegetables such as potatoes and turnips should be kept in cold water in the coldest part of the refrigerator. (However, vitamin C, which is water soluble, starts to diminish.) Celeriac, Jerusalem artichokes and salsify need to be soaked in water with lemon juice or vinegar added to prevent discoloration.

Many vegetables need only to be cooked briefly before serving. Some, like carrots, green beans or cabbage, are best when they are still crisp and almost crunchy and in this way more nutrients are retained. They can be slightly undercooked, then rinsed under

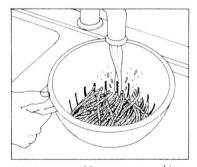

*Rinsing vegetables to arrest cooking*

cold running water to retain color and arrest further cooking. Reheat quickly in butter just before serving.

Vegetable dishes can be cooked in a number of different

ways to help keep last-minute preparations to a minimum.

*Braised* Vegetables like red cabbage, celery, endive and celeriac are delicious when braised, that is, slowly cooked in very little liquid until they become soft. Leave until cold, cover and refrigerate, then reheat slowly.

*Stewed* Ratatouille (vegetable ragout) is the classic example of a dish which improves greatly if made well ahead of serving (see recipe on page 22). Stewed vegetable dishes will keep for 2–3 days in the refrigerator. They are also good served cold (allow them to come to room temperature for best flavor).

*Stuffed* Serve vegetables as an accompaniment stuffed with breadcrumbs, or as a main course stuffed with rice and chopped meat. The stuffing can be made in advance and the case filled up to 12 hours ahead. Bake in the oven to finish. Choose from tomatoes, eggplants, mushrooms and onions.

*Puréed* Most vegetables can be puréed, either as a convenient way of storing them in the freezer for later use in soups, or as a vegetable dish accompaniment. Boiled or steamed vegetables can be quickly puréed in a blender or food processor or put through a sieve or vegetable mill. Leave until cold, cover and refrigerate. To reheat, season, add a dash of cream and heat slowly, stirring often. Root vegetables can be put in the oven.

# *Cook-Ahead Vegetable Dishes*

## LAYERED FRENCH-STYLE POTATOES

*Serves 4–6*

| 2 lb potatoes, peeled |
| 2 Tbsp Dijon mustard |
| 2 Tbsp snipped chives |
| 1¼ cups milk or chicken stock |
| salt and freshly ground pepper |
| 2 Tbsp butter, melted |

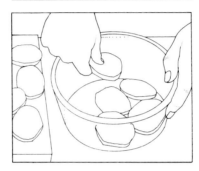

*1* Cut the potatoes into ½-inch slices and arrange one layer in a greased 5-cup ovenproof dish.

*2* Combine the mustard, chives, liquid and seasoning. Pour some over the potato layer. Repeat layers of potato and mustard/chive dressing, finishing with potato.

*3* Brush the top layer of potato with butter, and sprinkle with salt and pepper. Cover the dish with foil and leave in a cool place until required.

*4* When ready to serve, bake in the oven at 350°F for 1¾–2 hours until the potatoes are tender when pierced with a fork.

## STUFFED PEPPERS

*Serves 4*

| 3 Tbsp butter |
| 1 onion, chopped |
| 4 oz bacon, chopped |
| 4 tomatoes, peeled and sliced |
| 1 cup long-grain rice, cooked |
| 4 Tbsp grated Cheddar cheese |
| salt and freshly ground pepper |
| 4 large green peppers |
| ¾ cup fresh breadcrumbs |
| ⅔ cup chicken stock |

*1* Melt 2 Tbsp of the butter in a heavy-based saucepan, add the onion and bacon and fry gently until golden brown. Add the tomatoes, cooked rice, half of the cheese and seasoning to taste.

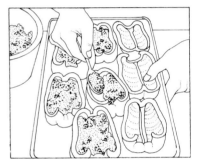

*2* Halve the green peppers lengthwise; remove pith and seeds. Place them in a single layer in a greased ovenproof dish and spoon in the stuffing.

*3* Mix the remaining cheese with the breadcrumbs and sprinkle over the stuffing. Pour the stock around the peppers and top each with a pat of butter. Leave in a cold place until required.

*4* When ready to serve, bake in the oven at 375°F for 15–20 minutes, or until the peppers are tender.

# RICE AND PASTA

Rice and pasta are essential store-cupboard items to add variety to meals. They can be served in place of potatoes as an accompaniment to meat or poultry, or as a main course in their own right. They are both an excellent way to stretch leftover meat and vegetables.

## RICE

Rice takes very well to a number of seasonings and flavorings so that family members need never tire of it. Cook extra rice to use cold in a rice salad or as part of a stuffing for vegetables or meat. Allow $\frac{1}{4}$ cup raw rice per serving.

*Fluffing up rice before serving*

Plain boiled rice can be made up to 24 hours ahead of serving. To reheat, dot with butter or margarine and place in a 350°F oven for 20 minutes. Fluff up with a fork and serve. Risottos, paellas and pilafs can be reheated in the same way.

## PASTA

Along with dried pasta, a good supply of fresh pasta, now so readily available, is a good reserve in the freezer. It takes only 1–2 minutes to cook from frozen and with a good pasta sauce on hand you can quickly serve a delicious no-fuss dinner party dish. Cook extra pasta shapes to add to soups and salads (pasta to be served cold should not be tossed in butter which hardens it).

Many pasta sauces can be made in advance and gently reheated. Delicious dishes can also be made in minutes by tossing pasta in such basics as cheese, eggs and cream and topping with grated Parmesan cheese. Fresh herbs, canned fish or crisp bacon are good last-minute additions.

Cooked pasta is best stored coated in a sauce, and in made-up dishes such as macaroni cheese and lasagne (which also freeze well). It will keep for several days in the refrigerator and can be reheated in a 350°F oven for 20 minutes or so until bubbling.

# COOK-AHEAD SAUCES TO SERVE WITH PASTA

## MILANESE SAUCE

*Serves 4*

| |
|---|
| 2 Tbsp butter |
| $\frac{1}{2}$ onion, chopped |
| 2 oz mushrooms, chopped |
| 8 oz tomatoes, peeled and chopped, or 15 oz can tomatoes, drained |
| 1 tsp sugar |
| 1 bay leaf |
| few sprigs of thyme |
| pinch of grated nutmeg |
| salt and freshly ground pepper |
| 2 oz ham, chopped |
| 2 oz tongue, chopped |

*1* Melt the butter in a heavy-based saucepan, add the onion and mushrooms and fry gently for 3–5 minutes until soft. Stir in the tomatoes, sugar, herbs, nutmeg and seasoning to taste. Cover and simmer gently for about 20 minutes, until the sauce has thickened and developed a good flavor.

*2* Add the ham and tongue and simmer, uncovered, for a further 5–10 minutes. Cool, then chill in the refrigerator or freeze until required. Reheat for 5–10 minutes until bubbling, then taste and adjust seasoning before serving.

## BOLOGNESE SAUCE

*Serves 4*

| |
|---|
| 1 Tbsp butter |
| 2 oz bacon, chopped |
| 1 small onion, chopped |
| 1 carrot, peeled and chopped |
| 1 celery stalk, washed, trimmed and chopped |
| 8 oz lean ground beef |
| 4 oz chicken livers, chopped |
| 1 level Tbsp tomato paste |
| $\frac{3}{4}$ cup dry white wine |
| $1\frac{1}{4}$ cups beef stock |
| salt and freshly ground pepper |

*1* Melt the butter in a large saucepan, add the bacon and fry for 2–3 minutes. Add the onion, carrot and celery and fry for a further 5 minutes until just browned.

*2* Add the beef and brown lightly, then stir in the chicken livers and cook for a further 3 minutes. Add the tomato paste and wine and simmer for a few minutes more.

*3* Stir in the stock and seasoning to taste and simmer for 30–40 minutes, until the meat is tender. Cool, then chill in the refrigerator or freeze until required. Reheat for 5–10 minutes until bubbling, then taste and adjust seasoning before serving.

# CHRISTMAS COUNTDOWN

To ensure that you have a festive but calm Christmas, start shopping and planning for your holiday entertaining well in advance. There's no substitute for a complete holiday checklist covering Christmas lunch and all the traditional Christmas goodies plus table decorations. It may seem daunting at first, but with foresight and organization Christmas time can be the pleasure it is supposed to be.

The best way to plan a Christmas period of eating without frustration in the kitchen is to keep meals, other than Christmas lunch, flexible. A roast ham or ham along with leftover turkey will provide several meals if you plan a good selection of winter salads to serve with them. Have some cold desserts such as a fruit compote or brandied peaches on hand or make a Christmas cheesecake with a cranberry topping, or a chestnut pavlova—meringue layers can be made several days before assembling and stored in an airtight container.

A freezer will be of enormous help when preparing for Christmas. All baking can be done about 3 months in advance. Freeze pies and breads uncooked and bake them nearer the time of serving . . . part of the enjoyment of Christmas is the delicious smells wafting from the kitchen. Make your own mincemeat; providing brandy is added it can be made at the beginning of December or even earlier. Plum puddings are traditionally made at the end of November.

- Buy a bird large enough to serve your guests with leftovers. Calculate the size of bird you need on the basis of 12 oz–1 lb for small birds, 12 oz for medium birds, 8 oz for large birds per serving. Order it early.

- Make sure you allow shelf space in the freezer for Christmas food. Mark packages for Christmas.

- If you make your own preserves and pickles, pot some in small attractive jars and set aside for entertaining over Christmas; they also make excellent last-minute gifts.

- Make your sauces in advance and have a few on hand to enliven leftovers. Keep all sauces in the refrigerator.

| Sauce | In advance |
|---|---|
| Brandy Butter | 2 weeks |
| Cumberland Sauce | 1 week |
| Cranberry Sauce | 1 week |
| Bread Sauce | 2 days |
| Horseradish Sauce | 1 day (using fresh cream) |
| Vinaigrette | 1 week |

- Make a large quantity of white sauce and store in $\frac{1}{2}$ pint portions. It will keep for up to 5 days in the refrigerator. Add cheese or herbs to it when reheating and serve with vegetables or use as the basis for a turkey casserole.

- Peel potatoes up to 24 hours in advance. Soak in cold water and keep in the coldest part of the refrigerator.

- Peel chestnuts and cook the day before serving. Leave to cool and store tightly wrapped in the refrigerator along with ready-trimmed Brussels sprouts.

- Check drinks cupboard and take advantage of Christmas specials frequently offered. *Buy or order early.* There are usually special offers for buying wine by the case. Remember to stock up on ice cubes. Turn them into plastic bags; to keep cubes separate spray them with soda water.

## CHRISTMAS PLUM PUDDING

*Makes 1 pudding to serve 8*

| |
|---|
| 1 cup prunes |
| $1\frac{1}{2}$ cups currants |
| $1\frac{1}{2}$ cups seedless raisins |
| $1\frac{1}{2}$ cups light raisins |
| $\frac{3}{4}$ cup flour |
| $\frac{1}{4}$ tsp grated nutmeg |
| $\frac{1}{4}$ tsp ground cinnamon |
| $\frac{1}{2}$ tsp salt |
| $\frac{3}{4}$ cup fresh breadcrumbs |
| $\frac{1}{2}$ cup shredded suet |
| $\frac{2}{3}$ cup dark brown sugar |
| $\frac{1}{4}$ cup chopped blanched almonds |
| finely grated rind of $\frac{1}{2}$ lemon |
| $\frac{2}{3}$ cup stout ale |
| 2 eggs, beaten |

*1* Snip the prunes into small pieces into a large bowl, discarding any pits.

*2* Half-fill a steamer or large saucepan with water and put it on to boil. Grease a 6-cup pudding basin or bowl.

*3* Add the remaining ingredients to the prunes and stir well until evenly mixed.

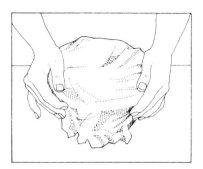

*4* Spoon the mixture into the prepared bowl, pushing down well. Cover with greased, pleated waxed paper and foil. Steam for about 8 hours.

*5* Remove the foil covering, but leave the paper in position. Allow to cool, then cover with a clean dry cloth or foil and store in a cool place for at least 2 weeks before serving.

*6* To reheat, steam for $2\frac{1}{2}$ hours. Turn out onto a warmed serving plate and serve with brandy or rum butter.

## MINCEMEAT

*Makes about $5\frac{1}{2}$ lb*

| |
| --- |
| 1 lb currants |
| 1 lb light raisins |
| 1 lb seedless raisins |
| 2 cups chopped mixed peel |
| 2 cups hard cooking apples, peeled, cored and grated |
| 1 cup chopped blanched almonds |
| 1 lb dark brown sugar |
| 12 Tbsp shredded suet |
| 1 tsp grated nutmeg |
| 1 tsp ground cinnamon |
| finely grated rind and juice of 1 lemon |
| finely grated rind and juice of 1 orange |
| $1\frac{1}{4}$ cups brandy |

*1* Place the dried fruits, peel, apples and almonds in a large bowl. Add all the remaining, ingredients and mix thoroughly.

*2* Cover the mincemeat and leave to stand for 2 days. Stir well and put into jars. Cover. Leave for at least 2 weeks to mature before using.

## FESTIVE CHRISTMAS CAKE

| |
| --- |
| 8-inch round fruit cake |
| apricot glaze |
| $1\frac{1}{2}$ lb marzipan or almond paste |
| 2 lb royal icing |
| ribbon and Christmas cake decorations such as Santa Claus, snowmen, robins, reindeer or Christmas trees, to finish |

*1* At least 14–20 days before required, place the cake on a 9-inch cake board. Brush with apricot glaze and cover with marzipan. Loosely cover the cake and store in a cool dry place for 4–5 days.

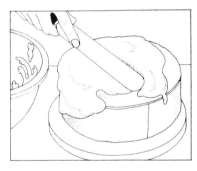

*2* Using half the royal icing, roughly spread the icing over the top and side of the cake. Leave to dry for 24 hours. Keep the remaining icing in a covered container.

*3* Spoon the remaining icing on top and roughly smooth it over with a palette knife.

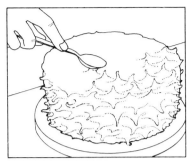

*4* Using a palette knife or the back of a teaspoon, pull the icing into well-formed peaks.

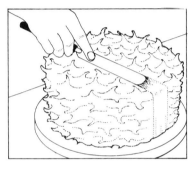

*5* Using a palette knife, smooth a path down the center of the top and side of the cake. Leave to dry for about 24 hours.

*6* Place a piece of ribbon along the pathway, securing the ends with pins. Arrange the decorations on top, securing them if necessary with little dabs of freshly made icing. Leave to dry for at least another 24 hours, ideally about 1 week before Christmas.

*7* Once iced, the cake will keep fresh without an airtight tin, but when dry, protect it by covering with a cake dome or box.

## TO COVER A CAKE WITH MARZIPAN

Cover the cake with marzipan 1 week or—at the latest—2 days before applying the first coat of royal icing. If the marzipan is not given enough time to dry out, oil from the paste may discolor the icing.

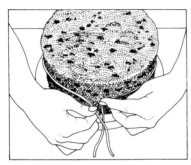

*1* To cover a round or square cake, first measure round the cake with a piece of string.

*2* Dust your work surface liberally with confectioners sugar and roll out two thirds of the marzipan to a rectangle, half the length of the string and twice the depth of the cake.

*3* Trim the edges of the marzipan neatly with a knife, then cut the rectangle in half lengthwise.

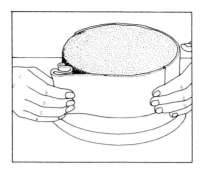

*4* Place the cake upside down on a board and brush the sides with apricot glaze. Gently lift the marzipan and place it firmly in position round the cake. Smooth seams with a palette knife and roll a jam jar lightly round the cake.

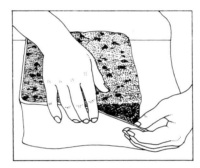

*5* For a square cake, position one strip of marzipan on one side of the cake and fold it round to cover a second side. Repeat for the other two sides. Keep the top edge of the cake square with the marzipan.

*6* Smooth the seams with a palette knife and mold any surplus marzipan into the bottom edge.

*7* Brush the top of the cake with apricot glaze. Dust your working surface with confectioners sugar and roll out the remaining marzipan to a round or square the same size as the top of the cake.

*8* Lift the marzipan onto the top of the cake with the rolling pin. Lightly roll with the rolling pin, then smooth the seam and leave to dry for at least 2 days.

## APRICOT GLAZE

*Makes 1 cup*

1 cup apricot jam

2 Tbsp water

Put the jam and water in a saucepan and heat gently, stirring, until the jam softens. Bring to the boil and simmer for 1 minute. Sieve the glaze and use while still warm.

## ROYAL ICING

*Makes about 2 lb*

4 egg whites

2 lb confectioners sugar

1 Tbsp lemon juice

2 tsp glycerine

*1* Whisk the egg whites in a bowl until slightly frothy. Then sift and stir in about a quarter of the confectioners sugar with a wooden spoon. Continue adding more sugar gradually, beating well after each addition, until about three quarters of the sugar has been added.

*2* Beat in the lemon juice and continue beating for about 10 minutes until the icing is smooth.

*3* Beat in the remaining sugar until the required consistency is achieved, depending on how the icing will be used.

*4* Finally, stir in the glycerine to prevent the icing from hardening. Cover and keep for 24 hours to allow air bubbles to rise to the surface.

# QUICK MEALS

With a well-stocked cupboard, last-minute dishes can be fun to put together, and very satisfying for the cook.

The following ideas are based on cupboard ingredients, with a few fresh foods as well.

# SOUPS

## SHRIMP AND ASPARAGUS BISQUE

Mix canned asparagus soup with a little white wine; add peeled shrimp (frozen or canned). Heat through and swirl in cream.

## QUICK VICHYSSOISE

Blend drained canned celery with drained canned new potatoes; add chicken stock and cream to give a smooth souplike consistency.

# APPETIZERS

## MARINATED ARTICHOKE WITH MUSHROOMS

Make a dressing with orange juice, olive oil, chopped mint (fresh or dried) and seasoning. Add drained canned artichoke hearts and button mushrooms and chill. Serve with bread.

# MAIN DISHES

## MEAT

### CHINESE CHICKEN

Cook chicken drumsticks until tender. Add canned sweet and sour sauce and sliced canned water chestnuts. Heat through.

### SAUSAGE CASSEROLE

Mix cooked sausages with canned red cabbage, canned red wine sauce, sliced green peppers, dill seeds and seasoning. Heat through in the oven.

## FISH

### FISHERMAN'S PIE

Mix a can of flaked salmon with a can of mushroom soup and some fried sliced onion; top with made up instant mashed potato mixed with egg yolk and grated cheese. Bake until golden.

### SMOKED SALMON FONDUE

Heat canned smoked salmon soup with a little white wine, cream and chopped fresh herbs.

## EGG

### EGG RISOTTO

Heat ready-cooked canned rice in butter with chopped spring onion; add chopped hard-boiled egg, chopped parsley and a little cream and heat through.

## PASTA

### NOODLE BAKE

Mix cooked green noodles with sour cream, thawed frozen peas, chopped ham, grated Parmesan cheese and seasoning. Place in a gratin dish, sprinkle with extra cheese and bake until golden.

# SUPPERS AND SNACKS

## CHICKEN AND POTATO GRATIN

Mix canned chicken soup with chopped canned chicken breast and finely chopped red pepper. Put into a gratin dish and top with frozen potato balls. Sprinkle with grated cheese and a few dried breadcrumbs. Bake until golden.

## PIZZA-STYLE FRENCH BREAD

Cut lengths of bread and split in half; brush with or dip in oil. Top with drained canned tomatoes, slivers of cheese and/or salami, anchovy fillets and black olives. Brush with oil and bake.

# VEGETABLES

Wrap frozen potato croquettes in bacon strips, and bake until crisp.
Mix thawed and drained frozen spinach purée with bottled tartar sauce; heat through in the oven in a covered dish.
Toss blanched almonds in melted butter until lightly golden; add frozen Brussels sprouts, and heat through.
Lightly cook button mushrooms and stir in sufficient canned curry sauce to bind lightly. Delicious with steak and other broiled meats.

# DESSERTS

## BUTTERED PINEAPPLE PASTRY

Roll out thawed frozen puff pastry to a rectangle; brush with beaten egg white. Top with canned pineapple slices, well drained (or slices of fresh pineapple) and knobs of butter. Scatter with light brown sugar and bake until well puffed and golden. Serve hot with cream.

## PEACHES WITH MELBA SAUCE

Use canned whole peaches or skinned fresh ones. Blend raspberry jam with orange juice and a little brandy until smooth. Put peaches into glass dishes and spoon over the sauce.

## RASPBERRY ROMANOFF

Crush ready-made meringues coarsely or, alternatively, use lady fingers. Mix with lightly whipped cream and well drained canned raspberries. Spoon into stemmed glasses and garnish with a twist of orange.

# PRESERVES

Putting food by is an age-old tradition which ensures that seasonal fruits and vegetables do not get wasted and are available all year round. Making jams, jellies and marmalade, or spicy pickles, relishes and chutneys is still one of a cook's most rewarding tasks, as the results should be not only less expensive but better than anything in the shops.

Special equipment is not essential for making preserves, but some help to make the job easier. Preserving pans are thick-based with slanting sides which help prevent overboiling of a hot mixture. Choose a good one made from heavy aluminium or stainless steel; it can double as a pan for making pickles and chutneys which contain a lot of vinegar. Brass, copper and iron react with vinegar causing a metallic flavor, so pans of these metals must not be used when making pickles and chutneys. A nylon sieve should be used as metal can discolor fruit and it also reacts adversely with vinegar. A long-handled wooden spoon makes stirring easier and if you make jellies, then a jelly bag is worth having. Other useful aids for regular jam-makers are a sugar thermometer and a jam funnel.

Jars must be in perfect condition with no cracks or chips. Use only jars made expressly for canning, and always use new lids for a proper seal. Sterilizing the jars before use is essential—make sure they are thoroughly clean by washing in hot soapy water and rinsing well. Use while warm so that they do not crack when filled with boiling jam or chutney.

## JAMS, JELLIES AND MARMALADES

Which preserve you make is largely a matter of family preference, but there are several points that the busy cook needs to consider. When a favorite fruit is abundant, it may not be a convenient time for you to make preserves. If you have a freezer, then most fruits can be frozen for use later (raspberries, for example, have a short season) otherwise only buy a large amount if you know you will have the time to preserve them immediately.

Jams, jellies and maramalades all require patience and time—time to clean and trim fruits, time to cook, and time to process. Use only top-quality fruit and be careful dealing with hot liquids.

## FRUIT

There must be sufficient quantities of pectin, acid and sugar present in fruit for preserves to get their characteristic firm set. Getting the balance right is what successful preserve making is all about, so it is important to follow recipes exactly until you get the knack of creating your own combinations of fruits. Fruit which is just ripe or only slightly underripe should be used; pectin content diminishes in overripe fruit. Fruits low in acid or pectin can still be used, but they require the addition of a fruit high in pectin, commercial pectin, and/or acid. Lemon juice helps to bring out the flavor of the fruit but commercially bottled pectin may be used according to manufacturer's instructions. Allow 2 Tbsp lemon juice for every 4 lb fruit.

*Equipment needed for making preserves*

# SUGAR

Once the fruit has softened, sugar is added; sugar not only affects setting quality, it also acts as a preservative. If too little sugar is used, then the preserve may not set properly. Too much sugar and the preserve may crystallize and become sticky. To ensure that the preserve sets well, the sugar must be added after the fruit has sufficiently softened—which is why uncooked fruit for preserving should not be frozen in a sugar pack.

First dissolve the sugar slowly in the hot fruit, then boil briskly until setting point is reached. To help retain the natural color and flavor of the fruit, it is important that you do not greatly exceed the stated time for boiling in the recipe testing.

## TESTING FOR A SET

A sugar thermometer can be placed in, or stood in or attached to, the

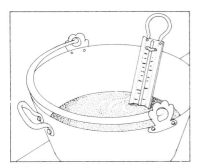

*Using a sugar thermometer*

side of the pan. When the temperature reaches 220°F, a set should be obtained. Or use the saucer test: place a little spoonful of the preserve on a chilled saucer, leave to cool, then push your finger gently through it. If the surface wrinkles, setting point has been reached. The pan should be removed from the heat during this

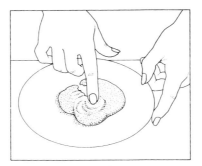

*Using finger to test for a set*

test. If setting point has not been reached, then return to the boil for a few more minutes and test again. Once setting point has been reached, remove any scum from the surface with a skimmer or slotted spoon before potting.

## JELLIES

To make a clear, firmly set jelly, strain the fruit and add the sugar to the extracted juice. Fruit is cooked to a pulp and left to drip through a jelly bag (though you

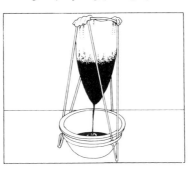

*Straining fruit pulp through jelly bag*

can improvise by using a double thickness of fine cloth, the four corners tied to an upturned chair) until all the juice is strained off. Fruit high in pectin can be re-cooked after the first straining in a little water and then strained again. Measure the juice and for every 2½ cups juice, add 1 lb sugar to fruit juices high in pectin and 2 cups sugar for juice with a medium pectin content. The fruit juice and sugar are then boiled until setting point is reached.

# MARMALADE

To prepare citrus fruits, the juice is squeezed out and the peel is cut thinly or thickly according to how you like your marmalade. The seeds and pith, which are rich in pectin, are loosely tied in a piece of muslin and cooked along with the citrus juice, peel and water. A large amount of water is used with marmalade because of the long cooking, during which it should reduce by about half. After

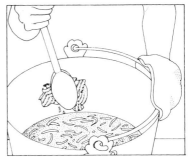

*Squeezing muslin bag to extract liquid*

cooking, squeeze the muslin bag with a wooden spoon to extract as much liquid as possible. An alternative method is to cook the fruit whole: after simmering the fruit is cut and the seeds and pith boiled for a few minutes before adding the sugar.

When cooking frozen oranges, use the whole-fruit cooking method and add one-eighth extra weight of fruit to offset pectin loss during freezing.

## CANNING, SEALING AND STORING

Jars holding around ½ pint or 1 pint are the usual choices. The jars should be warm and placed on a heat-resistant surface such as a chopping board or a pile of newspapers to prevent cracking when ladling in the hot preserve. Fill the jars up to the bottom of the neck. Some wholefruit jams and marmalades should cool for about 15 minutes before potting, otherwise the fruit will rise. Some people still cover jellies with

parafin, but most recommendations nowadays are to process
jellies, jams, and preserves in a hot
water bath. If using only a parafin
seal, limit it to jellies (no jams or
preserves) that have a very firm
set. Then immediately cover with a
lid. Label with contents and date.

Store in a cool, dry, dark place
for up to 1 year. If stored for
longer, the flavor and color will
start to deteriorate although the
preserve is perfectly safe to eat. If
mold growth occurs on the top of
a jam, it is not safe to eat.

# PICKLES, CHUTNEYS AND RELISHES

All of these are a good way to add
interest to any meal, be it hot or
cold, elaborate or plain.

Many kinds of fruit and
vegetables are used, ranging from
onions, red cabbage, cucumbers,
cauliflower, apples and dried fruit
to eggplants, bananas and pears.

Pickles are preserved either raw
or lightly cooked. They should
look attractive, so produce must
be perfect. For most types no
more than washing and trimming
is needed. Chutneys and relishes
need more preparation as ingredients must be finely chopped.
Chutneys are cooked long and

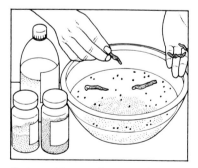

*Spices add extra flavor to vinegar*

slowly to produce a jam-like
consistency. Relishes are cooked
briefly or not at all.

All are preserved in vinegar,
which must have an acidic content
of at least 5%. Distilled (white)
vinegar is best for light-colored
pickles; cider vinegar is traditional
for pickled onions and perfectly
good for chutneys. The more
expensive wine vinegars give the
best flavor.

Spices add the finishing touch.
They are usually ground for
chutneys and relishes, left whole
for pickles.

## MAKING PICKLES
Before vinegar is added, many
vegetables and some fruits are first
salted to remove excess water,
which would dilute the strength of
the vinegar during storage, and
therefore diminish the keeping
qualities. Vegetables with a high

*Layer with salt before adding
vinegar*

water content like squash,
tomatoes and cucumbers are
layered with salt. Use 1 Tbsp salt
for every 1 lb vegetables. Other
vegetables like cauliflower and
onions are covered with a brine
solution of $\frac{1}{3}$ cup salt dissolved in
$2\frac{1}{2}$ cups water for every 1 lb
vegetables. The vegetables are left,
covered, for up to 24 hours, then
drained and rinsed. Fruits do not
require brining as they are usually
lightly cooked to evaporate the
surplus moisture before pickling.

*Pouring vinegar on pickles*

Pack vegetables loosely and
attractively in warmed jars. Pour
over cold vinegar for crisp pickles
and hot vinegar for softer ones.
Fill jars leaving only a small space
for expansion during processing
and making sure that the vinegar
covers the contents. Cover
immediately with canning lids and
process as directed by jar
manufacturer.

For sweet fruit pickles, sugar is
added to the vinegar, the liquid is
reduced to concentrate the flavor
and poured over the fruit.

Leave pickles to mature for 3
months before serving. Most will
keep for up to 1 year, but red
cabbage pickles should be served
within 2–3 weeks.

## MAKING CHUTNEYS AND RELISHES
These are the simplest preserves
to make. All the ingredients,
including sugar which gives the
sweet-sour flavor, are simmered
until there are no pools of liquid
left on the surface. For chutneys
this can take as long as 4 hours.
Only occasional stirring is needed.
Jar and process as pickles.

## USING THE PRESSURE COOKER

Use the pressure cooker to save time when making preserves. It is especially good for making marmalade and softening hard fruits for jellies. Not only is there a great time saving but the fruit retains its flavor and color beautifully. Always consult manufacturer's instructions before using your pressure cooker for preserving. Although the entire preserve can be made in the pressure cooker pan, only the preliminary cooking and softening of the fruit can be done actually under pressure. After adding the sugar and any lemon juice the preserve must be boiled in the open pan for about 15 minutes. Never fill the pan more than half full; use half the amount of water given in a standard recipe. Add half of this when the fruit is cooked under pressure. The second half is added with the sugar. Cook citrus fruits for 20 minutes at medium (10 lb) pressure. Release pressure at room temperature.

## FRUITS IN ALCOHOL

For a delicious dessert that you can boast is homemade, fruits in alcohol are well worth making. They are made by preserving lightly poached fruits like peaches, apricots and plums in equal parts of sugar and alcohol. Brandy is usually used, but try more unusual mixtures containing kirsch or orange-flavored liqueurs. The sugar syrup can be flavored with whole spices like cinnamon and cloves, and for an attractive appearance the spices can be added to the jar. Fruits in alcohol should be filled and covered in the same way as jams.

## BUSY COOK'S GUIDE TO JAMS, JELLIES AND MARMALADE

- Cook frozen fruit from frozen to prevent discoloration.

- Chop citrus fruit peel in the chopper attachment of a food mixer or in a food processor. Do not use a coarse grinder as it produces a paste-like marmalade.

- Soak citrus peel overnight to help soften it.

- For jams made with pitted fruits, the pits will float to the surface after cooking and can be removed with a slotted spoon. Cherries are an exception, however, and their pits should be removed beforehand, with a cherry pitter.

- Grease the bottom of the preserving pan with butter to help prevent sticking during cooking.

- Warm the sugar in a 275°F oven before adding it to the fruit and it will dissolve more quickly when stirred into the fruit.

- Have saucers chilling in the refrigerator ready for testing.

- Adding a pat of butter after the sugar has dissolved helps reduce foaming.

- Scald a jelly bag so the fruit juice runs clean through and is not absorbed by the fabric.

- Don't rush the straining by squeezing the bag—this results in a cloudy mixture.

- Wipe filled jars clean while they are still warm with a cloth that has been wrung out in hot water.

---

### PECTIN CONTENT OF FRUITS AND VEGETABLES USED IN PRESERVING

| Good | Medium | Poor |
|------|--------|------|
| Cooking apples | Dessert apples | Bananas |
| Crabapples | Apricots | Carrots |
| Cranberries | Blueberries | Cherries |
| Fresh currants | Blackberries | Elderberries |
| Gooseberries | Greengage plums | Figs |
| Lemons | Loganberries | Grapes |
| Limes | Mulberries | Squash |
| Oranges | Raspberries | Melons |
| Plums (some varieties) | | Nectarines |
| Quinces | | Peaches |
| | | Pineapple |
| | | Rhubarb |
| | | Strawberries |

# PRESERVE RECIPES

## GOOSEBERRY JELLY

*Makes about 4 lb*

4½ lb gooseberries, washed

water

sugar

*1* Put the gooseberries in a preserving pan with water to cover. Bring to the boil, then simmer gently for ¾–1 hour until the fruit is soft and pulpy. Stir from time to time.

*2* Spoon the fruit pulp into a jelly bag or cloth attached to the legs of an upturned stool and leave to strain into a large bowl for at least 12 hours.

*3* Discard the pulp remaining in the jelly bag. Measure the extract and return it to the pan with 1 lb sugar for each 2½ cups extract. Heat gently, stirring, until the sugar has dissolved, then boil rapidly for about 15 minutes.

*4* Test for a set, then remove any scum with a slotted spoon. Cover and seal.

——— VARIATIONS ———

### GOOSEBERRY MINT JELLY

Cook the gooseberries with a few sprigs of mint and add finely chopped mint to the jelly before sealing.

### GOOSEBERRY AND ELDERFLOWER JELLY

Tie two large elderflower heads in a piece of muslin. When the jelly has reached setting point, remove from the heat, add the muslin bag and stir around in the hot jelly for about 3 minutes. This will produce a good flavor that is not over-dominant.

## STRAWBERRY JAM

*Makes about 5 lb*

3½ lb strawberries, washed and hulled

3 Tbsp lemon juice

3 lb sugar

pat of butter

*1* Put the strawberries in a preserving pan with the lemon juice. Simmer gently, stirring occasionally, for 20–30 minutes until really soft.

*2* Take the pan off the heat, add the sugar and stir until dissolved. Add butter and boil rapidly for about 20 minutes.

*3* Test for a set, then remove any scum with a slotted spoon.

*4* Allow the jam to cool for 15–20 minutes, stir gently, fill jars and cover; process.

## APRICOT CONSERVE

*Makes about 5 lb*

1 lb dried apricots, soaked in 8 cups water overnight

juice of 1 lemon

3 lb sugar

½ cup blanched almonds, split

pat of butter

*1* Put the apricots in a preserving pan with the soaking water and lemon juice. Simmer for about 30 minutes until soft, stirring from time to time.

*2* Remove the pan from the heat and add the sugar and almonds. Stir until the sugar has dissolved, then add butter and boil rapidly for 20–25 minutes, stirring frequently to prevent sticking.

*3* Test for a set, then remove any scum with a slotted spoon. Fill jars, cover, and process.

## ORANGE MARMALADE

*Makes about 10 lb*

3 lb oranges, washed

juice of 2 lemons

4 quarts water

6 lb sugar

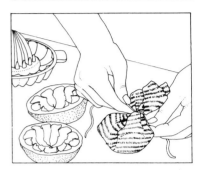

*1* Halve the oranges and squeeze out the juice and seeds. Tie the seeds, and any membrane that has come away during squeezing, in a piece of muslin.

*2* Slice the orange peel thinly or thickly, as preferred, and put it in a preserving pan with the fruit juices, water and muslin bag. Simmer gently for about 2 hours until the peel is really soft and the liquid reduced by about half.

*3* Remove the muslin bag, squeezing it well and allowing the juice to run back into the pan. Add the sugar, stirring until it has dissolved, then boil the mixture rapidly for about 15–20 minutes. Test for a set, then remove any scum with a slotted spoon.

*4* Allow the marmalade to cool for 15–20 minutes, stir gently, then fill jars and process.

# LEMON CURD

*Makes about 1½ lb*

finely grated rind and juice of 4
   medium lemons

4 eggs

½ cup butter

2 cups sugar

*1* Place all the ingredients in the
top of a double saucepan or in
a bowl standing over a pan of
simmering water. Stir until the
sugar has dissolved and continue
heating gently for about 20
minutes until the curd thickens.

*2* Strain into jars and cover.
Process. Store for about
1 month only.

--- VARIATION ---

The fresh lemon juice can be
replaced with ¾ cup reconstituted
lemon juice. To give extra tang,
add the grated rind of 1 fresh
lemon.

# CORN RELISH

*Makes about 5½ lb*

6 ears corn

½ a small green cabbage, trimmed
   and roughly chopped

2 medium onions, halved

1½ sweet red peppers, seeded and
   quartered

2 tsp salt

2 Tbsp flour

½ tsp turmeric

1 cup sugar

2 tsp powdered mustard

2½ cups distilled white vinegar

*1* Cook the corn in boiling water
for 3 minutes, then drain.
Using a sharp knife, cut the
kernels from the cobs.

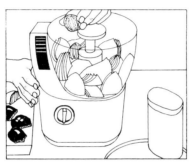

*2* Coarsely mince the cabbage,
onions and red peppers and
combine with the corn.

*3* Blend the salt, flour, turmeric,
sugar and mustard together in
a saucepan, then gradually stir in
the vinegar. Heat gently, stirring,
until the sugar has dissolved, then
bring to the boil. Add the
vegetables and simmer for 25–30
minutes, stirring occasionally.
Cover and refrigerate.

# BEET AND HORSERADISH RELISH

*Makes about 3 lb*

2 oz fresh horseradish

1 lb beets

1 medium onion

8 oz cooking apples

2 cups cider vinegar

1½ cups sugar

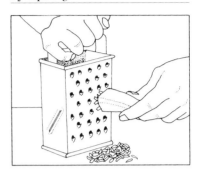

*1* Peel and grate the horseradish.
Peel the beets, then shred or
grate coarsely. Chop the onion.
Peel, quarter, core and roughly
chop the apples.

*2* Place all the ingredients in a
medium-sized saucepan and
heat gently until the sugar
dissolves.

*3* Boil gently, uncovered, for
about 1¼ hours until the
ingredients are tender and the
contents well reduced. Cover and
refrigerate.

333

## PICKLED RED CABBAGE

about 3 lb firm red cabbage, finely shredded

2 large onions, sliced

4 Tbsp salt

2½ quarts spiced vinegar (see below)

1 Tbsp light brown sugar

*1* Layer the cabbage and onion in a large bowl, sprinkling each layer with salt, then cover and leave overnight.

*2* Next day drain the cabbage and onion thoroughly, rinse off the surplus salt and drain again. Pack into jars.

*3* Pour the vinegar into a pan and heat gently. Add the sugar and stir until dissolved. Leave to cool, then pour over the cabbage and onion and cover immediately. Use within 2–3 weeks as the cabbage tends to lose its crispness.

## SPICED VINEGAR

*Makes 5 cups*

5 cups vinegar

2 Tbsp mace

1 Tbsp whole allspice

1 Tbsp whole cloves

7 inches cinnamon stick

6 peppercorns

1 small bay leaf

*1* Place the vinegar, spices and bay leaf in a saucepan, bring to the boil and pour into a bowl or bottles. Cover to preserve the flavor and leave to marinate for 2 hours.

*2* Strain through muslin, pour into clean bottles and seal with airtight and vinegar-proof tops. An even better result is obtained if the spices are left to stand in unheated vinegar for 1–2 months.

## DRIED FRUIT PICKLE

*Makes about 3 lb*

1 lb sugar

1¼ cups distilled white vinegar

2 tsp whole cloves

2 tsp whole allspice

1 cinnamon stick

pared rind of 1 small lemon

½ tsp ground ginger

2 lb dried mixed fruit, soaked in cold water overnight

*1* Put the sugar and vinegar in a preserving pan and heat gently until the sugar dissolves.

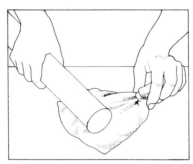

*2* Place the cloves, allspice, cinnamon stick and lemon rind in a muslin bag. Crush lightly.

*3* Add the bag to the vinegar and sugar. Stir in the ground ginger and bring to the boil. Cook for 5–7 minutes until reduced and syrupy, with about 3 cups remaining.

*4* Put the dried fruit in a separate pan with the soaking water. Cover and simmer until tender. Drain, then pack into warm jars. Cover completely with the hot reduced vinegar. Process.

*5* Keep for several weeks before eating. Store in the refrigerator after opening.

## PICKLED ONIONS

*Makes about 4 lb*

4 lb pickling onions

1 lb salt

5 quarts water

5 cups spiced vinegar (see below left)

*1* Place the onions, without peeling, in a large bowl. Dissolve half the salt in half the water, pour the brine over the onions and leave for 12 hours.

*2* Peel the onions, then cover with fresh brine, made with the remaining salt and water. Leave for a further 24–36 hours.

*3* Drain and rinse the onions well and pack them into jars. Pour the spiced vinegar over the onions and cover the jars immediately with airtight and vinegar-proof tops. Process.

## TOMATO AND SWEET RED PEPPER CHUTNEY

*Makes about 3 lb*

2 lb ripe tomatoes

4 medium onions

1 red chili

1 sweet red pepper

1¼ cups distilled white vinegar

⅔ cup raw sugar

1 tsp salt

1 tsp paprika

¼ tsp chili powder

*1* Peel and roughly chop the tomatoes and onions. Seed and finely chop the chili and pepper.

*2* Place all the ingredients in a medium saucepan and heat gently until the sugar dissolves.

*3* Boil gently, uncovered, for about 1½ hours until the vegetables are tender and the chutney of a thick pulpy consistency, stirring occasionally. Cover and refrigerate.

# *Making the Most of Your Freezer*

Freezers are not just for large families needing an endless supply of ice cream and hamburgers. Nor are they only for country dwellers who live miles from the stores. Single people and couples will also find that a freezer, once bought, becomes an integral and necessary part of their way of life.

A freezer is primarily a convenient and healthy method of food storage. If the food is fresh when it goes into the freezer, it will be fresh when it comes out—unlike in a refrigerator where the chill is only sufficient to slow down deterioration, not to stop it.

## HEALTH

Food values change very little while food is stored in the freezer, in sharp contrast to other methods of preservation such as canning, which relies on heat to destroy the spoilage organisms. With this method, the heat also destroys a high proportion of the food value, especially vitamins. In some cases food which is frozen while at the peak of freshness will have a higher food value than that which may have stood in the village store for a day or two, and then in your vegetable rack for a day or two more before it finally reaches your plate.

## CONVENIENCE

If the nutritional value of frozen food gives you some satisfaction when you happen to think about it, the convenience factor will quite simply change your life. With a freezer in the home you are no longer dependent on daily or even weekly shopping, and you can even regulate your cooking to fit in more conveniently with other demands on your time. Meat, vegetables, fruit, snacks, bread— they and a whole lot more foods can all be frozen, cutting down on the bulk of your regular shopping.

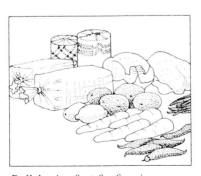

*Bulk buying food for freezing*

If you own a freezer you can shop monthly where you used to shop weekly. For many seasonal foods such as fruit and vegetables it can even become a once a year event, when you pick, freeze and store enough fresh produce to last you through till next year. Of course there are foods which do not freeze well, and you will want to vary your diet with fresh foods. But the peace of mind that comes from knowing there is always something available to eat is precious to freezer owners.

If all this shopping sounds expensive, remember that buying in bulk is usually less expensive than buying in small quantities. You have to balance these economies against the actual cost of running the freezer—electricity, packaging materials and so on— but in the long run your freezer should not actually cost you money if you run it carefully. What it will do is to improve your standard of living by adding to the variety of foods that are easily accessible to you.

As well as shopping, the freezer can make your cooking more convenient. If when you are

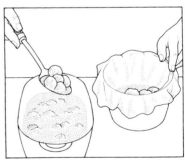

*Divide and separate meat to freeze*

cooking a casserole you prepare enough for two meals and freeze half, this will save time on another day when you may have less time or energy. You could also actually choose to cook when you otherwise would not need to. If you enjoy cooking you might like to while away a wet Sunday afternoon cooking for the freezer—then on working days

335

reheating is the only work required.

At first thought this may seem the way to repetitive eating, but in practice it usually turns out to be the opposite. In a busy household it is all too easy to get into the habit of existing on a limited diet of quickly cooked foods—steaks and chops, chicken, omelettes. The freezer will encourage you to vary your diet with more complicated dishes. It will also save waste, as leftovers can be stored properly for use another day.

## BULK BUYING

One of the prime advantages of freezer ownership is the facility it gives you for bulk buying. Whether you snap up a cheap offer at the local butcher, or pick your own raspberries in July to enjoy in December, you will appreciate this extension to your normal shopping patterns. But be disciplined. Be sure you want what you are buying and will use it up within a reasonable time. Otherwise the storage will be costing you more than you can possibly save on the purchase price of fresh food.

Watch particularly that you are buying the quality of food that you would normally want—buying inferior goods is no saving. If possible, and particularly if you do not know the supplier, taste a small sample first. This may not be possible with meat, so you are probably best to stick to a supplier you know and trust. But it is often possible for fruit and vegetables; buy enough for one meal first, then go back for more if the quality is good.

Remember that although frozen foods stay healthy almost indefinitely, the eating quality does start to deteriorate with long storage. This is because no packaging is completely vapor-proof and the foods do begin gradually to dry out. This may affect only the surface at first but will eventually penetrate right through the food. Water content

makes up quite a large part of many foods and if this is allowed to evaporate, the foods may become tough, chewy, stringy or simply less tasty.

For prepared foods that are easily replaced, plan no more than about 3 months storage. This is particularly important for commercially packed foods, where you are going to open and reseal the pack; resealing is never as airtight as the original seal. When you are cooking for the freezer at home, it is a matter of pride. You will be less than pleased if a homemade chicken pot pie is allowed to dry out until it tastes no better than one you could have bought at the corner store.

Meat is less vulnerable. You can buy it from a freezer center or have it freshly frozen (ask the butcher to flash freeze it for you if buying fresh meat). Most meats will remain in good condition for a comfortable six months. This period will probably see you through several seasonal price rises, so watch the prices and buy carefully. The exceptions are variety meats, bacon and ground meats. Variety meats are best kept for no more than three months, and ground meat deteriorates quickly because of the large number of cut surfaces exposed to the air. Bacon with other cured and smoked meats, goes rancid and is best eaten within one or two months.

Fresh, seasonal fruit and vegetables are different. It is worth buying a year's supply so long as you are sure the quality is good and you pack it well. On the other hand, don't overdo any one food. Even asparagus can become boring if served too often!

Portioning is important when you buy or cook in bulk. Wherever possible, divide large packs into smaller ones, in meal-size portions. Foods will keep much better if a pack is not frequently opened and closed again. And for foods that freeze into a solid block, it is almost impossible to cut off portions when needed.

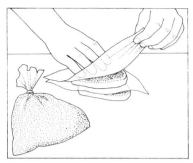

*Divide chops with plastic wrap*

When buying meat, make sure that it is cut into roasts or pieces to suit you. Divide chops with plastic wrap or freezer paper in ones or twos, so that you can separate off what is required as you need it. Pack ground meat in $\frac{1}{2}$ lb or 1 lb bags, suitable for one meal or for one cooking session with some left over to freeze away.

When freezing fresh fruit and vegetables, it is possible to achieve a free-flow pack from which you can empty out a little at a time, but it is difficult. It's much better to buy a supply of small bags and divide up the fruit before freezing.

Take care when freezing fresh food not to put too much into the freezer at once or you will raise the temperature in the unit above a safe level. Fast freezing always achieves the best results (small packs help here again), and most freezers have a "fast freeze" switch which cuts out the thermostat, allowing the temperature to drop well below the normal storage temperature. Most manufacturers recommend that you freeze only 10 percent of the freezer's total capacity in any 24-hr period. If you do not have a separate fast freeze compartment, which is the case with many small models, try to keep a separate shelf or find some other method of preventing the fresh unfrozen foods from touching the surfaces of those already in the freezer.

## BATCH COOKING

Another joy of the freezer owner is that of cooking two, or several, meals at one time. This rarely takes more time than a single meal of the same dish, and yet saves considerable time when it comes to serving the frozen dish on later occasions. In a small household there are also considerable financial economies to be made in savings of fuel. Many people hesitate to switch on the oven to cook one or two portions of casserole for two or three hours—but if the oven can be filled with several portions of the same or similar dishes, then it is well worthwhile. For thawing and reheating, a pan on top of the stove or in the microwave is often adequate.

There are two main approaches to bulk cooking. The first is the simplest: you cook one big dish such as a stew or pot of soup, divide it into suitable portions and pack them into the freezer. The other is more complicated and could be thought of as chain cooking. This way you cook a basic item in bulk but turn it into several different dishes for freezing. So a bag full of windfall apples will make stewed apple and also apple sauce, apple pie, blackberry or raspberry and apple pie, apple crumble or apple tarts, as you wish. For speed, you will appreciate the help of gadgets such as a food processor to slice the apples and rub in the pastry and crumble mixtures quickly, or an electric mixer for beating and creaming cake mixtures.

*Batch cooking with ground beef*

If you have been tempted by a special offer on ground beef, start by cooking it all together as a basic seasoned mixture. You could then, for example, turn one quarter of it into lasagne, another into shepherd's pie, a third portion into meat loaf, and eke out any left over with beans to make chili con carne. Whether you make up all these dishes in the first cooking session, or whether you cook and pack the basic mixture ready for use later is a matter of choice—either way you save considerable time.

Use chain cooking to add variety to your meals. If you live alone you probably are used to buying single chicken portions to bake or broil. With a freezer installed, try buying two whole chickens. First take off the breasts; these can be frozen flat, for stir frying, or stuffed and rolled ready for frying. Pack them in ones or twos as appropriate. Use the leg and wing portions for casseroles or cook the complete carcasses together, remove the meat and use it for fricassée, curry or chicken pot pies. Stew the bones and giblets for stock and save the livers for pâté or sautés. You will be able to buy whole chickens much more cheaply per 1 lb than individual portions, and nothing will be wasted.

The end result of all these ploys is more variety than is otherwise reasonable when cooking for one or two. You also have the fun of cooking when you want to, with reduced work when you don't want it.

## PACKAGING

Freezing converts water to ice within the cell structure of the food. If careless packaging allows moisture to be withdrawn from other foods, or from the inside of the freezer, then frosting will appear on the outside of the food. And if it is allowed to continue, moisture will eventually be withdrawn from the food itself, causing dehydration and loss of nutrients.

With meat and poultry this can be particularly noticeable, with exposed areas developing "freezer burn." This is the name given when tissues go tough and spongy—so tough and spongy that no amount of clever cooking can correct it. And with any kind of food, strong smells can travel from one faulty package to another, so that a delicate lemon water ice could come out with the flavor of curried beef.

So the basic requirements of freezer packaging are to exclude air from the food, preventing oxidation, and to contain water vapor within the package. The other important thing to remember is labelling; wrapped foods quickly become totally anonymous in the freezer, leading to possibly disastrous, often comic, results when you come to prepare a meal.

There are many different packaging materials on the market; it is important to use those labelled especially for freezer use. These will be thicker and more completely vapor-proof than those intended for general kitchen use.

**Plastic wrap** is not really suitable for freezer use as it is not thick enough and quickly ceases to cling at freezer temperatures. However, it may be useful as an inner wrap for awkwardly shaped foods.

**Foil** is useful as an inner wrap for awkward shapes such as meat, fish or pies. It can be pressed firmly against the surface of the food to exclude virtually all air. But it punctures easily, so always overwrap with a plastic bag.

**Foil dishes** These are another favorite standby. They come in all sorts of shapes and sizes—square, round, pie dishes, casserole dishes or pudding molds—and some come with a fitting lid. Beware of buying a manufacturer's pack of foil dishes of mixed sizes—there will be lots you will not use. Much better to buy a few individual dishes until you find which ones best suit your needs, then buy

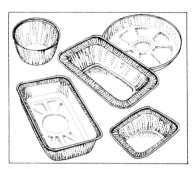

*Foil containers for freezing*

those in bulk. If thoroughly washed and checked for holes, foil dishes can be reused several times. The lids cannot be reused, however, as they are backed with cardboard which is not washable, so for second use they must be covered with foil and overwrapped with a plastic bag.

**Labelling** Waterproof labels are vital. Anything else will fall off in the freezer and you will be left not knowing what is what. Equally important is a waterproof pen that will not smudge and become illegible.

**Microwave dishes** If you intend using your freezer in combination with a microwave oven, look for microwave-safe plastic dishes. These can be used for storage in the freezer and transferred directly to the microwave for thawing and reheating.

**Reusable plastic boxes** Rigid plastic boxes with an airtight snap-on lid are expensive but useful for fragile pastries and cakes, and they last for years. If you save manufacturer's plastic boxes you may be able to avoid the expense of buying these. Some frozen dessert cartons are good, and last well. Margarine tubs, yogurt containers and cottage cheese tubs, etc., are all useful, but they do become brittle in the freezer so cannot be reused indefinitely.

**Plastic bags** Many people manage almost entirely with plastic bags. Always choose heavy duty bags, and they can be

washed, dried and reused several times. But do check that they have not been punctured during use. Buy a selection of different sizes to start with and you will soon learn which you find most useful.

Fasten bags with paper or plastic covered twist ties, excluding as much air as possible from the package.

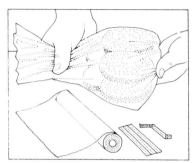

*Exclude air from bag before tying*

Boilable bags are more expensive but are especially useful for microwave owners. They must be sealed with the special plastic ties provided if you are going to use them in the microwave (metal ties will cause arcing). With these bags the food can be thawed and reheated without removing it from the bag.

**Waxed or freezer paper** is primarily useful for portioning. You can use it to interleave individual chops or fillets of fish, or individual portions of cake or pâté, so that you can pack a large quantity in one bag or box, removing individual portions as required.

## THAWING AND REHEATING

Most cooked dishes can be re-heated from frozen and this helps to preserve flavor, texture and color. Cooking from frozen is essential for vegetables, but other cooked dishes can be thawed before reheating. This is more of an economy measure than any-thing else, for example, to reheat a stew from frozen needs 1 hour in

a 400°F oven, then a further 40 minutes at 350°F. A thawed stew will only need 20–40 minutes at 350°F. Reheating can also be done on the stove. If frozen, break up chunks with a fork to speed up reheating. Do not re-freeze thawed raw food unless it is cooked first, cooled quickly, then frozen.

## FREEZER STANDBYS

Have these on hand to save time on last-minute preparations. This is a great way to use up leftovers.
### STOCKS AND SAUCES
Make your own bouillon cubes by

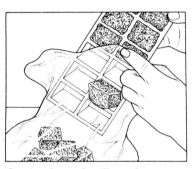

*Storing frozen bouillon cubes*

freezing stock in ice-cube trays until solid, then storing them in plastic bags (a well-reduced stock will be concentrated in flavor). Use as a convenient way to flavor soups and stews. Cubes of left-over sauces are also handy for flavoring.
### CHEESE
Pack grated cheese in a plastic bag; the cheese will stay separate so you can shake out only as much as needed.
### CHOCOLATE
When you feel like indulging in a little chocolate cookery, make chocolate squares, curls or leaves; freeze in rigid containers, inter-leaving layers to prevent crushing.

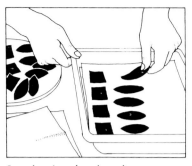

*Interleaving chocolate shapes*

Use for decoration while still very cold, but allow 10 minutes to thaw.

## WHIPPED CREAM
Freeze leftover cream by piping in rosettes onto baking parchment

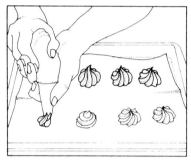

*Piping rosettes onto baking parchment*

on a tray. Open freeze until solid, then pack in rigid containers, interleaving layers to prevent crushing. Use from frozen to decorate, but allow 10 minutes to thaw.

## JUICE OR RIND OF ORANGES AND LEMONS
When using just the rind or the juice of citrus fruits in a recipe, freeze the unused parts in a small container. For convenience in later recipes, make sure you state the quantity for each portion frozen. Grate rind before freezing.

## BREADCRUMBS
Make fresh breadcrumbs and pack in plastic bags—the crumbs will stay separate. Thaw for 30 minutes if using to coat for frying, otherwise use from frozen. Buttered crumbs can also be frozen ready for use as toppings to

be browned under the grill. Open freeze, then pack in plastic bags in useable quantities.

## CROUTONS
Open freeze on trays until solid, then pack in a plastic bag. Reheat from frozen for 5–10 minutes in the oven at 400°F.

## HERBS
Freeze whole sprigs of herbs, then, to avoid chopping them, crumble while still frozen into soups and stews; herbs will be too wet to use as a garnish.

*Crumbling frozen herbs into soup*

Alternatively, freeze chopped herbs with water in ice-cube trays (as for stock above), then transfer to a plastic bag.

Use straight from the freezer as an addition to stews, casseroles and sauces.

## BUTTER BALLS
These take time to make when needed, but a few stored in the freezer—even those left over from a party—are handy for almost instant use.

## PARSLEY BUTTER
This is ideal for topping steaks, chops and other grills such as fish. Cream $\frac{1}{2}$ cup unsalted butter until smooth. Beat in the grated rind and juice of 1 lemon, 4 Tbsp chopped fresh parsley, and salt and pepper. Form into a long sausage shape between sheets of waxed or non-stick paper. Refirm in the fridge or freezer and cut into 4-Tbsp portions. Wrap each in foil. Alternatively, freeze the butter roll whole and cut off slices as required. Make a neat parcel, seal and label. Use straight from the freezer.

# *FREEZING SUMMER PRODUCE*

Summer and early autumn are the peak times of year for fruit and vegetables and, whether you grow your own in the garden or have access to cheap supplies from a local farm or market, if you own a freezer it should be the busiest time of year for stocking up.

Freezer owners can take advantage of gluts and bargain bulk buys so that when dreary late autumn and winter comes they can enjoy the luxury of out-of-season produce.

What's more, a lot of the time-consuming work of peeling, pitting, slicing and dicing the fruits and vegetables will have already been done months ago. So making up some quick soup, a simple casserole, fruit compote or pie will be almost as easy as defrosting a few containers of food.

The trick to efficient freezing of fruits and vegetables is time and management. Set aside some time when you have nothing else that must be done so you can devote yourself completely to the task at hand and not feel frazzled. Then get everything you'll need all lined up so it's right there at the crucial moment: the knives, the potato peeler, the pots, sieve, dish towels, freezer bags or containers, and whatever else. Once you've begun, don't put things aside to finish later; the quality of your frozen food will suffer if it's not prepared and put into the freezer right away.

# *HOW TO FREEZE VEGETABLES*

Most vegetables freeze successfully unless they have a very high water content such as cucumbers or tomatoes. Only freeze the very youngest and freshest of produce — ideally all vegetables should be frozen just as they reach maturity.

## PREPARATION
The only disadvantage to freezing vegetables is the amount of time you need to set aside for preparation before you can actually put them in the freezer, so when you have lots of vegetables to freeze, allow yourself plenty of time. All vegetables must be fully prepared, that is scrubbed or peeled, with roots, leaves and damaged parts removed. Vegetables in the pod should be shelled before freezing (except in the case of snow peas and very young broad beans, which can be frozen whole). The blanching of vegetables is recommended (see below) and, although time-consuming, is well worth the trouble in the long run because it increases the storage life of vege-

## HOW TO BLANCH VEGETABLES

Blanching is a scalding process which halts enzyme activity in vegetables. Though not absolutely essential, it is advisable. Enzymes are naturally present in food; they are not harmful, but if they are not halted in this way, they will continue to work during storage in the freezer and after a period of time will cause the vegetables to lose color, flavor and texture and, most important of all, ascorbic acid (vitamin C). Obviously the blanching process itself causes loss of ascorbic acid, but this is only slight compared with the amount which would be lost during storage if the vegetables are not blanched.

**Short-term storage** In times of glut and/or when you are too busy to blanch vegetables before freezing they can be frozen unblanched, but in this case storage times will be shortened by as much as one-quarter. Plan to use these vegetables as soon as you possibly can after freezing. Special blanching sets are available which are worth buying if you freeze a lot of vegetables, otherwise use a large saucepan and a colander or wire basket.

*1* Bring 4 quarts *unsalted* water to the boil in the pan, place 1 lb vegetables in the basket and immerse in the boiling water. Bring the water back to the boil immediately, then blanch the vegetables for the recommended length of time (see chart).

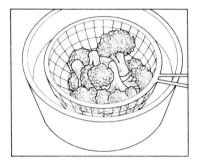

*2* Have ready a large bowl of ice water. As soon as the blanching time is up, remove the basket from the boiling water. Quickly plunge the basket of vegetables into the water and leave until the vegetables are cold (cooling time is usually the same as scalding time).

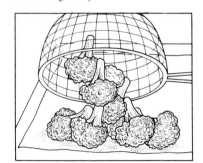

*3* Remove the basket from the water, drain the vegetables, then tip them out onto a clean towel or absorbent paper. Dry, then pack immediately to avoid discoloration.

tables in the freezer and also maintains their fresh quality. For example, a notable change in the eating quality of unblanched Brussels sprouts can be detected after only 3 days; in broad beans after 3 weeks; in runner beans after 1 month; in peas after 6 months.

One plus point with blanching which cuts down on time is that the same blanching water doesn't have to be renewed with every batch of vegetables —the same water can be used six or seven times, and by doing so you will in fact achieve a build-up of vitamin C in the blanching water and less loss of minerals, though the iced water for cooling after blanching should be renewed with each batch.

## PACKING VEGETABLES FOR THE FREEZER

Vegetables can be packed in either rigid plastic containers or freezerproof plastic bags, whichever is most convenient for you. Vegetables such as peas, beans and corn are best frozen as free-flow packs in plastic bags so that they do not stick together as one solid mass and you can use as many or as few as you like. Open-freeze them on trays before packing in this way (see open-freezing method for fruit, right).

## THAWING AND COOKING VEGETABLES

*Always* cook vegetables from frozen to avoid overcooking (this is especially important when they have been blanched before freezing). Plunge them into a minimum amount of boiling salted water (about $1\frac{1}{4}$ cups water) and $\frac{1}{2}$ tsp salt to every 1 lb vegetables.

Alternatively, frozen vegetables can be cooked in a covered pan with butter, seasoning and herbs; or added to soups and stews without prior cooking.

# HOW TO FREEZE FRUIT

All fruits are suitable for freezing, either whole or sliced, mashed or puréed to a pulp. Possible exceptions are bananas, which can only be frozen if mashed to a purée and combined with other ingredients, and pomegranates, which are too watery. As with vegetables, it is only worth freezing top-quality produce. Ideally, fruits should be frozen just at the point when they become ready for eating, but slightly over-ripe fruits can still be used for purées.

## PREPARATION

Rinse all fruits (except for soft fruits) in ice-cold water, a few at a time, then drain. If slicing fruits which are likely to discolor, drop them into a bowl of acidulated water during preparation.

## PACKING FRUIT FOR THE FREEZER

There are four ways of packing fruit for the freezer. Use only the methods recommended for each individual type (see chart) or you will have disappointing results.

**Dry pack method** Suitable for small, whole fruits with perfect, undamaged skins which are not likely to discolor: examples are blackberries, cherries, currants, gooseberries and strawberries. Fruits frozen in this way can become mis-shapen through freezing together in a solid mass and are best used in pies and preserves where perfect shape is not important.

*To dry pack:* pick over fruits; wash, then dry. Pack in rigid containers.

**Open-freezing method** Recommended for small whole fruits or pieces of fruit which need to keep their shape during storage: examples are apple slices, cherries, and strawberries which are used in open tarts and flans or as decorations for desserts and cakes.

*To open-freeze:* pick over fruits, prepare as necessary (see chart), then spread out on a tray. Freeze until solid, then remove and pack in rigid

containers or freezer bags for free-flow packs.

**Dry sugar pack method** This method helps soft, juicy fruits retain their shape and texture during freezing; ideal for berries which produce a sweetened juice on thawing—perfect for mousses, fruit salads, or for serving with cream or ice cream.

*To make a dry sugar pack:* put a layer of fruit in the bottom of a rigid container, then sprinkle with sugar. Repeat layers to fill container, leaving $\frac{3}{4}$ inch headspace.

**Sugar syrup pack method** Best for non-juicy fruits which have a low vitamin C content and pitted fruits which discolor easily (such as apricots, peaches and pears).

When preparing fruits, make sure you have enough syrup to make it a day in advance and refrigerate overnight.

*To make sugar syrup:* dissolve the sugar in the water by heating gently. Bring to the boil, then remove from the heat, strain, cover and cool. Allow $1\frac{1}{4}$ cups syrup for every 1 lb fruit.

Prepare fruit quickly (see chart), place in rigid containers and immediately pour over cold sugar syrup, leaving $\frac{3}{4}$ inch headspace.

## THAWING AND COOKING FRUIT

If the fruit is served raw, thaw in unopened container and eat chilled. Pitted fruits frozen in a sugar syrup should be kept submerged when thawing—open the container just before serving or fruits will discolor.

### Thawing times for fruit

| | |
|---|---|
| In a refrigerator | 6–8 hours |
| At room temperature | 2–4 hours |

Dry packs and dry sugar packs thaw more quickly than sugar syrup packs. For quick, emergency thawing, place the container in a bowl of slightly warm water for 30 minutes–1 hour. If fruit is cooked, thaw until pieces are just loosened. Cook as for fresh fruit, but if it is packed in sugar or sugar syrup, decrease or omit sugar.

| VEGETABLE | PREPARATION | PACKAGING AND STORAGE TIME | THAWING |
|---|---|---|---|
| **Artichoke** | Remove outer leaves and stalks. Trim tops and stems. Wash. Blanch in water with lemon juice for 5–7 mins. Drain and cool upside down. | Pack in rigid containers. 6 months | Cook from frozen in boiling salted water for approx. 7 mins according to size. |
| **Asparagus** | Cut off woody ends. Scrape off fibrous scales. Grade into thick and thin stems. Wash. Blanch thin stems 2 mins, thick 4 mins. Drain and cool. | Tie into small bundles. Pack bundles tips to stalks in rigid containers, separating them with freezerproof non-stick paper. 9 months | Cook from frozen to avoid over-cooking. Plunge into boiling salted water and cook for 2 mins according to size. |
| **Avocado** | Will not freeze whole, so prepare in pulp form. Peel and mash with 1 Tbsp lemon juice to each avocado. | Quickly pack pulp in rigid containers. Seal and freeze immediately to prevent discoloration. 2 months maximum | Thaw in unopened containers for approx. 2 hrs. Use as soon as possible or flesh will discolor. |
| **Bean (Broad/French/ Runner)** | Broad: Shell and blanch 3 mins. French: Trim ends and blanch 2–3 mins; runner: Slice thickly and blanch 2 mins. Drain and cool. | Pack in usable quantities in freezer-proof plastic bags, or open-freeze and pack as free-flow packs. 12 months | Cook from frozen in boiling salted water: broad beans 3–5 mins; French and runner 5–7 mins. |
| **Beet** | Only freeze small whole beet. Boil in water with 1 tsp vinegar 5–10 mins until tender. Drain and rub off skins. Cool. | Pack in rigid containers either whole or in slices. 6 months maximum | Thaw in unopened containers at room temperature approx. 4 hrs. Use in salads or heat through as a hot vegetable. |
| **Broccoli** | Remove outer leaves and trim stem. Divide into sprigs and remove woody stalks. Wash in salted water. Blanch thin sprigs 3 mins, medium 4 mins, thick 5 mins. Drain and cool. | Pack sprigs of similar size in rigid containers, alternating heads. 12 months | Cook from frozen in boiling salted water 3–7 mins according to size. |
| **Cabbage (hard green/red/ white)** | Remove outer leaves. Wash. Shred. Blanch 1½ mins. Drain and cool. | Pack in usable quantities in freezer-proof plastic bags. 6 months | Cook from frozen in a little salted water with butter for 5 mins. |
| **Carrot** | Scrub or scrape. Leave whole if young, otherwise slice or dice. Blanch whole carrots 3 mins, slices and dice 2 mins. Drain and cool. | Pack in usable quantities in freezer-proof plastic bags or open-freeze and pack as free-flow packs. 12 months | Cook from frozen in boiling salted water 3–5 mins according to size. Slices and dice can be added frozen to casseroles and soups. |
| **Cauliflower** | Only freeze the head as individual florets, approx. 2 inches in diameter. Blanch 2–3 mins according to size with 1 Tbsp lemon juice to each 2½ cups water. Drain and cool. | Open-freeze and pack as free-flow packs. 6 months | Cook from frozen in boiling salted water 4–6 mins according to size. |
| **Celery** | Scrub separated stalks and cut into 2 inch lengths. Blanch 3 mins. Drain and cool. | Pack in usable quantities in freezer-proof plastic bags. 9 months | Use frozen in casseroles and soups, etc, or thaw at room temperature 2–4 hrs and use in made-up cooked dishes. |
| **Corn** | Only freeze young corn. Remove silks and husks. Trim stalks. Blanch whole corn-on-the-cob 4–8 mins according to size. Drain and cool. Kernels can be stripped off cob with a sharp knife, if desired. | Wrap cobs individually in foil or plastic, then open-freeze and pack together in freezerproof plastic bags. Open-freeze kernels and pack as free-flow packs. 12 months | Thaw whole cobs overnight in re-frigerator, then boil in unsalted water with a little sugar 5 mins or until tender. Cook kernels from frozen 4 mins in boiling water, or add frozen to casseroles, soups, etc. |
| **Eggplant** | Peel if liked. Slice into 1 inch rounds or dice. Sprinkle with salt, leave 30 mins. Rinse and drain. Blanch 3–4 mins. Drain and cool. | Pack in layers in rigid containers, separating layers with freezerproof non-stick paper. 12 months | Thaw in unopened containers until just beginning to soften, then use as fresh. |
| **Fennel** | Trim off frondy top. Cut bulb lengthwise into quarters. Blanch 3 mins. Drain and cool. | Pack in usable quantities in freezer-proof plastic bags. 6 months | Cook from frozen in boiling salted water 7 mins, or leave in bags at room temperature until soft enough to slice, then use in dishes. |

| VEGETABLE | PREPARATION | PACKAGING AND STORAGE TIME | THAWING |
|---|---|---|---|
| **Fresh herbs** | Only freeze freshly gathered herbs. Wash only if absolutely necessary and shake dry. Separate into sprigs; then strip off leaves, or chop leaves finely (but not bay, rosemary, sage and thyme). To increase storage leave on sprigs. Blanch 1 min. Drain and cool. | Pack sprigs in freezerproof plastic bags or rigid containers; keep all one kind together or combine them in *bouquets garnis*. Pack whole and chopped leaves in ice cube trays, fill with water, open-freeze until solid, then remove from trays and pack together in freezerproof plastic bags. 6 months (9 months for blanched) | Use sprigs from freezer for cooking, either whole or by crumbling leaves with fingers. Add frozen cubes of herbs to cooked dishes, or thaw 1 hr at room temperature and use as fresh. |
| **Garlic** | Only freeze whole bulbs—do not separate into cloves. | Wrap bulbs individually in foil or plastic wrap, then pack several cloves together in a freezerproof plastic bag. Overwrap. 3 months maximum | Break individual cloves from frozen whole bulb and thaw approx. 2 hrs at room temperature before using as fresh. |
| **Kohlrabi (small roots only)** | Cut off leaves. Peel. Slice or dice. Blanch 1½–2 mins. Drain and cool. | Open-freeze and pack as free-flow packs. 12 months | Steam from frozen 10–12 mins, or stir-fry from frozen, or thaw 2–4 hrs and deep-fry in batter. |
| **Leek** | Remove green tops, roots and outer leaves. Cut into ½ inch slices and wash thoroughly. Blanch 3 mins. Drain and cool. Or sauté 4 mins in butter or oil and cool. | Pack in usable quantities in plastic bags. 6 months | Use frozen in made-up cooked dishes. |
| **Mushroom (only small button)** | Wipe clean (do not wash or peel). Trim stalks. Sauté in butter 1 min. Cool. | Open-freeze and pack as free-flow packs. 3 months | Sauté from frozen in butter. |
| **Onion** | Peel small pickling onions and leave whole. Peel large onions, then slice or dice. Blanch whole onions 2 mins, slices or dice 1 min. Drain and cool. | Open-freeze whole onions and pack as free-flow packs. Pack slices and dice in usable quantities in freezer-proof plastic bags. Overwrap. 3 months | Use frozen in casseroles, etc, or thaw in bags 2 hrs at room temperature, then use as fresh. |
| **Pea (including snowpeas)** | Freeze only very young peas. Shell and blanch 1 min, shaking basket to distribute heat evenly. Drain and cool. Top and tail snowpeas. Blanch 30–60 secs. | Open-freeze and pack as free-flow packs. 12 months | Cook shelled peas from frozen 4 mins in boiling salted water, or add frozen to casseroles and soups, etc. Sauté frozen snowpeas in butter for few minutes only. |
| **Pepper, sweet** | Wash and dry. Halve, then remove core, seeds and stalk. Leave as halves, or slice or dice. Do not blanch. | Open-freeze and pack as free-flow packs. 6 months | Add frozen to casseroles, soups and other cooked made-up dishes. Thaw halves in bags 2 hrs at room tem-perature, then stuff as fresh. |
| **Potato (new)** | Only freeze small, even-sized potatoes. Scrape. Cook in boiling salted water until just tender. Drain and cool. | Pack in usable quantities in freezer-proof plastic bags. 12 months | Steam from frozen with butter and mint. Take care not to overcook. |
| **Spinach (including sorrel and Swiss chard)** | Wash individual leaves thoroughly and remove thick stalks. Leave whole or tear. Blanch 2 mins. Drain and cool. Purée if liked. | Pack in usable quantities in plastic bags. 12 months | Cook from frozen in a heavy pan with butter and seasonings until thawed. |
| **Summer Squash** | Peel. Cut into chunks, discarding seeds. Blanch 2 mins. Drain and cool. | Pack in rigid containers. 6 months | Steam from frozen 2 mins. |
| **Tomato** | Whole and halved tomatoes can be frozen, but as they can only be used in cooking, they are most useful frozen as a purée: skin and core, simmer 5 mins then purée through sieve or in blender. | Pack whole tomatoes in usable quantities in freezerproof plastic bags. Pack halves in rigid containers, separating layers. Pack purée in rigid containers, leaving headspace. 12 months | Thaw whole tomatoes 2 hrs at room temperature, then use as fresh in cooking. Grill halves from frozen. Thaw purée at room temperature until usable consistency. |

| VEGETABLE | PREPARATION | PACKAGING AND STORAGE TIME | THAWING |
|---|---|---|---|
| **Turnip** | Only freeze small, young turnips. Trim and peel. Slice or dice. Blanch 2½ mins. Drain and cool. Or cook 10 mins until tender, then drain and mash. | Open-freeze slices and dice and pack as free-flow packs. Pack mashed turnip in rigid containers, leaving headspace. 12 months | Cook slices and dice from frozen 5 mins in boiling salted water. Or add frozen to casseroles, soups, etc. Re-heat frozen mashed turnip in a double boiler. |
| **Zucchini** | Do not peel. Leave small, young zucchini whole or halve lengthwise. Cut large into ½ inch slices. Blanch whole 2 mins, halves and slices 1 min. Drain and cool. | Pack in usable quantities in freezer-proof plastic bags or open-freeze and pack as free-flow packs. 6 months | Thaw in bags 2 hrs at room temperature then use as fresh. Slices can be added frozen to casseroles, soups and made-up cooked dishes. |

| FRUIT | PREPARATION | PACKAGING AND STORAGE TIME | THAWING |
|---|---|---|---|
| **Apple** | Peel, core and slice. Keep in water with lemon juice added (to prevent discoloration). Blanch cooking apples 1 min. Drain and cool. Can also be cooked to a purée—cool before packing. | Immediately pack drained slices in rigid containers or freezerproof bags. Pack purée in rigid containers, leaving headspace. 12 months (8 months for apple purée) | Thaw in unopened containers 1 hr at room temperature. Or use from frozen in pies, puddings and sauces, etc. |
| **Apricot** | Prepare quickly to avoid discoloration. Peel whole fruit after plunging into boiling water 30 secs. Leave fruit whole or cut in halves or slices. Or cook to a purée with or without sugar and cool. | Pack whole fruit, halves and slices in rigid containers in sugar syrup made from 1 lb sugar to 5 cups water plus 4 tsp lemon juice. Immerse fruit by placing crumpled paper under lid of container. Pack purée in rigid containers, leaving headspace. 12 months | Thaw in unopened containers 3–4 hrs in refrigerator, then use as soon as possible to avoid discoloration. Or use from frozen in cooked pies and puddings, etc. Fruit frozen in syrup can be poached in syrup after thawing. |
| **Avocado** | SEE CHART FOR VEGETABLES | | |
| **Blackberry** | Pick over and remove stalks. Wash only if absolutely necessary. Leave whole, or cook with a little water and sugar to taste, then purée if liked. Cool. | Whole fruit: dry pack; or open-freeze and pack as free-flow packs; or dry sugar pack allowing ⅔ cup sugar to 1 lb fruit. Pour cooked and puréed fruit into rigid containers, leaving headspace. 12 months | Tip dry and dry sugar packs into a bowl and thaw approx. 2 hrs at room temperature. Thaw purée in container overnight in refrigerator, or heat from frozen in heavy pan. |
| **Blueberry** | Wash and drain thoroughly. Leave whole or crush lightly with ⅔ cup sugar to 1–1½ lb fruit. | Whole fruit: dry pack; or open-freeze and pack as free-flow packs; or pack in rigid containers with sugar syrup made from 2 lb sugar to 5 cups water, leaving headspace. Pack crushed fruit in rigid containers. 12 months | Thaw in unopened containers 2½ hrs at room temperature. Poach fruit in syrup after thawing. |
| **Cherry** | Remove stalks. Wash and dry. Remove pits. Leave raw, or poach in water until tender. Cool. | Whole sweet cherries: dry pack; or open-freeze and pack as free-flow packs; or dry sugar pack allowing ⅔ cup sugar to 1 lb fruit. Pack sour cherries in rigid containers with sugar syrup made from 1 lb sugar to 5 cups water plus ½ tsp ascorbic acid, leaving headspace. Pack poached cherries in rigid containers, leaving headspace. 12 months (raw); 8 months (poached) | Thaw raw and poached cherries in unopened package 3 hrs at room temperature. Use immediately package is opened or fruit will discolor. |

| FRUIT | PREPARATION | PACKAGING AND STORAGE TIME | THAWING |
|---|---|---|---|
| **Currant** | Remove stalks. Wash and dry fruit. Top and tail. Leave whole or crush lightly with sugar to taste. Or cook with a little water and sugar to taste, then purée or sieve if liked. Cool. | Whole currants: dry pack; or open-freeze and pack as free-flow packs; or pack in rigid containers with sugar syrup made from $1\frac{1}{2}$ lb sugar to 5 cups water, leaving headspace. Pack crushed, cooked and puréed fruit in rigid containers, leaving headspace. 12 months | Cook from frozen or thaw in containers 1–2 hrs at room temperature. |
| **Damson Plum** | Wash and dry fruit. Do not freeze whole as skins will toughen. Halve fruit and remove pits. Or cook with a little water and sugar to taste, then sieve to remove skins and pits. Cool. | Pack halves in rigid containers with sugar syrup made from 1 lb sugar to 5 cups water, leaving headspace. Pack purée in rigid containers, leaving headspace. 12 months | Thaw halves in syrup $2\frac{1}{2}$ hrs at room temperature, then poach until tender. Thaw purée in containers 1 hr at room temperature or cook from frozen. |
| **Fig** | Wipe or wash gently to avoid bruising. Remove stems. Peel if liked. | Wrap unpeeled figs individually in foil, then pack together in freezer-proof bags. Pack peeled figs immediately in rigid containers with sugar syrup made from $1\frac{1}{2}$ cups sugar to 5 cups water, leaving headspace. 12 months | Thaw in bags or containers approx. 2 hrs at room temperature, then use as fresh. |
| **Gooseberry** | Wash. Top and tail if freezing as dry sugar pack, in syrup sugar or as stewed whole fruit. Leave raw or cook with a little water and sugar to taste, then sieve if liked. | Whole raw gooseberries: dry pack; or open-freeze and pack as free-flow packs; or dry sugar pack allowing 1 cup sugar to 1 lb fruit; or pack in rigid containers with sugar syrup made from $1\frac{1}{2}$ lb sugar to 5 cups water leaving headspace. Pour cooked and puréed fruit into rigid containers, leaving headspace. 12 months | Rub off tops and tails from frozen dry and free-flow packs, then cook from frozen. Cook dry sugar and sugar syrup packs from frozen or thaw in containers $2\frac{1}{2}$ hrs at room temperature, then cook. Thaw cooked and puréed fruit in containers $2\frac{1}{2}$ hrs at room temperature. |
| **Grape** | Leave seedless varieties whole, in bunches if liked. All other grapes should be peeled, halved and seeded. | Whole grapes and bunches: open-freeze and pack as free-flow packs. Halves: pack in rigid containers with sugar syrup made from 1 lb sugar to 5 cups water, leaving headspace. 12 months | Thaw in bags or containers approx. 2 hrs at room temperature. |
| **Mango** | Only freeze ripe (not green) fruit. Peel and slice, discarding pit. | Immediately pack sliced flesh in rigid containers with sugar syrup made from $1\frac{1}{2}$ lb sugar to 5 cups water plus 4 tsp lemon juice, leaving headspace. 12 months | Thaw in unopened containers 1–2 hrs at room temperature, then use as soon as possible while still slightly chilled—to avoid discoloration. |
| **Melon (Cantaloupe and Honeydew varieties—not Watermelon)** | Only freeze perfectly ripe fruit. Cut in half, remove seeds and fibers. Cut flesh into pieces or use a melon baller to make even-sized balls. | Dry sugar pack allowing 1 cup sugar to 1 lb fruit, or pack in rigid containers with sugar syrup made from 1 lb sugar to 5 cups water, leaving headspace. 12 months | Thaw in unopened bags or containers 1–2 hrs at room temperature, then serve chilled to preserve firm texture as much as possible. |
| **Papaya** | Peel. Halve lengthwise. Scoop out and discard seeds. Slice flesh thinly. Purée ripe fruit with sugar and lemon juice to taste, if liked. | Freeze unripe slices in savory dishes, e.g. casseroles. Freeze ripe slices as for mango above. Pour purée into rigid containers, leaving headspace. 12 months | Thaw slices as for mango above. Thaw purée in unopened containers overnight in refrigerator. |

| FRUIT | PREPARATION | PACKAGING AND STORAGE TIME | THAWING |
|---|---|---|---|
| **Peach (including nectarine)** | Prepare quickly to avoid discoloration. Fruit must be peeled before freezing: peel firm fruit as for apricot above, ripe fruit by holding under cold running water and rubbing off with fingers. Halve fruit and remove pits. Leave as halves or slice. | Pack halves and slices in rigid containers with sugar syrup made from 1 lb sugar to 5 cups water plus juice of 1 lemon, leaving headspace. Pour purée into rigid containers, leaving headspace. 12 months | Thaw in unopened containers 3–4 hrs in refrigerator, then use as soon as possible to avoid discoloration. Fruit frozen in syrup can be poached in syrup after thawing. |
| **Pear** | Prepare quickly to avoid discoloration. Cooking pears: peel, core and leave whole, or cut into halves or quarters. Immediately poach in water, sugar and flavorings or spices until just tender. Cool. Dessert pears: peel. Cut into halves or quarters, removing cores. Brush with lemon. | Cooking pears: pack in rigid containers with cooking liquid, leaving headspace. Dessert pears: immediately pack in rigid containers with sugar syrup made from 1½ lb sugar to 5 cups water, leaving headspace. 12 months | Thaw in unopened containers 2½ hrs at room temperature, then use as soon as possible to avoid discoloration. Poached pears can be reheated gently in cooking liquid after thawing. |
| **Pineapple** | Only freeze ripe fruit. Peel and core. Cut flesh into rings or chunks. Flesh can also be crushed, with or without sugar. | Dry pack rings and chunks, interleaving layers with freezerproof paper; or pack in rigid containers with sugar syrup made from 1 lb sugar to 5 cups water, leaving headspace. Pack crushed pineapple in rigid containers, leaving headspace. 12 months | Thaw in unopened containers 2½ hrs at room temperature. |
| **Plum (including greengage)** | Wipe clean and remove stalks. Halve and remove pits. Leave as raw halves or poach until tender in sugar syrup made from 1 lb sugar to 5 cups water plus ½ tsp ascorbic acid. Cool. Halves can also be cooked in a little water with sugar to taste, then sieved and cooled. | Pack raw halves in rigid containers with sugar syrup made from 1½ lb sugar to 5 cups water plus juice of 1 lemon, leaving headspace. Pack poached plums in rigid containers with cooking liquid, leaving headspace. Pour purée into rigid containers, leaving headspace. 12 months | Thaw raw and poached halves as for pear above. Thaw purées in unopened containers overnight in refrigerator. |
| **Raspberry (including loganberry)** | Do not wash. Hull. Leave whole if perfect, otherwise crush or purée with or without sugar according to future use. | Whole fruit: dry pack; or open-freeze and pack as free-flow packs; or dry sugar pack allowing 1 cup sugar to 1 lb fruit. Pack crushed and puréed raspberries in rigid containers, leaving headspace. 12 months | Thaw whole and crushed fruit in unopened bags or containers 2 hrs at room temperature. Serve whole fruit chilled to preserve shape and texture as much as possible. Thaw purées in unopened containers overnight in refrigerator. |
| **Rhubarb** | Trim off leaves and root ends. Wash and dry stalks. Cut into 1-inch lengths. Blanch 1 min. Drain and cool. Rhubarb can also be poached in water with sugar and flavorings or spices until just tender. Cool and purée, if liked. | Blanched rhubarb: open-freeze and pack as free-flow packs; or dry sugar pack, allowing 1 cup sugar to 1 lb fruit. Poached rhubarb: pack in rigid containers with cooking liquid, leaving headspace. Puréed rhubarb: pour into rigid containers, leaving headspace. 12 months | Use uncooked rhubarb from frozen in pies and other puddings, allowing extra cooking time. Thaw poached rhubarb in container 3 hrs at room temperature, then reheat gently in cooking liquid. Thaw puréed rhubarb in container overnight in refrigerator. |
| **Strawberry** | Do not wash. Hull, then slice, crush or purée. (Whole strawberries do *not* freeze successfully.) Add sugar to taste to crushed and puréed fruit. | Pack slices in rigid containers with sugar syrup made from 1½ lb sugar to 5 cups water, leaving headspace. Pack crushed and puréed fruit in rigid containers, leaving headspace. Add ½ tsp ascorbic acid. 12 months | Thaw sliced and crushed fruit in containers 1–2 hrs at room temperature. Serve slices chilled to preserve shape and texture as much as possible. Thaw purées in unopened containers overnight in refrigerator. |

# STORING AND FREEZING CAKES

When the cake is cold, store in a tin with an airtight seal. Wrap fruitcakes in waxed paper and foil first. If no tin is available, store un-iced cakes wrapped first in waxed paper then in foil or plastic wrap. Cakes with a fresh cream filling or decoration should be kept in the refrigerator. Store cakes and cookies separately or cookies will go soft.

Most undecorated cakes freeze well. Wrap plain cakes in freezer wrapping and seal before freezing.

Freeze decorated cakes without wrapping until firm, then wrap. Store in a rigid plastic container. Unwrap before thawing.

Freeze pastry cakes unfilled and refresh in the oven at 375°F for 5 minutes before filling and serving.

## BASIC CAKE FREEZING KNOW-HOW

| Storage time | Preparation | Freezing | Thawing and serving |
|---|---|---|---|
| **CAKES** *cooked* including sponge cakes, jelly rolls and layer cakes: 6 months *Iced cakes:* 2 months | Bake in usual way. Leave until cold on a wire rack. Jelly rolls are best rolled up in cornstarch, not sugar, if they are to be frozen without a filling. Do not spread or layer cakes with jam before freezing. Keep flavorings to a minimum and go lightly on the spices. | Wrap plain cake layers separately, or together with waxed paper between layers. Quick-freeze iced cakes (whole or cut) until icing has set, then wrap. Seal and pack in boxes to protect the icing. | Iced cakes: unwrap before thawing so the wrapping will not stick to the icing. Cream cakes: may be sliced while frozen for a better shape and quick thawing. Plain cakes: leave in package and thaw at room temperature. Un-iced large cakes thaw in about 3–4 hours at room temperature, layer cakes take about 1–2 hours and small cakes about 30 minutes; iced layer cakes take up to 4 hours. |
| **CAKE MIXTURES** *uncooked* 2 months | Whisked sponge mixtures do not freeze well uncooked. Put rich creamed mixtures into containers, or line the pan to be used later with greased foil and add the cake mixture. | Freeze uncovered. When frozen, remove from pan, package in foil and overwrap. Return to freezer. | To thaw, leave at room temperature for 2–3 hours, then fill pans to bake. Preformed cake mixtures can be returned to the original pan, without wrapping but still in foil lining. Place frozen in preheated oven and bake in usual way, but allow longer cooking time. |
| **PASTRY\*** *uncooked* *Short pastries:* 3 months *Flaky pastries:* 3–4 months | Roll out to size required. Fast-freeze pie shells until hard, to avoid damage. Rounds of pastry can be stacked with waxed paper between for pie bases or tops. | Stack pastry shapes with two pieces of waxed paper between layers: if needed, one piece of pastry can be removed without thawing the whole batch. Place the stack on a piece of cardboard, wrap and seal. | Thaw flat rounds at room temperature, fit into pie plate and proceed with recipe. Unbaked pie shells or flat cases should be returned to their original container before cooking: they can go into the oven from the freezer (ovenproof glass that has been in the freezer should first stand for 10 minutes at room temperature); add about 5 minutes to baking time. |
| **PASTRY** *cooked* *Pastry cases:* 6 months | Prepare as usual. Empty cases freeze satisfactorily, but with some change in texture. | Wrap carefully — very fragile. | Tart shells should be thawed at room temperature for about 1 hour. Refresh if desired, by heating, uncovered, in the oven at 325°F for 10 minutes. |
| **CREAM** *Whipped:* 3 months *Commercially frozen:* up to 1 year | Use only pasteurized cream, with a butterfat content of 40% or more (heavy cream). For best results, half-whip cream with 1 tsp sugar to each $\frac{2}{3}$ cup. Whipped cream may be piped into rosettes on waxed paper. | Transfer cream to suitable container, e.g., waxed carton, leaving head space for expansion. Quick-freeze rosettes; when firm, pack in a single layer in foil. | Thaw in refrigerator, allowing 24 hours, or 12 hours at room temperature. Put rosettes in position as decoration before thawing, as they cannot be handled once thawed. Rosettes take less time to thaw. |

\**Note* there is little advantage in bulk-freezing uncooked shortcrust pastry, as it takes about 3 hours to thaw before it can be rolled out. For bulk-freezing flaky pastries — prepare up to the last rolling; pack in freezer bags or foil and overwrap. To use, leave for 3–4 hours at room temperature, or overnight in the refrigerator.

# Cakes, Pastry and Cookies

Baking can never be a hit-and-miss affair. There are a few golden rules to success: read your recipe before you start, select and measure ingredients carefully, make sure your oven temperature is accurate and baking time is followed according to the recipe. Most cakes need to go into the oven as soon as they are mixed, so turn on the oven before you start mixing.

# *INGREDIENTS*

## FLOUR

Most cakes are made with all-purpose or self-rising flour. Self-rising flour is popular for simple mixtures because it contains rising agents already blended into it. It contains too much rising agent for many rich cakes, however, so for these use either a mixture of self-rising and all-purpose flours, or all-purpose flour with the exact amount of rising agent specified. If a recipe calls for self-rising flour and you have none, use all-purpose flour with baking powder added (1 Tbsp to each 2 cups flour).

Some recipes use cake flour, which is softer than all-purpose flour. Cake flour is sold in most supermarkets.

For cakes made with yeast, use bread flour. This gives a large volume and light, open texture.

*Wholewheat* flour can be used for variety of texture and flavor except in very light, delicate mixtures. When using this flour, add extra liquid to the recipe to give the right consistency.

Sift flours before using to incorporate air and make them easier to mix in.

## FATS

*Butter* and *margarine* are interchangeable, although butter gives a richer flavor and cakes made with butter keep well. *Soft tub margarines* are *not* suitable for baking. If possible, use unsalted butter or margarine. Vegetable oil can be used in recipes that call for it.

Do not use butter or margarine direct from the refrigerator. If the fat for a creamed mixture is too firm, beat it alone until softened, then add the sugar and cream them together. If melted fat is required, heat it very gently, as it quickly turns brown.

## SUGARS

Sugar is not just a sweetener; it also helps produce a soft, spongy texture and improves the keeping qualities of a cake.

*Granulated sugar* is the best white sugar for most cakes, as it dissolves quickly and easily.

*Confectioners sugar* is very fine and powdery, giving a poor volume and hard crust if used in cake mixtures. It is, however, ideal for icing and decorating.

*Raw sugar* has coarse crystals that make it unsuitable for creamed mixtures. It is fine for cakes made when ingredients are melted together. It gives a golden color and distinctive syrup flavor.

*Dark brown sugar* creams well and, when used in place of granulated sugar, gives an equally good volume. It gives a rich flavor and color.

## RISING AGENTS

*Baking powder* reacts with moisture to produce carbon dioxide. The bubbles of gas expand during baking, making the cake rise. The heat then sets the mixture so that the bubbles are trapped. *One part baking soda to two parts cream of tartar* is sometimes used as a substitute.

*Baking soda* is often used in place of or in addition to baking powder. It must be mixed with an acid such as buttermilk to work well.

*Yeast* is a living organism that ferments in a warm, moist atmosphere to produce carbon dioxide. The yeast is then killed in the hot oven and the bubbles remain trapped in the structure of the flour. Most recipes are written using *dried yeast*, which is easily available.

*Eggs* used for baking should be at room temperature. A large egg is suitable for most recipes.

# MEASURING INGREDIENTS

When making cakes it is important to weigh and measure quantities accurately to achieve the correct balance of ingredients. Use standard measuring spoons, available in sets and standard measuring cups, also sold in sets. For dry ingredients dip the spoon in and level the surface with a knife. Liquids, of course, level themselves. For larger quantities of liquid use a measuring cup. Always measure liquid at eye level; looking down on the markings gives a distorted view and an inaccurate measure.

## CAKE PANS

Choose good-quality, strong cake pans in a variety of shapes and sizes. Non-stick surfaces clean most easily and are particularly useful in small, awkwardly shaped pans. Some cake pans have a loose bottom or a loosening device to make it easier to remove the cake.

Use the pan size specified in the recipe. Using too large a pan will tend to give a pale, flat and shrunken-looking cake; cakes baked in too small a pan will bulge over and lose their contours. If you do not have the pan specified, choose a slightly larger one. The mixture will be shallower and will take less time to cook, so test for doneness 5–10 minutes early.

If using a pan of a different shape from the one in the recipe, choose one with the same liquid capacity (test by filling right to the brim with water).

*Tart rings and quiche pans* come in many forms. Round pans with plain or fluted sides and removable bases are primarily for pastry cases.

*Loaf pans* are used for cakes as well as bread. Two sizes are available: 1 lb and 2 lb.

*Small cake pans and molds* come in sheets of 6, 9 or 12, or individually. There are shapes for buns, éclairs, sponge fingers etc.

*Spring-form pans* come complete with different loose bottoms.

*Standard cake pans* For everyday use, 8-inch, 9-inch and 10-inch pans are standard, for celebration cakes you may need larger sizes.

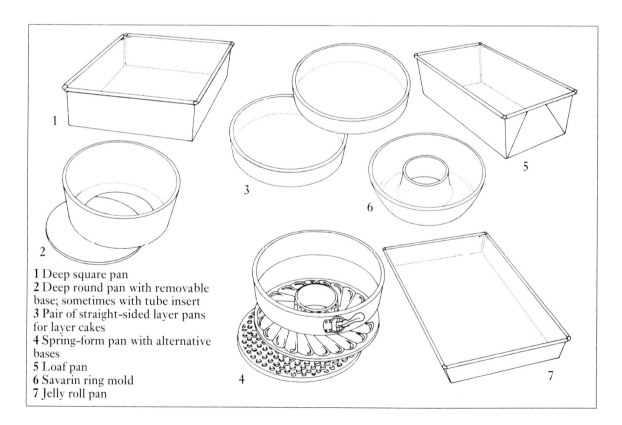

1 Deep square pan
2 Deep round pan with removable base; sometimes with tube insert
3 Pair of straight-sided layer pans for layer cakes
4 Spring-form pan with alternative bases
5 Loaf pan
6 Savarin ring mold
7 Jelly roll pan

# PREPARING CAKE PANS

Pans without a non-stick finish should be greased and lined before use. Non-stick pans do not need lining but may need greasing; follow the manufacturer's instructions. For a good finish to a sponge baked in a non-stick pan, grease the pan and then coat with a light mixture of sifted flour and sugar.

**Grease the pan** by brushing with oil or melted fat and line it with waxed paper or non-stick parchment paper.

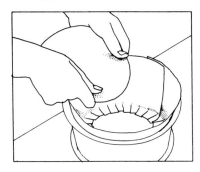

**Lining a deep pan** Cut a piece of waxed paper long enough to reach round the pan and wide enough to extend about 2 inches above the top. Cut another piece to fit the bottom. Fold up one edge of the long strip about 1 inch, then snip the folded portion at intervals. Grease the pan, place the strip in position and then place the bottom piece over the snipped edge of the band to make a neat lining. Waxed paper should then be greased; non-stick paper does not require greasing.

**Lining a loaf pan** Line the base only, cutting a round of waxed paper or non-stick paper to fit the base exactly.

---

## TRICKS OF THE TRADE

- **Preheating the oven**
  Before starting to mix the cake, turn the oven to the correct setting so that it will be up to temperature by the time it is needed.

- **Testing whether a cake is done**
  Small cakes should be well risen, golden and just firm to the touch. They should start to shrink from the sides of the pan when taken out of the oven.
  A larger cake made with a light mixture should be spongy and give only very slightly when pressed in the center with a finger; the surface should rise again immediately, leaving no impression.
  For a fruitcake, lift gently from the oven and listen to it. A sizzling sound indicates that the cake is not cooked through. Or insert a warmed thin skewer into the center of the cake. It should come out perfectly clean.

- **Cooling the cake**
  Leave in the pan for a few minutes, then turn out gently and remove any lining paper. Turn the right way up on a wire rack and leave until quite cold.

- **To skin hazelnuts**
  Heat through in the oven or under the broiler, shaking them occasionally to turn. Then place in a clean cloth or plastic bag and rub the papery skins off.

- **To help prevent candied cherries sinking**
  Cut cherries in half, rinse under cold running water, then pat dry and toss lightly in a little of the measured flour.

- **To shred or chop candied peel**
  Remove the sugar and cut the peel into fine shreds with scissors or chop with a sharp knife. If very hard, soak in boiling water for 1–2 minutes.

- **To blanch almonds**
  Put the nuts in a pan with cold water to cover, bring just to the boil, strain and run cold water over them. Rub between the finger and thumb to remove skins.

- **To toast nuts**
  Spread nuts in a shallow pan and brown lightly under a medium broiler, turning occasionally; or bake in the oven at 350°F for 10–12 minutes.

- **To clean dried fruit**
  Most dried fruit is sold ready cleaned, washed and dried. If not, rub fruit in a towel with a little flour, then pick over to remove any stalks. Discard surplus flour.

- **To separate an egg**
  Knock the egg sharply against the rim of a basin and break the shell in half. Pass the yolk back and forth from one half-shell to the other, letting the white drop into the basin. Put the yolk in another basin.

- **To melt chocolate**
  Break the chocolate into a bowl and stand it over hot (not boiling) water until melted. Do not allow to become too hot and only stir once or twice toward the end of melting.

- **To layer a cake**
  Measure the depth of the layers up the side of the cake and insert toothpicks at intervals as a cutting guide. Use a long, sharp-bladed knife, resting it above and against the toothpicks while cutting.

# CAKE-MAKING TECHNIQUES

Plain or rich, fruity, spicy or laden with cream, cakes are pure fun. Wholly superfluous to our nutritional needs, they represent all that is sociable and pleasing about food. If you can master the techniques to produce a really beautiful cake you will give your family and friends a real treat— and yourself a lot of creative pleasure into the bargain.

There's more chemistry to making cakes than most people realize. When you follow a recipe you're taking into consideration the relationship between the gluten in the flour, raising agents like baking soda and baking powder and the raising power of eggs. You're also controlling the amount of fat and the ratio of liquid to dry ingredients. The sugar you add will influence the texture of the cake and certainly how it tastes. How long your cake bakes in the oven and at what temperature plays a big role in determining how all the ingredients interact with one another to affect texture, taste and appearance.

# RUBBED-IN CAKES

For plain cakes, in which the proportion of fat to flour is half or less, the fat is literally rubbed into the flour with the fingertips and thumbs. Cakes made like this have a soft, light texture; they are easy to make and economical too. Just because they are called "plain" doesn't mean these cakes can't be varied with fruits and spices, but icings and fillings are generally kept to a minimum as these are the cakes that naturally form everyday dessert fare for the family.

To make cakes by the "rubbing in" method, first sift the dry ingredients into a bowl. Cut the firm fat into pieces and add to the bowl. Then rub the fat lightly into the flour between the fingertips and

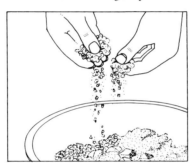

thumbs. Lift your hands well up over the bowl and work lightly to incorporate air into the mixture; this helps to make the cake light, though the main leavening agents are chemical. Shake the bowl occasionally to bring any large lumps to the surface and rub in until the mixture resembles fine bread crumbs.

Sugar and flavoring go in next, then the liquid. Adding the liquid is a crucial stage in the making of a rubbed-in mixture. Too much liquid can cause a heavy, doughy texture, while insufficient gives a dry cake. Beaten egg and milk are the commonest liquids; add them cautiously, using just enough to bring the mixture to the right consistency. For cakes baked in a pan, the mixture should have a soft dropping consistency. That is, it

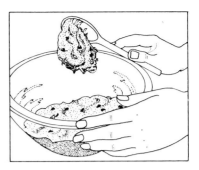

should drop easily from the spoon when the handle is tapped against the side of the bowl. For small cakes that are baked flat on a baking sheet, the mixture should be stiff enough to hold its shape without spreading too much

during the baking time. A stiff consistency describes a mixture which clings to the spoon.

Because they are low in fat, these cakes do not keep well. They are best eaten the day they are made.

## ALTERNATIVE LEAVENING AGENTS

If all-purpose flour and baking powder are used instead of self rising flour, allow 1 tsp baking powder to 1 cup flour and sift them together twice before using. If you use cream of tartar and baking soda in place of baking powder, allow 1 tsp cream of tartar and $\frac{1}{2}$ tsp baking soda to 1 cup flour with ordinary milk, or $\frac{1}{2}$ tsp baking soda and $\frac{1}{2}$ tsp cream of tartar with sour milk.

# CREAMED CAKES

Cakes that contain half as much fat as flour, or more, are made by creaming the fat and sugar at the start. These cakes are rich and moist, firm to touch and they are excellent iced. They cut easily into fancy shapes, so make good children's party cakes.

Use butter or block margarine and take it out of the refrigerator a while before you want to use it. Choose a large mixing bowl, to give you room for vigorous beating and warm it a little to make creaming easier. Beat the fat and sugar together with a wooden spoon until they are as pale and fluffy as whipped cream. If the fat is a little hard to start with, beat it alone until well softened before adding the sugar. An electric mixer makes creaming easier.

Next beat in the eggs. These too should be at room temperature, and add them a little at a time to prevent curdling. If the mixture starts to curdle, add a little sifted flour with each portion of egg and beat in. Fold in the remaining flour with a large metal spoon.

Quicker to make than creamed cakes are those made by the 'all-in-one' method. For these you need soft 'tub' margarine, which is soft enough to beat straight from the refrigerator and which has been developed to give the best results with the 'all-in-one' method. You can use butter or block margarine but it must be soft; leave it at room temperature for at least 1 hour first.

For all-in-one cakes simply beat all the ingredients together with a wooden spoon for 2–3 minutes, or with a mixer for even less time. Use self-rising flour, to give the cake an extra boost, and granulated or brown sugar, which dissolve quicker than other sugars. The result of this method is a cake that is similar to one made by creaming, but it won't keep as well. Put it in an airtight container or wrap tightly in foil as soon as it is cold to prevent it going stale.

## VICTORIA LAYER

*Serves 6–8*

| |
|---|
| $\frac{1}{2}$ **cup butter or margarine** |
| $\frac{3}{4}$ **cup sugar** |
| **2 eggs, beaten** |
| **1 cup self-rising flour** |
| **sugar, to dredge** |
| **4 Tbsp jam or $\frac{2}{3}$ cup heavy cream, whipped or $\frac{1}{2}$ quantity butter cream, to fill** |

*1* Grease two 7-inch layer pans and line the base of each with greased waxed paper.

*2* Put the fat and sugar into a warmed mixing bowl and cream together with a wooden spoon until pale and fluffy. Scrape mixture down from sides of bowl from time to time to ensure that no sugar crystals are left.

*3* Add the eggs one at a time; beat well after each addition. Gradually sift the flour onto the mixture and fold it in as quickly and lightly as possible.

*4* Place half the mixture in each of the prepared layer pans. Lightly smooth the surface of the mixture with a palette knife. Bake both cakes on the same shelf of the oven at 375°F for about 20 minutes until they are well risen and begin to shrink away from sides of pans.

*5* Turn out and leave the cakes to cool on a wire rack, then sandwich them together with jam.

——— VARIATIONS ———

**Chocolate layer** Replace 3 Tbsp flour with 3 Tbsp cocoa powder. For a more moist cake, blend the cocoa with a little water to give a thick paste and beat it into the creamed ingredients with the eggs. Use chocolate butter cream as filling.
**Coffee layer** Dissolve 2 tsp instant coffee in a little water and add it to the creamed mixture with the egg, or use 2 tsp coffee extract. Use coffee butter cream as filling.
**Orange or lemon layer** Add the finely grated rind of one orange or lemon to the mixture and use orange or lemon marmalade or orange or lemon butter cream as filling. Use some of the juice from the orange or lemon to make glacé icing.

**Cup cakes** Divide the mixture among 18 paper cases and bake as above. If liked, fold $\frac{1}{2}$ cup chocolate morsels, raisins, chopped walnuts or candied cherries into the mixture with

the flour. When cold, top each cup cake with glacé icing.

# MADEIRA CAKE

*Serves 6–8*

$\frac{3}{4}$ cup all-purpose flour

1 cup self-rising flour

$\frac{3}{4}$ cup butter or margarine

1 cup sugar

1 tsp vanilla extract

3 eggs, beaten

1–2 Tbsp milk (optional)

2–3 thin slices citron peel

*1* Grease and line a 7-inch round cake pan. Sift the flours together.

*2* Cream the butter or margarine and the sugar together until pale and fluffy, then beat in the vanilla extract.

*3* Add the eggs one at a time, beating well after each addition.

*4* Fold in the sifted flour with a metal spoon, adding a little milk if necessary to give a dropping consistency.

*5* Turn the mixture into the prepared pan and bake in the oven at 350°F for 20 minutes.

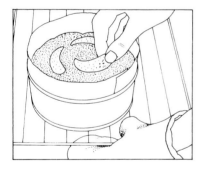

*6* Lay the citron peel on top of the cake, return it to the oven and bake for a further 40 minutes until firm to the touch. Turn out and leave to cool on a wire rack.

# CHOCOLATE BATTENBERG CAKE

*Serves 10*

$\frac{3}{4}$ cup butter or margarine

1 cup sugar

a few drops of vanilla extract

3 eggs, beaten

1$\frac{1}{2}$ cups self-rising flour

2 Tbsp cocoa powder

a little milk, to mix (optional)

8 oz almond paste

1 cup apricot jam, melted

sugar, to dredge

*1* Grease and line a $12 \times 8$-inch jelly roll pan and divide it lengthwise with a "wall" of waxed paper.

*2* Cream fat and sugar together until pale and fluffy, then beat in vanilla extract. Add the eggs one at a time, beating well.

*3* Gradually sift the flour over the mixture and fold it in lightly. Turn half the mixture into one side of the pan and level the surface. Sift the cocoa over the other half and fold in, adding a little milk if necessary to give a dropping consistency.

*4* Turn the chocolate mixture into the pan and level surface. Bake in the oven at 375°F for 40–45 minutes until well risen and firm. Turn out and leave to cool on a wire rack.

*5* When cold, trim cakes to an equal size and cut each in half lengthways. On a working surface sprinkled with sugar, roll out the almond paste to a $12 \times 16$-inch rectangle.

*6* Place one strip of cake on the almond paste so that it lies up against the edge of paste. Place an alternate colored strip next to it.

*7* Brush top and sides of cake with melted jam and layer up with alternate colored strips.

*8* Bring almond paste up and over cake to cover it. Press paste firmly on to cake, then seal and trim join. Place cake seam-side down and trim both ends with a sharp knife. Crimp top edges of paste with the thumb and forefinger and mark the top in a criss-cross pattern with a knife. Dredge lightly with sugar.

# APPLE SAUCE CAKE

*Serves 8*

1$\frac{1}{2}$ cups self-rising flour

$\frac{1}{2}$ tsp salt

1 tsp ground cinnamon

$\frac{1}{2}$ tsp ground nutmeg

$\frac{1}{2}$ tsp ground cloves

1 tsp baking soda

2 cups apple sauce

$\frac{1}{2}$ cup butter or margarine

1$\frac{1}{4}$ cups light brown sugar

1 egg, separated

$\frac{3}{4}$ cup seedless raisins

*1* Grease and line with greased waxed paper an 8-inch round cake pan. Sift together the flour, salt and spices.

*2* Add the baking soda to the apple sauce and stir until dissolved.

*3* Cream the butter or margarine and the sugar together until pale and fluffy, then beat in the egg yolk.

*4* Fold in the flour and apple sauce alternately, then stir in the seedless raisins.

*5* Whisk the egg white until stiff, and fold in with a large metal spoon.

*6* Turn the mixture into the prepared pan. Bake in the oven at 350°F for about 1–1$\frac{1}{2}$ hours until firm to the touch. Turn out and leave to cool on a wire rack.

353

# ONE-STAGE CAKES

These cake recipes show you just how easy it is to achieve stunning results. Once you've mastered the basic recipes, the variations are endless and soon you will have a whole repertoire of teatime and party treats.

## ONE-STAGE FRUIT CAKE

| |
|---|
| 1½ cups self-rising flour |
| 2 tsp mixed spice |
| 1 tsp baking powder |
| ½ cup soft tub margarine |
| ¾ cup dark brown sugar |
| 1⅓ cups mixed dried fruit |
| 2 eggs |
| 2 Tbsp milk |

*1* Grease a 7-inch round cake pan and line it with waxed paper. Grease the paper.

*2* Sift together the flour, spice and baking powder into a large bowl. Add the remaining ingredients, mix well and beat for 2–3 minutes until well blended.

*3* Turn the mixture into the prepared pan and bake in the oven at 325°F for 1¾ hours. Leave the cake in the pan to cool for 1 hour, then turn out onto a wire rack. When the cake is cold, store in an airtight tin for at least a day before cutting.

## ONE-STAGE FRUIT CAKE MADE WITH OIL

| |
|---|
| 1½ cups plain flour |
| 2 tsp baking powder |
| ¼ tsp salt |
| 1 cup sugar |
| ⅔ cup vegetable oil |
| 2 eggs |
| 3 Tbsp milk |
| 1⅔ cups mixed dried fruit |
| ⅔ cup candied cherries, quartered |
| ½ cup chopped mixed peel |

*1* Grease and line a 7-inch round cake pan and line it with waxed paper. Grease the paper.

*2* Sift together the flour, baking powder and salt into a large bowl. Stir in the sugar. Add the remaining ingredients, mix well and beat for 2–3 minutes until well blended.

*3* Turn the mixture into the prepared pan and bake in the oven at 325°F for 1 hour. Reduce the oven temperature to 300°F and bake for a further 1¼–1½ hours.

*4* Leave the cake to cool in the pan for 1 hour, then turn onto a wire rack. When the cake is cold, store in an airtight tin for at least 1 day before cutting.

## ONE-STAGE SANDWICH CAKE

This is a very quick method of making a cake without rubbing in or creaming the fat first, but you must use a soft tub margarine.

| |
|---|
| ¾ cup self-rising flour |
| 1 tsp baking powder |
| ½ cup soft tub margarine |
| ¾ cup sugar |
| 2 eggs |
| jelly |
| sugar, to dredge |

*1* Grease two 7-inch sandwich pans and line the base of each with waxed paper. Grease the paper.

*2* Sift the flour and baking powder into a large mixing bowl. Add the remaining ingredients, except the filling and dredging sugar, mix well and beat for 2–3 minutes until well blended.

*3* Divide the mixture equally between the two prepared pans, smoothing the surface with a palette knife. Bake in the oven at 325°F for 25–35 minutes until well risen and firm to the touch.

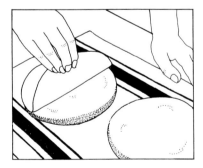

*4* Turn the cakes out onto a clean cloth, remove the lining paper, turn onto a wire rack and leave to cool. When cold, sandwich the sponges together with jelly and dredge the top with caster sugar.

# *RICH FRUITCAKES*

A rich fruitcake is traditional for family celebrations. At weddings and christenings, anniversaries and Christmas, the centerpiece will most often be a beautiful cake decorated with royal icing; beneath the sugar coating will be a dark, glossy cake loaded with fruit, candied peel, nuts and spices and deliciously soaked with brandy.

Like other rich cakes, fruitcakes are made by the creaming method, but the mixture is slightly stiffer to support the weight of the fruit. If the mixture is too wet fruit is inclined to sink to the bottom. Remember that all dried fruit should be thoroughly cleaned and dried before use; glacé cherries should be rinsed to remove excess syrup, then dried. Toss all fruit in a little of the measured flour.

You will find that creaming and mixing a rich fruitcake is quite hard work, especially if it is a large cake, and the baking times are long. So it is useful to know that you can mix one day and bake the next if it is more convenient. Put the prepared mixture in the pan, cover it loosely with a clean cloth and leave it in a cool place until you are ready to bake.

Protect the outside of a rich fruitcake from overbrowning during the long cooking by wrapping a double thickness of brown paper round the outside of the pan. Stand the pan on several thicknesses of brown paper or newspaper in the oven and cover the top of the cake towards the end of cooking if necessary.

All fruitcakes keep well, but the richest actually improve if kept for two or three months before you cut them. When the cake is cold, wrap it in waxed paper and put it in an airtight container or wrap in foil; every two or three weeks, get it out, prick the surface with a fine skewer and spoon over a little brandy or other spirit.

## RICH FRUITCAKE

*1* Grease and line the cake pan for the size of cake you wish to make, using a double thickness of waxed paper. Tie a double band of brown paper round the outside.

*2* Prepare the ingredients for the appropriate size of cake according to the chart (page 356). Wash and dry all the fruit, if necessary chopping any over-large pieces, and mix well together in a large bowl. Add the flaked almonds. Sift flour, baking powder and spices into another bowl with a pinch of salt.

*3* Put the butter, sugar and lemon rind into a warmed mixing bowl and cream together with a wooden spoon until pale and fluffy. Add the beaten eggs, one at a time, beating well after each addition.

*4* Gradually fold the flour lightly into the mixture with a metal spoon, then fold in the brandy. Finally fold in the fruit and nuts.

*5* Turn the mixture into the prepared pan, spreading it evenly and making sure there are no air pockets. Make a hollow in the center to ensure an even surface when cooked.

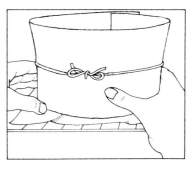

*6* Stand the pan on newspaper or brown paper in the oven and bake at 300°F for the required time, until a fine skewer inserted in the center comes out clean. To prevent the cake from overbrowning, cover it with waxed paper after about $1\frac{1}{2}$ hours.

*7* When cooked, leave the cake to cool in the pan before turning out onto a wire rack. Prick the top of the cake all over with a fine skewer and slowly pour 2–3 Tbsp brandy over it before storing.

*8* Wrap the cake in a double thickness of waxed paper and place upside down in an airtight tin. Cover with foil to store.

# Quantities and Sizes for Square and Round Rich Fruitcakes

If you want to make a formal cake, this chart shows you the amount of ingredients required to fill the chosen cake pans.

| | | | | | | | |
|---|---|---|---|---|---|---|---|
| Square Pan Size | 6 inch | 7 inch | 8 inch | 9 inch | 10 inch | | 12 inch |
| Round Pan Size | 7 inch | 8 inch | 9 inch | 10 inch | | 12 inch | |
| Raisins | $\frac{2}{3}$ cup | $\frac{3}{4}$ cup | 1 cup | $1\frac{1}{3}$ cups | 2 cups | $2\frac{1}{3}$ cups | $3\frac{1}{4}$ cups |
| Glacé Cherries | $\frac{1}{2}$ cup | $\frac{3}{4}$ cup | 1 cup | $1\frac{1}{2}$ cups | $2\frac{1}{4}$ cups | $2\frac{1}{2}$ cups | 3 cups |
| Chopped Mixed Fruit | $\frac{1}{4}$ cup | $\frac{1}{2}$ cup | $\frac{2}{3}$ cup | $\frac{3}{4}$ cup | $1\frac{1}{4}$ cups | $1\frac{3}{4}$ cups | $2\frac{1}{4}$ cups |
| Sliced Almonds | $\frac{1}{4}$ cup | $\frac{1}{2}$ cup | $\frac{3}{4}$ cup | $\frac{3}{4}$ cup | $1\frac{1}{4}$ cups | $1\frac{3}{4}$ cups | $2\frac{1}{4}$ cups |
| All-purpose Flour | $1\frac{1}{4}$ cups | $1\frac{1}{2}$ cups | 2 cups | $3\frac{1}{2}$ cups | $4\frac{1}{2}$ cups | 6 cups | 8 cups |
| Baking Powder | 1 tsp | $1\frac{1}{2}$ tsp | 2 tsp | 1 Tbsp | $1\frac{1}{2}$ Tbsp | 2 Tbsp | $2\frac{1}{2}$ Tbsp |
| Mixed Spices | $\frac{1}{4}$ tsp | $\frac{1}{2}$ tsp | $\frac{1}{2}$ tsp | 1 tsp | 1 tsp | 2 tsp | $2\frac{1}{2}$ tsp |
| Cinnamon | $\frac{1}{4}$ tsp | $\frac{1}{2}$ tsp | $\frac{1}{2}$ tsp | 1 tsp | 1 tsp | 2 tsp | $2\frac{1}{2}$ tsp |
| Butter | 6 Tbsp | $\frac{3}{4}$ cup | 1 cup | $1\frac{1}{2}$ cups | 1 lb | $1\frac{1}{2}$ lb | 2 lb |
| Sugar | $\frac{3}{4}$ cup | 1 cup | $1\frac{1}{3}$ cups | $1\frac{1}{2}$ cups | 2 cups | 3 cups | 4 cups |
| Lemon Rind | a little | a little | $\frac{1}{4}$ lemon | $\frac{1}{4}$ lemon | $\frac{1}{2}$ lemon | $\frac{1}{2}$ lemon | 1 lemon |
| Large Eggs | 2 | 2 | 3 | 4 | 6 | 8 | 10 |
| Brandy | 1 Tbsp | 1–2 Tbsp | 2 Tbsp | 2–3 Tbsp | 3 Tbsp | 3 Tbsp | 4 Tbsp |
| Baking Time (approx) | $2\frac{1}{2}$–3 hours | 3 hours | $3\frac{1}{2}$–4 hours | 4 hours | $5\frac{1}{2}$ hours | 7 hours | 8 hours |

# *MERINGUES*

If you want the simplest possible cake for a special dessert, a meringue is a good choice. Light as air and sweet as sugar, they are easy to make and few people can refuse them.

All meringues are based on stiffly whisked egg whites. The most common type is made by folding in granulated sugar; when baked this gives a crisp, off-white meringue with a very slightly soft inside. It can be formed into rounds or mounds or piped — either in the traditional "shell" shape or in nests to hold fruit or cream fillings. Using the same method but substituting confectioners sugar gives a much drier, whiter meringue. For a firm meringue for elaborate baskets, the sugar is added in the form of a hot syrup. Finally, a really soft meringue can be made by adding a little vinegar and cornstarch. This is used to make a pavlova.

Meringues are best made with eggs that are 2–3 days old. Separate the whites from the yolks carefully, making sure that no trace of yolk gets into the whites. If possible, keep the separated whites in a covered container in the refrigerator for up to 24 hours before use — this makes them more gelatinous and whisk more quickly to a greater volume. Otherwise use them directly after separating, but the colder the better; a pinch of salt or cream of tartar can be added to help them hold their shape.

Whisk until the whites are stiff enough to stand in peaks, then add the sugar. For a basic meringue, whisk in half the sugar first, then fold the rest in lightly with a large metal spoon. Shape the meringue quickly, before the mixture separates, on a baking sheet lined with non-stick paper. Dry out or bake in a low oven for several hours until crisp. When cool, store in an airtight container; meringues keep well unfilled for 2–3 weeks; they also freeze very successfully in rigid plastic containers.

## SMALL MERINGUES

2 egg whites
$\frac{1}{2}$ cup sugar
$\frac{2}{3}$ cup heavy cream

*1* Line a large baking sheet with non-stick paper. Whisk the egg whites until very stiff.

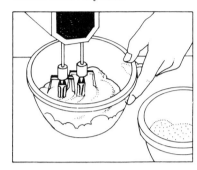

*2* Add half the sugar and whisk again until the mixture regains its former stiffness. Fold the remaining sugar into the mixture very lightly with a metal spoon.

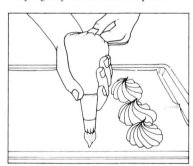

*3* Spoon the mixture into a piping bag fitted with a large star nozzle and pipe small mounds onto the prepared baking sheet.

*4* Dry out in the oven at 250°F for 2–3 hours until the meringues are firm and crisp but still white. If they begin to color, prop the oven door open slightly. Ease the meringues off the paper and leave to cool on a wire rack. Whip cream until stiff and use to sandwich meringues in pairs.

## MOCHA MERINGUE

3 egg whites
1 cup sugar
1 Tbsp instant coffee powder
*For the filling*
1$\frac{1}{3}$ cups heavy cream
2 egg whites
1 tsp instant coffee powder
1 oz chocolate, grated
$\frac{1}{4}$ cup finely chopped almonds
chopped almonds and grated chocolate, to decorate

*1* Draw two 8-inch circles on non-stick paper and place on two baking sheets.

*2* Whisk the egg whites until very stiff. Whisk in half the sugar, add the instant coffee and whisk until the mixture is really stiff and no longer speckled with coffee. Carefully fold in the remaining sugar with a metal spoon.

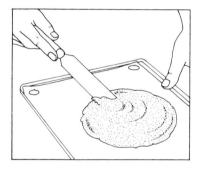

*3* Divide the mixture between the baking sheets and spread evenly to fill the circles. Bake in the oven at 300°F for about 2 hours until dry. Leave to cool on the baking sheets before carefully lifting them off.

*4* To make up the filling, whip the cream until thick. Whisk the egg whites until stiff, then carefully fold into the cream. Fold in the coffee, chocolate and nuts.

*5* Sandwich the meringue layers together with half the cream mixture. Spread remainder on top; decorate with nuts and chocolate 30 minutes before serving.

357

# MELTED CAKES

If honey, molasses, syrup or chocolate are included in a recipe, the cake is made by melting these ingredients with the sugar and fat before mixing with the flour. This ensures that they blend in evenly. The result is a cake with a moist and irresistibly sticky texture. The method is a very easy one, traditionally used for gingerbreads and brownies.

The rising agent in cakes made by this method is usually baking soda, which reacts with the natural acids present in liquid sweeteners, and spices are often added to enhance the flavor and counteract any soda taste.

Measure molasses, syrup and honey carefully, as too much of these products can cause a heavy, sunken cake. Warm the fat, sugar and liquid sweetener gently, just until the sugar is dissolved and the fat melted. Do not let the mixture boil or it will be unusable.

Let the mixture cool slightly and add any other liquids such as milk and eggs before adding to the flour. If a hot liquid is added to the flour, it will begin to cook and the cake will be hard.

If the recipe includes chocolate, break the chocolate into a bowl and add the fat, cut into pieces. Place the bowl over a saucepan of hot, but not boiling, water and heat it gently until melted. The chocolate and butter should blend to a smooth cream when stirred together. Let it cool a little before adding to the flour.

The final mixture will be a thick, heavy batter that can be poured into the pan. It will not need smoothing, as it will find its own level. Cakes made by this method are generally baked at a low to moderate temperature until just risen and firm to the touch. They are best left for a day or two before cutting, to allow the crust to soften and the flavor to mellow, and they keep well if stored in an airtight container.

## GINGERBREAD

*Serves 8–10*

| |
|---|
| 3½ cups all-purpose flour |
| 1 tsp salt |
| 1 Tbsp ground ginger |
| 1 Tbsp baking powder |
| 1 tsp baking soda |
| 1½ cups light brown sugar |
| ¾ cup butter or margarine |
| ¾ cup molasses |
| ¾ cup corn syrup |
| 1⅓ cups milk |
| 1 egg, beaten |

*1* Grease and line a 9-inch square cake pan. Sift together the flour, salt, ginger, baking powder and baking soda into a large mixing bowl.

*2* Put the sugar, fat, molasses and syrup in a saucepan and warm gently over a low heat until melted and well blended. Do not allow the mixture to boil. Then remove the pan from the heat and leave to cool slightly, until you can hold your hand comfortably against the side of the pan.

*3* Mix in the milk and beaten egg. Make a well in the center of the dry ingredients, pour in the liquid and mix very thoroughly.

*4* Pour the mixture into the prepared pan and bake in the oven at 325°F for about 1½ hours until firm but springy to the touch.

*5* Leave the gingerbread in the pan for about 10 minutes after baking, then turn out onto a wire rack, remove the lining paper and leave to cool.

## BROWNIES

*Makes about 16*

| |
|---|
| 2 oz semisweet chocolate |
| 5 Tbsp butter or margarine |
| 1 cup sugar |
| ½ cup self-rising flour |
| ¼ tsp salt |
| 2 eggs, beaten |
| ½ tsp vanilla extract |
| ½ cup chopped walnuts |

*1* Grease and line a shallow 8-inch square cake pan. Then break up the chocolate and put it in a bowl with the butter, cut into pieces. Stand the bowl over a pan of hot water and heat gently, stirring occasionally, until melted. Add the sugar.

*2* Sift together the flour and salt into a bowl. Add the chocolate mixture, eggs, vanilla extract and walnuts. Mix thoroughly.

*3* Pour the mixture into the prepared pan and bake in the oven at 350°F for 35–40 minutes until the mixture is risen and just beginning to leave the sides of the cake pan.

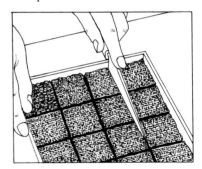

*4* Leave in the pan to cool, then cut the brownies into squares with a sharp knife.

# SPONGE CAKES

The classic sponge cake is light and feathery, made by whisking together eggs and sugar, then folding in the flour. There is no fat in the mixture, and the cake rises simply because of the air incorporated during whisking. For an even lighter cake the egg yolks and sugar can be whisked together, with the whites whisked separately and folded in afterwards.

The whisking method produces the lightest of all cakes. Sponges are perfect for filling with whipped cream and fruit and are used for many layer cakes, dessert cakes and Swiss rolls. Because they have no fat they always need a filling, and they do not keep well. Bake a sponge the day you wish to eat it.

A moister version of a whisked sponge is a Genoese sponge. This is also made by the whisking method, but melted butter is added with the flour. This gives a delicate sponge, lighter than a Victoria layer, but with a moister texture than the plain whisked sponge, and a delicious buttery taste. Don't try to substitute margarine for butter in this recipe or the flavor and texture will be lost. A Genoese sponge keeps better than a plain whisked sponge.

To make a really good sponge, don't rush. The eggs and sugar must be whisked until thick enough to leave a trail when the whisk is lifted from the surface. If you use a rotary whisk or a hand-held electric mixer, place the bowl over a saucepan of hot water to speed the thickening process and make it less hard work. Do not let the bottom of the bowl touch the water or the mixture will become too hot. When the mixture is really thick and double in volume, take the bowl off the heat and continue to whisk until it is cool.

Add the flour carefully. Sift it first, then add a little at a time to the whisked mixture and fold it in until evenly blended. Do not stir or you will break the air bubbles and the cake will not rise.

## WHISKED SPONGE CAKE

*Serves 6–8*

**3 eggs**
**¾ cup sugar**
**½ cup all-purpose flour**

*1* Grease and line two 7-inch layer pans and dust with a little flour or with a mixture of flour and sugar.

*2* Put the eggs and sugar in a large deep bowl and stand it over a pan of hot water. The bowl should fit snugly over the pan and the bottom of the bowl should not touch the bottom of the pan.

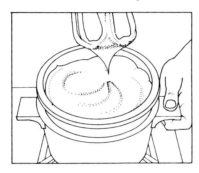

Whisk the eggs and sugar together until doubled in volume and thick enough to leave a trail on the surface when the whisk is lifted. If whisking by hand, this will take 15–20 minutes; if a hand-held electric mixer is used, 7–10 minutes will be enough.

*3* Remove the bowl from the heat and continue whisking for a further 5 minutes until the mixture is cooler and creamy looking.

*4* Sift half the flour over the mixture and fold it in very lightly, using a large metal spoon. Sift and fold in the remaining flour in the same way.

*5* Pour the mixture into the prepared pans, tilting the pans to spread the mixture evenly. Do not use a palette knife or spatula to smooth the mixture as this will crush out the air bubbles.

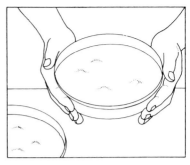

*6* Bake the cakes in the oven at 375°F for 20–25 minutes until firm but springy to the touch. Turn out and leave to cool on a wire rack for 30 minutes.

*7* When the cakes are cold, sandwich them together with strawberry or apricot jam, whipped cream or butter cream and dredge with sugar or cover the top with glacé icing (see page 152).

## SWISS ROLL

*Serves 6–8*

**3 eggs**
**¾ cup sugar**
**¾ cup all-purpose flour**
**1 Tbsp hot water**
**sugar, to dredge**
**½ cup jam, warmed**

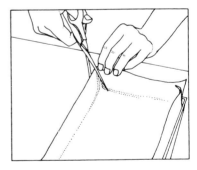

*1* Grease a 13 × 9-inch jelly roll pan. Cut a piece of waxed paper about 2 inches larger all round than the pan. Place it on the pan, creasing it to fit, and make cuts from corners of paper to corners of creases. Put in pan and grease.

*2* Put the eggs and sugar in a large bowl, stand this over a pan of hot water and whisk until thick, creamy and pale in color. The mixture should be stiff enough to leave a trail on the surface when the whisk is lifted.

*3* Remove the bowl from the heat and whisk until cool. Sift half the flour over the mixture and fold in very lightly with a metal spoon. Sift and fold in the remaining flour, then lightly stir in the hot water.

*4* Pour the mixture into the prepared pan and tilt the pan backwards and forwards to spread the mixture in an even layer. Bake in the oven at 425°F for 7–9 minutes until golden brown, well risen and firm to the touch.

*5* Meanwhile, place a sheet of waxed paper over a tea towel lightly wrung out in hot water. Dredge the paper thickly with sugar.

*6* Quickly turn out the cake onto the paper, trim off the crusty edges; spread with warmed jam.

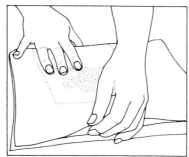

*7* Roll up the cake with the aid of the paper. Make the first turn firmly so that the whole cake will roll evenly and have a good shape when finished, but roll more lightly after this turn.

*8* Place seam-side down on a wire rack and dredge with sugar. Leave to cool for 30 minutes before serving.

––––––––– VARIATION –––––––––

**Chocolate Swiss roll** Replace 1 Tbsp flour with 1 Tbsp cocoa powder. Turn out the cooked sponge and trim as above, then cover with a sheet of waxed paper and roll with the paper inside. When the cake is cold, unroll and remove the paper. Spread with whipped cream or butter cream and re-roll. Dust with confectioners sugar.


# GENOESE SPONGE

*Serves 6–8*

| |
|---|
| **3 Tbsp butter** |
| **3 eggs** |
| **$\frac{1}{2}$ cup sugar** |
| **$\frac{1}{2}$ cup all-purpose flour** |
| **1 Tbsp cornstarch** |

*1* Grease and line two 7-inch layer pans or one 7-inch deep cake pan.

*2* Put the butter into a saucepan and heat gently until melted, then remove from the heat and leave to stand for a few minutes to cool slightly.

*3* Put the eggs and sugar in a bowl, stand it over a pan of hot water and whisk until thick, creamy and pale in color. The mixture should be stiff enough to leave a trail on the surface when the whisk is lifted. Remove from the heat and continue whisking until cool.

*4* Sift the flours together into a bowl. Fold half the flour into the egg mixture with a metal spoon.

*5* Pour half the cooled butter round the edge of the mixture. Gradually fold in the remaining butter and flour alternately. Be sure to fold in very lightly or the fat will sink to the bottom and cause a heavy cake.

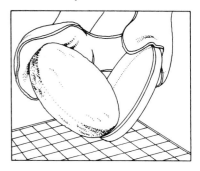

*6* Pour the mixture into the prepared pans. Bake cakes in the oven at 350°F for 25–30 minutes, or a deep cake for 35–40 minutes, until golden brown and firm to the touch. Turn out and leave to cool on a wire rack for 30 minutes before serving.

––––––––– VARIATION –––––––––

**Chocolate Genoese** For either cake, replace 2 Tbsp flour with 2 Tbsp cocoa powder.

# *Yeast Cakes*

Cakes baked with yeast have a magic of their own. The lively rising of the dough before it is cooked and the characteristic yeasty smell during baking make this type of baking a special pleasure.

Dried yeast keeps well in an airtight container in a cool dry place for at least 6 months.

Yeast needs warmth in which to grow, so all the cake ingredients should be at warm room temperature. Dried yeast must be activated in advance by mixing with a proportion of the recipe liquid (usually a third) and a little sugar; leave for 15 minutes before use.

In plain mixtures the yeast liquid can be blended straight into the flour and fat, kneaded and left to rise. Rich mixtures containing larger proportions of fat and eggs retard the growth of the yeast, so to help it you start it off with a "sponge batter." This is made with about a third of the flour and all the liquid; the yeast is blended into the batter and it is left until frothy before blending with remaining ingredients. With the sponge batter method there is no need to activate dried yeast ahead.

Always use hard flour for recipes made with yeast; the extra gluten helps give the cake a light, open texture. With a plain mixture, kneading will help develop the gluten and give a better rise.

## DOUGHNUTS

*Makes 10–12*

| 2 tsp dried yeast |
| 4 Tbsp tepid milk |
| pinch of sugar (optional) |
| 1½ cups bread flour |
| ½ tsp salt |
| pat of butter or block margarine |
| 1 egg, beaten |
| jam |
| fat, for deep frying |
| sugar and ground cinnamon |

*1* Sprinkle yeast on the milk and add the sugar; leave for about 15 minutes until frothy.

*2* Sift the flour and salt into a bowl and rub in the fat. Add the yeast liquid and egg and mix to a soft dough, adding a little more milk if necessary. Beat well until smooth. Cover with a clean cloth and leave to rise in a warm place until doubled in size.

*3* Knead lightly on a lightly floured working surface and divide into ten–twelve pieces.

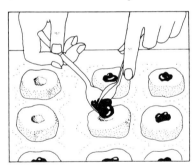

*4* Shape each piece into a round, with a small hole in the middle. Put 1 tsp jam in the center and draw up edges to form a ball.

*5* Heat the fat to 360°F or until it will brown a 1-inch cube of bread in 1 minute. Fry the doughnuts for 5–10 minutes until golden. Drain and toss in sugar mixed with cinnamon.

## RUM BABAS

*Makes 16*

| 1 Tbsp dried yeast |
| 6 Tbsp tepid milk |
| 1½ cups bread flour |
| ½ tsp salt |
| 2 Tbsp sugar |
| 4 eggs, beaten |
| ½ cup butter, softened |
| ⅔ cup currants |
| 1⅓ cups heavy cream |
| 8 Tbsp clear honey |
| 8 Tbsp water |
| a little rum |

*1* Lightly grease sixteen 3½-inch ring pans with lard and place them on baking sheets.

*2* Put the yeast, milk and ¼ cup flour into a bowl and blend until smooth. Cover with a clean cloth and leave in a warm place for 15 minutes until frothy.

*3* Add the remaining flour, the salt, sugar, eggs, butter and currants and beat well with a wooden spoon for 3–4 minutes.

*4* Half-fill the prepared pans with the dough, cover with a cloth and leave to rise in a warm place until pans are two-thirds full.

*5* Bake in the oven at 400°F for 15–20 minutes until well risen, golden and just beginning to shrink away from the sides of the pans. Leave to cool in the pans for a few minutes.

*6* Meanwhile, make the rum syrup. Put the honey and water together in a pan and warm gently. Add rum to taste.

*7* Turn the rum babas out onto a wire rack and put a tray underneath. While the babas are still hot, spoon rum syrup over each one until well soaked. Cool. To serve, whip the cream until thick and spoon or pipe some in to the center of each baba.

# WHAT WENT WRONG

### Too close a texture
1 Too much liquid.
2 Too little rising agent.
3 Insufficient creaming of the fat and sugar–air should be well incorporated at this stage.
4 Curdling of the creamed mixture when the eggs are added (a curdled mixture holds less air than one of the correct consistency).
5 Over-stirring or beating the flour into a creamed mixture when little or no rising agent is present.

### Uneven texture with holes
1 Over-stirring or uneven mixing in of the flour.
2 Putting the mixture into the cake pan in small amounts — pockets of air trapped in the mixture.

### Dry and crumbly texture
1 Too much rising agent.
2 Too long a cooking time in too cool an oven.

### Fruitcakes dry and crumbly
1 Cooking at too high a temperature.
2 Too stiff a mixture.
3 Not lining the pan thoroughly —for a large cake, double waxed paper should be used.

### Fruit sinking to the bottom of the cake
1 Damp fruit.
2 Sticky candied cherries.
3 Too soft a mixture: a rich fruit cake mixture should be fairly stiff, so that it can support the weight of the fruit.
4 Opening or banging the oven door while the cake is rising.
5 Using self-rising flour where the recipe requires regular, or using too much baking powder —the cake over-rises and cannot carry the fruit with it.

### "Peaking" and "cracking"
1 Too hot an oven.
2 The cake being placed too near top of the oven.
3 Too stiff a mixture.
4 Too small a cake pan.

### Close, heavy-textured whisked sponge
1 The eggs and sugar being insufficiently beaten, so that not enough air is enclosed.
2 The flour being stirred in too heavily or for too long—very light folding movements are required and a metal spoon should be used.

### Cakes sinking in the middle
1 Too soft a mixture.
2 Too much rising agent.
3 Too cool an oven, which means that the center of the cake does not rise.
4 Too hot an oven, which makes the cake appear to be done on the outside before it is cooked through, so that it is taken from the oven too soon.
5 Insufficient baking.

### Burnt fruit on the outside of a fruitcake
1 Too high a temperature.
2 Lack of protection: as soon as the cake begins to color, a piece of brown paper or a double thickness of waxed paper should be placed over the top for the remainder of the cooking time to prevent further browning.

### A heavy layer at the base of a Genoese sponge
1 The melted fat being too hot —it should be only lukewarm and just flowing.
2 Uneven or insufficient folding in of fat or flour.
3 Pouring the fat into the center of the mixture instead of round the edge.

# DISGUISING THE DAMAGE

If a cake goes wrong in the baking, there is no way of going back and putting it right without baking a new cake. But there are ways of disguising the damage so that only you will know.

● If a chocolate cake turns out rather too moist, call it a pudding and serve it with a fluffy sauce.

● If homemade cookies crumble badly, use them to make a cracker crumb tart shell.

● If the top of a fruitcake gets burnt, cut it off and use a well flavored almond paste to disguise it.

● If meringues break as you lift them off the baking sheet, serve large pieces on top of fruit and cream.

● If a sponge cake turns out a thin, flat layer, cut into fancy shapes with a cookie cutter and sandwich together with jam and cream.

● If your cake rises unevenly, level the top, turn it over and ice the bottom.

● If a cake breaks as you take it out of the pan, disguise it as a pudding with custard sauce or fruit.

● If a cake sinks in the middle, cut out the center and turn it into a ring cake. Ice it with butter cream or almond paste and royal icing, according to type, or decorate with whipped cream and fill the center with fruit for a dessert.

● If a sponge or plain cake is dry, crumbly or heavy, use it as the base for a trifle and soak it in plenty of booze!

# PERFECT PASTRY AND COOKIES

There is no doubt that making your own pastry does take time, but the results are usually worth it. There are many different types of pastry and each has its own distinctive texture, flavor and use. The art of producing good pastry lies in understanding the basic rules by which each one is made and sticking to them.

Good cookies should look as good as they taste, for each is an individual treat to eye and palate. Making cookies is not as difficult as making pastry but because you're making so many little "cakes," they can be time-consuming. If you have little time, little patience, or both, then choose to make the simpler cookies. Bars are the easiest, but refrigerator cookies are simple, too, because there is little hand-shaping involved.

# PASTRY CAKES

For successful pastry, work in a cool kitchen with cool utensils and ingredients. As you work, handle the pastry as little as possible and use just your finger and thumb tips for rubbing in fat.

For most pastries, use all-purpose flour. For puff pastry use bread flour, to help give it a light, open structure. Butter and margarine are interchangeable in short pastries, and give good results when mixed with lard. Proprietary vegetable shortenings and pure vegetable oils can also be used, but follow the manufacturer's directions as the quantities required may be less. In richer pastries stick to butter. Add liquid to a pastry mixture gradually, using just enough to bind it.

*Pâte sucrée* is a really rich shortcrust that keeps its shape well; use it for sweet tarts and pies. *Shortcrust* is probably the most widely used pastry, and is quick and easy to prepare. Use it for vegetable pies and quiches. *Flan pastry* is a slightly richer pastry made by the same method. It is usually sweetened, and it is ideal for flans and tarts.

*Puff pastry* is the richest of all and rises to layer upon layer of crisp, delicate flakes. Because it takes so long to make most people make it only occasionally, mixing up a large batch and freezing it in small quantities for future use.

*Flaky pastry* is used where a rich pastry is required but when the rise is not so important. *Rough puff* is quicker and easier to make and similar in appearance to flaky, but the texture is not so even.

*Choux pastry* is made by melting the fat and beating in the flour and the resulting paste is piped to shape. The result is a light, crisp shell, almost hollow inside. Used mostly for cream puffs.

# PÂTE SUCRÉE

| |
|---|
| $\frac{3}{4}$ cup all-purpose flour |
| pinch of salt |
| $\frac{1}{4}$ cup granulated sugar |
| 4 Tbsp butter, at room temperature |
| 2 egg yolks |

*1* Sift the flour and salt together onto a working surface or, preferably, a marble slab.

*2* Make a well in the center of the mixture and add the sugar, butter and egg yolks.

*3* Using the fingertips of one hand, pinch and work the sugar, butter and egg yolks together until well blended. Gradually work in all the flour, adding a little water if necessary to bind it together.

*4* Knead lightly until smooth, then wrap the pastry in foil or plastic wrap and leave to rest in the refrigerator or a cool place for about 1 hour.

*5* Roll out the pastry on a lightly floured surface and use as required. *Pâte sucrée* is usually cooked at 375°F.

## SHORTCRUST PASTRY

1¼ cups all-purpose flour
pinch of salt
6 Tbsp butter or margarine
 and lard
about 2 Tbsp cold water

*1* Mix the flour and salt together in a bowl. Cut the fat into small pieces and add it to the flour.

*2* Using both hands, rub the fat into the flour between finger and thumb tips until the mixture resembles fine bread crumbs.

*3* Add the water, sprinkling it evenly over the surface. Stir it in with a round-bladed knife until the mixture begins to stick together in large lumps.

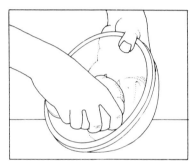

*4* With one hand, collect the mixture together and knead lightly for a few seconds to give a firm, smooth dough. The pastry can be used right away but is better allowed to rest for about 30 minutes. It can also be wrapped in plastic wrap and kept in the refrigerator for a day or two.

*5 To roll out:* sprinkle a very little flour on a working surface and the rolling pin, not on the pastry, and roll out the dough evenly in one direction only, turning it occasionally. The ideal thickness is usually about ⅛ inch. Do not pull or stretch the pastry. When cooking shortcrust pastry, the usual oven temperature is 400–425°F.

## FLAN PASTRY

¾ cup all-purpose flour
pinch of salt
6 Tbsp butter or margarine and
 lard
1 tsp granulated sugar
1 egg, beaten

*1* Mix the flour and salt together in a bowl. Cut the fat into small pieces, add it to the flour and rub it in as for shortcrust pastry until the mixture resembles fine bread crumbs. Stir in the sugar.

*2* Add the egg, stirring with a round-bladed knife until the ingredients begin to stick together in large lumps.

*3* With one hand, collect the mixture together and knead lightly for a few seconds to give a firm, smooth dough.

*4* Roll out as for shortcrust pastry and use as required. When cooking flan pastry the usual oven temperature is 400°F.

## BAKING BLIND

Baking blind is the process of baking a pastry case without the filling—essential if the filling is to be uncooked or if it only requires a short cooking time. First shape the pastry into the baking pan. Prick the pastry base with a fork. For large cases, cut a round of waxed paper rather larger than

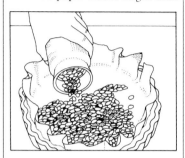

the pan. Use this to line the pastry and weight it down with some dried beans, pasta or rice. Alternatively, screw up a piece of foil and use that to line the base of the pastry case. Bake the pastry at the temperature given in the recipe for 10–15 minutes, then remove the baking beans and paper or foil lining and return the pan to the oven for a further 5 minutes to crisp the pastry. Leave the baked case to cool and shrink slightly before removing it from the pan. (The baking beans can be kept for use again.)

For small cases, it is usually sufficient to prick the pastry well with a fork before baking.
 Baked unfilled pastry cases can be kept for a few days in an airtight container.

# ROUGH PUFF PASTRY

1½ cups all-purpose flour
pinch of salt
6 Tbsp butter or margarine
6 Tbsp lard
about ⅔ cup cold water
a squeeze of lemon juice
beaten egg, to glaze

*1* Mix the flour and salt together in a bowl. Cut the fat (which should be quite firm) into cubes about ¾ inch across.

*2* Stir the fat into the flour without breaking up the pieces. Add enough water and lemon juice to mix to a fairly stiff dough.

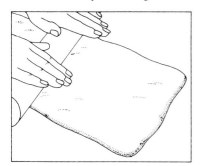

*3* On a lightly floured surface, roll out into an oblong three times as long as it is wide.

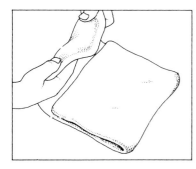

*4* Fold the bottom third up and the top third down, then turn the pastry so that the folded edges are at the sides. Seal the ends of the pastry by pressing lightly with a rolling pin.

*5* Repeat this rolling and folding process three more times, turning the dough so that the folded edge is on the left hand side each time.

*6* Wrap the pastry in waxed paper and leave to rest in the refrigerator or a cool place for about 30 minutes before using.

*7* Roll out the pastry on a lightly floured surface to ⅛ inch thick and use as required. Brush with beaten egg before baking. The usual oven temperature is 425°F.

# PUFF PASTRY

3½ cups bread flour
pinch of salt
1 lb butter
1¼ cups cold water
1 Tbsp lemon juice
beaten egg, to glaze

*1* Mix the flour and a pinch of salt together in a large mixing bowl.

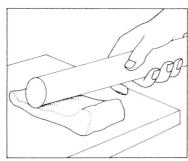

*2* Cut off 4 Tbsp butter and pat the remaining butter with a rolling pin to a slab ¾ inch thick.

*3* Rub the 4 Tbsp butter into the flour with the finger and thumb tips. Stir in enough water and lemon juice to make a soft, elastic dough.

*4* Knead dough until smooth and shape into a round. Cut through half the depth in a cross shape.

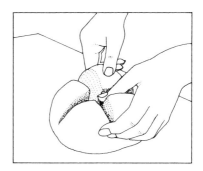

*5* Open out the flaps to form a star. Roll out, keeping the center four times as thick as the flaps.

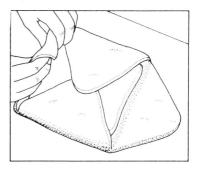

*6* Place the slab of butter in the center of the dough and fold over the flaps, envelope-style. Press gently with a rolling pin.

*7* Roll out into a rectangle measuring about 16 × 8 inches. Fold the bottom third up and the top third down, keeping the edges straight. Seal the edges by pressing with the rolling pin.

*8* Wrap the pastry in waxed paper and leave in the refrigerator to rest for 30 minutes.

*9* Put the pastry on a lightly floured working surface with the folded edges to the sides and repeat the rolling, folding and resting sequence five times.

*10* After the final resting, roll out the pastry on a lightly floured surface and shape as required. Brush with beaten egg. The usual oven temperature is 450°F.

## FLAKY PASTRY

1½ cups all-purpose flour
pinch of salt
6 Tbsp butter or margarine
6 Tbsp lard
about ⅔ cup cold water
a squeeze of lemon juice
beaten egg, to glaze

*1* Mix the flour and salt together in a bowl. Soften the fat by working it with a knife on a plate, then divide it into four equal portions.

*2* Add one quarter of the fat to the flour and rub it in between finger and thumb tips until the mixture resembles fine breadcrumbs.

*3* Add enough water and lemon juice to make a soft elastic dough, stirring it in with a round-bladed knife.

*4* Turn the dough onto a lightly floured surface and roll out into an oblong three times as long as it is wide.

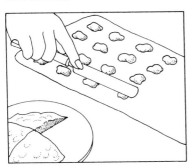

*5* Using a round-bladed knife, dot another quarter of the fat over the top two-thirds of the pastry in flakes, so that it looks like buttons on a card.

*6* Fold the bottom third of the pastry up and the top third down and turn it so that the folded edges are at the side. Seal the edges of the pastry by pressing with a rolling pin.

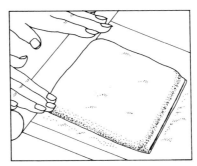

*7* Re-roll as before and repeat the process twice more until the remaining portions of fat have been used up.

*8* Wrap the pastry loosely in waxed paper and leave it to rest in the refrigerator or a cool place for at least 30 minutes before using.

*9* Roll out the pastry on a lightly floured working surface to ⅛ inch thick and use as required. Brush with beaten egg before baking to give the characteristic glaze. When cooking flaky pastry, the usual oven temperature is 400–425°F.

## CHOUX PASTRY

4 Tbsp butter or margarine
⅔ cup water
½ cup all-purpose flour
2 eggs, lightly beaten

---

### BEATING CHOUX PASTRY

Add the beaten egg gradually to choux pastry, taking care to add only just enough to give a piping consistency. When beating by hand with a wooden spoon the arm tends to tire, the beating speed is reduced and the final consistency is often too slack to retain its shape. In this case a little less egg should be added.

---

*1* Put the fat and water together in a pan, heat gently until the fat has melted, then bring to the boil. Remove pan from heat.

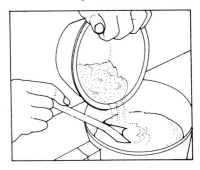

*2* Tip all the flour into the hot liquid at once. Beat thoroughly with a wooden spoon, then return the pan to the heat.

*3* Continue beating the mixture until it is smooth and forms a ball in the center of the pan. (Take care not to overbeat or the mixture will become fatty.) Remove from the heat and leave the mixture to cool for a minute or two.

*4* Beat in the egg, a little at a time, adding only just enough to give a piping consistency. Beat the mixture vigorously at this stage to trap in as much air as possible. Continue beating until the mixture develops an obvious sheen, then use as required. When cooking choux pastry the usual oven temperature is 400–425°F.

# COOKIES

Homemade cookies beat bought ones any day, and they are so simple to make it is a pity to pass them by. Choose to make the thin and crisp type, or softer, thicker and more crumbly ones. They will all be equally popular.

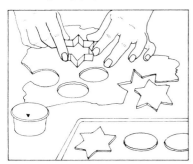

The traditional cookie mixture makes a dough that you roll out thinly and cut to shape before baking. If you find the dough sticky or difficult to handle, chill it a little, or roll it between sheets of non-stick parchment. Don't add extra flour to the working surface as this will spoil the texture of the cookies.

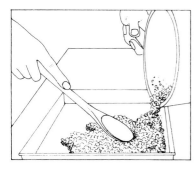

*Bar cookies* are especially easy and quick to make. You mix the ingredients and press it all firmly into a baking pan. It is then cut into bars after baking.

*Icebox cookies* are quick and easy to make. Make up the dough and shape it into a neat roll, then wrap it and place in the refrigerator or freezer. Then you just

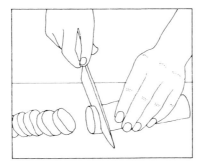

cut off thin slices, thaw slightly if frozen dough, and bake them, as and when you want freshly baked cookies. The dough will keep quite happily for about 2 weeks in the refrigerator or 3 months in the freezer.

*Dropped and piped* recipes are a little more difficult to handle as the mixture is softer. These are either dropped from a spoon or piped onto baking sheets. They are inclined to spread, so leave plenty of space between each one.

Cook all cookies on good-quality, flat baking sheets with no sides, to ensure even browning. Bake them in the center of the oven, or if baking two sheets at a time, swap them over half way through. Leave soft cookies on the baking sheet for a few minutes after taking out of the oven, to firm up a little, then transfer carefully to a wire rack to cool.

Store cookies in an airtight container. Most keep well for 2–3 weeks, but keep different varieties separate, so the flavors don't mix, and keep them separate from cakes. If you plan to ice cookies, do it shortly before serving.

## ICEBOX COOKIES

*Makes 22*

| |
|---|
| $\frac{3}{4}$ **cup sugar** |
| $\frac{1}{2}$ **cup soft margarine** |
| **vanilla extract** |
| **grated rind of 1 lemon** |
| **1 egg, beaten** |
| **1$\frac{1}{2}$ cups all-purpose flour** |

*1* Cream together the sugar and margarine until very pale. Beat in a few drops of vanilla extract, the lemon rind and egg.

*2* Stir in the flour and mix to a firm paste. Knead lightly, wrap and chill for 30 minutes.

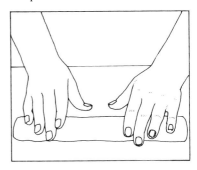

*3* Roll the dough to a sausage shape, 2 inches in diameter, 8 inches long. Wrap in waxed paper. Refrigerate for at least 30 minutes before baking.

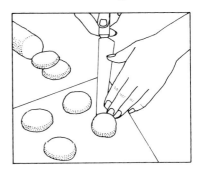

*4* When required, cut $\frac{1}{4}$-inch slices, place on lightly greased baking sheets and bake in the oven at 375°F for 12–15 minutes. Cool on a wire rack.

## OAT STRIPS

*Makes 16–18*

| |
|---|
| 4 Tbsp butter or margarine |
| $\frac{1}{4}$ cup light brown sugar |
| 3 Tbsp corn syrup |
| $\frac{3}{4}$ cup rolled oats |

*1* Grease a 7-inch square cake pan. Then melt the butter with the sugar and syrup, pour it onto the rolled oats and mix well.

*2* Turn the mixture into the prepared pan and press down well. Bake in the oven at 350°F for 20–25 minutes until golden brown.

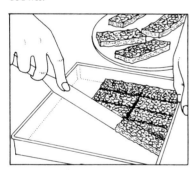

*3* Cool slightly in the pan, mark into fingers with a sharp knife and loosen round the edges. When firm, cut right through and using a palette knife, remove the cookies from the pan.

## LEMON AND NUTMEG SHORTIES

*Makes 24*

| |
|---|
| $\frac{1}{2}$ cup butter or margarine, softened |
| $\frac{1}{4}$ cup sugar |
| 1 cup all-purpose flour |
| $\frac{1}{4}$ cup ground rice |
| $\frac{1}{4}$ tsp ground nutmeg |
| grated rind of 1 lemon |
| 1 tsp lemon juice |
| sugar and nutmeg, to finish |

*1* Cream together the butter and sugar until very pale. Stir in the flour, ground rice, nutmeg, lemon rind and juice. Knead very well to form a smooth, workable paste.

*2* On a lightly sugared surface, roll out the cookie dough to slightly more than $\frac{1}{4}$ inch thick.

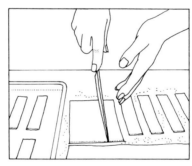

*3* With a sharp knife, cut into $3 \times \frac{3}{4}$-inch fingers. Place on lightly greased baking sheets and chill for 30 minutes.

*4* Bake in the oven at 375°F for about 25 minutes until just changing color.

*5* Dredge with sugar and ground nutmeg while still warm. Leave to cool completely on a wire rack.

## CHERRY GARLANDS

*Makes 24*

| |
|---|
| 1 cup soft margarine |
| $\frac{3}{4}$ cup confectioners sugar |
| $1\frac{1}{2}$ cups all-purpose flour |
| $\frac{1}{4}$ cup cornstarch |
| vanilla extract |
| $\frac{1}{2}$ cup candied cherries, very finely chopped |
| whole cherries and angelica, to decorate |
| confectioners sugar |

*1* Cream the margarine and sugar together until pale and fluffy.

*2* Beat in the flours, a few drops of vanilla extract and the chopped cherries. (If using an electric handmixer, beat for 3–4 minutes; by hand, beat until the mixture is very soft.)

*3* Spoon half the mixture into a piping bag fitted with a $\frac{1}{2}$-inch star nozzle. Pipe 2-inch rings onto lightly greased baking sheets allowing room for spreading.

*4* Decorate with a quartered cherry and pieces of angelica. Repeat with the remaining mixture.

*5* Bake in the oven at 375°F for about 20 minutes until pale golden. Allow to firm up slightly on the baking sheets for about 30 seconds before sliding onto a wire rack to cool. Dredge with confectioners sugar.

# DECORATING CAKES

"The icing on the cake" is the finishing touch that turns a workaday cake into a loving creation. Decorations for informal cakes may be anything from a light dusting of sugar, a smooth coat of glacé icing or merely a simple fresh flower adorning the top. Whirls of butter cream interspersed with nuts or colored sweets results in something showier. For formal cakes you need to master piping techniques and the method of flat icing with royal icing.

## EQUIPMENT

Simple decorations need no special equipment, but the right tools do help when you start to attempt more elaborate work. It can often make the difference between an amateur-looking job and a polished, professional one. If you like showing off and treating your guests to something very special now and then, cake decorating tools will be a good investment for years to come.

*An icing comb* helps with icing the sides of a deep cake.

*An icing nail* is a small metal or plastic nail with a large head that is designed to hold decorations such as icing roses, while you make them. It enables you to hold the rose securely, and turn it without damaging it.

*An icing ruler* is useful for flat icing a large cake. You can substitute anything with a fine straight edge, long enough to extend both sides of the cake.

*An icing turntable* gives you clearance from the working surface and enables you to turn the cake freely. If you do not have a turntable, place the cake board on an upturned plate, to give it a little lift from the working surface.

*Nozzles* can be used with paper or fabric piping bags. A fine plain nozzle for writing and piping straight lines and simple designs, plus a star or shell nozzle, are the basics; more advanced piping work demands a whole range of different shapes and sizes. For use with paper piping bags, choose nozzles without a screw band; the band is useful with a fabric bag.

*Piping bags* can be made from parchment paper, or bought ready-made in fabric. Special icing pumps are also available.

*A silver cake board or plate* sets off any iced cake. Some are made from thin card, or stronger ones are about $\frac{1}{2}$ inch thick. Choose a board that is 2 inches larger than the cake, so that a border shows all round.

Apart from the above, the only tools you will need are everyday kitchen equipment: a frosting knife, a table fork and a wire rack; for flat icing with royal icing you will need some fine sandpaper.

## ICING

The cake must be completely cold before you start icing. The surface must be level; if necessary, turn the cake upside down and ice the flat bottom.

If making a layer cake, put the filling in first. Then apply any decorations to the sides. Ice the top last.

For simple icings, place the cake on a wire rack to decorate it. Lifting it from one plate to another may crack the icing, and you are sure to make drips on the plate.

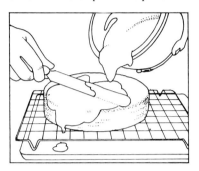

*To use glacé icing,* if coating both the top and sides of the cake, stand it on a wire rack with a tray underneath to catch the drips. As soon as the icing reaches a coating consistency and looks smooth and glossy, pour it from the bowl onto the center of the cake. Allow the icing to run down the sides, guiding it with a palette knife. Keep a little icing back to fill the gaps.

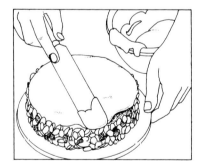

If the sides are decorated and only the top is to have glacé icing, pour the icing onto the center of the cake and spread it with a palette knife, stopping just inside the

369

edges to prevent it dripping down the sides. If the top is to be iced and the sides left plain, protect them with a band of waxed paper tied round the cake and projecting a little above it. Pour on the icing and let it find its own level. Peel off the paper when the icing is hard.

Arrange any ready-made decorations such as nuts, cherries, sweets, silver balls etc in position as soon as the icing has thickened and formed a skin. Except for feather icing, leave the icing until quite dry before applying piped decorations.

*To feather ice*, make a quantity of glacé icing and mix to a coating consistency. Make up a second batch of icing using half the quantity of sugar and enough warm water to mix it to a thick piping consistency; tint the second batch with food coloring. Spoon the colored icing into a waxed paper piping bag.

Coat the top of the cake with the larger quantity of icing. Working quickly, before it has time to form a skin, snip the end off the piping bag and pipe parallel lines of colored icing about $\frac{1}{2}-\frac{3}{4}$ inches apart over the surface. Then quickly draw the point of a skewer or a sharp knife across the piped lines, first in one direction then in the other, spacing them evenly apart.

*Butter cream* can be used as a filling or icing. Spread it over the top only, or over the top and sides. Decorate by making swirl marks

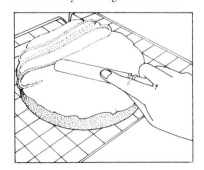

with the flat of a knife blade, or spread it evenly with a palette knife

and mark with the prongs of a fork. Add any extra decorations before it sets. For more elaborate decoration, butter cream pipes well.

*Crème au beurre* is a richer form of butter cream suitable for more elaborate cakes.

*Boiled frosting* is a fluffy, soft icing. You need a sugar thermometer to make it. *Seven-minute frosting* is similar but can be made without the help of a thermometer.

*Almond paste* is used on fruitcakes either as a decoration in its own right, when it may be shaped and colored as you wish, or as a firm base for royal icing.

*Royal icing* is the hard icing used on fruitcakes for formal occasions.

## CAKE DECORATIONS

Add ready-made decorations before the icing hardens completely, or stick them in place with a little dab of fresh icing.

Nuts of all sorts, but particularly walnuts, hazelnuts, almonds and pistachios, are popular. Buy crystallized violets and roses in small quantities and keep them in a dark place to avoid bleaching. When buying angelica, look for a really good color and a small amount of sugar. To remove sugar, soak briefly in hot water, then drain and dry well.

Chocolate and colored vermicelli stale quickly and become speckled, so buy in small quantities as needed. Silver dragees (balls) keep well in a dry place; use tweezers for handling. They come in colors other than silver. Hundreds and thousands are useful for children's cakes, as are all sorts of colored sweets. For more sophisticated decorations, look for candy coffee beans.

When decorating with chocolate, choose semisweet eating chocolate for chopping and grating. Chocolate-flavored cake covering is useful for shavings and melting, but the flavor is not so good. Crumbled chocolate flake makes a useful last minute decoration.

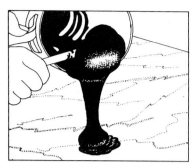

**Chocolate caraque** Melt 4 oz chocolate in a bowl over a pan of hot water. Pour it in a thin layer onto a marble slab or cold baking tray and leave to set until it no longer sticks to your hand when you touch it. Holding a large knife with both hands, push the blade

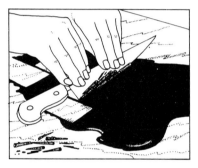

across the surface of the chocolate to roll pieces off in long curls. Adjust the angle of the blade to get the best curls.
**Chocolate shapes** Make a sheet of chocolate as above and cut into neat triangles or squares with a sharp knife, or stamp out circles with a small round cutter.

**Chocolate shavings** Using a potato peeler, pare thin layers from the edge of the block.

# GLACÉ ICING

*Makes about ½ cup*

½ cup confectioners sugar

a few drops of vanilla or almond extract (optional)

1 Tbsp warm water

coloring (optional)

*1* Sift the sugar into a bowl. If you wish, add a few drops of vanilla or almond extract.

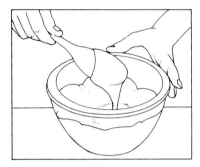

*2* Gradually add the warm water. The icing should be thick enough to coat the back of a spoon. If necessary add more water or sugar to adjust consistency. Add coloring, if liked, and use at once.

——————— VARIATIONS ———————

**Orange or lemon** Replace the water with 1 Tbsp strained orange or lemon juice.

**Chocolate** Dissolve 2 tsp cocoa powder in a little hot water and use instead of the same amount of water.

**Coffee** Flavor with 1 tsp coffee extract or dissolve 2 tsp instant coffee in a little hot water and use instead of the same amount of water.

**Mocha** Dissolve 1 tsp cocoa powder and 2 tsp instant coffee in a little hot water and use instead of the same amount of water.

**Liqueur** Replace 2–3 tsp of the water with the same amount of any liqueur.

# BUTTER CREAM

*Makes about 1 cup*

6 Tbsp butter

1 cup confectioners sugar

a few drops of vanilla extract

1–2 Tbsp milk or warm water

Put the butter in a bowl and cream until soft. Gradually sift and beat in the sugar, adding the vanilla flavoring and milk or water.

——————— VARIATIONS ———————

**Orange or lemon** Replace the vanilla extract with a little finely grated orange or lemon rind. Add a little juice from the fruit, beating well to avoid curdling the mixture.

**Almond** Add 2 Tbsp finely chopped toasted almonds and mix.

**Coffee** Replace the vanilla extract with 2 tsp instant coffee blended with some of the liquid, or replace 1 Tbsp of the liquid with the same amount of coffee extract.

**Chocolate** Dissolve 1 Tbsp cocoa powder in a little hot water and cool before adding to the mixture.

**Mocha** Dissolve 1 tsp cocoa powder and 2 tsp instant coffee in a little warm water taken from the measured amount. Cool before adding to the mixture.

# APRICOT GLAZE

*Makes about ⅔ cup*

½ cup apricot jam

2 Tbsp water

Put the jam and water in a saucepan and heat gently, stirring, until the jam softens. Bring to the boil and simmer for 1 minute. Sieve the glaze and use while still warm.

# CRÈME AU BEURRE
(Rich Butter Cream)

*Makes about 1¼ cups*

½ cup sugar

4 Tbsp water

2 egg yolks, beaten

¾ cup butter

*1* Place the sugar in a heavy-based saucepan, add the water and heat very gently to dissolve the sugar, without boiling.

*2* When completely dissolved, bring to boiling point and boil steadily for 2–3 minutes, to reach a temperature of 225°F.

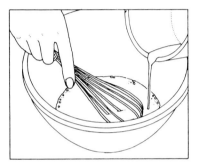

*3* Pour the syrup in a thin stream onto the egg yolks in a deep bowl, whisking all the time. Continue to whisk until the mixture is thick and cold.

*4* In another bowl, cream the butter until very soft and gradually beat in the egg yolk mixture.

——————— VARIATIONS ———————

**Chocolate** Melt 2 oz semisweet chocolate with 1 Tbsp water. Cool slightly and beat in.

**Coffee** Beat in 1–2 Tbsp coffee extract.

**Fruit** Crush 8 oz fresh strawberries, raspberries etc, or thaw, drain and crush frozen fruit. Beat into the basic mixture.

**Orange or lemon** Add freshly grated rind and juice to taste.

## CRÈME PÂTISSIÈRE

*Makes about 1 cup*

2 eggs
$\frac{1}{4}$ cup sugar
2 Tbsp all-purpose flour
2 Tbsp cornstarch
$1\frac{1}{3}$ cups milk
a few drops of vanilla extract

*1* Cream the eggs and sugar together until really pale and thick. Sift the flour and cornstarch in to the bowl and beat in with a little cold milk until smooth.

*2* Heat the rest of the milk until almost boiling and pour onto the egg mixture, stirring well all the time.

*3* Return the custard to the saucepan and stir over a low heat until the mixture boils. Add vanilla extract to taste and cook for a further 2–3 minutes. Cover and allow to cool before using.

## SEVEN-MINUTE FROSTING

*Makes about $\frac{3}{4}$ cup*

1 egg white
1 cup sugar
pinch of salt
pinch of cream of tartar
2 Tbsp water

*1* Put all the ingredients into a bowl and whisk lightly. Then place the bowl over a pan of hot water and heat, whisking continuously, until the mixture thickens sufficiently to stand in peaks. This will take about 7 minutes depending on the whisk used and the heat of the water.

*2* Pour the frosting over the top of the cake and spread with a palette knife.

——— VARIATIONS ———

Use the same flavorings as for Boiled frosting.

## ROYAL ICING

*Makes about 4 cups*

4 egg whites
2 lb confectioners sugar
1 Tbsp lemon juice
2 Tbsp glycerine

*1* Whisk the egg whites in a bowl until slightly frothy. Then sift and stir in about a quarter of the sugar with a wooden spoon. Continue adding more sugar gradually, beating well after each addition, until about three quarters of the sugar has been added.

*2* Beat in the lemon juice and continue beating for about 10 minutes until the icing is smooth.

*3* Beat in the remaining sugar until the required consistency is achieved, depending on how the icing will be used.

*4* Finally, stir in the glycerine to prevent the icing hardening. Cover and keep for 24 hours to allow air bubbles to rise to the surface.

## ALMOND PASTE

*Makes 4 cups*

5 cups confectioners sugar
$1\frac{1}{4}$ cups sugar
1 lb almonds, ground
1 tsp vanilla extract
2 eggs, lightly beaten
2 tsp lemon juice

*1* Sift the confectioners sugar into a bowl and mix in the granulated sugar and ground almonds.

*2* Add the vanilla extract, egg and lemon juice and mix to a stiff dough. Knead lightly and into a ball.

## BOILED FROSTING

*Makes about 1 cup*

1 egg white
$1\frac{1}{4}$ cups granulated sugar
4 Tbsp water
pinch of cream of tartar

*1* Whisk the egg white until stiff. Then gently heat the sugar with the water and cream of tartar, stirring until dissolved. Then, without stirring, boil to 240°F.

*2* Remove the syrup from the heat and, immediately the bubbles subside, pour it onto the egg white in a thin stream, beating the mixture continuously.

*3* When it thickens, shows signs of going dull round the edges and is almost cold, pour the frosting quickly over the cake and spread evenly with a palette knife.

——— VARIATIONS ———

**Orange** Beat in a few drops of orange extract and a little orange food coloring before it thickens. **Lemon** Beat in a little lemon juice before the mixture thickens. **Caramel** Substitute light brown sugar for the white sugar. **Coffee** Beat in 1 tsp coffee extract before mixture thickens.

## CHOCOLATE FROSTING

*Makes just less than 1 cup*

1 oz semisweet chocolate
4 cups confectioners sugar
1 egg
$\frac{1}{2}$ tsp vanilla extract
2 Tbsp butter

*1* Break the chocolate into pieces and put in a bowl over a pan of hot water. Heat gently, stirring, until the chocolate has melted.

*2* Sift in the sugar, add the egg, vanilla extract and butter and beat until smooth.

# Basic Recipes

We conclude with a collection of recipes that we think you'll turn to time and time again. Many, particularly the stocks, dressings and both sweet and spicy sauces, are basic recipes that every cook should have on hand; they form the foundation of so many popular dishes. Others, like the breads, vegetables and salads, hors d'oeuvres, and drinks are recipe classics. Master them and you can skillfully add special touches to menus of all kinds, for all occasions.

## *SAUCES AND DRESSINGS*

### WHITE SAUCE (POURING)

**One-stage method**

*Makes 1¼ cups*

1 Tbsp butter or margarine

1½ Tbsp flour

1¼ cups milk

salt and freshly ground pepper

*1* Place the butter or margarine, flour and milk in a saucepan. Heat, whisking continuously, until the sauce thickens. Season with salt and pepper.

### WHITE SAUCE (COATING)

*1* Follow the recipe for Pouring Sauce (above), but use 2 Tbsp butter and 3 Tbsp flour.

**Blender or food processor method**

*1* Use the ingredients in the same proportions as for Pouring or Coating Sauce (above).

*2* Put the butter, flour, milk and seasoning in the machine and blend until smooth.

*3* Pour into a saucepan and bring to a boil, stirring, until the sauce thickens.

**Roux method**

*1* Use the ingredients in the same quantities as for Pouring Sauce or Coating Sauce (above).

*2* Melt the butter in a saucepan. Add the flour and cook over a low heat, stirring with a wooden spoon, for 2 minutes. Do not allow the mixture (roux) to brown.

*3* Remove the pan from the heat and gradually blend in the milk, stirring after each addition to prevent lumps from forming. Bring to a boil slowly and continue to cook, stirring all the time, until the sauce comes to a boil and thickens.

*4* Simmer very gently for another 2–3 minutes. Season with salt and freshly ground pepper.

——————— VARIATIONS ———————

**Parsley Sauce**
A traditional sauce for ham and fish dishes.

*1* Follow the recipe for the Pouring Sauce or Coating Sauce (above).

*2* After seasoning with salt and pepper, stir in 1–2 Tbsp **finely chopped fresh parsley.**

**Onion Sauce**
For broiled and roast lamb.

*1* Add **1 large onion,** skinned and finely chopped, to the ingredients for Pouring or Coating Sauce (above) and use the roux method.

*2* Cook the onion until soft in the butter before adding the flour.

*3* Reheat gently before serving.

**Cheese Sauce**
For fish, poultry, ham, egg and vegetable dishes.

*1* Follow the recipe for Pouring or Coating Sauce (above).

*2* Before seasoning with salt and pepper, stir in ½ cup **finely grated Cheddar cheese** or any other hard cheese, **½–1 tsp prepared mustard and a pinch of cayenne pepper.** Cook gently until the cheese melts.

### Lemon Sauce

For fish, poultry, egg and veal dishes.

*1* Follow the recipe for Pouring or Coating Sauce (previous page).

*2* Before seasoning with salt and pepper stir in the **finely grated rind of 1 small lemon and 1 Tbsp lemon juice.** Reheat gently before serving.

## BASIC VINAIGRETTE

*Makes 9 Tbsp*

**6 Tbsp olive oil**

**3 Tbsp wine vinegar, cider vinegar or lemon juice**

**$\frac{1}{2}$ tsp sugar**

**$\frac{1}{2}$ tsp wholegrain, Dijon or French mustard**

**salt and freshly ground pepper**

*1* Place all the ingredients in a bowl or screw-topped jar and whisk or shake together.

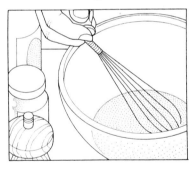

*2* Before use, whisk or shake dressing again, as the oil separates out on standing. Taste and adjust seasoning.

Note: If a recipe calls for $\frac{2}{3}$ cup of dressing, add an extra 1 Tbsp oil.

## MAYONNAISE MADE IN A BLENDER OR FOOD PROCESSOR

Most blenders and food processors need at least a two-egg quantity in order to ensure that the blades are covered. Remember to have all the ingredients at room temperature.

*Makes 1$\frac{1}{4}$ cups*

**2 egg yolks**

**1 tsp mustard powder or 1 tsp Dijon mustard**

**1 tsp salt**

**$\frac{1}{2}$ tsp freshly ground pepper**

**1 tsp sugar (optional)**

**2 Tbsp white wine vinegar or lemon juice**

**1$\frac{1}{4}$ cups vegetable oil**

*1* Put the egg yolks, mustard, salt, freshly ground pepper, sugar, if using, and 1 Tbsp of the vinegar or lemon juice into the blender container or food processor bowl fitted with the metal blade. Blend well together.

*2* If your machine has a variable speed control, run it at a slow speed. Add the oil drop by drop through the top of the blender container or the feed tube of the processor while the machine is running, until the egg and oil emulsify and become thick. Continue adding the oil gradually in a thin, steady stream. If the mayonnaise becomes too thick, add a little more of the vinegar or of the lemon juice.

*3* When all the oil has been added, gradually add the remaining vinegar or lemon juice with the machine still running and blend thoroughly. Taste and adjust seasoning before serving.

### STORING MAYONNAISE

Homemade mayonnaise does not keep as long as bought varieties as it is free from added emulsifiers, stabilizers and preservatives. The freshness of the eggs and oil used and the temperature at which it is stored also affect how long it will keep. Mayonnaise keeps for 1 week in the refrigerator in a screw-topped glass jar.

### RESCUE REMEDIES

If the mayonnaise separates while you are making it, don't worry— there are ways to save it. All these ways involve beating the curdled mixture into a fresh base.

This base can be any one of the following: 1 tsp hot water; 1 tsp vinegar or lemon juice; 1 tsp Dijon mustard or $\frac{1}{2}$ tsp mustard powder (the mayonnaise will taste more strongly of mustard than usual); or a fresh egg yolk to every 1$\frac{1}{4}$ cups of mayonnaise. Add the curdled mixture to the base, beating hard. When the mixture is smooth, continue adding the oil as above. (If you use an extra egg yolk you may find that you need to add extra oil.)

————— VARIATIONS —————

These variations are made by adding the ingredients to 1$\frac{1}{4}$ cups mayonnaise.

**Caper mayonnaise** Add **4 tsp chopped capers, 2 tsp chopped pimento** and **1 tsp tarragon vinegar.** Caper mayonnaise makes an ideal accompaniment for fish.

**Celery mayonnaise** Add **2 Tbsp chopped celery** and **2 Tbsp snipped fresh chives.**

**Cucumber mayonnaise** Add **4 Tbsp finely chopped cucumber.** This mayonnaise goes well with fish salads, especially crab, lobster or salmon.

**Herb mayonnaise** Add **4 Tbsp snipped fresh chives** and **2 Tbsp chopped fresh parsley.** This mayonnaise goes well with hard-boiled eggs.

**Horseradish mayonnaise** Add **2 Tbsp horseradish sauce.**

**Piquant mayonnaise** Add **2 tsp tomato ketchup, 2 tsp chopped stuffed olives** and **a pinch of paprika.**

# HOLLANDAISE SAUCE MADE IN A BLENDER OR FOOD PROCESSOR

*Makes about ⅔ cup*

2 egg yolks

salt and freshly ground pepper

2 Tbsp wine or tarragon vinegar or lemon juice

1 Tbsp water

½ cup butter

*1* Put the egg yolks and seasoning into the blender container or food processor bowl fitted with the metal blade. Blend well together.

*2* Put the vinegar or lemon juice and water in a small pan and boil until reduced to about 1 Tbsp. At the same time, melt the butter in another pan and bring to a boil.

*3* With the machine running, add the boiling vinegar then most but not all of the butter in a slow, steady stream through the top of the machine or through the feeder tube, then mix well.

*4* Taste the sauce—if it is too sharp, add a little more butter—it should be slightly piquant, almost thick enough to hold its shape.

*5* Turn into a warmed serving dish. Serve warm rather than hot. It is excellent with fish in particular but it is also good with asparagus, broccoli or poached eggs.

——— VARIATION ———

**Mousseline Sauce**
Stir 1–2 Tbsp heavy cream into the sauce before serving.

# QUICK TOMATO SAUCE

*Makes about 2 cups*

14-oz can tomatoes

1 tsp tomato paste

1 small onion, skinned and chopped

1 clove garlic, skinned and crushed (optional)

pinch of dried basil

pinch of sugar

freshly ground pepper

1 Tbsp vegetable oil

*1* Put all the ingredients in a blender or food processor and blend until smooth.

*2* Heat in a saucepan for 10–15 minutes until slightly thickened. Serve on pasta or use in prepared dishes.

# BARBECUE SAUCE

*Makes about 2 cups*

1 medium onion, skinned and chopped or 2 Tbsp dried onions

4 Tbsp cider vinegar

7 Tbsp brown sugar

1 tsp mustard powder

2 Tbsp Worcestershire sauce

⅔ cup ketchup

1¼ cups water

salt and freshly ground pepper

1 tsp lemon juice

*1* Put all ingredients in a pan. Bring to a boil and simmer gently for 15 minutes, stirring occasionally, until slightly thickened.

*2* Strain through a sieve. Heat in a saucepan before serving with sausages, hamburgers or chops.

# PIMENTO AND PAPRIKA SAUCE

*Makes 2 cups*

3 Tbsp butter

1 Tbsp paprika

3 Tbsp flour

2 cups stock

salt and freshly ground pepper

1 tsp lemon juice

2 Tbsp red wine

4-oz jar pimento, drained and thinly sliced

*1* Melt the butter in a saucepan, stir in the paprika and flour and cook gently for 2 minutes.

*2* Remove the pan from the heat and gradually stir in the stock, beating well after each addition.

*3* Bring to a boil and continue to cook, stirring until the sauce thickens. Simmer for 5 minutes.

*4* Season. Add lemon juice, red wine and pimentos. Reheat and check for seasoning. Serve with cauliflower, celeriac and zucchini.

# SWEET AND SOUR SAUCE

*Makes about 2 cups*

7 Tbsp sugar

4 Tbsp cider vinegar

3 Tbsp soy sauce

2 Tbsp cornstarch

1¼ cups water

1 green pepper, blanched and cut into thin strips

½ lb tomatoes, skinned and quartered

11-oz can crushed pineapple

*1* Put the sugar, vinegar and soy sauce in a saucepan. Blend the cornstarch with the water and add to the pan. Bring to a boil, stirring; simmer gently for 5 minutes. Add the remaining ingredients and simmer for another 5 minutes.

# STOCKS AND FLAVORINGS

Stocks are the basis of good soups. They are easy to make and freeze extremely well. Here are recipes for meat, fish and vegetable stocks.

## BROWN BEEF STOCK

*Makes about 6 cups*

| |
|---|
| 1 lb shin of beef, cut into pieces |
| 1 lb beef bones, cracked |
| bouquet garni |
| 1 onion, skinned and sliced |
| 1 carrot, peeled and sliced |
| 1 stick celery, washed, trimmed and sliced |
| 6 black peppercorns |

*1* Put the bones, meat and vegetables on a roasting pan and brown in the oven at 400°F for 30–40 minutes, stirring frequently.

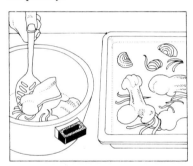

*2* With a slotted spoon, transfer to a large pan, cover with 7 cups cold water and add the peppercorns. Bring to a boil. With a slotted spoon, skim off any scum that forms. Cover and simmer for 5–6 hours. Strain the stock into a bowl and leave to cool.

*3* When cold, lift off any fat that has risen to the surface of the stock. Cover and chill in the refrigerator. Beef stock will keep for several weeks in the refrigerator if brought to a boil and boiled for 10 minutes every 3–4 days. It can be frozen for up to 6 months.

---
VARIATIONS
---

## BROWN VEAL STOCK

Substitute **2 lb veal bones** for the shin of beef and bones, and continue as per basic recipe, adding **1 Tbsp tomato paste**, if desired.

## BROWN LAMB STOCK

Substitute **2 lb scraps of lamb** (raw or cooked) including at least **1 lb lamb bones**. Continue as per basic recipe, adding **1 Tbsp tomato paste**, if desired.

---

## WHITE STOCK

*Makes about 7½ cups*

| |
|---|
| 2 lb knuckle of veal, chopped |
| juice of ½ a lemon |
| 1 onion, skinned and sliced |
| 2 carrots, peeled and sliced |
| bouquet garni |
| 6 black peppercorns |

*1* Put the bones in a large pan, add 2½ quarts cold water and lemon juice and bring to a boil. With a slotted spoon, skim off any scum that forms.

*2* Add the vegetables, bouquet garni and peppercorns and bring back to a boil. Half cover and simmer for 5–6 hours. Strain the stock and leave to cool.

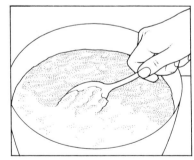

*3* When cold, lift off any fat that has risen to the surface of the stock. Cover and refrigerate. Refrigerated it will keep for 2–3 weeks if it is boiled for 10 minutes every 2–3 days. It can be frozen for up to 6 months.

## LAMB STOCK

*Makes about 6 cups*

| |
|---|
| 2 lb lamb scraps, cut into pieces |
| 1 lb lamb bones, chopped |
| 1 onion, skinned and sliced |
| 1 carrot, peeled and sliced |
| 1 celery stick, trimmed and sliced |
| 1 Tbsp tomato paste (optional) |
| 1 bouquet garni |
| 6 black peppercorns |

*1* Put the meat, bones and vegetables in a roasting pan. Brown in the oven at 400°F for 30–40 minutes, stirring frequently.

*2* With a slotted spoon, transfer to a large saucepan. Cover with 7½ cups cold water, add the tomato paste, if desired, the bouquet garni and peppercorns. Bring to a boil.

*3* Skim off any scum that forms with a slotted spoon. Half cover the pan and simmer very gently for 5–6 hours.

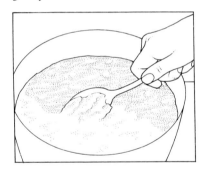

*4* Strain the stock into a bowl. Leave until cold, then lift off any fat that has risen and set on the surface.

*5* Cover and chill until required. Store for up to 4 days. It can be kept for longer but should then be boiled for at least 10 minutes every day.

# CHICKEN STOCK

*Makes 5–6 cups*

carcass and bones of a cooked or
   raw chicken and any chicken
   scraps

1 onion, skinned and sliced

1 carrot, peeled and sliced

1 celery stick, trimmed and sliced

6 black peppercorns

bouquet garni

*1* Break down the carcass and
bones of the chicken, and make
sure to include any skin and
chicken scraps.

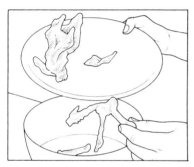

*2* Put in a large pan with
6–7 cups cold water, the
onion, carrot, celery, peppercorns
and bouquet garni and bring to a
boil.

*3* With a slotted spoon, skim off
any scum that forms. Half
cover and simmer for 3 hours.

*4* Strain the stock into a bowl
and leave to cool. When cold,
lift off any fat that has risen to the
surface of the stock. Cover and
chill in the refrigerator. Chicken
stock will keep in the refrigerator
for 2–3 weeks if brought to a boil
and boiled for 10 minutes every
2 days. It can be frozen for up to
6 months.

# FISH STOCK

*Makes about 4 cups*

1 lb fish heads, bones and
   trimmings

6 white peppercorns

bouquet garni

1 onion, skinned and sliced

*1* Put the fish bones in a large
pan with the peppercorns,
bouquet garni and onion. Cover
with 4 cups cold water. Bring to a
boil.

*2* With a slotted spoon, skim off
any scum that forms.

*3* Lower the heat, cover and
simmer for no longer than 20
minutes.

*4* Strain the stock into a bowl.
Use on the same day, or store
in a covered container in the
refrigerator for no longer than
2 days, thereafter it must be
brought to a boil and boiled for 10
minutes every 2 days if it is to be
kept longer. It will keep in this
manner for 2–3 weeks as long as it
is boiled every 2 days. It can be
frozen for up to 6 months. Use for
fish soups.

# VEGETABLE STOCK

*Makes about 5 cups*

2 Tbsp vegetable oil

1 medium onion, skinned and
   finely chopped

1 tsp sugar

1 medium carrot, washed and
   diced

$\frac{1}{8}$ lb (about $\frac{1}{2}$ cup) turnip, washed
   and diced

$\frac{1}{8}$ lb (about $\frac{1}{2}$ cup) parsnip, washed
   and diced

4 celery sticks, roughly chopped

celery tops

cabbage leaves

mushroom peelings

tomato skins

potato peelings

onion skins (optional)

bouquet garni

6 whole black peppercorns

*1* Heat the oil in a large pan, add
the onion and fry gently for
5 minutes until soft. Stir in the
sugar and continue to cook for
another 5 minutes, stirring
occasionally until beginning to
caramelize.

*2* Add the vegetables to the pan
with any trimmings, outer
leaves or peelings available.

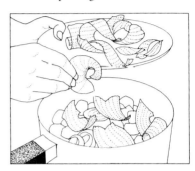

*3* If a dark brown colored stock
is required, add onion skins.
Cover the vegetables with $7\frac{1}{2}$ cups
cold water and add the bouquet
garni and peppercorns. Bring to a
boil.

*4* Half cover and simmer for $1\frac{1}{2}$
hours, skimming occasionally
with a slotted spoon.

*5* Strain and leave to cool. Cover
and refrigerate for up to
2 days. Freeze for up to 6 months.

# MEAT, CHICKEN OR FISH GLAZE

*Makes about $\frac{2}{3}$ cup*

1 gallon good stock

*1* Skim the stock and place it in a
heavy saucepan. Bring to a boil
and continue boiling for several
hours, until the stock is reduced
and is glazelike.

*2* Leave to cool then pour into a
bowl, cover and store in the
refrigerator. It will keep for several
months.

*3* To reconstitute, add 1 tsp
glaze to each $2\frac{1}{2}$ cups water.

# HORS D'OEUVRES

When you are in a rush and you are entertaining, it is good to have a few hors d'oeuvres up your sleeve that are easy and quick to prepare. Here are a few suggestions. Simple garnishes of lemon and cucumber twists or sprigs of parsley finish them off well.

## QUICK HUMMUS

*Serves 8*

two 14-oz cans chick peas

juice of 2 large lemons

$\frac{2}{3}$ cup tahini (paste of finely ground sesame seeds)

4 Tbsp olive oil

1–2 garlic cloves, crushed

salt and freshly ground pepper

black olives and chopped fresh parsley, to garnish

warm pita bread, to serve

*1* Put the chick peas in a blender or food processor, reserving a few for garnish, and gradually add the reserved liquid and the lemon juice, blending well after each addition in order to form a smooth purée.

*2* Add the tahini paste, oil (reserving 2 tsp) and garlic and salt and pepper to taste. Blend again until smooth.

*3* Spoon into a serving dish and sprinkle with the reserved oil. Garnish with the reserved chick peas, and the olives and chopped parsley.
   Serve with warm pita bread.

## AVOCADO RAMEKINS

*Serves 4*

1 large ripe avocado

finely grated rind and juice of 1 lemon

1 cup cottage cheese

4 Tbsp yogurt

1 small garlic clove, skinned and crushed

salt and freshly ground pepper

sprigs of parsley, to garnish

*1* Halve, pit and peel the avocado. Put the flesh in a bowl and mash with a fork, then add the cottage cheese, yogurt, garlic and salt and pepper to taste. Blend until smooth.

*2* Spoon the mixture into 4 ramekins and chill in the refrigerator for about 30 minutes.

*3* Garnish each dish with a sprig of parsley and serve immediately.
   Serve with slices of wholewheat toast.

## MARINATED MUSHROOMS

*Serves 4–6*

1 lb small button mushrooms, wiped

$\frac{2}{3}$ cup vinaigrette

chopped fresh parsley, to garnish

*1* Place the mushrooms in a bowl and pour over the vinaigrette. Cover and marinate in the refrigerator for 6–8 hours, stirring occasionally.

*2* Serve chilled, in individual shallow dishes, sprinkled with chopped parsley.
   Serve with wholewheat rolls and butter, or garlic bread.

## SMOKED MACKEREL PÂTÉ

*Serves 4*

$\frac{3}{4}$ lb smoked mackerel fillets

$\frac{1}{4}$ cup butter, softened

4 Tbsp mayonnaise

finely grated rind and juice of $\frac{1}{2}$ lemon

1 tsp snipped chives

pinch of ground mace or nutmeg

freshly ground pepper

parsley sprigs and lemon slices, to garnish

*1* Remove the skin and any bones from the mackerel fillets. Place the flesh in a bowl and add the butter, mayonnaise, lemon rind and juice, chives, mace or nutmeg and pepper to taste. Mix well together.

*2* Divide the pâté equally between 4 ramekins and garnish with parsley sprigs and lemon slices. Chill in the refrigerator for 1 hour before serving.
   Serve with slices of hot toast or Melba toast.

## TUNA PÂTÉ

*Serves 8*

$\frac{3}{4}$ cup butter, softened

7-oz can tuna fish, drained and mashed

1 tsp anchovy paste

a squeeze of lemon juice

salt and freshly ground pepper

*1* Put the butter in a bowl and beat until creamy. Add the tuna fish and anchovy paste and beat well to mix.

*2* Add lemon juice and salt and pepper to taste. Turn into a serving bowl and chill in the refrigerator for 1 hour before serving.
   Serve with wholewheat toast or crispbreads.

# *Vegetables and Salads*

## CHESTNUT AND BRUSSELS SPROUT SAUTÉ

*Serves 8*

2 lb fresh chestnuts or 1 lb 15-oz can whole chestnuts

2½ cups chicken stock

1½ lb Brussels sprouts

salt and freshly ground pepper

1 lb medium onions, skinned

8 oz celery, trimmed

½ cup butter

finely grated rind of 1 lemon

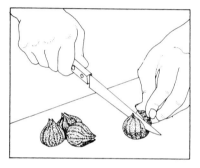

*1* If using fresh chestnuts, snip the brown outer skins, or nick with a sharp knife. Place in boiling water for 3–5 minutes.

*2* Lift the chestnuts out a few at a time, then peel off both the brown and inner skins. Put the nuts in a saucepan, cover with the stock and simmer for 40–45 minutes until tender. Drain well.

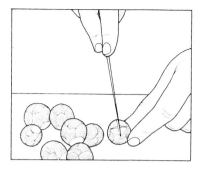

*3* Meanwhile, trim off the sprouts and pull off any damaged or discolored outer leaves. With a sharp knife, make a cross in the stalk end of each one.

*4* Cook the sprouts in boiling salted water for 3–4 minutes only; drain well.

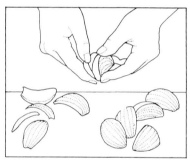

*5* Quarter the onions and separate out the layers. Cut the celery into 1-inch pieces.

*6* Melt the butter in a large sauté or frying pan. Add the onions and celery with the lemon rind and sauté for 2–3 minutes until softened. Add the cooked chestnuts, Brussels sprouts and salt and pepper to taste. Sauté for a further 1–2 minutes until heated through. Serve immediately.

## BAKED PARSNIPS IN ORANGE

*Serves 4*

1 lb parsnips, peeled

⅔ cup unsweetened orange juice

¼ cup butter

salt and freshly ground pepper

1 Tbsp light brown sugar

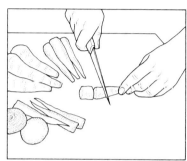

*1* Cut the parsnips into bite-sized pieces, removing the woody core if they are old and large.

*2* Place the parsnips and orange juice in a pan, bring to a boil and simmer gently for 5 minutes.

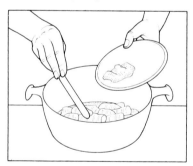

*3* Turn into a greased casserole, dot with butter, season and sprinkle with the sugar.

*4* Cover and cook in the oven at 375°F for 1 hour until tender.

## PARSNIP AND CARROT AU GRATIN

*Serves 4–6*

1 lb parsnips, peeled

1 lb carrots, peeled

2½ cups chicken stock

salt and freshly ground pepper

2 Tbsp butter

1 cup fresh breadcrumbs

2 Tbsp chopped fresh parsley, to garnish

*1* Chop the parsnips and carrots coarsely and place in a saucepan with the stock and salt and pepper to taste. Bring to a boil, cover and simmer gently for 15–20 minutes until well cooked. Drain and cool slightly.

*2* Purée the vegetables in a blender or rub through a sieve. Add the butter and turn into a flameproof dish. Sprinkle the breadcrumbs over the surface and cook under a hot broiler until golden brown. Garnish with parsley and serve hot.

## DIJON POTATOES

*Serves 6*

2 lb potatoes, peeled

2 large onions, skinned

2 Tbsp snipped chives

2 Tbsp Dijon mustard

1¼ cups chicken stock

salt and freshly ground pepper

2 Tbsp butter

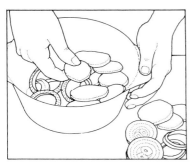

*1* Slice the potatoes and onion thinly and arrange in alternate layers in a casserole dish. Sprinkle each layer with the chives and end with a potato layer.

*2* Blend the mustard and stock together with salt and pepper to taste. Pour over the potatoes.

*3* Melt the butter in a pan and brush over the top. Cover and bake in the oven at 350°F for 2 hours.

*4* Remove the lid 30 minutes before the end of the cooking time to brown the top. Serve hot.

## GOLDEN OVEN-FRIED POTATOES

*Serves 6*

2½ lb medium potatoes (about 6)

salt and freshly ground pepper

4 Tbsp vegetable oil

2 Tbsp butter

*1* Peel the potatoes, place in a large saucepan and cover with cold water. Add a good pinch of salt and bring to a boil. Cover and simmer for 8–10 minutes only, then drain.

*2* Cut the potatoes into ¼–½ inch slices and score the surfaces in both directions with a sharp-pronged fork.

*3* Heat the oil and butter in a roasting pan measuring about 12 × 9 inches. Add the potato slices, turn them over in the fat, then sprinkle with salt and pepper to taste.

*4* Bake the potatoes in the oven at 400°F for about 1¼ hours, turning once. Drain off the fat before serving.

## POTATO AND CARROT RÖSTI

*Serves 2*

1 lb even-sized potatoes

salt and freshly ground pepper

½ lb carrots, peeled

1 Tbsp snipped chives

¼ cup butter or margarine

*1* Scrub the potatoes and place in a large saucepan. Cover with cold water, add a good pinch of salt and bring to a boil. Cover and simmer for 7 minutes only.

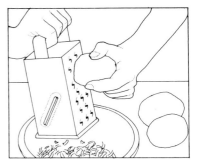

*2* Drain the potatoes well, remove the skins and grate the flesh into a bowl.

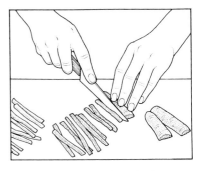

*3* Cut the carrots lengthwise, into fine, stumpy matchsticks. Blanch in boiling salted water for 5 minutes. Drain well.

*4* Combine the carrots with the potato, chives and plenty of salt and pepper.

*5* Melt the butter in a frying pan, add the potato mixture and form into a 6-inch cake. Fry for 7 minutes a side.

## DUCHESSE POTATOES

*Serves 6*

2 lb floury potatoes

salt and freshly ground pepper

$\frac{1}{4}$ cup butter or margarine

pinch of grated nutmeg

2 eggs, beaten

*1* Cook the potatoes in boiling salted water for 15 minutes or until just tender. Drain and mash. Beat in butter with nutmeg and salt and pepper. Gradually beat in eggs, reserving a little for glazing.

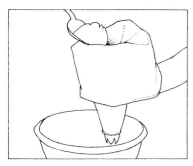

*2* Cool the potato mixture then spoon into a piping bag fitted with a large star nozzle. Pipe the mixture in pyramids onto a greased baking sheet.

*3* Brush carefully with the remaining egg to which a pinch of salt has been added. bake in the oven at 400°F for about 25 minutes or until golden brown and set.

## ROAST POTATOES

*Serves 4*

$1\frac{1}{2}$–2 lb floury potatoes, peeled

2 Tbsp lard or dripping

*1* Cut the potatoes into even-sized pieces, place them in boiled salted water. Cook for 2–3 minutes and drain.

*2* Heat lard in a roasting pan in the oven. Add the potatoes, baste with the fat and cook at 425°F for 45 minutes or until golden brown.

## *SALADS*

Whether cooked or raw, salads make a welcome contribution to any meal.

## POTATO SALAD

*Serves 6*

2 lb waxy potatoes

4 spring onions, trimmed and chopped

salt and freshly ground pepper

$\frac{2}{3}$ cup mayonnaise

snipped fresh chives, to garnish

*1* Quarter any large potatoes and put the potatoes in boiling salted water, and cook for about 15 minutes or until tender. Drain, remove the skins and leave until quite cold.

*2* Cut the potatoes into small dices and place in a bowl. Add the onions to the potatoes and season with salt and pepper.

*3* Stir the mayonnaise into the potatoes and toss gently. Leave the salad to stand for at least 1 hour so that the flavors can blend. To serve, sprinkle with snipped chives.

## WALDORF SALAD

*Serves 4*

1 lb eating apples

juice of 1 lemon

1 tsp sugar

$\frac{2}{3}$ cup mayonnaise

$\frac{1}{2}$ bunch celery, trimmed and sliced

$\frac{1}{2}$ cup walnuts, chopped

1 lettuce

few walnut halves, to garnish (optional)

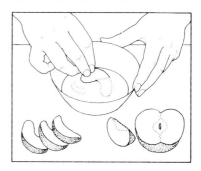

*1* Core the apples, slice one and dice the rest. Dip the slices in a little of the lemon juice to prevent discoloration of the fruit.

*2* Toss the diced apples in the remaining lemon juice, the sugar and 1 Tbsp mayonnaise. Leave to stand for about 30 minutes.

*3* Just before serving, add the sliced celery, chopped walnuts and the remaining mayonnaise. Toss the ingredients together.

*4* Serve in a bowl lined with lettuce leaves, and garnish with the apple slices and a few walnut halves, if desired.

## CAESAR SALAD

*Serves 4*

1 large garlic clove, skinned and
 crushed

$\frac{2}{3}$ cup olive oil

2 slices stale white bread

1 lettuce

salt and freshly ground pepper

2 Tbsp lemon juice

$\frac{1}{4}$ cup grated Parmesan cheese

8 anchovy fillets, drained and
 chopped

1 egg

*1* Add the garlic to the oil and
 leave to stand for 30 minutes.
Cut the stale white bread into
$\frac{1}{4}$-inch dices.

*2* Heat a little of the garlic oil in
 a frying pan and fry the bread
until golden brown on all sides.
Remove with a slotted spoon and
drain on paper towels.

*3* Carefully wash the lettuce in
 cold running water. Drain it
well and pat dry with paper
towels.

*4* Tear into bite-sized pieces and
 place in a salad bowl. Pour
over the remaining garlic oil and
toss until the leaves are completely
coated. Season well with salt and
pepper to taste.

*5* Add the lemon juice, cheese,
 anchovies and croûtons and
toss well to mix.

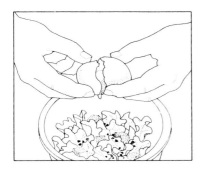

*6* Boil the egg for 1 minute only,
 crack into the salad and give
the salad a final toss. Serve
immediately.

## SALADE NIÇOISE
### *(FRENCH TUNA AND VEGETABLE SALAD)*

*Serves 4*

7-oz can tuna fish, drained

8 oz tomatoes, quartered

$\frac{1}{3}$ cup black olives, pitted

$\frac{1}{2}$ small cucumber, thinly sliced

8 oz cooked French beans

2 hard-boiled eggs, shelled and
 quartered

1 Tbsp chopped fresh parsley

1 Tbsp chopped fresh basil

$\frac{1}{3}$ cup garlic vinaigrette

8 anchovy fillets, drained and
 halved

French bread, to serve

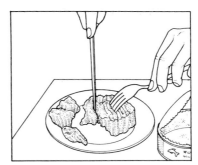

*1* Flake the canned tuna into
 fairly large chunks. Arrange
the tuna chunks in a salad bowl
with the tomatoes, olives, slices of
cucumber, beans and eggs.

*2* Add the parsely and basil to
 the garlic vinaigrette, mix well
and pour dressing over salad.

*3* Arrange the anchovy fillets in a
 lattice pattern over the salad
and allow to stand for 30 minutes
before serving. Serve with crusty
French bread.

## GREEN SALAD

Use 2 or more green salad
 ingredients such as lettuce,
 mustard and cress, watercress,
 endive, chicory, peppers,
 cucumber, cabbage, etc.

*1* Wash and drain the
 ingredients well. Just before
serving, toss lightly in a bowl with
French dressing, adding a little
finely chopped onion if desired.

*2* Sprinkle with chopped fresh
 parsley, chives, mint, tarragon
or other herbs, as available.

## TOMATO SALAD

*Serves 6*

$1\frac{1}{2}$ lb ripe tomatoes, skinned

9 Tbsp olive oil

3 Tbsp wine vinegar

1 small garlic clove, crushed

2 Tbsp chopped fresh parsley

salt and freshly ground pepper

*1* Slice the tomatoes thinly and
 arrange on 6 individual serving
plates. Put the oil, vinegar, garlic,
parsley and salt and pepper in a
bowl or screw-topped jar and
whisk or shake well together.
Spoon over the tomatoes.

*2* Cover the plates tightly with
 plastic wrap and chill in the
refrigerator for about 2 hours.

# DUMPLINGS AND BREADS

Soups can be set off by the garnishes in them, like dumplings and croûtons. Bread can be made in many shapes and can be varied by different flavorings. They can be fried or toasted, be white or wholewheat, plain or herbed. Here are a few suggestions.

## HERB DUMPLINGS

*Makes 24 small dumplings*

$\frac{3}{4}$ **cup self-rising flour**
$\frac{1}{2}$ **cup fine breadcrumbs**
$\frac{1}{3}-\frac{1}{2}$ **cup shredded suet**
**salt and freshly ground pepper**
**1 Tbsp chopped fresh parsley**
**1 Tbsp chopped fresh herbs**
   **(thyme, marjoram etc.) or 1 tsp**
   **dried mixed herbs**
**1 egg, beaten (optional)**
**milk, to mix**

*1* Put the flour and breadcrumbs in a bowl. Add the shredded suet and mix together. Add the parsley, herbs and salt and pepper. Stir in the egg (if using) and enough milk to give a soft dough. Mix lightly.

*2* Form the dough into 24 small dumplings and flour these lightly. Add the dumplings to the boiling soup 20–30 minutes before serving.

## MELBA TOAST

*Serves 4*

**4 slices of thick cut ready-sliced**
   **bread, white or wholewheat**

*1* Preheat the broiler and toast the bread on both sides until golden brown.

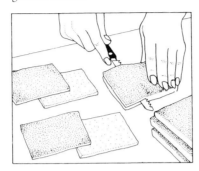

*2* Using a serrated knife, cut off the crusts and slide the knife between the toasted edges to split the bread.

*3* Cut each piece in half diagonally. Place on a baking sheet and bake in the oven at 300°F for 15–20 minutes until curled dry and brittle.
   Homemade Melba toast has the edge on the bought packaged variety. It is at its nicest served while still a little warm, in a basket or on a napkin-lined plate. If it is made ahead, store it in an airtight container, then refresh it for a short time in the oven.

## CHEESE CROÛTES

*Makes 4*

**4 slices of French bread**
**4 oz Cheddar cheese, grated**

*1* Broil the slices of bread on one side only.

*2* Turn the slices over, sprinkle the cheese on top and broil until golden brown.

*3* Float the croûtes on top of soup just before serving.

## CROÛTONS

*Serves 4*

**2 slices of stale bread**
**oil or butter and oil**

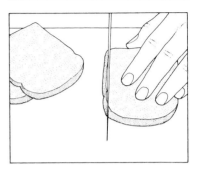

*1* Trim the crusts off the bread slices and cut them into $\frac{1}{4}-\frac{1}{2}$ inch cubes.

*2* Heat at least $\frac{1}{4}$ inch of oil or butter and oil in a heavy-based frying pan and fry the bread cubes until crisp and golden. Keep stirring the croûtons while they are frying.

*3* Lift the croûtons out of the pan all at once and drain on paper towels.
   Croûtons should be passed around in a separate bowl to be added to each bowl of soup at the last moment; otherwise they may get soggy.

———— VARIATIONS ————

Use **bacon fat** or **lard** for frying instead of oil or butter.
   Add a skinned **clove of garlic** to the fat and remove when the croûtons are done.

## GARLIC BREAD

*Makes 1 loaf*

$\frac{1}{2}$ cup butter, softened
2 garlic cloves, skinned
$\frac{1}{4}$ tsp salt
freshly ground pepper
1 long French loaf

*1* Beat the butter until smooth. Crush the garlic with the salt to a smooth paste and beat into the butter with pepper to taste.

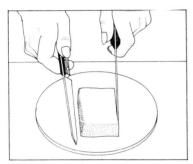

*2* Shape the garlic butter into a neat block and chill in the refrigerator for 15 minutes before using.

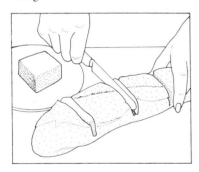

*3* Partially cut through a French loaf at 2-inch intervals. Place a pat of garlic butter in each incision.

*4* Wrap the whole loaf in foil and bake in the oven at 350°F for 15–20 minutes, until the butter has melted and flavored the bread. Serve hot.

## BABY LOAVES WITH TARRAGON BUTTER

*Makes 4*

$\frac{3}{4}$ cup butter, softened
2 Tbsp chopped fresh tarragon or 2 tsp dried
squeeze of lemon juice
4 small individual wholewheat loaves

*1* Put the butter in a bowl with the tarragon and lemon juice. Beat together until well combined.

*2* Slash the loaves diagonally 4 or 5 times and spread the cut surfaces generously with the tarragon butter.

*3* Place the loaves on a baking sheet and cover loosely with foil. Warm them through in the oven at 350°F for about 10 minutes. Serve immediately.

## QUICK WHOLEWHEAT ROLLS

*Makes 12*

1 cake fresh yeast or 2 tsp dried
2 tsp sugar
1$\frac{1}{2}$ cups white bread flour
1$\frac{1}{2}$ cups wholewheat flour
2 tsp salt
1 Tbsp lard
cracked wheat, for the topping

*1* Blend in the yeast with 1 tsp sugar and 1$\frac{1}{4}$ cups tepid water and leave in a warm place to froth.

*2* Mix both flours together in a bowl with the salt and the remaining 1 tsp sugar. Rub in the fat.

*3* Add the yeast mixture and mix to a soft dough. Turn onto a lightly floured surface and knead for about 2 minutes until smooth.

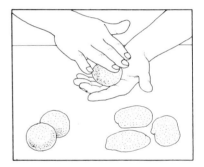

*4* Divide the dough into 12 equal pieces and roll into rounds. Place on a greased baking sheet, brush with water and sprinkle the tops with cracked wheat.

*5* Cover the rolls with a clean, damp tea towel and leave to rise in a warm place for about 1 hour or until doubled in size.

*6* Bake the rolls in the oven at 450°F for 15–20 minutes or until golden brown. Cool on a wire rack.

## POPPY-SEED ROLLS

*Makes 12*

3 cups white bread flour
2 tsp salt
2 Tbsp butter
1 cake fresh yeast or 2 tsp dried
$1\frac{1}{4}$ cups tepid milk and water
  mixed
1 tsp sugar
1 egg, beaten, to glaze
poppy seeds, for the topping

*1* Sift the flour and salt into a bowl and rub in the butter. Blend the yeast with the warmed milk and water mixture and sugar. Stir into the flour and mix to a soft dough.

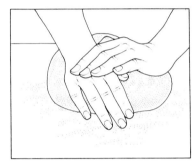

*2* Turn the dough onto a lightly floured surface and knead for about 10 minutes until smooth.

*3* Cover the dough with a clean, damp tea towel and leave to rise in a warm place for about 1 hour or until doubled in size.

*4* Turn the dough onto a floured surface and knead for 2–3 minutes. Divide into 12 equal pieces. Roll each piece into a sausage shape about 8 inches in length.

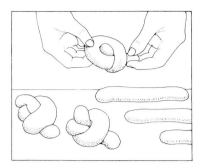

*5* Tie the pieces of dough in loose knots. Place the knots on a greased baking sheet and cover with a clean damp tea towel. Leave to prove in a warm place for 15–20 minutes.

*6* Brush the knots with the beaten egg, then sprinkle with the poppy seeds. Bake in the oven at 425°F for 15–20 minutes. Cool on a wire rack.

## POTATO ROLLS

*Makes 8*

$\frac{1}{4}$ cup butter or margarine
1 lb potatoes, cooked and mashed
2 cakes fresh yeast
$\frac{2}{3}$ cup tepid milk
$4\frac{1}{2}$ cups white bread flour
1 Tbsp salt
2 cups tepid water

*1* Grease two baking sheets. Add the fat to the potatoes while they are still warm and blend well. Mix the yeast with the milk and stir into the potatoes. Sift the flour and salt into a bowl and add the potato mixture and water and mix to a smooth dough. Knead for 5 minutes. Cover with a clean damp tea towel and leave to rise in a warm place for about 1 hour until doubled in size.

*2* Turn onto a floured surface and knead for 10 minutes. Divide the dough into 8 equal pieces and shape into rolls. Place on the baking sheets and bake in the oven at 375°F for 25–30 minutes until golden brown. Cool on a wire rack.

## BREADSTICKS

*Makes about 24*

$4\frac{1}{2}$ cups white bread flour
2 tsp salt
$1\frac{1}{2}$ cakes fresh yeast
2 tsp sugar
$1\frac{3}{4}$ cups tepid milk
$\frac{1}{4}$ cup butter, melted

*1* Grease a large baking sheet. Sift the flour and salt into a warmed bowl. Blend the yeast with the sugar and half the tepid milk. Make a well in the center of the flour and pour in the yeast mixture. Sprinkle with flour and leave in a warm place for 15 minutes, until spongy. Add the remaining milk and melted butter and mix to a firm dough.

*2* Turn onto a lightly floured surface and knead for 5 minutes until smooth. Cover with a clean damp tea towel and leave to rise for 15–20 minutes.

*3* Turn onto a lightly floured surface and knead for 2–3 minutes. Divide the dough into 24 small pieces and roll into sticks 6–8 inches long and as thick as a finger. Place on the baking sheet, cover with a clean damp tea towel and leave to prove in a warm place for 15–20 minutes.

*4* Bake in the oven at 400°F for 10 minutes then reduce the oven temperature to 350°F for a further 20–25 minutes. For salted bread sticks, brush over with milk and water before baking and sprinkle with crushed rock salt. Cool on a wire rack.

## ANCHOVY TWISTERS

**8-oz packet frozen puff pastry, thawed**

**beaten egg, to glaze**

**two 1¾-oz cans anchovies**

*1* Roll out the pastry to an 8-inch square. Glaze it with beaten egg and cut it into ¾-inch wide strips.

*2* Lay the drained anchovies in the center of each strip, pressing lightly to make them stick.

*3* Lightly grease an 11-inch swiss-roll tin. Lift the strips and twist them along their length several times. Lay them across the short side of the tin and attach the edges over the rim (this stops untwisting). Repeat with each strip.

*4* At this stage you can leave the twisters loosely covered in a cool place. Bake them in the oven at 425°F for about 12 minutes. Cool. Halve to serve.

## MUSTARD BAKE-UPS

If it is a little on the thick side, roll out the sliced bread once or twice; this makes the texture more pliable. Before baking, store wrapped in the fridge for a couple of days, or in the freezer for up to a month.

*Serves 4*

**4 thin slices white bread**

**½ cup butter**

**2 tsp wholegrain mustard**

*1* Generously butter the bread. Spread it with the mustard, and cut off the crusts. Roll up each slice inside waxed paper and refrigerate for at least 1 hour to firm up.

*2* Remove paper, halve each roll lengthwise and place seam-side down on baking sheets. Bake in the oven at 425°F for about 12 minutes, until golden and crisp. Serve hot.

## SHAPED MILK ROLLS

*Makes 8*

**1 cake fresh yeast**

**1 tsp sugar**

**⅔ cup tepid milk**

**1½ cups white bread flour**

**1 tsp salt**

**2 Tbsp block margarine or lard**

**beaten egg, to glaze**

*1* Grease a baking sheet. In a small bowl cream together the yeast, sugar and tepid milk. Sift the flour and salt into a bowl and rub in the fat. Add the yeast liquid to form a fairly soft dough, adding a little more milk if necessary.

*2* Turn onto a lightly floured surface and knead the dough for 10 minutes until smooth. Cover with a clean damp tea towel and leave to rise in a warm place for about 45 minutes until doubled in size.

*3* Knead on a lightly floured surface, divide into 8 equal pieces and shape into small braids, twists, loaves, knots, trefoils, rounds or rings. Place on the greased baking sheet, cover with a clean damp tea towel and leave to prove for 15–20 minutes.

*4* Glaze with beaten egg and bake in the oven at 425°F for 15 minutes until golden brown. Cool on a wire rack.

### ROLL SHAPES

Rolls can be made in any of the traditional bread shapes by dividing the basic white dough into small egg-sized pieces and shaping in the following way.

**Knots** Shape each piece of dough into a thin roll and tie into a knot.

**Round** Place the pieces on a very lightly floured board and roll each into a ball. To do this, hold the hand flat almost at table level and move it round in a circular motion, gradually lifting the palm to get a good round shape.

**Rings** Make a thin roll with each piece of dough and bend it around to form a ring; dampen the ends and mold them together.

**Trefoil** Divide each piece of dough into three pieces and roll each into a ball. Place the three balls grouped together.

**Twist** Divide each piece of dough into two and shape into thin rolls. Hold one end of the two pieces of dough together and twist. Dampen the ends and tuck under.

## PIQUANT PALMIERS

Really quick to make, they look as though you've spent hours producing them.

**½ lb packet frozen puff pastry, thawed**

**4 Tbsp tomato paste**

**freshly ground pepper**

*1* Roll out the pastry to an oblong about 12 × 10 inches. Lightly spread it with tomato paste, and season with the freshly ground pepper.

*2* Roll up from the two narrow edges so that the rolls meet in the center. Trim off the edges and slice into twelve pieces. Place cut-side down on greased baking sheets, leaving room to spread. Press down lightly with the heel of the hand to flatten a little.

*3* Bake in the oven at 425°F for about 12 minutes.

# SWEET SOUFFLÉS, PANCAKES AND DESSERT TOPPINGS

## SOUFFLÉS

Hot soufflés are based either on a sweet white sauce to which egg yolks and flavorings are added, or on a crème pâtissière, in which the egg yolks are already incorporated. Cold soufflés are usually based on fruit purées.

## HOT VANILLA SOUFFLÉ

*Serves 4–6*

| |
|---|
| $\frac{1}{3}$ cup sugar |
| 4 eggs, separated |
| 4 Tbsp all-purpose flour |
| $1\frac{1}{3}$ cups milk |
| $\frac{1}{2}$ tsp vanilla extract |
| confectioners sugar (optional) |

*1* Butter a 7 inch, 2-quart capacity soufflé dish. Cream the sugar with one whole egg and one yolk until pale cream in color. Stir in the flour. Pour on the milk and mix until smooth.

*2* Pour the mixture into a saucepan and bring to boiling point, stirring, and simmer for 2 minutes. Cool slightly. Beat in remaining yolks and extract.

*3* Whisk the egg whites until stiff then fold into the mixture. Pour into the prepared soufflé dish and bake in the oven at 350°F for about 45 minutes until well risen, firm to the touch and pale golden. Serve at once.

## STRAWBERRY SOUFFLÉ

*Serves 4–6*

| |
|---|
| $\frac{3}{4}$ lb strawberries |
| 2 Tbsp powdered gelatine |
| 4 Tbsp sugar |
| 4 tsp lemon juice |
| 3 egg whites |
| pinch of salt |
| $\frac{3}{4}$ cup cream |

*1* Reserve six strawberries for decoration. Purée the remainder in a blender.

*2* Put gelatine and 1 Tbsp sugar in a saucepan, add one third of purée and stir over gentle heat until gelatine dissolves.

*3* Remove from the heat, stir in the remaining purée and the lemon juice and pour into a bowl. Chill until the mixture mounds slightly when dropped from spoon.

*4* Prepare a paper collar (see page 48) for a 5-cup soufflé dish. Place dish on a baking sheet for easier handling.

*5* Whisk egg whites and salt until soft peaks form. Add remaining sugar a little at a time, whisking well, until stiff peaks form.

*6* Beat the chilled strawberry mixture in a mixer until fluffy. Whip cream until soft peaks form and combine with strawberry mixture. Carefully fold in egg whites.

*7* Spoon soufflé mixture into dish and smooth the top. Chill for 4 hours until set. Peel off the collar from dish. Decorate with reserved strawberries.

# CRÊPES

Crêpes are made with a batter of pouring consistency. Most batters will improve if they are left to rest in a cool place for at least 30 minutes before using; this will help make a lighter crêpe. If the crêpe mixture thickens after resting it can be thinned with a little milk. Crêpe batters made with a whisked egg white must be used straight away.

## CRÊPES

*Makes 8 crêpes*

| |
|---|
| $\frac{3}{4}$ cup all-purpose flour |
| pinch of salt |
| 1 egg |
| $1\frac{1}{3}$ cups milk |
| vegetable oil |

*1* Mix the flour and salt together, make a well in the center and break in the egg. Add half the liquid. Beat until smooth.

*2* Add the remaining liquid gradually. Beat until the ingredients are well mixed.

*3* Heat a little oil in a small frying pan running it around pan to coat sides. Raise handle side of pan slightly. Pour a little batter in from raised side, tilting pan to form an evenly round crêpe.

*4* Place over a moderate heat and cook until golden underneath, then turn with a palette knife and cook the other side. Slide the crêpe on to a plate lined with wax paper. Repeat.

## DESSERT TOPPINGS

### CRUMBLE TOPPING

*Serves 4–6*

| 1 cup plus 3 Tbsp flour |
| --- |
| $\frac{1}{3}$ cup margarine or butter |
| $\frac{1}{4}$ cup sugar |

Put the flour in a bowl, then rub in the fat with the fingertips until the mixture is the texture of fine crumbs. Stir in the sugar.

This mixture may be kept in the refrigerator for 3–4 days; it can also be frozen—pack in a plastic bag and freeze for up to 3 months. Use it as a topping for fruit crumbles and for single crust fruit pies.

—————— VARIATIONS ——————

Add 1 tsp **ground cinnamon, mixed spice** or **ginger** to the flour before rubbing in the fat.

Add 2 oz chopped **crystallized ginger** to the crumb mixture before using.

Add the finely **grated rind of 1 orange** or **lemon** to the crumb mixture before using.

Roughly crush 2 Tbsp **cornflakes** and add them to the rubbed-in mixture with **light brown sugar** in place of granulated sugar.

# SWEET BUTTERS AND SAUCES

## SWEET BUTTERS

### BRANDY BUTTER

*Makes 6–8 servings*

| $\frac{1}{2}$ cup butter, softened |
| --- |
| $1\frac{3}{4}$ cups confectioners sugar, sifted |
| $\frac{2}{3}$ cup sugar |
| 1 Tbsp milk |
| 1 Tbsp brandy |

*1* Beat the butter until pale and light. Gradually beat in the sugars, alternately with the milk and brandy. Continue beating until light and fluffy. Pile into a small dish and leave to harden before serving.

—————— VARIATIONS ——————

**Rum Butter** Use brown sugar instead of granulated sugar, replace the brandy with 3 Tbsp rum and add the grated rind of $\frac{1}{2}$ a lemon and a squeeze of lemon juice.

**Lemon or Orange Butter** Omit the milk and brandy and add the grated rind and juice of 1 lemon or a small orange.

## CHOCOLATE NUT BUTTER

| $\frac{1}{2}$ cup butter |
| --- |
| 2 tsp sugar |
| 1 Tbsp grated semisweet chocolate |
| 2 Tbsp chopped walnuts |

*1* Beat the butter until light and fluffy, then beat in the remaining ingredients.

## SWEET SAUCES

### SWEET WHITE SAUCE

| $1\frac{1}{2}$ Tbsp cornstarch |
| --- |
| $1\frac{1}{4}$ cups milk |
| $1\frac{1}{2}$ Tbsp sugar |

*1* Blend the cornstarch with 1–2 Tbsp of the milk to a smooth paste.

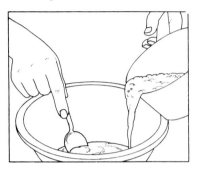

*2* Heat the remaining milk until boiling and add to mixture, stirring. Return to pan and bring to the boil, stirring. Cook for 1–2 minutes after the mixture has thickened to a glossy sauce. Add sugar to taste.

—————— VARIATIONS ——————

When adding extra liquid to the sauce make a thicker sauce by increasing the quantity of cornstarch to 2 Tbsp.

Flavor with any of the following when sauce has thickened:

1 tsp allspice
2 Tbsp jam
grated rind of $\frac{1}{2}$ an orange or lemon
1–2 Tbsp rum
1 egg yolk (reheat but do not boil)

### CHOCOLATE SAUCE

*Makes about $1\frac{1}{3}$ cups*

| 6 oz semisweet chocolate in pieces |
| --- |
| 1 Tbsp butter |
| 3 Tbsp milk |
| 3 Tbsp light corn syrup |

*1* Put the chocolate in a small bowl with the butter. Add the milk and syrup.

2 Stand the bowl over a pan of warm water and heat gently, stirring, until the chocolate has melted and the sauce is warm.

## FUDGE SAUCE

*Makes about 2 cups*

| 2 oz semisweet chocolate |
| 2 Tbsp butter |
| 4 Tbsp warm milk |
| 1½ cups brown sugar |
| 2 Tbsp light corn syrup |
| 1 tsp vanilla extract |

1 Break up the chocolate and put into a bowl standing over a saucepan of hot water. Add the butter. Leave until the chocolate and butter have melted, stirring once or twice.

2 Off the heat, blend in the milk and transfer the chocolate mixture to a saucepan. Add sugar and syrup.

3 Stir over a low heat until the sugar has dissolved. Bring to the boil and boil steadily without stirring for 5 minutes. Remove pan from heat. Add vanilla extract and mix well. Serve hot with ice cream, and steamed puddings.

## BUTTERSCOTCH NUT SAUCE

*Makes about ½ cup*

| 2 Tbsp butter |
| 2 Tbsp brown sugar |
| 1 Tbsp light corn syrup |
| 3 Tbsp chopped nuts |
| squeeze of lemon juice (optional) |

1 Warm the butter, sugar, and syrup in a saucepan until well blended. Boil for 1 minute and stir in the nuts and lemon juice.

## JAM SAUCE

*Makes about 1 cup*

| 4 Tbsp jam, seeds removed |
| ⅔ cup juice, drained from a can of fruit |
| 2 tsp arrowroot |
| 2 Tbsp cold water |
| squeeze of lemon juice, optional |

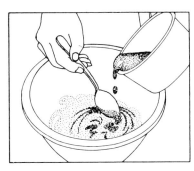

1 Warm the jam with the fruit juice and simmer gently for 5 minutes, stirring to blend well. Blend the arrowroot and cold water to a smooth cream and stir in the jam mixture.

2 Return to the pan and heat gently until it thickens and clears, stirring constantly. Add the lemon juice.

——— VARIATION ———

**Thick jam sauce** Omit the fruit juice and arrowroot. Heat the jam gently in a heavy-based saucepan until just melted and stir in a little lemon juice.

## LEMON SAUCE

*Makes about 1½ cups*

| juice and grated rind of 1 large lemon |
| 1 Tbsp cornstarch |
| 2 Tbsp sugar |
| 1 Tbsp butter |
| 1 egg yolk, optional |

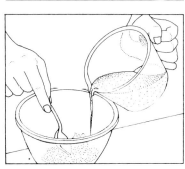

1 Add enough water to the lemon juice to measure 1⅓ cups. Add the lemon rind. Blend a little of the liquid with the cornstarch and the sugar until smooth.

2 Bring the remaining liquid to the boil and stir into the creamed cornstarch. Return all the liquid to the pan and bring to the boil, stirring until the sauce thickens and clears. Add butter.

3 Cool, beat in the egg yolk if used and reheat without boiling, stirring all the time.

——— VARIATION ———

**Orange sauce** Use the juice and rind of an orange instead of a lemon.

# DRINKS

## APERITIFS

Before dinner, it is customary to serve an aperitif or cocktail, with hors d'oeuvre or canapés. The aperitif may be a traditional drink such as sherry—dry, sweet or amontillado as you prefer—or a standard spirit-based drink such as gin or vodka and tonic, or whiskey with soda or dry ginger.

Other possibilities are drinks flavored with aromatic herbs such as Campari (with ice, soda and a slice of orange), and the many types of vermouth. Vermouth may be served on its own with ice and lemon or orange, made into a long drink with tonic or mineral water or used to spark up gin or vodka.

You can also make a huge variety of cocktails. For a professional touch, try frosting cocktail glasses with sugar or salt: first dip the rims in very lightly beaten egg white, then dip them in sugar or salt and leave them for several hours to dry.

Other aperitifs include Champagne and drinks more often served after dinner, such as port or Madeira, usually served chilled in this case.

## WINE

Good wine is the perfect complement to good food, but there is a great deal of mystique surrounding the subject of which wines should be served with particular foods.

The cardinal rule used to be that white wine should accompany the first course or fish or chicken, and that red wines were for serving with red meat and game. A sweet wine, it was decreed, should accompany the dessert course. Nowadays, however, it is much more important to consider the taste and "weight" of the food you are serving and to choose your wines accordingly. A light food such as fish needs an equally light wine, while heavier dishes such as casseroles need richer, more full-bodied wines. While white wines certainly go well with light starters and have an acidity which offsets the flavor of fish perfectly, a young, light-bodied red wine will often do just as well; similarly, a full-bodied white wine, such as a white Burgundy can be as good with a beef casserole or game pie as a rich red. A sweet wine is, of course, still best for desserts. See our chart below.

## WHITE WINE CUP

*Makes about 4 quarts*

crushed ice

3 bottles white wine

$\frac{3}{4}$ bottle dry sherry

4 Tbsp curaçao

4 "splits" tonic water

3 slices of cucumber, a slice of apple and a sprig of borage per cup

Mix all the ingredients together in one or more jars and chill before serving.

## PINEAPPLE CIDER CUP

*Makes about 6 quarts*

8 pints dry hard or beer cider

$2\frac{1}{2}$ cups soda water

orange

lemon

12-oz can pineapple pieces, drained

12 maraschino cherries

$\frac{3}{4}$ cup dry sherry

sprigs of mint, to decorate

*1* Chill the cider and the soda water in the bottles. Pare the orange and lemon rind free of all the white pith and put in a bowl with the pineapple pieces, cherries, sherry, orange juice and lemon juice and chill.

*2* Just before serving, pour the cider and soda water over this mixture and decorate with sprigs of fresh mint.

---

# WINE WITH FOOD

**First courses (not soups), salads, cold meats:** Any dry to medium white wine, but particularly Muscadet, Chablis, Pouilly Fumé

**Soups:** Sherry, Madeira, any dry white wine or light dry red wine but particularly dry Sauternes, Graves

**Fish:** Any light dry or medium white wine or a light red, particularly Muscadet, Mosel, Meursault, Chablis, Hermitage Blanc

**Red meat, game:** Any sturdy, full-bodied red, particularly Bordeaux, Chianti, Barolo, Côtes du Rhône, Valpolicella, Médoc, St Emilion

**White meat (not stuffed or served with heavy sauce):** Any full-bodied white or a medium-bodied red, particularly Chianti Classico, Alsatian Riesling

**Cheese:** Port, or a young red wine such as Beaujolais Nouveau

**Dessert:** Any sweet white wine, particularly Asti Spumante, sweet Sauternes, Vouvray, Marsala, Sweet Muscatel, Champagne

---

*These are, of course, only guidelines. Do not be afraid to experiment and take advantage of special offers and bin ends when out wine shopping, or if you order wine by mail order. Equally, make use of friends' recommendations.

# SUMMER PUNCH

*Serves 18–20*

3 bottles medium white wine, chilled

$\frac{3}{4}$ bottle dry sherry

4 Tbsp Grand Marnier

4 small bottles tonic water

crushed ice

3 cucumber slices, a slice of apple and a fresh mint sprig per cup, to garnish

*1* Mix the wine, sherry, orange-flavored liqueur and tonic in one or more cups and chill the liquid before serving.

*2* To serve, add crushed ice and garnish with the cucumber, apple and mint.

# BRANDY CIDER CUP

*Makes about 6 cups*

$2\frac{1}{2}$ cups weak China tea

$\frac{1}{4}$ cup sugar

juice of 2 oranges

6–8 Tbsp brandy

$4\frac{1}{2}$ cups cider

lemon, thinly sliced

Infuse the tea and strain it on to the sugar in a bowl. Cool and add the orange juice and brandy. Just before serving add the cider and decorate with the lemon slices.

# SANGRIA

3 pints red wine

bottle Champagne or sparkling white wine

4 Tbsp brandy

1 Tbsp Cointreau

juice of 1 lemon

assorted fruit—1 sliced orange and lemon

bananas, apples and grapes (without skin or seeds)

Let mixture stand for 2 or 3 hours to allow flavors of the fruits to be thoroughly absorbed. Serve the sangria well iced.

# ICED COFFEE

*Serves 4–6*

6 Tbsp ground coffee

$3\frac{3}{4}$ cups water

sugar, to taste

ice cube and whipped cream, to serve

Make some strong black coffee. While it is still hot, add sugar to taste. Cool and chill. To serve, pour into glasses, add an ice cube and top with whipped cream.

# ICED TEA

*Serves 4–6*

5–7 tsp China tea

$3\frac{3}{4}$ cups water

crushed ice

sugar, to taste

lemon slice, to serve

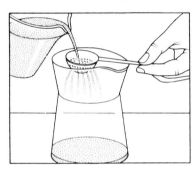

Make China tea in the usual way and strain into a cup. Add sugar to taste and chill. Serve in glasses which have been half filled with ice and a slice of lemon. Add a sprig of mint, if desired.

# MILK SHAKES

Mix chilled milk with strong coffee, cocoa, fruit juice or syrup, or use a special milk shake flavoring; blend until frothy either with a rotary whisk or in an electric blender.

For an ice-cold milk shake, add 1–2 Tbsp ice cream to each glass before serving.

# ICE CREAM SODA

1 glass soda water per person

1 Tbsp ice cream per person

Whisk the soda water and ice cream together with a rotary whisk until frothy or blend them at maximum speed for 1 minute in an electric blender. Pour into a large glass and serve at once.

# ICED BANANA SHAKE

*Makes $1\frac{1}{4}$ cups*

$1\frac{1}{4}$ cups milk

banana, peeled and mashed

2 Tbsp ice cream

Whisk all the ingredients together with a rotary whisk until frothy, or blend at maximum speed for 1 minute in an electric blender or food processor. Pour the shake into a large glass.

# COFFEE MILK SHAKE

Make as above, using 1 cup milk, $\frac{1}{4}$ cup espresso and 2 Tbsp ice cream.

# PINEAPPLE CRUSH

*Serves 8*

19-fl oz can pineapple juice

juice of 1 orange

juice of 1 lemon

sugar

1 quart ginger ale, chilled

pineapple sage or mint, to garnish (optional)

Combine the fruit juices, sweeten to taste and chill. Just before serving, add the ginger ale. Garnish with the sage, if liked.

# INDEX